SPIDER-MAN

SAGA OF THE SANDMAN

SPIDER-MAN

SAGA OF THE SANDMAN

Amazing Spider-Man #4 & #18-19
September 1963 & November-December 1964
Writer: Stan Lee
Artist: Steve Ditko
Letterer: Sam Rosen

Fantastic Four #61 - April 1967
Writer: Stan Lee
Penciler: Jack Kirby
Inker: Joe Sinnott
Letterer: Sam Rosen

Incredible Hulk #138 - April 1971
Writer: Roy Thomas
Penciler: Herb Trimpe
Inker: Sam Grainger
Letterer: Sam Rosen

Marvel Team-Up #1 - March 1972
Writer: Roy Thomas
Penciler: Ross Andru
Inker: Mike Esposito
Letterer: Art Simek

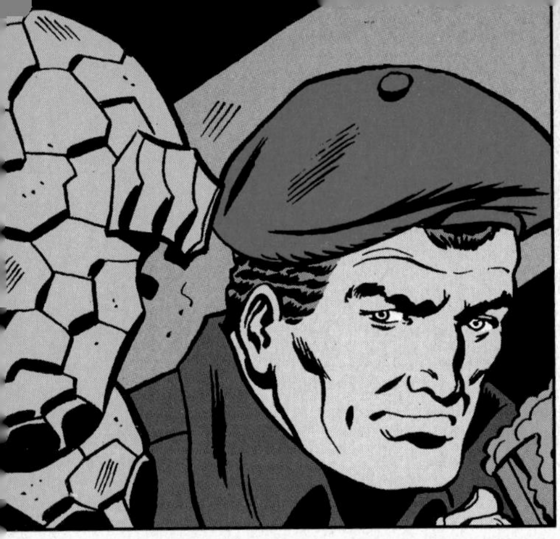

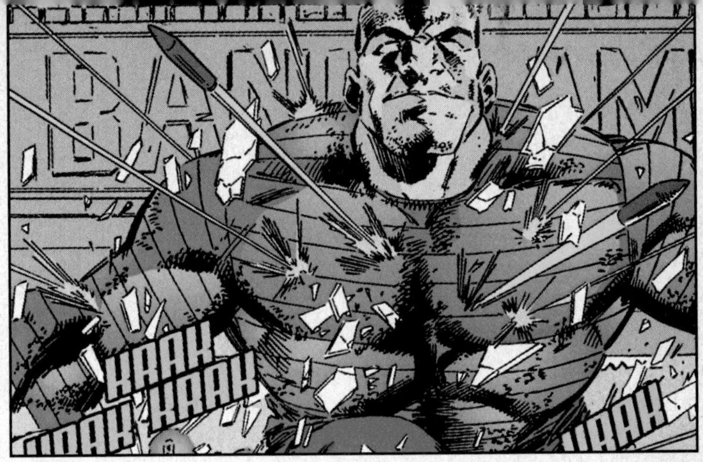
KRAK
KRAK
KRAK

Marvel Two-In-One #86 - April 1982

Writer: Tom DeFalco
Penciler: Ron Wilson
Inker: Chic Stone
Letterer: Jim Novak
Colorist: George Roussos
Editor: Jim Salicrup

Untold Tales of Spider-Man #3 - November 1995

Writer: Kurt Busiek
Penciler: Pat Olliffe
Inkers: Al Vey with Pam Eklund
Letterers: Richard Starkings & Comicraft
Colorist: Steve Mattsson
Editor: Tom Brevoort

Select Color Reconstruction: Jerron Quality Color
Cover Art: Mark Brooks, Jaime Mendoza & Danimation

Senior Editor, Special Projects: Jeff Youngquist
Associate Editors: Jennifer Grünwald & Mark D. Beazley
Assistant Editor: Michael Short
Vice President of Sales: David Gabriel
Production: Jerron Quality Color
Vice President of Creative: Tom Marvelli

Editor in Chief: Joe Quesada
Publisher: Dan Buckley

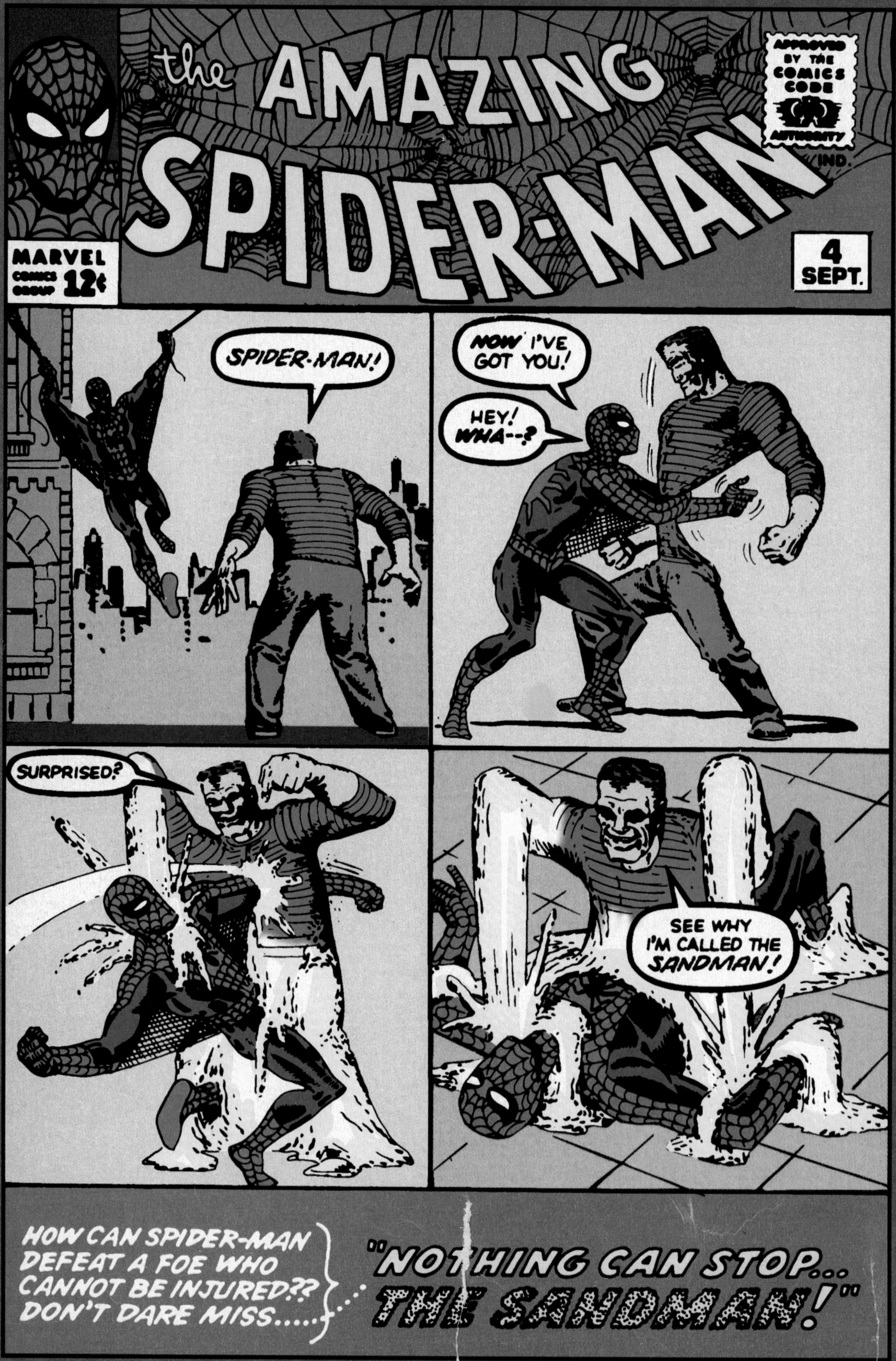

the AMAZING SPIDER-MAN
APPROVED BY THE COMICS CODE AUTHORITY
IND.
MARVEL COMICS GROUP 12¢
4 SEPT.
SPIDER-MAN!
NOW I'VE GOT YOU!
HEY! WHA--?
SURPRISED?
SEE WHY I'M CALLED THE SANDMAN!
HOW CAN SPIDER-MAN DEFEAT A FOE WHO CANNOT BE INJURED?? DON'T DARE MISS.....
"NOTHING CAN STOP... THE SANDMAN!"

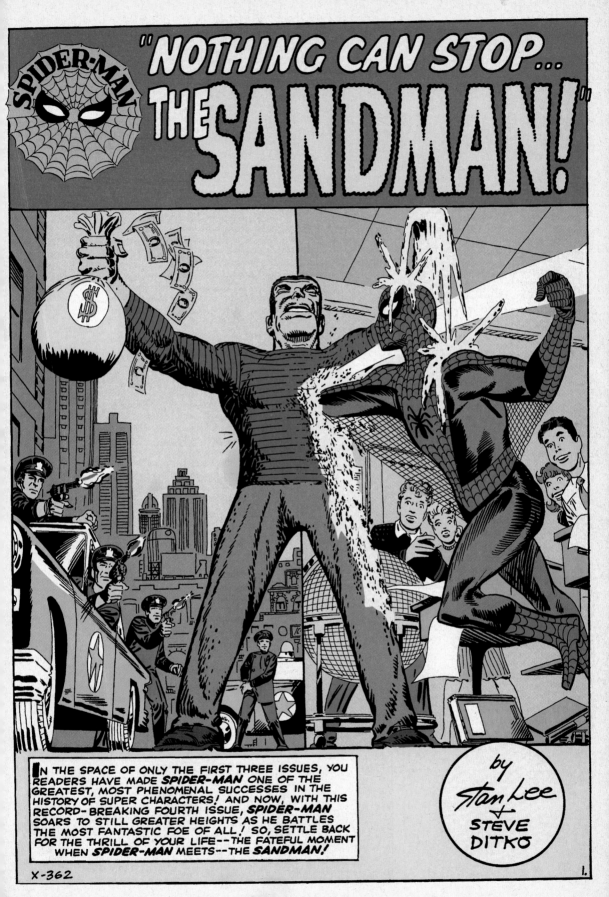

SPIDER-MAN

"NOTHING CAN STOP... THE SANDMAN!"

IN THE SPACE OF ONLY THE FIRST THREE ISSUES, YOU READERS HAVE MADE **SPIDER-MAN** ONE OF THE GREATEST, MOST PHENOMENAL SUCCESSES IN THE HISTORY OF SUPER CHARACTERS! AND NOW, WITH THIS RECORD-BREAKING FOURTH ISSUE, **SPIDER-MAN** SOARS TO STILL GREATER HEIGHTS AS HE BATTLES THE MOST FANTASTIC FOE OF ALL! SO, SETTLE BACK FOR THE THRILL OF YOUR LIFE--THE FATEFUL MOMENT WHEN **SPIDER-MAN** MEETS--THE **SANDMAN!**

by
Stan Lee
+
STEVE DITKO

X-362

1.

5

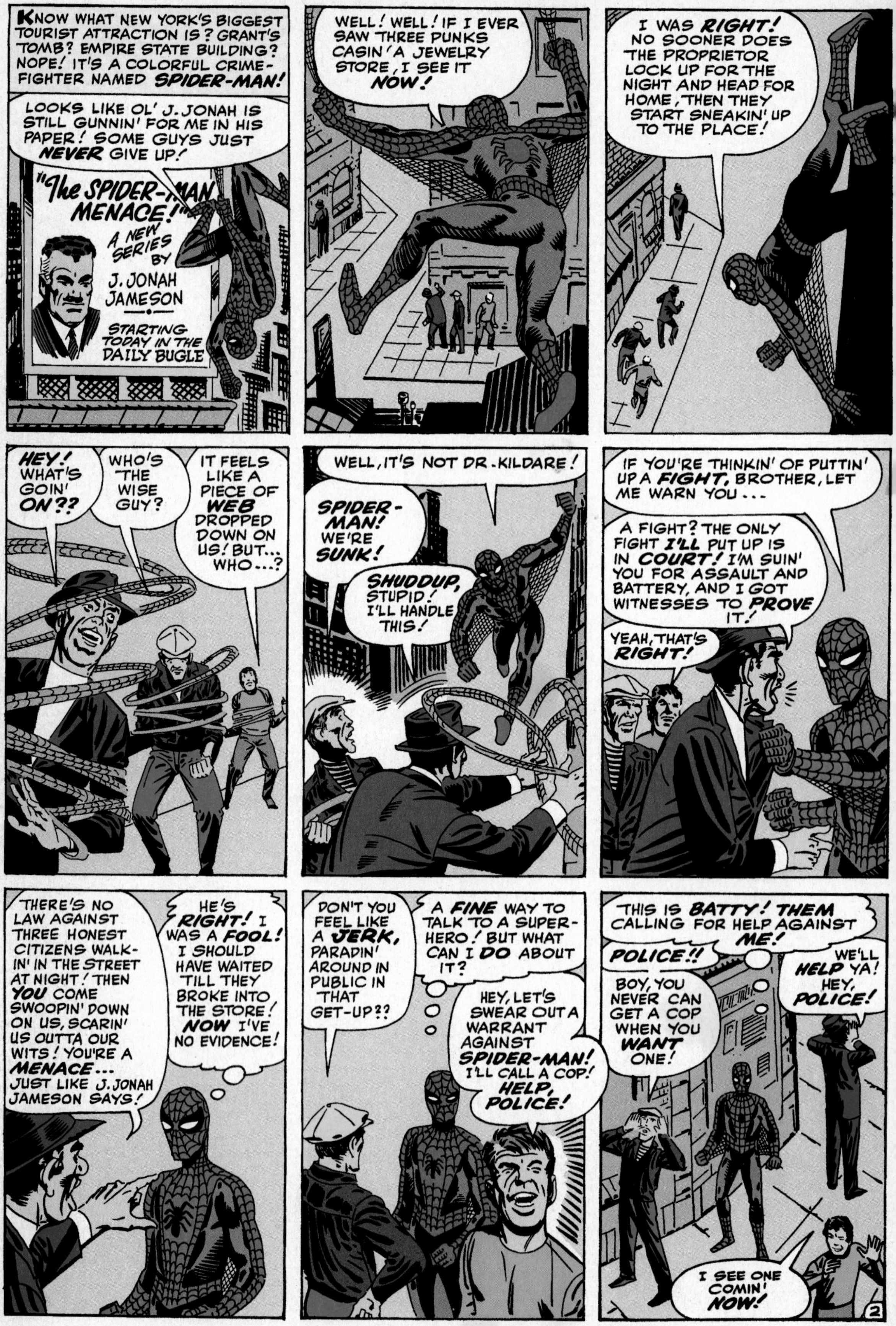
KNOW WHAT NEW YORK'S BIGGEST TOURIST ATTRACTION IS? GRANT'S TOMB? EMPIRE STATE BUILDING? NOPE! IT'S A COLORFUL CRIME-FIGHTER NAMED SPIDER-MAN!
LOOKS LIKE OL' J. JONAH IS STILL GUNNIN' FOR ME IN HIS PAPER! SOME GUYS JUST NEVER GIVE UP!
"The SPIDER-MAN MENACE!" A NEW SERIES BY J. JONAH JAMESON STARTING TODAY IN THE DAILY BUGLE
WELL! WELL! IF I EVER SAW THREE PUNKS CASIN' A JEWELRY STORE, I SEE IT NOW!
I WAS RIGHT! NO SOONER DOES THE PROPRIETOR LOCK UP FOR THE NIGHT AND HEAD FOR HOME, THEN THEY START SNEAKIN' UP TO THE PLACE!
HEY! WHAT'S GOIN' ON??
WHO'S THE WISE GUY?
IT FEELS LIKE A PIECE OF WEB DROPPED DOWN ON US! BUT... WHO...?
WELL, IT'S NOT DR. KILDARE!
SPIDER-MAN! WE'RE SUNK!
SHUDDUP, STUPID! I'LL HANDLE THIS!
IF YOU'RE THINKIN' OF PUTTIN' UP A FIGHT, BROTHER, LET ME WARN YOU...
A FIGHT? THE ONLY FIGHT I'LL PUT UP IS IN COURT! I'M SUIN' YOU FOR ASSAULT AND BATTERY, AND I GOT WITNESSES TO PROVE IT!
YEAH, THAT'S RIGHT!
THERE'S NO LAW AGAINST THREE HONEST CITIZENS WALKIN' IN THE STREET AT NIGHT! THEN YOU COME SWOOPIN' DOWN ON US, SCARIN' US OUTTA OUR WITS! YOU'RE A MENACE... JUST LIKE J. JONAH JAMESON SAYS!
HE'S RIGHT! I WAS A FOOL! I SHOULD HAVE WAITED TILL THEY BROKE INTO THE STORE! NOW I'VE NO EVIDENCE!
DON'T YOU FEEL LIKE A JERK, PARADIN' AROUND IN PUBLIC IN THAT GET-UP??
A FINE WAY TO TALK TO A SUPER-HERO! BUT WHAT CAN I DO ABOUT IT?
HEY, LET'S SWEAR OUT A WARRANT AGAINST SPIDER-MAN! I'LL CALL A COP! HELP, POLICE!
THIS IS BATTY! THEM CALLING FOR HELP AGAINST ME!
POLICE!!
WE'LL HELP YA! HEY, POLICE!
BOY, YOU NEVER CAN GET A COP WHEN YOU WANT ONE!
I SEE ONE COMIN' NOW!
2

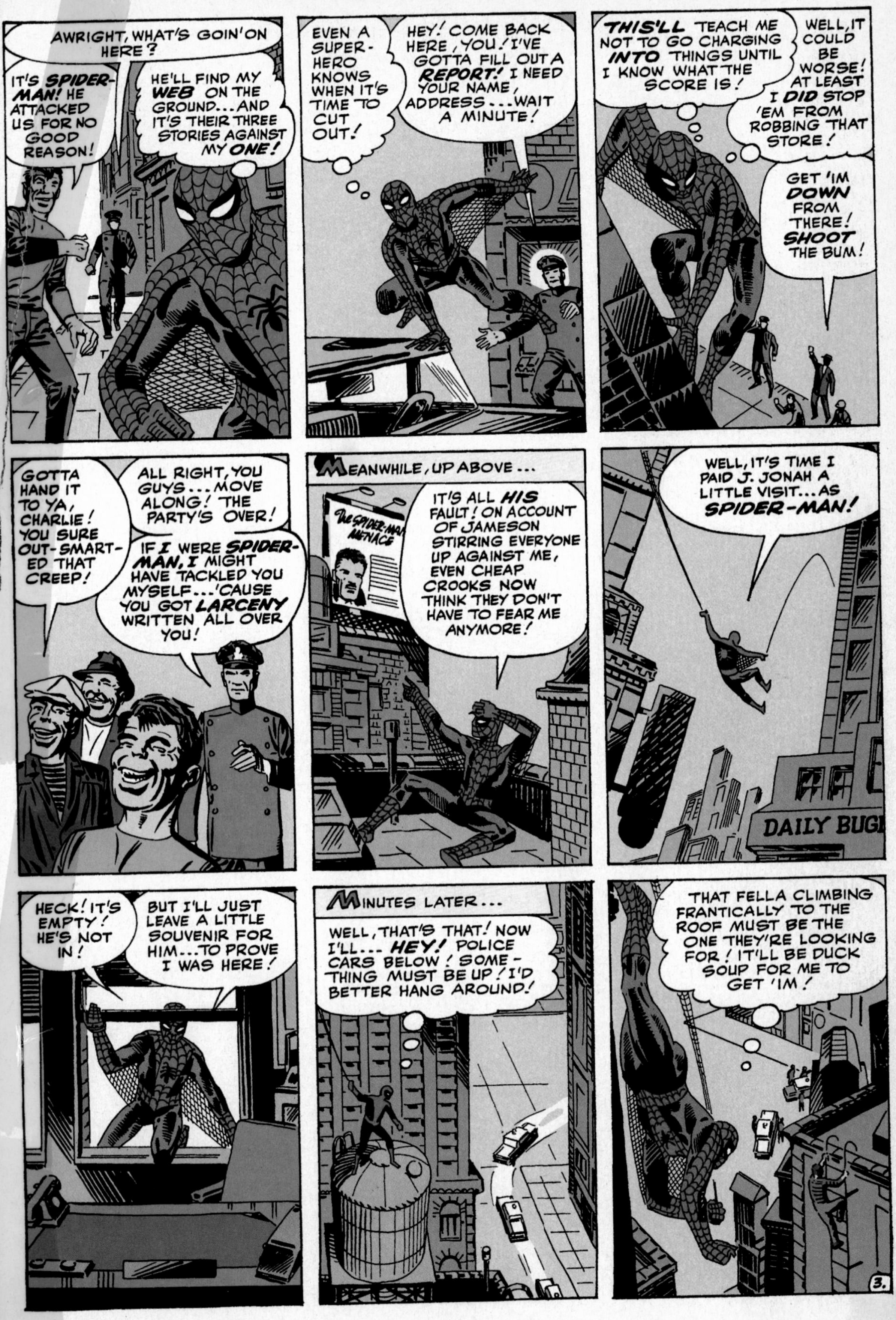
AWRIGHT, WHAT'S GOIN' ON HERE?
IT'S SPIDER-MAN! HE ATTACKED US FOR NO GOOD REASON!
HE'LL FIND MY WEB ON THE GROUND... AND IT'S THEIR THREE STORIES AGAINST MY ONE!
EVEN A SUPER-HERO KNOWS WHEN IT'S TIME TO CUT OUT!
HEY! COME BACK HERE, YOU! I'VE GOTTA FILL OUT A REPORT! I NEED YOUR NAME, ADDRESS... WAIT A MINUTE!
THIS'LL TEACH ME NOT TO GO CHARGING INTO THINGS UNTIL I KNOW WHAT THE SCORE IS!
WELL, IT COULD BE WORSE! AT LEAST I DID STOP 'EM FROM ROBBING THAT STORE!
GET 'IM DOWN FROM THERE! SHOOT THE BUM!
GOTTA HAND IT TO YA, CHARLIE! YOU SURE OUT-SMARTED THAT CREEP!
ALL RIGHT, YOU GUYS... MOVE ALONG! THE PARTY'S OVER!
IF I WERE SPIDER-MAN, I MIGHT HAVE TACKLED YOU MYSELF...'CAUSE YOU GOT LARCENY WRITTEN ALL OVER YOU!
MEANWHILE, UP ABOVE...
THE SPIDER-MAN MENACE
IT'S ALL HIS FAULT! ON ACCOUNT OF JAMESON STIRRING EVERYONE UP AGAINST ME, EVEN CHEAP CROOKS NOW THINK THEY DON'T HAVE TO FEAR ME ANYMORE!
WELL, IT'S TIME I PAID J. JONAH A LITTLE VISIT... AS SPIDER-MAN!
DAILY BUG
HECK! IT'S EMPTY! HE'S NOT IN!
BUT I'LL JUST LEAVE A LITTLE SOUVENIR FOR HIM... TO PROVE I WAS HERE!
MINUTES LATER...
WELL, THAT'S THAT! NOW I'LL... HEY! POLICE CARS BELOW! SOME-THING MUST BE UP! I'D BETTER HANG AROUND!
THAT FELLA CLIMBING FRANTICALLY TO THE ROOF MUST BE THE ONE THEY'RE LOOKING FOR! IT'LL BE DUCK SOUP FOR ME TO GET 'IM!
3.

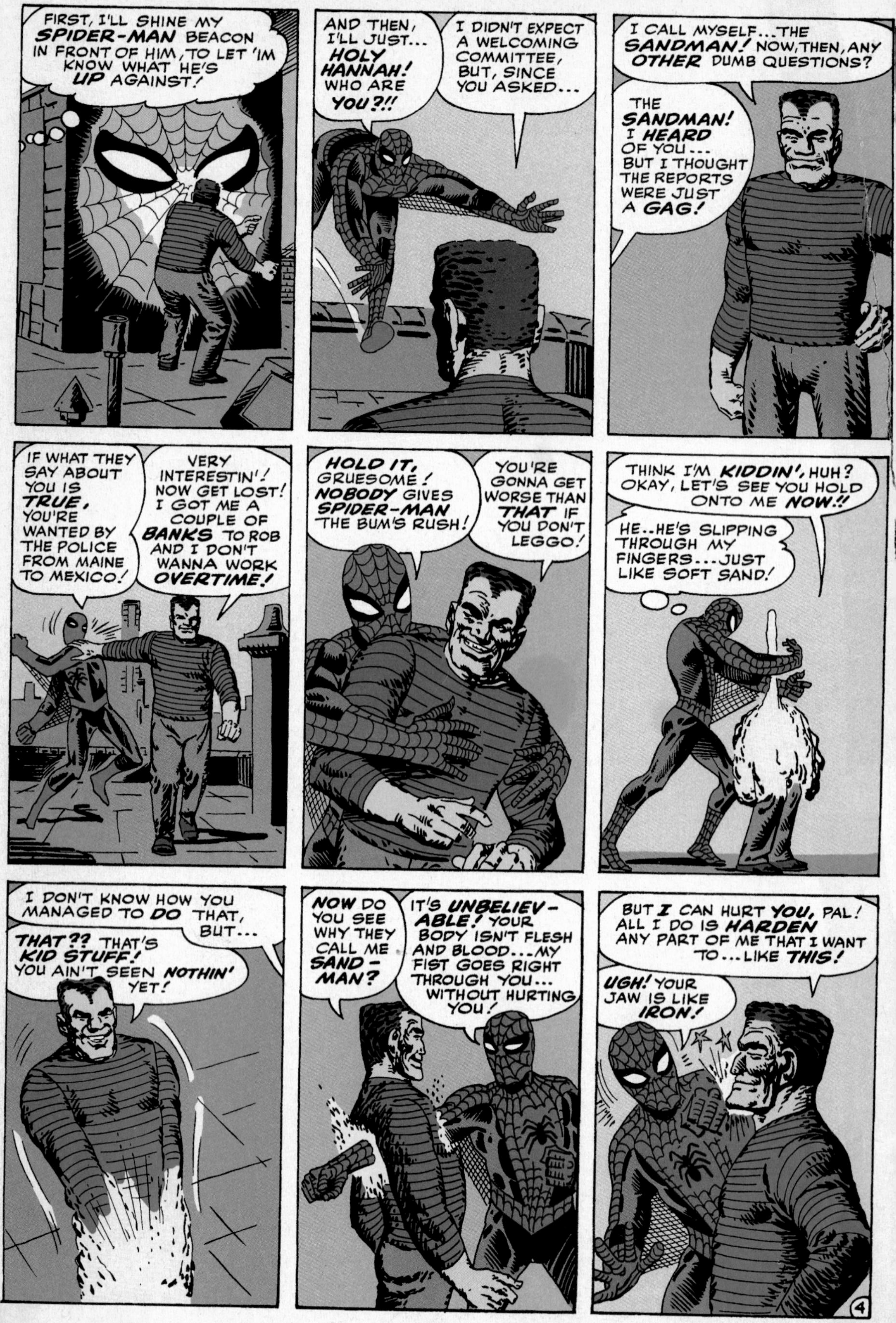

FIRST, I'LL SHINE MY SPIDER-MAN BEACON IN FRONT OF HIM, TO LET 'IM KNOW WHAT HE'S UP AGAINST!
AND THEN, I'LL JUST... HOLY HANNAH! WHO ARE YOU?!!
I DIDN'T EXPECT A WELCOMING COMMITTEE, BUT, SINCE YOU ASKED...
I CALL MYSELF... THE SANDMAN! NOW, THEN, ANY OTHER DUMB QUESTIONS?
THE SANDMAN! I HEARD OF YOU... BUT I THOUGHT THE REPORTS WERE JUST A GAG!
IF WHAT THEY SAY ABOUT YOU IS TRUE, YOU'RE WANTED BY THE POLICE FROM MAINE TO MEXICO!
VERY INTERESTIN'! NOW GET LOST! I GOT ME A COUPLE OF BANKS TO ROB AND I DON'T WANNA WORK OVERTIME!
HOLD IT, GRUESOME! NOBODY GIVES SPIDER-MAN THE BUM'S RUSH!
YOU'RE GONNA GET WORSE THAN THAT IF YOU DON'T LEGGO!
THINK I'M KIDDIN', HUH? OKAY, LET'S SEE YOU HOLD ONTO ME NOW!!
HE..HE'S SLIPPING THROUGH MY FINGERS... JUST LIKE SOFT SAND!
I DON'T KNOW HOW YOU MANAGED TO DO THAT, BUT...
THAT?? THAT'S KID STUFF! YOU AIN'T SEEN NOTHIN' YET!
NOW DO YOU SEE WHY THEY CALL ME SAND-MAN?
IT'S UNBELIEV-ABLE! YOUR BODY ISN'T FLESH AND BLOOD... MY FIST GOES RIGHT THROUGH YOU... WITHOUT HURTING YOU!
BUT I CAN HURT YOU, PAL! ALL I DO IS HARDEN ANY PART OF ME THAT I WANT TO... LIKE THIS!
UGH! YOUR JAW IS LIKE IRON!
4

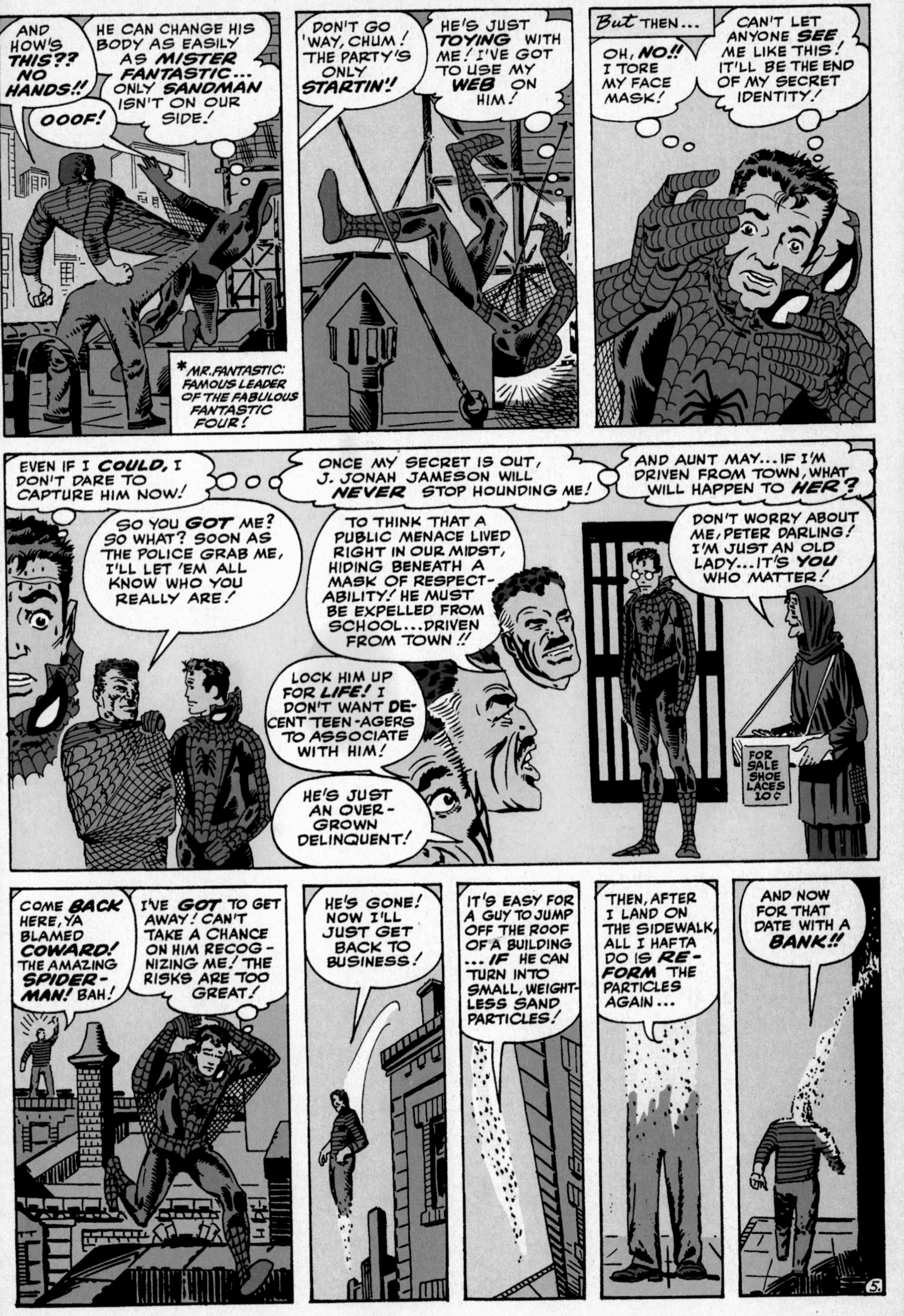
AND HOW'S THIS?? NO HANDS!!
HE CAN CHANGE HIS BODY AS EASILY AS MISTER FANTASTIC... ONLY SANDMAN ISN'T ON OUR SIDE!
OOOF!
*MR. FANTASTIC: FAMOUS LEADER OF THE FABULOUS FANTASTIC FOUR!
DON'T GO 'WAY, CHUM! THE PARTY'S ONLY STARTIN'!
HE'S JUST TOYING WITH ME! I'VE GOT TO USE MY WEB ON HIM!
But THEN...
OH, NO!! I TORE MY FACE MASK!
CAN'T LET ANYONE SEE ME LIKE THIS! IT'LL BE THE END OF MY SECRET IDENTITY!
EVEN IF I COULD, I DON'T DARE TO CAPTURE HIM NOW!
ONCE MY SECRET IS OUT, J. JONAH JAMESON WILL NEVER STOP HOUNDING ME!
AND AUNT MAY... IF I'M DRIVEN FROM TOWN, WHAT WILL HAPPEN TO HER?
SO YOU GOT ME? SO WHAT? SOON AS THE POLICE GRAB ME, I'LL LET 'EM ALL KNOW WHO YOU REALLY ARE!
TO THINK THAT A PUBLIC MENACE LIVED RIGHT IN OUR MIDST, HIDING BENEATH A MASK OF RESPECTABILITY! HE MUST BE EXPELLED FROM SCHOOL...DRIVEN FROM TOWN!!
LOCK HIM UP FOR LIFE! I DON'T WANT DECENT TEEN-AGERS TO ASSOCIATE WITH HIM!
HE'S JUST AN OVER-GROWN DELINQUENT!
DON'T WORRY ABOUT ME, PETER DARLING! I'M JUST AN OLD LADY...IT'S YOU WHO MATTER!
FOR SALE SHOE LACES 10¢
COME BACK HERE, YA BLAMED COWARD! THE AMAZING SPIDER-MAN! BAH!
I'VE GOT TO GET AWAY! CAN'T TAKE A CHANCE ON HIM RECOGNIZING ME! THE RISKS ARE TOO GREAT!
HE'S GONE! NOW I'LL JUST GET BACK TO BUSINESS!
IT'S EASY FOR A GUY TO JUMP OFF THE ROOF OF A BUILDING ...IF HE CAN TURN INTO SMALL, WEIGHTLESS SAND PARTICLES!
THEN, AFTER I LAND ON THE SIDEWALK, ALL I HAFTA DO IS RE-FORM THE PARTICLES AGAIN...
AND NOW FOR THAT DATE WITH A BANK!!
5.

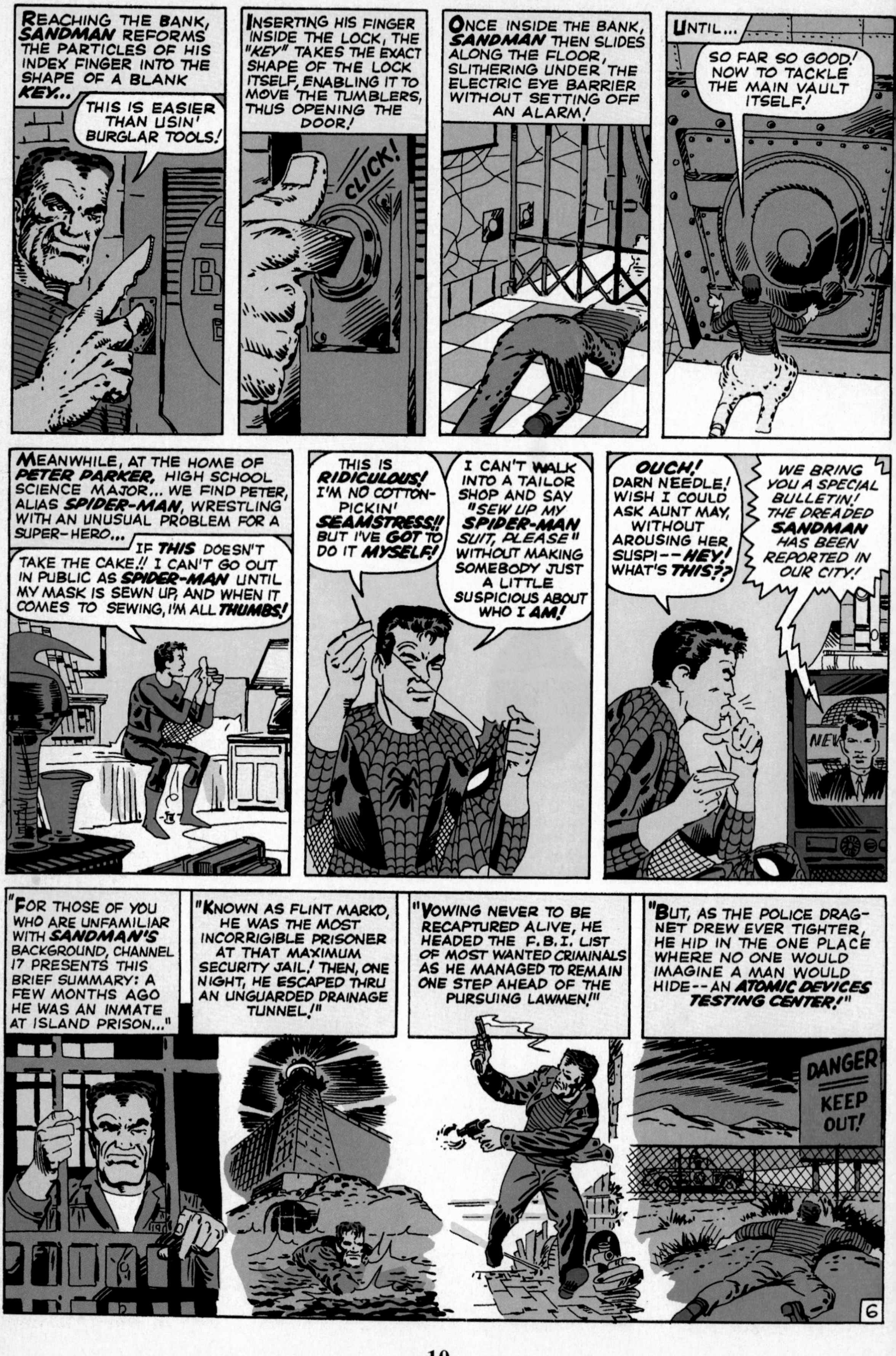

REACHING THE BANK, SANDMAN REFORMS THE PARTICLES OF HIS INDEX FINGER INTO THE SHAPE OF A BLANK KEY...
THIS IS EASIER THAN USIN' BURGLAR TOOLS!
INSERTING HIS FINGER INSIDE THE LOCK, THE "KEY" TAKES THE EXACT SHAPE OF THE LOCK ITSELF, ENABLING IT TO MOVE THE TUMBLERS, THUS OPENING THE DOOR!
CLICK!
ONCE INSIDE THE BANK, SANDMAN THEN SLIDES ALONG THE FLOOR, SLITHERING UNDER THE ELECTRIC EYE BARRIER WITHOUT SETTING OFF AN ALARM!
UNTIL...
SO FAR SO GOOD! NOW TO TACKLE THE MAIN VAULT ITSELF!
MEANWHILE, AT THE HOME OF PETER PARKER, HIGH SCHOOL SCIENCE MAJOR... WE FIND PETER, ALIAS SPIDER-MAN, WRESTLING WITH AN UNUSUAL PROBLEM FOR A SUPER-HERO...
IF THIS DOESN'T TAKE THE CAKE!! I CAN'T GO OUT IN PUBLIC AS SPIDER-MAN UNTIL MY MASK IS SEWN UP, AND WHEN IT COMES TO SEWING, I'M ALL THUMBS!
THIS IS RIDICULOUS! I'M NO COTTON-PICKIN' SEAMSTRESS!! BUT I'VE GOT TO DO IT MYSELF!
I CAN'T WALK INTO A TAILOR SHOP AND SAY "SEW UP MY SPIDER-MAN SUIT, PLEASE" WITHOUT MAKING SOMEBODY JUST A LITTLE SUSPICIOUS ABOUT WHO I AM!
OUCH! DARN NEEDLE! WISH I COULD ASK AUNT MAY, WITHOUT AROUSING HER SUSPI--HEY! WHAT'S THIS??
WE BRING YOU A SPECIAL BULLETIN! THE DREADED SANDMAN HAS BEEN REPORTED IN OUR CITY!
NEW
"FOR THOSE OF YOU WHO ARE UNFAMILIAR WITH SANDMAN'S BACKGROUND, CHANNEL 17 PRESENTS THIS BRIEF SUMMARY: A FEW MONTHS AGO HE WAS AN INMATE AT ISLAND PRISON..."
"KNOWN AS FLINT MARKO, HE WAS THE MOST INCORRIGIBLE PRISONER AT THAT MAXIMUM SECURITY JAIL! THEN, ONE NIGHT, HE ESCAPED THRU AN UNGUARDED DRAINAGE TUNNEL!"
"VOWING NEVER TO BE RECAPTURED ALIVE, HE HEADED THE F.B.I. LIST OF MOST WANTED CRIMINALS AS HE MANAGED TO REMAIN ONE STEP AHEAD OF THE PURSUING LAWMEN!"
"BUT, AS THE POLICE DRAG-NET DREW EVER TIGHTER, HE HID IN THE ONE PLACE WHERE NO ONE WOULD IMAGINE A MAN WOULD HIDE--AN ATOMIC DEVICES TESTING CENTER!"
DANGER
KEEP OUT!
6

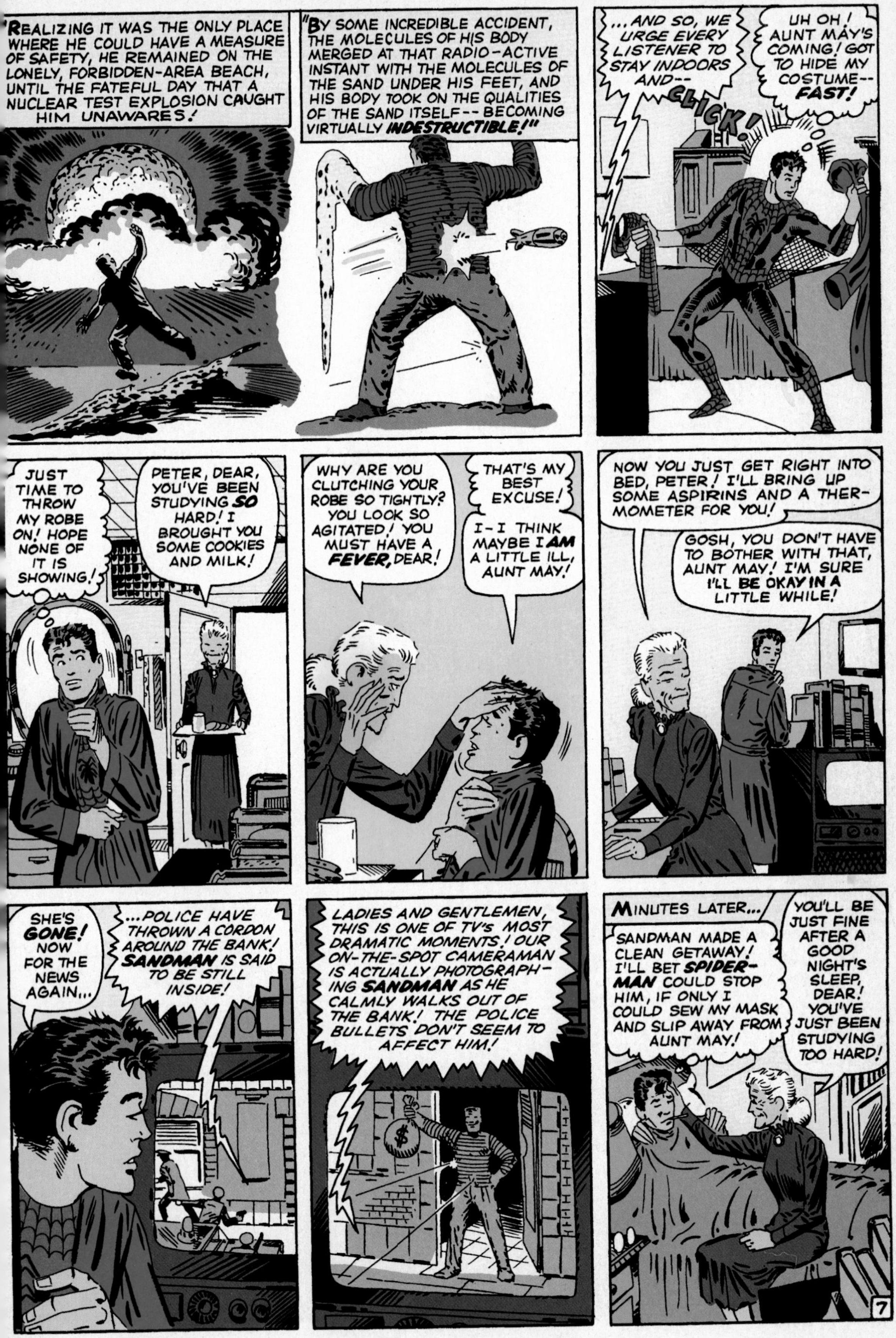
REALIZING IT WAS THE ONLY PLACE WHERE HE COULD HAVE A MEASURE OF SAFETY, HE REMAINED ON THE LONELY, FORBIDDEN-AREA BEACH, UNTIL THE FATEFUL DAY THAT A NUCLEAR TEST EXPLOSION CAUGHT HIM UNAWARES!
"BY SOME INCREDIBLE ACCIDENT, THE MOLECULES OF HIS BODY MERGED AT THAT RADIO-ACTIVE INSTANT WITH THE MOLECULES OF THE SAND UNDER HIS FEET, AND HIS BODY TOOK ON THE QUALITIES OF THE SAND ITSELF-- BECOMING VIRTUALLY INDESTRUCTIBLE!"
...AND SO, WE URGE EVERY LISTENER TO STAY INDOORS AND--
CLICK!
UH OH! AUNT MAY'S COMING! GOT TO HIDE MY COSTUME-- FAST!
JUST TIME TO THROW MY ROBE ON! HOPE NONE OF IT IS SHOWING!
PETER, DEAR, YOU'VE BEEN STUDYING SO HARD! I BROUGHT YOU SOME COOKIES AND MILK!
WHY ARE YOU CLUTCHING YOUR ROBE SO TIGHTLY? YOU LOOK SO AGITATED! YOU MUST HAVE A FEVER, DEAR!
THAT'S MY BEST EXCUSE!
I- I THINK MAYBE I AM A LITTLE ILL, AUNT MAY!
NOW YOU JUST GET RIGHT INTO BED, PETER! I'LL BRING UP SOME ASPIRINS AND A THERMOMETER FOR YOU!
GOSH, YOU DON'T HAVE TO BOTHER WITH THAT, AUNT MAY! I'M SURE I'LL BE OKAY IN A LITTLE WHILE!
SHE'S GONE! NOW FOR THE NEWS AGAIN...
...POLICE HAVE THROWN A CORDON AROUND THE BANK! SANDMAN IS SAID TO BE STILL INSIDE!
LADIES AND GENTLEMEN, THIS IS ONE OF TV'S MOST DRAMATIC MOMENTS! OUR ON-THE-SPOT CAMERAMAN IS ACTUALLY PHOTOGRAPHING SANDMAN AS HE CALMLY WALKS OUT OF THE BANK! THE POLICE BULLETS DON'T SEEM TO AFFECT HIM!
MINUTES LATER...
SANDMAN MADE A CLEAN GETAWAY! I'LL BET SPIDER-MAN COULD STOP HIM, IF ONLY I COULD SEW MY MASK AND SLIP AWAY FROM AUNT MAY!
YOU'LL BE JUST FINE AFTER A GOOD NIGHT'S SLEEP, DEAR! YOU'VE JUST BEEN STUDYING TOO HARD!
7

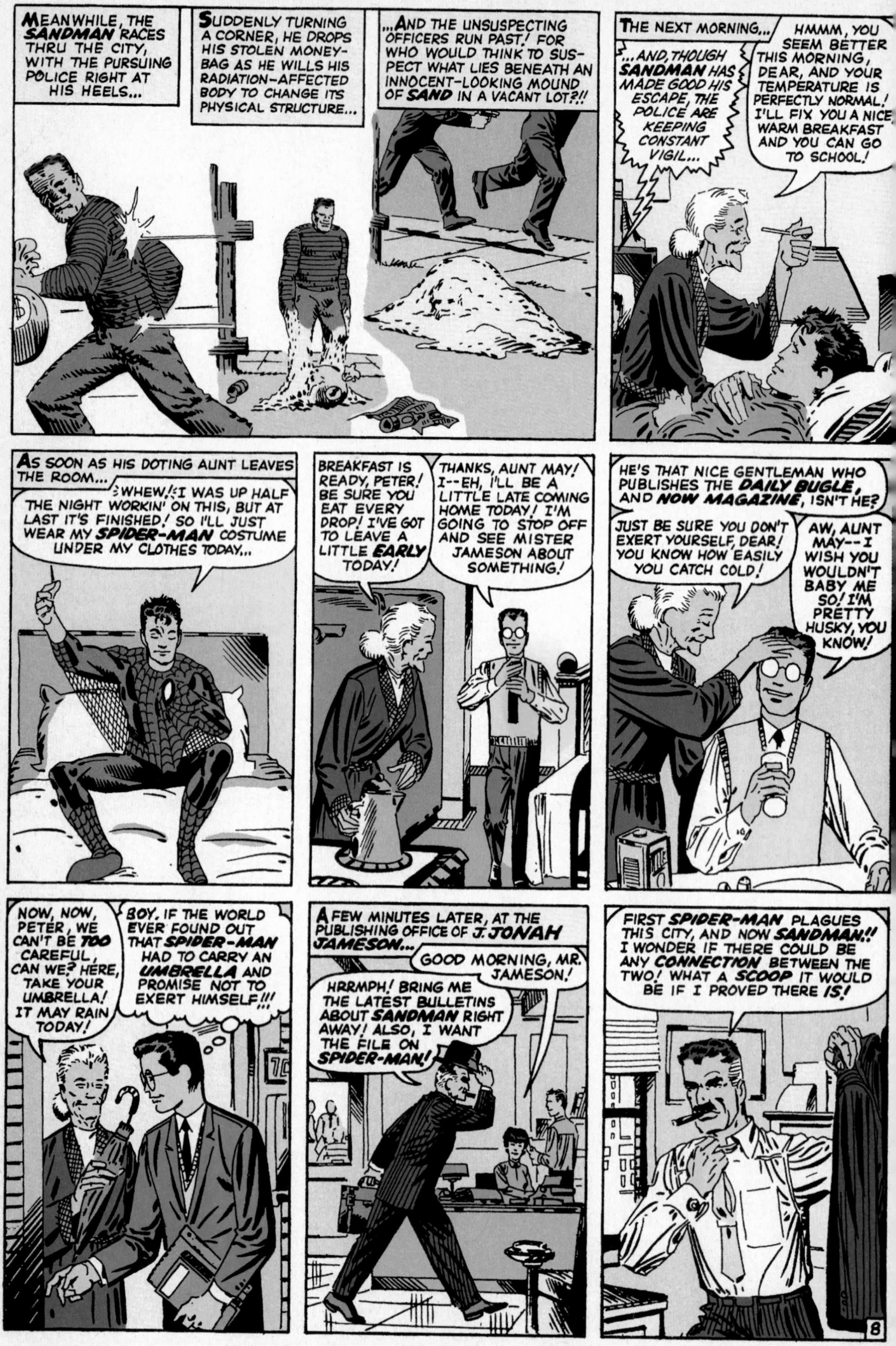
MEANWHILE, THE SANDMAN RACES THRU THE CITY, WITH THE PURSUING POLICE RIGHT AT HIS HEELS...
SUDDENLY TURNING A CORNER, HE DROPS HIS STOLEN MONEY-BAG AS HE WILLS HIS RADIATION-AFFECTED BODY TO CHANGE ITS PHYSICAL STRUCTURE...
...AND THE UNSUSPECTING OFFICERS RUN PAST! FOR WHO WOULD THINK TO SUSPECT WHAT LIES BENEATH AN INNOCENT-LOOKING MOUND OF SAND IN A VACANT LOT?!!
THE NEXT MORNING,...
...AND, THOUGH SANDMAN HAS MADE GOOD HIS ESCAPE, THE POLICE ARE KEEPING CONSTANT VIGIL...
HMMM, YOU SEEM BETTER THIS MORNING, DEAR, AND YOUR TEMPERATURE IS PERFECTLY NORMAL! I'LL FIX YOU A NICE WARM BREAKFAST AND YOU CAN GO TO SCHOOL!
AS SOON AS HIS DOTING AUNT LEAVES THE ROOM...
WHEW! I WAS UP HALF THE NIGHT WORKIN' ON THIS, BUT AT LAST IT'S FINISHED! SO I'LL JUST WEAR MY SPIDER-MAN COSTUME UNDER MY CLOTHES TODAY...
BREAKFAST IS READY, PETER! BE SURE YOU EAT EVERY DROP! I'VE GOT TO LEAVE A LITTLE EARLY TODAY!
THANKS, AUNT MAY! I--EH, I'LL BE A LITTLE LATE COMING HOME TODAY! I'M GOING TO STOP OFF AND SEE MISTER JAMESON ABOUT SOMETHING!
HE'S THAT NICE GENTLEMAN WHO PUBLISHES THE DAILY BUGLE, AND NOW MAGAZINE, ISN'T HE?
JUST BE SURE YOU DON'T EXERT YOURSELF, DEAR! YOU KNOW HOW EASILY YOU CATCH COLD!
AW, AUNT MAY-- I WISH YOU WOULDN'T BABY ME SO! I'M PRETTY HUSKY, YOU KNOW!
NOW, NOW, PETER, WE CAN'T BE TOO CAREFUL, CAN WE? HERE, TAKE YOUR UMBRELLA! IT MAY RAIN TODAY!
BOY, IF THE WORLD EVER FOUND OUT THAT SPIDER-MAN HAD TO CARRY AN UMBRELLA AND PROMISE NOT TO EXERT HIMSELF!!!
A FEW MINUTES LATER, AT THE PUBLISHING OFFICE OF J. JONAH JAMESON...
GOOD MORNING, MR. JAMESON!
HRRMPH! BRING ME THE LATEST BULLETINS ABOUT SANDMAN RIGHT AWAY! ALSO, I WANT THE FILE ON SPIDER-MAN!
FIRST SPIDER-MAN PLAGUES THIS CITY, AND NOW SANDMAN!! I WONDER IF THERE COULD BE ANY CONNECTION BETWEEN THE TWO! WHAT A SCOOP IT WOULD BE IF I PROVED THERE IS!
8

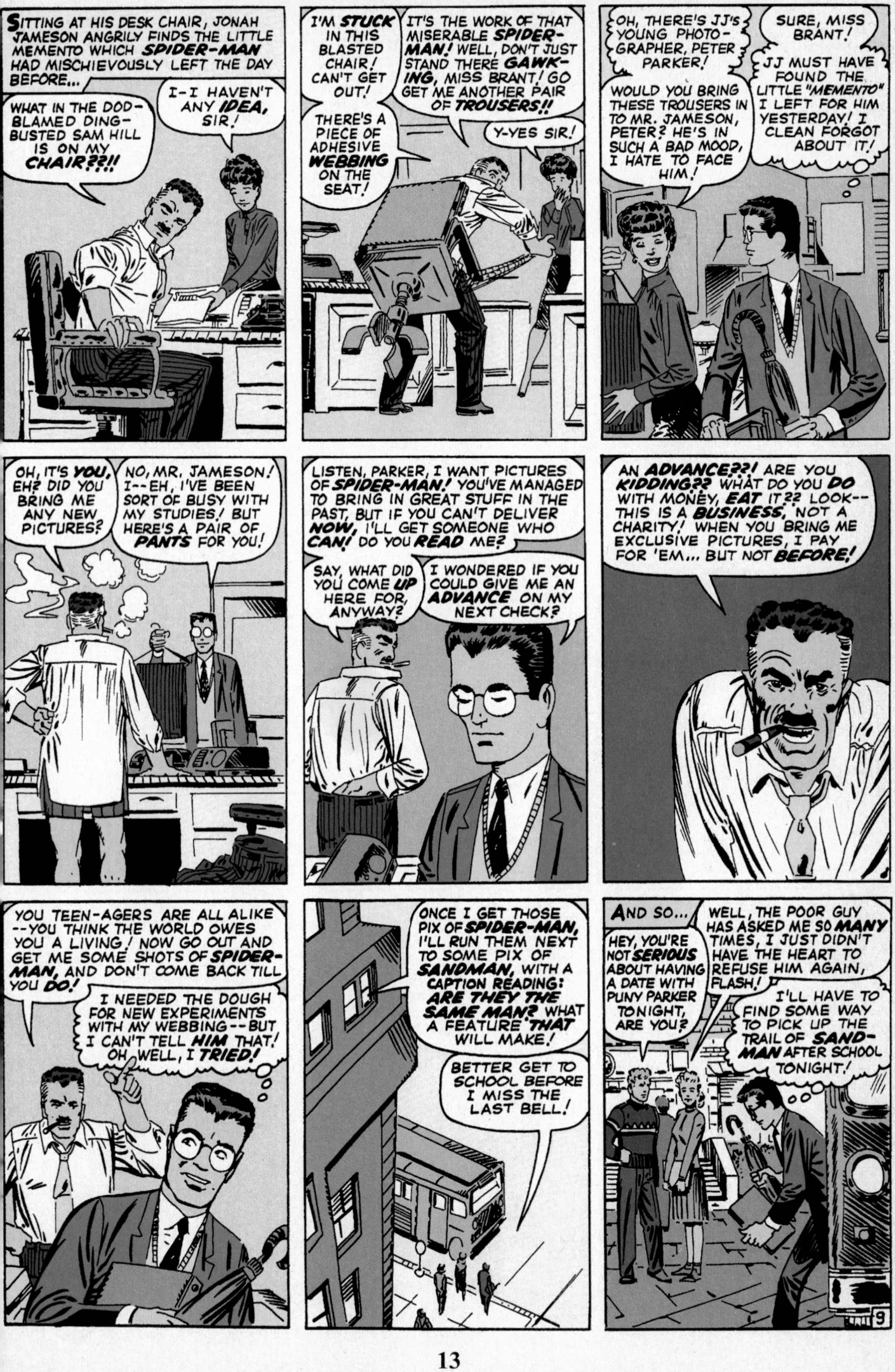
SITTING AT HIS DESK CHAIR, JONAH JAMESON ANGRILY FINDS THE LITTLE MEMENTO WHICH SPIDER-MAN HAD MISCHIEVOUSLY LEFT THE DAY BEFORE...
WHAT IN THE DOD-BLAMED DING-BUSTED SAM HILL IS ON MY CHAIR??!!
I-I HAVEN'T ANY IDEA, SIR!
I'M STUCK IN THIS BLASTED CHAIR! CAN'T GET OUT!
THERE'S A PIECE OF ADHESIVE WEBBING ON THE SEAT!
IT'S THE WORK OF THAT MISERABLE SPIDER-MAN! WELL, DON'T JUST STAND THERE GAWK-ING, MISS BRANT! GO GET ME ANOTHER PAIR OF TROUSERS!!
Y-YES SIR!
OH, THERE'S JJ'S YOUNG PHOTO-GRAPHER, PETER PARKER!
WOULD YOU BRING THESE TROUSERS IN TO MR. JAMESON, PETER? HE'S IN SUCH A BAD MOOD, I HATE TO FACE HIM!
SURE, MISS BRANT!
JJ MUST HAVE FOUND THE LITTLE "MEMENTO" I LEFT FOR HIM YESTERDAY! I CLEAN FORGOT ABOUT IT!
OH, IT'S YOU, EH? DID YOU BRING ME ANY NEW PICTURES?
NO, MR. JAMESON! I--EH, I'VE BEEN SORT OF BUSY WITH MY STUDIES! BUT HERE'S A PAIR OF PANTS FOR YOU!
LISTEN, PARKER, I WANT PICTURES OF SPIDER-MAN! YOU'VE MANAGED TO BRING IN GREAT STUFF IN THE PAST, BUT IF YOU CAN'T DELIVER NOW, I'LL GET SOMEONE WHO CAN! DO YOU READ ME?
SAY, WHAT DID YOU COME UP HERE FOR, ANYWAY?
I WONDERED IF YOU COULD GIVE ME AN ADVANCE ON MY NEXT CHECK?
AN ADVANCE??! ARE YOU KIDDING?? WHAT DO YOU DO WITH MONEY, EAT IT?? LOOK--THIS IS A BUSINESS, NOT A CHARITY! WHEN YOU BRING ME EXCLUSIVE PICTURES, I PAY FOR 'EM... BUT NOT BEFORE!
YOU TEEN-AGERS ARE ALL ALIKE--YOU THINK THE WORLD OWES YOU A LIVING! NOW GO OUT AND GET ME SOME SHOTS OF SPIDER-MAN, AND DON'T COME BACK TILL YOU DO!
I NEEDED THE DOUGH FOR NEW EXPERIMENTS WITH MY WEBBING--BUT I CAN'T TELL HIM THAT! OH, WELL, I TRIED!
ONCE I GET THOSE PIX OF SPIDER-MAN, I'LL RUN THEM NEXT TO SOME PIX OF SANDMAN, WITH A CAPTION READING: ARE THEY THE SAME MAN? WHAT A FEATURE THAT WILL MAKE!
BETTER GET TO SCHOOL BEFORE I MISS THE LAST BELL!
AND SO...
HEY, YOU'RE NOT SERIOUS ABOUT HAVING A DATE WITH PUNY PARKER TONIGHT, ARE YOU?
WELL, THE POOR GUY HAS ASKED ME SO MANY TIMES, I JUST DIDN'T HAVE THE HEART TO REFUSE HIM AGAIN, FLASH!
I'LL HAVE TO FIND SOME WAY TO PICK UP THE TRAIL OF SAND-MAN AFTER SCHOOL TONIGHT!
9

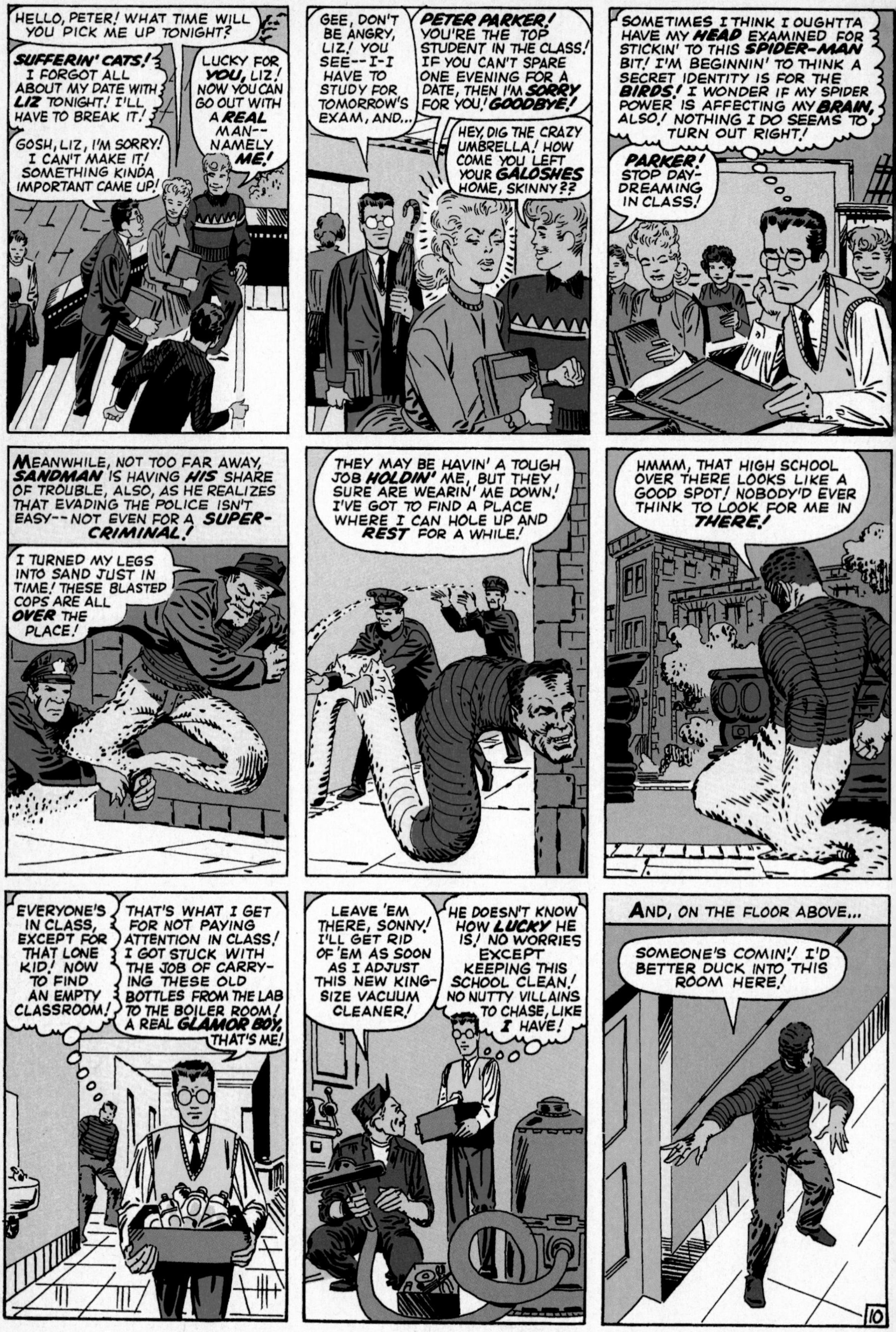
HELLO, PETER! WHAT TIME WILL YOU PICK ME UP TONIGHT?
SUFFERIN' CATS! I FORGOT ALL ABOUT MY DATE WITH LIZ TONIGHT! I'LL HAVE TO BREAK IT!
LUCKY FOR YOU, LIZ! NOW YOU CAN GO OUT WITH A REAL MAN-- NAMELY ME!
GOSH, LIZ, I'M SORRY! I CAN'T MAKE IT! SOMETHING KINDA IMPORTANT CAME UP!
GEE, DON'T BE ANGRY, LIZ! YOU SEE--I-I HAVE TO STUDY FOR TOMORROW'S EXAM, AND...
PETER PARKER! YOU'RE THE TOP STUDENT IN THE CLASS! IF YOU CAN'T SPARE ONE EVENING FOR A DATE, THEN I'M SORRY FOR YOU! GOODBYE!
HEY, DIG THE CRAZY UMBRELLA! HOW COME YOU LEFT YOUR GALOSHES HOME, SKINNY??
SOMETIMES I THINK I OUGHTTA HAVE MY HEAD EXAMINED FOR STICKIN' TO THIS SPIDER-MAN BIT! I'M BEGINNIN' TO THINK A SECRET IDENTITY IS FOR THE BIRDS! I WONDER IF MY SPIDER POWER IS AFFECTING MY BRAIN, ALSO! NOTHING I DO SEEMS TO TURN OUT RIGHT!
PARKER! STOP DAY-DREAMING IN CLASS!
MEANWHILE, NOT TOO FAR AWAY, SANDMAN IS HAVING HIS SHARE OF TROUBLE, ALSO, AS HE REALIZES THAT EVADING THE POLICE ISN'T EASY--NOT EVEN FOR A SUPER-CRIMINAL!
I TURNED MY LEGS INTO SAND JUST IN TIME! THESE BLASTED COPS ARE ALL OVER THE PLACE!
THEY MAY BE HAVIN' A TOUGH JOB HOLDIN' ME, BUT THEY SURE ARE WEARIN' ME DOWN! I'VE GOT TO FIND A PLACE WHERE I CAN HOLE UP AND REST FOR A WHILE!
HMMM, THAT HIGH SCHOOL OVER THERE LOOKS LIKE A GOOD SPOT! NOBODY'D EVER THINK TO LOOK FOR ME IN THERE!
EVERYONE'S IN CLASS, EXCEPT FOR THAT LONE KID! NOW TO FIND AN EMPTY CLASSROOM!
THAT'S WHAT I GET FOR NOT PAYING ATTENTION IN CLASS! I GOT STUCK WITH THE JOB OF CARRYING THESE OLD BOTTLES FROM THE LAB TO THE BOILER ROOM! A REAL GLAMOR BOY, THAT'S ME!
LEAVE 'EM THERE, SONNY! I'LL GET RID OF 'EM AS SOON AS I ADJUST THIS NEW KING-SIZE VACUUM CLEANER!
HE DOESN'T KNOW HOW LUCKY HE IS! NO WORRIES EXCEPT KEEPING THIS SCHOOL CLEAN! NO NUTTY VILLAINS TO CHASE, LIKE I HAVE!
AND, ON THE FLOOR ABOVE...
SOMEONE'S COMIN'! I'D BETTER DUCK INTO THIS ROOM HERE!
10

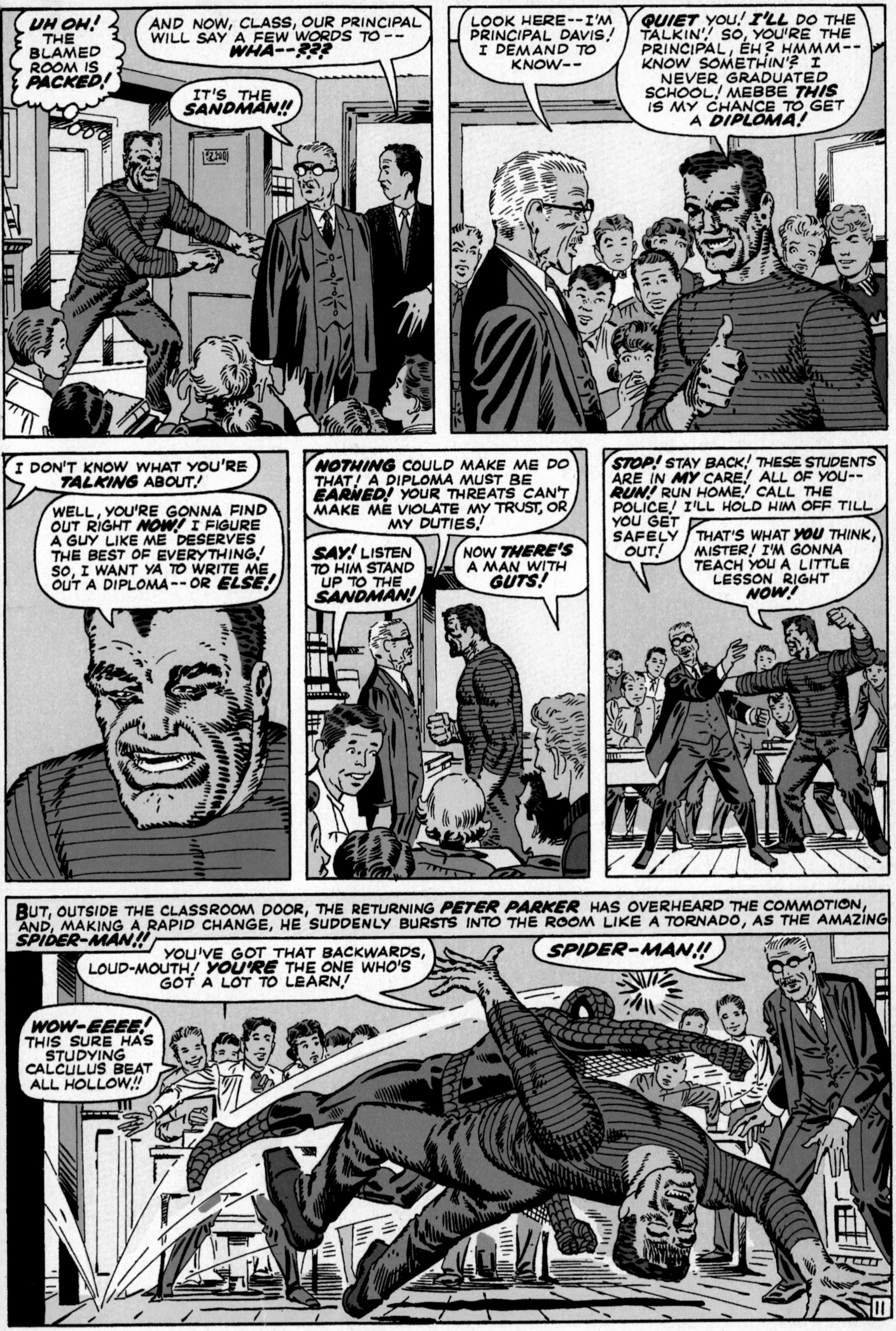
UH OH! THE BLAMED ROOM IS PACKED!
AND NOW, CLASS, OUR PRINCIPAL WILL SAY A FEW WORDS TO-- WHA--???
IT'S THE SANDMAN!!
LOOK HERE--I'M PRINCIPAL DAVIS! I DEMAND TO KNOW--
QUIET YOU! I'LL DO THE TALKIN'! SO, YOU'RE THE PRINCIPAL, EH? HMMM--KNOW SOMETHIN'? I NEVER GRADUATED SCHOOL! MEBBE THIS IS MY CHANCE TO GET A DIPLOMA!
I DON'T KNOW WHAT YOU'RE TALKING ABOUT!
WELL, YOU'RE GONNA FIND OUT RIGHT NOW! I FIGURE A GUY LIKE ME DESERVES THE BEST OF EVERYTHING! SO, I WANT YA TO WRITE ME OUT A DIPLOMA--OR ELSE!
NOTHING COULD MAKE ME DO THAT! A DIPLOMA MUST BE EARNED! YOUR THREATS CAN'T MAKE ME VIOLATE MY TRUST, OR MY DUTIES!
SAY! LISTEN TO HIM STAND UP TO THE SANDMAN!
NOW THERE'S A MAN WITH GUTS!
STOP! STAY BACK! THESE STUDENTS ARE IN MY CARE! ALL OF YOU--RUN! RUN HOME! CALL THE POLICE! I'LL HOLD HIM OFF TILL YOU GET SAFELY OUT!
THAT'S WHAT YOU THINK, MISTER! I'M GONNA TEACH YOU A LITTLE LESSON RIGHT NOW!
BUT, OUTSIDE THE CLASSROOM DOOR, THE RETURNING PETER PARKER HAS OVERHEARD THE COMMOTION, AND, MAKING A RAPID CHANGE, HE SUDDENLY BURSTS INTO THE ROOM LIKE A TORNADO, AS THE AMAZING SPIDER-MAN!!
YOU'VE GOT THAT BACKWARDS, LOUD-MOUTH! YOU'RE THE ONE WHO'S GOT A LOT TO LEARN!
SPIDER-MAN!!
WOW-EEEE! THIS SURE HAS STUDYING CALCULUS BEAT ALL HOLLOW!!
11

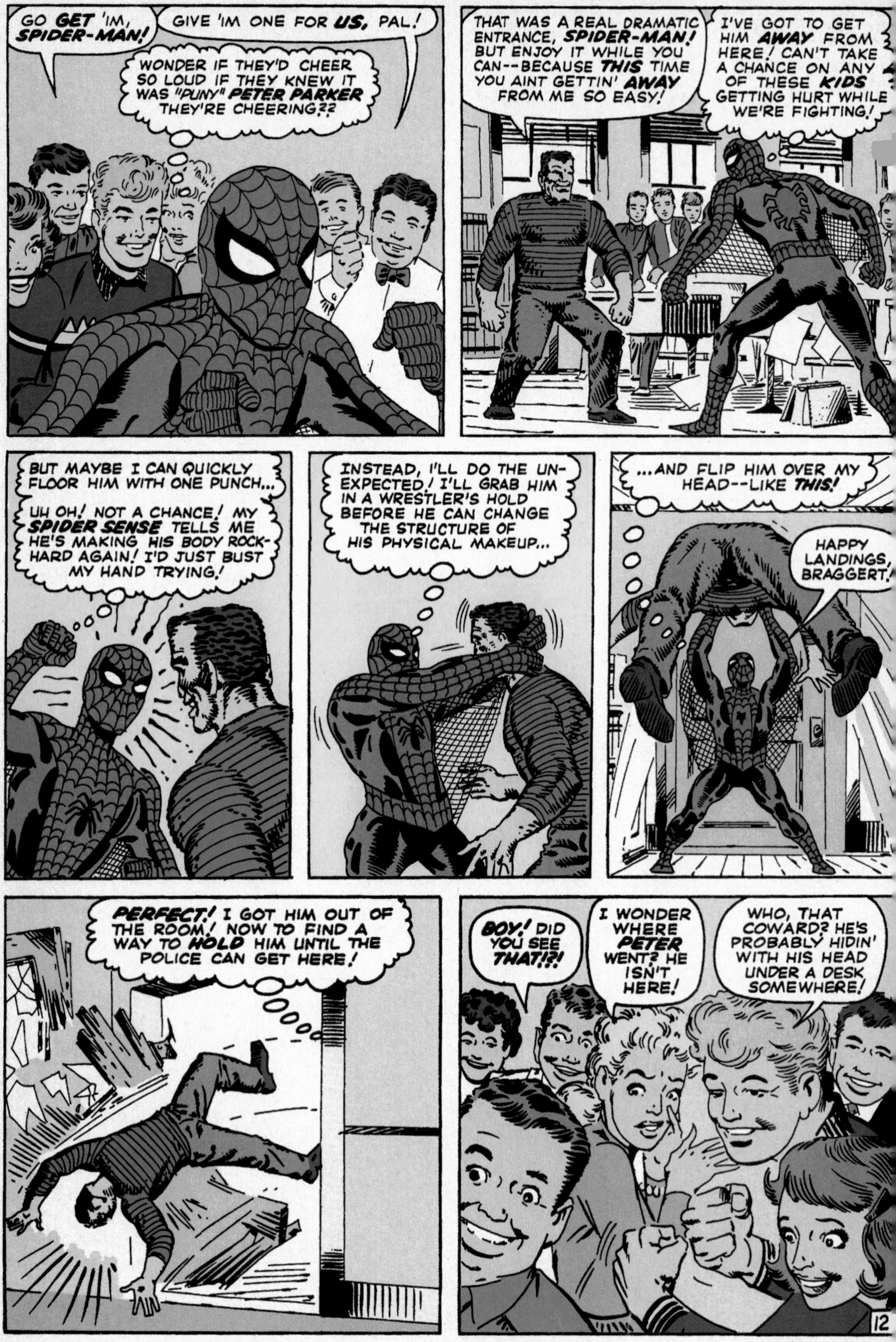
GO GET 'IM, SPIDER-MAN!
GIVE 'IM ONE FOR US, PAL!
WONDER IF THEY'D CHEER SO LOUD IF THEY KNEW IT WAS "PUNY" PETER PARKER THEY'RE CHEERING??
THAT WAS A REAL DRAMATIC ENTRANCE, SPIDER-MAN! BUT ENJOY IT WHILE YOU CAN--BECAUSE THIS TIME YOU AINT GETTIN' AWAY FROM ME SO EASY!
I'VE GOT TO GET HIM AWAY FROM HERE! CAN'T TAKE A CHANCE ON ANY OF THESE KIDS GETTING HURT WHILE WE'RE FIGHTING!
BUT MAYBE I CAN QUICKLY FLOOR HIM WITH ONE PUNCH...
UH OH! NOT A CHANCE! MY SPIDER SENSE TELLS ME HE'S MAKING HIS BODY ROCK-HARD AGAIN! I'D JUST BUST MY HAND TRYING!
INSTEAD, I'LL DO THE UN-EXPECTED! I'LL GRAB HIM IN A WRESTLER'S HOLD BEFORE HE CAN CHANGE THE STRUCTURE OF HIS PHYSICAL MAKEUP...
...AND FLIP HIM OVER MY HEAD--LIKE THIS!
HAPPY LANDINGS, BRAGGERT!
PERFECT! I GOT HIM OUT OF THE ROOM! NOW TO FIND A WAY TO HOLD HIM UNTIL THE POLICE CAN GET HERE!
BOY! DID YOU SEE THAT!?!
I WONDER WHERE PETER WENT? HE ISN'T HERE!
WHO, THAT COWARD? HE'S PROBABLY HIDIN' WITH HIS HEAD UNDER A DESK SOMEWHERE!
12

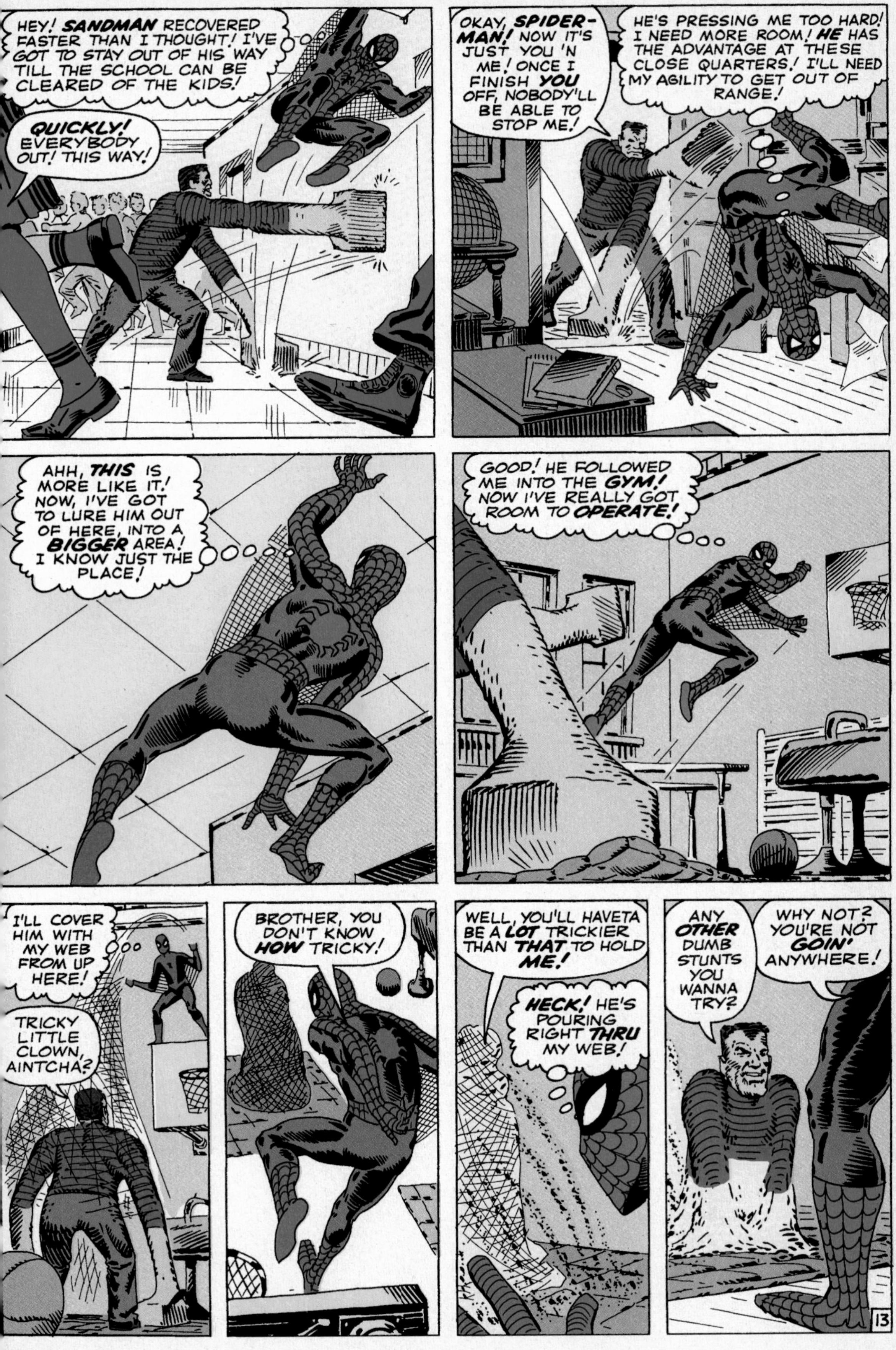
HEY! SANDMAN RECOVERED FASTER THAN I THOUGHT! I'VE GOT TO STAY OUT OF HIS WAY TILL THE SCHOOL CAN BE CLEARED OF THE KIDS!
QUICKLY! EVERYBODY OUT! THIS WAY!
OKAY, SPIDER-MAN! NOW IT'S JUST YOU 'N ME! ONCE I FINISH YOU OFF, NOBODY'LL BE ABLE TO STOP ME!
HE'S PRESSING ME TOO HARD! I NEED MORE ROOM! HE HAS THE ADVANTAGE AT THESE CLOSE QUARTERS! I'LL NEED MY AGILITY TO GET OUT OF RANGE!
AHH, THIS IS MORE LIKE IT! NOW, I'VE GOT TO LURE HIM OUT OF HERE, INTO A BIGGER AREA! I KNOW JUST THE PLACE!
GOOD! HE FOLLOWED ME INTO THE GYM! NOW I'VE REALLY GOT ROOM TO OPERATE!
I'LL COVER HIM WITH MY WEB FROM UP HERE!
TRICKY LITTLE CLOWN, AINTCHA?
BROTHER, YOU DON'T KNOW HOW TRICKY!
WELL, YOU'LL HAVETA BE A LOT TRICKIER THAN THAT TO HOLD ME!
HECK! HE'S POURING RIGHT THRU MY WEB!
ANY OTHER DUMB STUNTS YOU WANNA TRY?
WHY NOT? YOU'RE NOT GOIN' ANYWHERE!
13

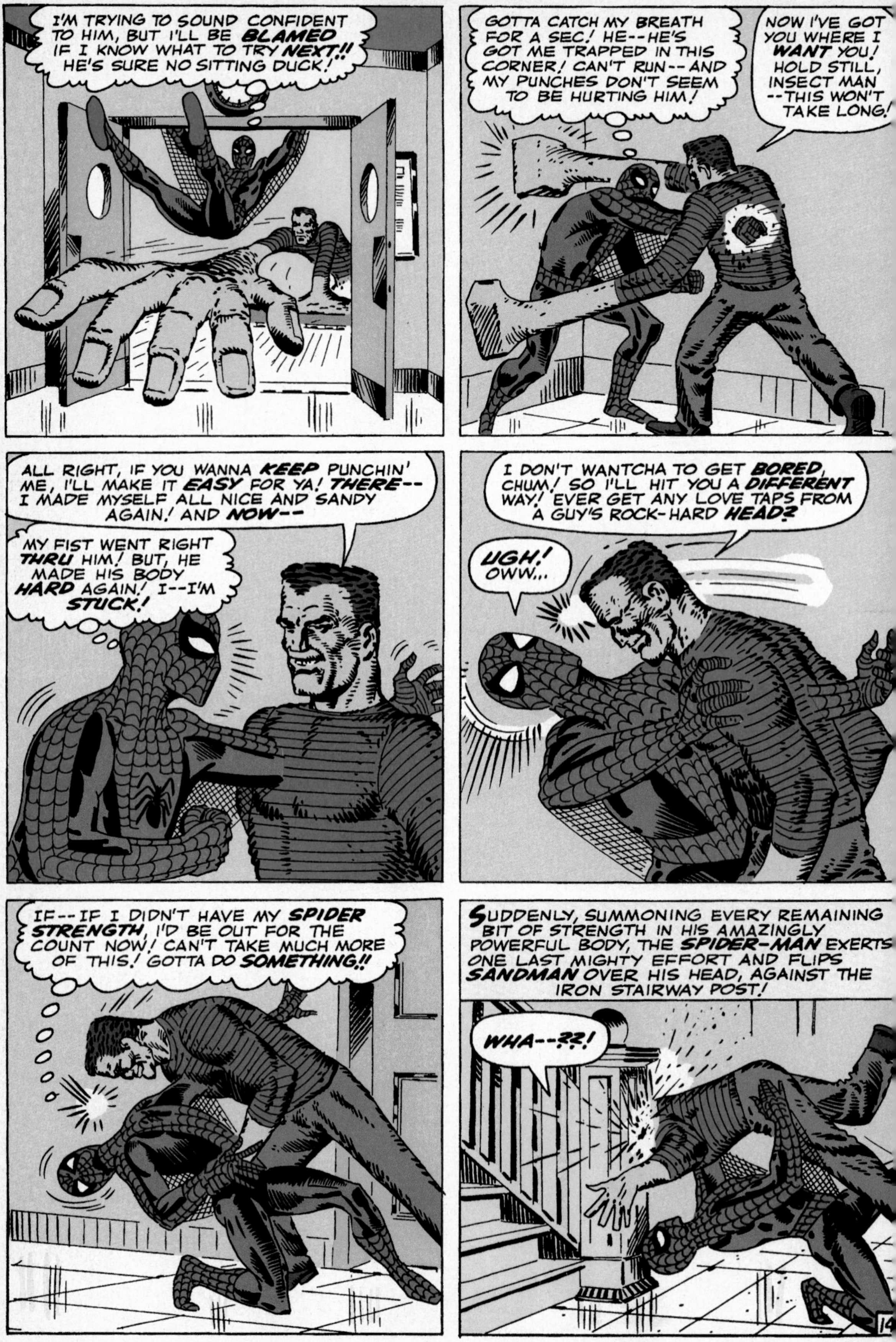
I'M TRYING TO SOUND CONFIDENT TO HIM, BUT I'LL BE BLAMED IF I KNOW WHAT TO TRY NEXT!! HE'S SURE NO SITTING DUCK!
GOTTA CATCH MY BREATH FOR A SEC! HE--HE'S GOT ME TRAPPED IN THIS CORNER! CAN'T RUN--AND MY PUNCHES DON'T SEEM TO BE HURTING HIM!
NOW I'VE GOT YOU WHERE I WANT YOU! HOLD STILL, INSECT MAN --THIS WON'T TAKE LONG!
ALL RIGHT, IF YOU WANNA KEEP PUNCHIN' ME, I'LL MAKE IT EASY FOR YA! THERE-- I MADE MYSELF ALL NICE AND SANDY AGAIN! AND NOW--
MY FIST WENT RIGHT THRU HIM! BUT, HE MADE HIS BODY HARD AGAIN! I--I'M STUCK!
I DON'T WANTCHA TO GET BORED, CHUM! SO I'LL HIT YOU A DIFFERENT WAY! EVER GET ANY LOVE TAPS FROM A GUY'S ROCK-HARD HEAD?
UGH! OWW...
IF--IF I DIDN'T HAVE MY SPIDER STRENGTH, I'D BE OUT FOR THE COUNT NOW! CAN'T TAKE MUCH MORE OF THIS! GOTTA DO SOMETHING!!
SUDDENLY, SUMMONING EVERY REMAINING BIT OF STRENGTH IN HIS AMAZINGLY POWERFUL BODY, THE SPIDER-MAN EXERTS ONE LAST MIGHTY EFFORT AND FLIPS SANDMAN OVER HIS HEAD, AGAINST THE IRON STAIRWAY POST!
WHA--??!
14

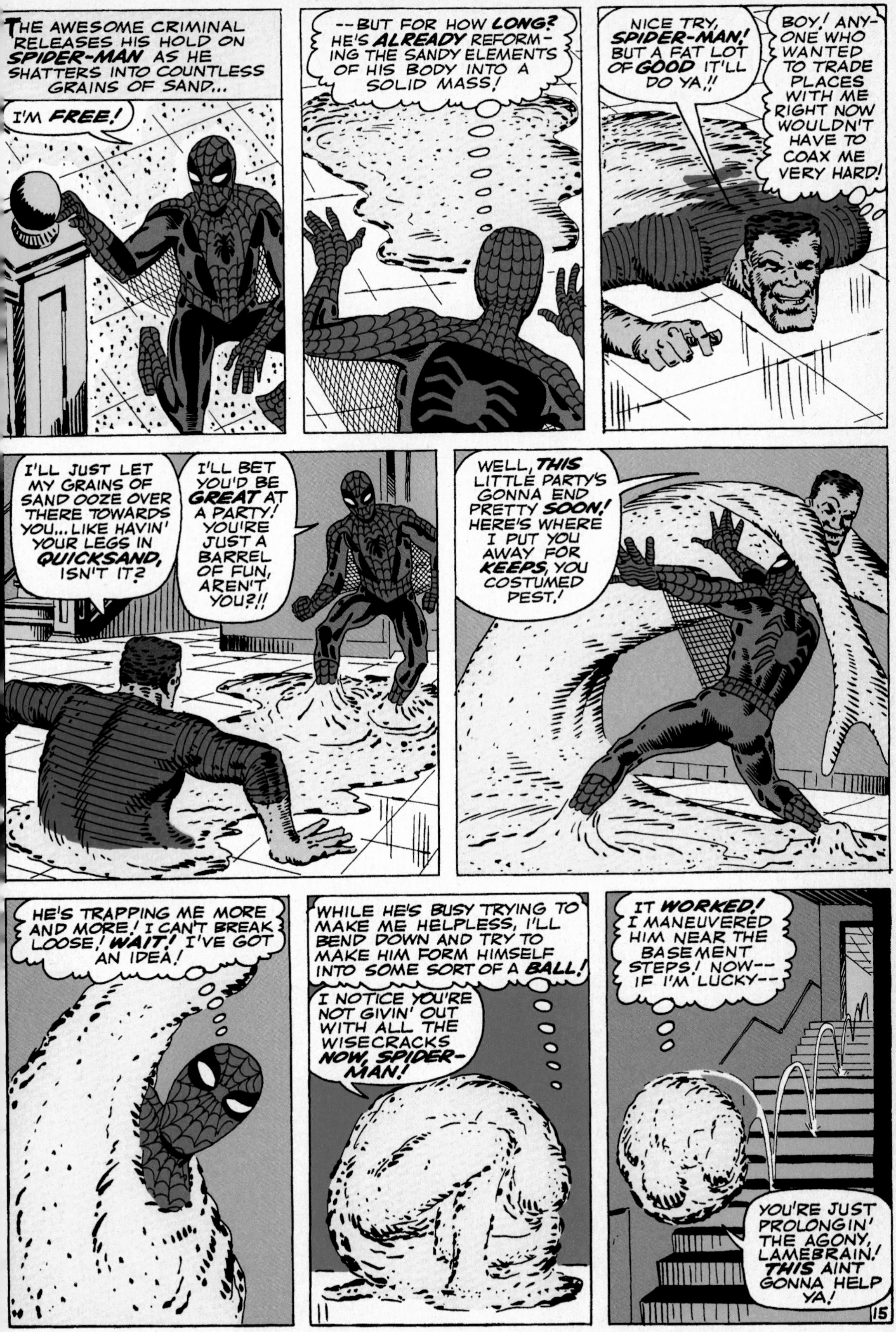
THE AWESOME CRIMINAL RELEASES HIS HOLD ON SPIDER-MAN AS HE SHATTERS INTO COUNTLESS GRAINS OF SAND...
I'M FREE!
--BUT FOR HOW LONG? HE'S ALREADY REFORMING THE SANDY ELEMENTS OF HIS BODY INTO A SOLID MASS!
NICE TRY, SPIDER-MAN! BUT A FAT LOT OF GOOD IT'LL DO YA!!
BOY! ANYONE WHO WANTED TO TRADE PLACES WITH ME RIGHT NOW WOULDN'T HAVE TO COAX ME VERY HARD!
I'LL JUST LET MY GRAINS OF SAND OOZE OVER THERE TOWARDS YOU... LIKE HAVIN' YOUR LEGS IN QUICKSAND, ISN'T IT?
I'LL BET YOU'D BE GREAT AT A PARTY! YOU'RE JUST A BARREL OF FUN, AREN'T YOU?!!
WELL, THIS LITTLE PARTY'S GONNA END PRETTY SOON! HERE'S WHERE I PUT YOU AWAY FOR KEEPS, YOU COSTUMED PEST!
HE'S TRAPPING ME MORE AND MORE! I CAN'T BREAK LOOSE! WAIT! I'VE GOT AN IDEA!
WHILE HE'S BUSY TRYING TO MAKE ME HELPLESS, I'LL BEND DOWN AND TRY TO MAKE HIM FORM HIMSELF INTO SOME SORT OF A BALL!
I NOTICE YOU'RE NOT GIVIN' OUT WITH ALL THE WISECRACKS NOW, SPIDER-MAN!
IT WORKED! I MANEUVERED HIM NEAR THE BASEMENT STEPS! NOW-- IF I'M LUCKY--
YOU'RE JUST PROLONGIN' THE AGONY, LAMEBRAIN! THIS AINT GONNA HELP YA!
15

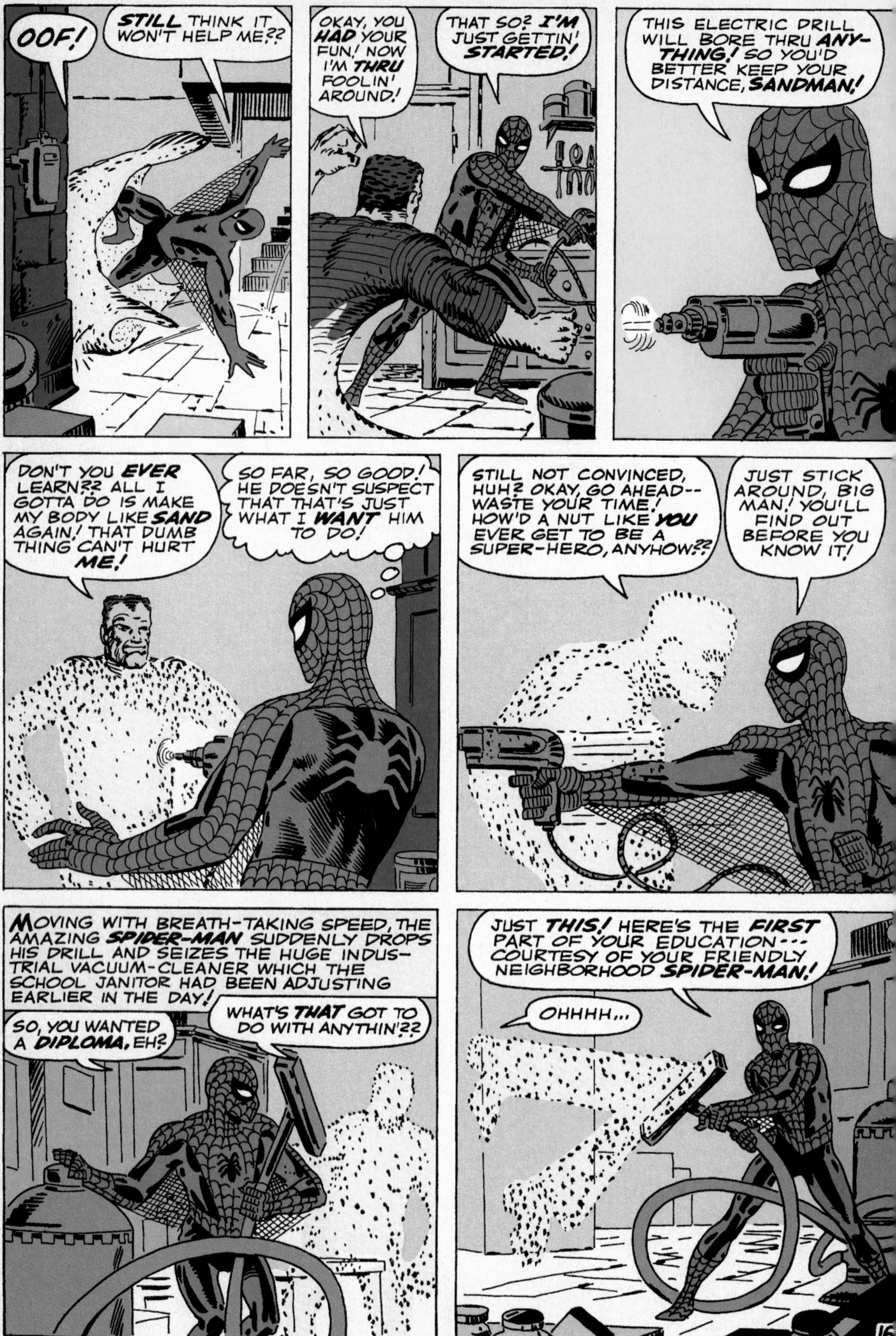
OOF!
STILL THINK IT WON'T HELP ME??
OKAY, YOU HAD YOUR FUN! NOW I'M THRU FOOLIN' AROUND!
THAT SO? I'M JUST GETTIN' STARTED!
THIS ELECTRIC DRILL WILL BORE THRU ANY-THING! SO YOU'D BETTER KEEP YOUR DISTANCE, SANDMAN!
DON'T YOU EVER LEARN?? ALL I GOTTA DO IS MAKE MY BODY LIKE SAND AGAIN! THAT DUMB THING CAN'T HURT ME!
SO FAR, SO GOOD! HE DOESN'T SUSPECT THAT THAT'S JUST WHAT I WANT HIM TO DO!
STILL NOT CONVINCED, HUH? OKAY, GO AHEAD-- WASTE YOUR TIME! HOW'D A NUT LIKE YOU EVER GET TO BE A SUPER-HERO, ANYHOW??
JUST STICK AROUND, BIG MAN! YOU'LL FIND OUT BEFORE YOU KNOW IT!
MOVING WITH BREATH-TAKING SPEED, THE AMAZING SPIDER-MAN SUDDENLY DROPS HIS DRILL AND SEIZES THE HUGE INDUS-TRIAL VACUUM-CLEANER WHICH THE SCHOOL JANITOR HAD BEEN ADJUSTING EARLIER IN THE DAY!
SO, YOU WANTED A DIPLOMA, EH?
WHAT'S THAT GOT TO DO WITH ANYTHIN'??
JUST THIS! HERE'S THE FIRST PART OF YOUR EDUCATION--- COURTESY OF YOUR FRIENDLY NEIGHBORHOOD SPIDER-MAN!
OHHHH...
16

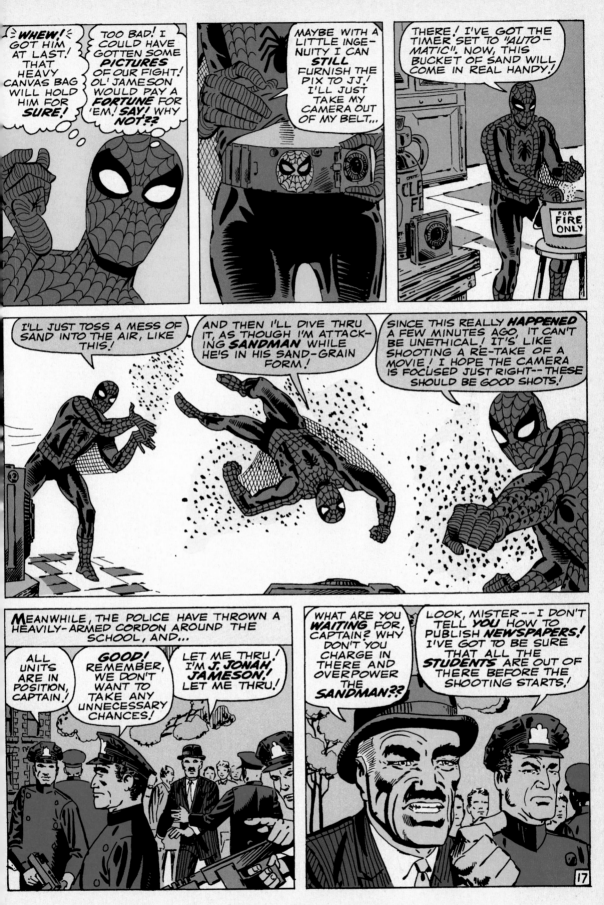

WHEW! GOT HIM AT LAST! THAT HEAVY CANVAS BAG WILL HOLD HIM FOR SURE!

TOO BAD! I COULD HAVE GOTTEN SOME PICTURES OF OUR FIGHT! OL' JAMESON WOULD PAY A FORTUNE FOR 'EM! SAY! WHY NOT??

MAYBE WITH A LITTLE INGE-NUITY I CAN STILL FURNISH THE PIX TO J.J.! I'LL JUST TAKE MY CAMERA OUT OF MY BELT...

THERE! I'VE GOT THE TIMER SET TO "AUTO-MATIC". NOW, THIS BUCKET OF SAND WILL COME IN REAL HANDY!

FOR FIRE ONLY

I'LL JUST TOSS A MESS OF SAND INTO THE AIR, LIKE THIS!

AND THEN I'LL DIVE THRU IT, AS THOUGH I'M ATTACK-ING SANDMAN WHILE HE'S IN HIS SAND-GRAIN FORM!

SINCE THIS REALLY HAPPENED A FEW MINUTES AGO, IT CAN'T BE UNETHICAL! IT'S LIKE SHOOTING A RE-TAKE OF A MOVIE! I HOPE THE CAMERA IS FOCUSED JUST RIGHT-- THESE SHOULD BE GOOD SHOTS!

MEANWHILE, THE POLICE HAVE THROWN A HEAVILY-ARMED CORDON AROUND THE SCHOOL, AND...

ALL UNITS ARE IN POSITION, CAPTAIN!

GOOD! REMEMBER, WE DON'T WANT TO TAKE ANY UNNECESSARY CHANCES!

LET ME THRU! I'M J. JONAH JAMESON! LET ME THRU!

WHAT ARE YOU WAITING FOR, CAPTAIN? WHY DON'T YOU CHARGE IN THERE AND OVERPOWER THE SANDMAN??

LOOK, MISTER-- I DON'T TELL YOU HOW TO PUBLISH NEWSPAPERS! I'VE GOT TO BE SURE THAT ALL THE STUDENTS ARE OUT OF THERE BEFORE THE SHOOTING STARTS!

17

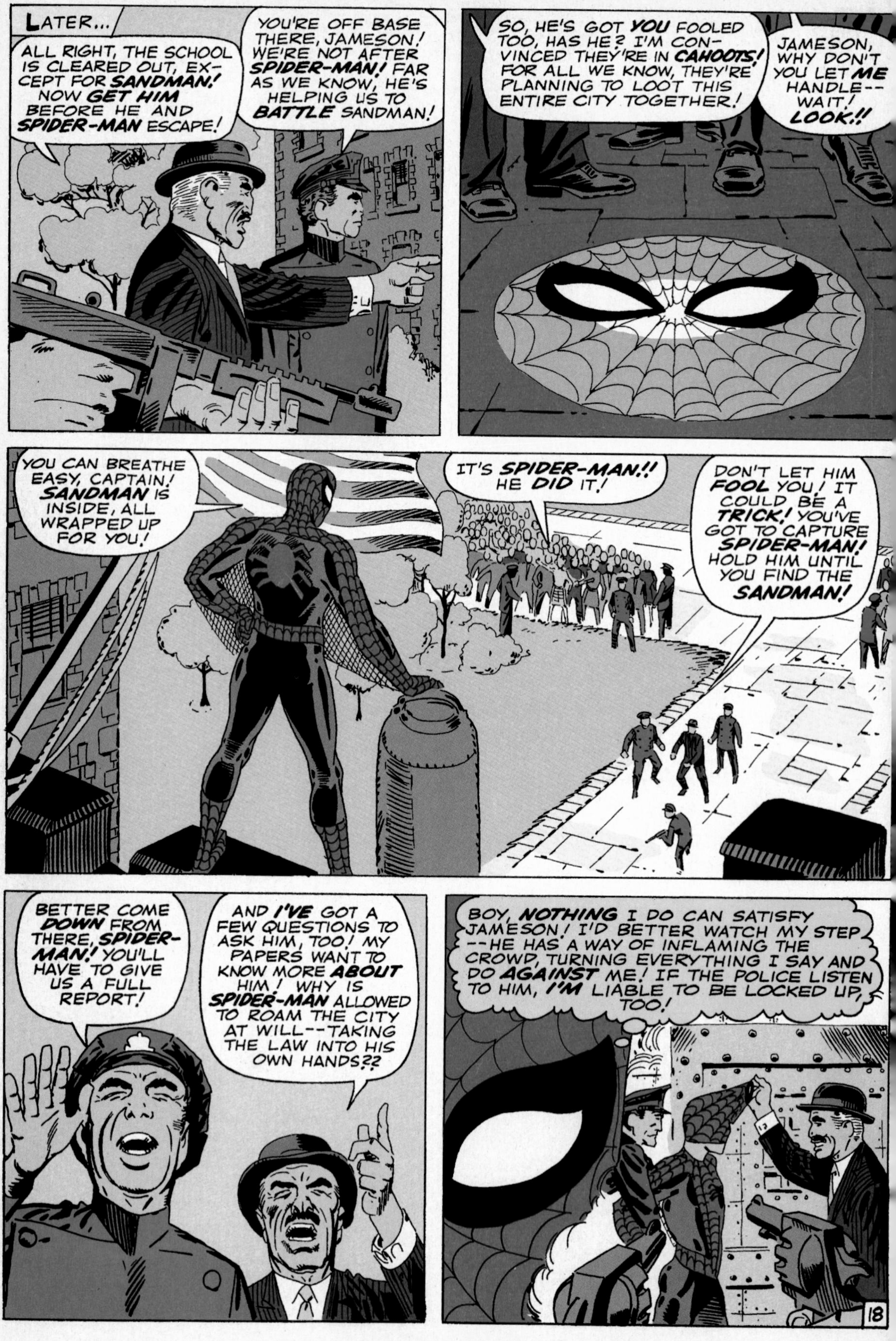
LATER...
ALL RIGHT, THE SCHOOL IS CLEARED OUT, EXCEPT FOR SANDMAN! NOW GET HIM BEFORE HE AND SPIDER-MAN ESCAPE!
YOU'RE OFF BASE THERE, JAMESON! WE'RE NOT AFTER SPIDER-MAN! FAR AS WE KNOW, HE'S HELPING US TO BATTLE SANDMAN!
SO, HE'S GOT YOU FOOLED TOO, HAS HE? I'M CONVINCED THEY'RE IN CAHOOTS! FOR ALL WE KNOW, THEY'RE PLANNING TO LOOT THIS ENTIRE CITY TOGETHER!
JAMESON, WHY DON'T YOU LET ME HANDLE-- WAIT! LOOK!!
YOU CAN BREATHE EASY, CAPTAIN! SANDMAN IS INSIDE, ALL WRAPPED UP FOR YOU!
IT'S SPIDER-MAN!! HE DID IT!
DON'T LET HIM FOOL YOU! IT COULD BE A TRICK! YOU'VE GOT TO CAPTURE SPIDER-MAN! HOLD HIM UNTIL YOU FIND THE SANDMAN!
BETTER COME DOWN FROM THERE, SPIDER-MAN! YOU'LL HAVE TO GIVE US A FULL REPORT!
AND I'VE GOT A FEW QUESTIONS TO ASK HIM, TOO! MY PAPERS WANT TO KNOW MORE ABOUT HIM! WHY IS SPIDER-MAN ALLOWED TO ROAM THE CITY AT WILL--TAKING THE LAW INTO HIS OWN HANDS??
BOY, NOTHING I DO CAN SATISFY JAMESON! I'D BETTER WATCH MY STEP --HE HAS A WAY OF INFLAMING THE CROWD, TURNING EVERYTHING I SAY AND DO AGAINST ME! IF THE POLICE LISTEN TO HIM, I'M LIABLE TO BE LOCKED UP, TOO!
18

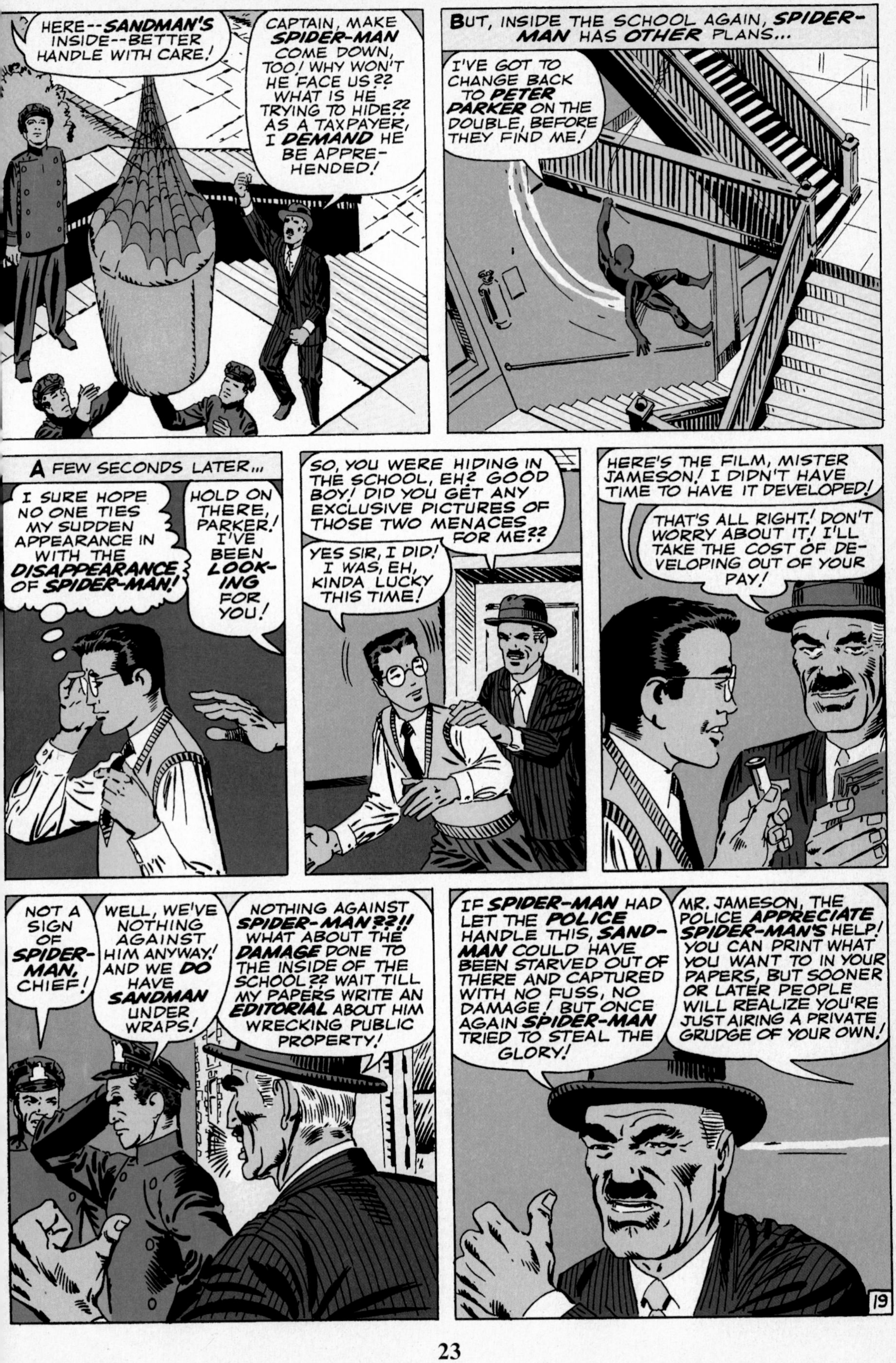
HERE--SANDMAN'S INSIDE--BETTER HANDLE WITH CARE!
CAPTAIN, MAKE SPIDER-MAN COME DOWN, TOO! WHY WON'T HE FACE US?? WHAT IS HE TRYING TO HIDE?? AS A TAXPAYER, I DEMAND HE BE APPREHENDED!
BUT, INSIDE THE SCHOOL AGAIN, SPIDER-MAN HAS OTHER PLANS...
I'VE GOT TO CHANGE BACK TO PETER PARKER ON THE DOUBLE, BEFORE THEY FIND ME!
A FEW SECONDS LATER...
I SURE HOPE NO ONE TIES MY SUDDEN APPEARANCE IN WITH THE DISAPPEARANCE OF SPIDER-MAN!
HOLD ON THERE, PARKER! I'VE BEEN LOOKING FOR YOU!
SO, YOU WERE HIDING IN THE SCHOOL, EH? GOOD BOY! DID YOU GET ANY EXCLUSIVE PICTURES OF THOSE TWO MENACES FOR ME??
YES SIR, I DID! I WAS, EH, KINDA LUCKY THIS TIME!
HERE'S THE FILM, MISTER JAMESON! I DIDN'T HAVE TIME TO HAVE IT DEVELOPED!
THAT'S ALL RIGHT! DON'T WORRY ABOUT IT! I'LL TAKE THE COST OF DEVELOPING OUT OF YOUR PAY!
NOT A SIGN OF SPIDER-MAN, CHIEF!
WELL, WE'VE NOTHING AGAINST HIM ANYWAY! AND WE DO HAVE SANDMAN UNDER WRAPS!
NOTHING AGAINST SPIDER-MAN??!! WHAT ABOUT THE DAMAGE DONE TO THE INSIDE OF THE SCHOOL?? WAIT TILL MY PAPERS WRITE AN EDITORIAL ABOUT HIM WRECKING PUBLIC PROPERTY!
IF SPIDER-MAN HAD LET THE POLICE HANDLE THIS, SANDMAN COULD HAVE BEEN STARVED OUT OF THERE AND CAPTURED WITH NO FUSS, NO DAMAGE! BUT ONCE AGAIN SPIDER-MAN TRIED TO STEAL THE GLORY!
MR. JAMESON, THE POLICE APPRECIATE SPIDER-MAN'S HELP! YOU CAN PRINT WHAT YOU WANT TO IN YOUR PAPERS, BUT SOONER OR LATER PEOPLE WILL REALIZE YOU'RE JUST AIRING A PRIVATE GRUDGE OF YOUR OWN!
19

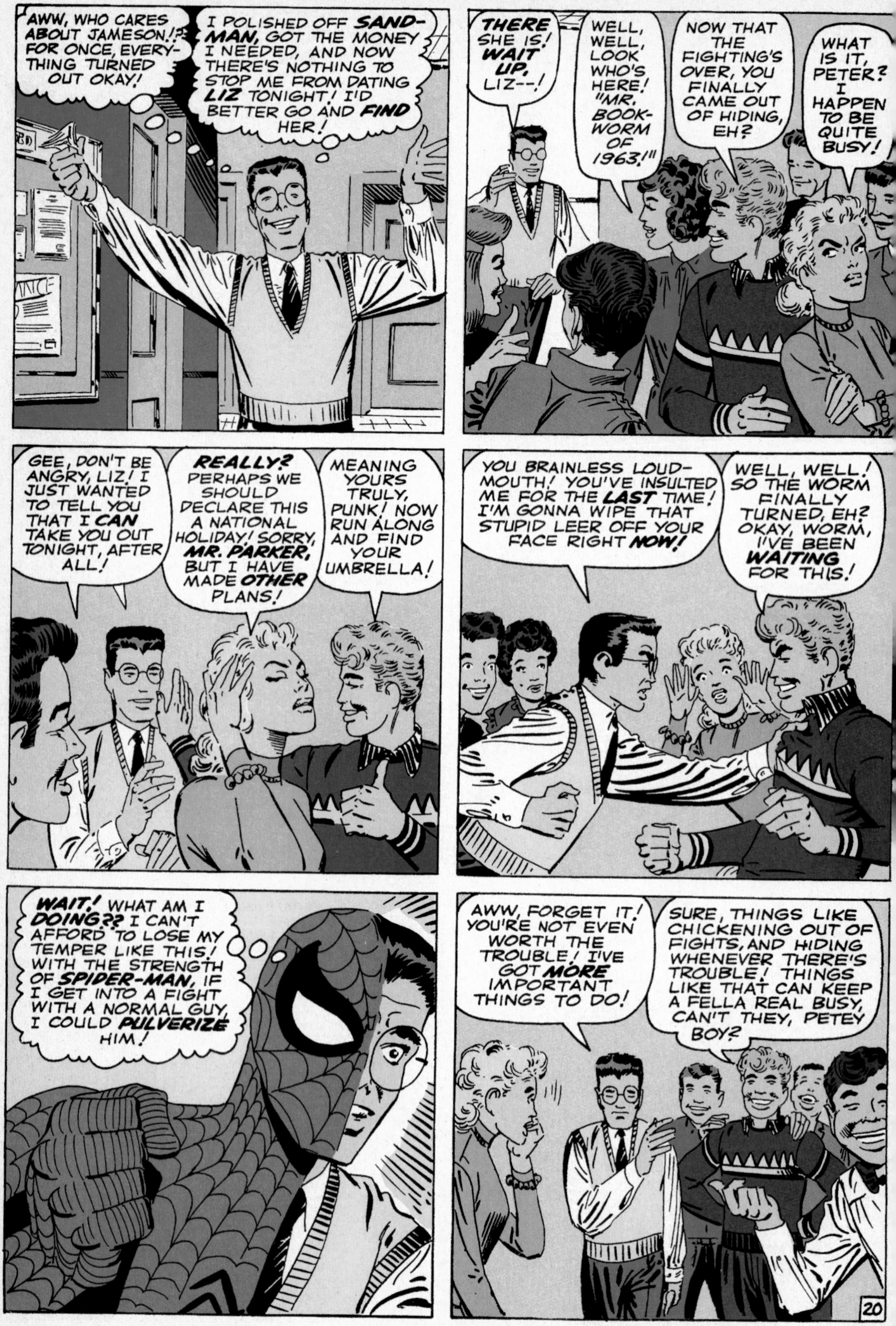
AWW, WHO CARES ABOUT JAMESON!? FOR ONCE, EVERYTHING TURNED OUT OKAY!
I POLISHED OFF SANDMAN, GOT THE MONEY I NEEDED, AND NOW THERE'S NOTHING TO STOP ME FROM DATING LIZ TONIGHT! I'D BETTER GO AND FIND HER!
THERE SHE IS! WAIT UP, LIZ--!
WELL, WELL, LOOK WHO'S HERE! "MR. BOOKWORM OF 1963!"
NOW THAT THE FIGHTING'S OVER, YOU FINALLY CAME OUT OF HIDING, EH?
WHAT IS IT, PETER? I HAPPEN TO BE QUITE BUSY!
GEE, DON'T BE ANGRY, LIZ! I JUST WANTED TO TELL YOU THAT I CAN TAKE YOU OUT TONIGHT, AFTER ALL!
REALLY? PERHAPS WE SHOULD DECLARE THIS A NATIONAL HOLIDAY! SORRY, MR. PARKER, BUT I HAVE MADE OTHER PLANS!
MEANING YOURS TRULY, PUNK! NOW RUN ALONG AND FIND YOUR UMBRELLA!
YOU BRAINLESS LOUDMOUTH! YOU'VE INSULTED ME FOR THE LAST TIME! I'M GONNA WIPE THAT STUPID LEER OFF YOUR FACE RIGHT NOW!
WELL, WELL! SO THE WORM FINALLY TURNED, EH? OKAY, WORM, I'VE BEEN WAITING FOR THIS!
WAIT! WHAT AM I DOING?? I CAN'T AFFORD TO LOSE MY TEMPER LIKE THIS! WITH THE STRENGTH OF SPIDER-MAN, IF I GET INTO A FIGHT WITH A NORMAL GUY, I COULD PULVERIZE HIM!
AWW, FORGET IT! YOU'RE NOT EVEN WORTH THE TROUBLE! I'VE GOT MORE IMPORTANT THINGS TO DO!
SURE, THINGS LIKE CHICKENING OUT OF FIGHTS, AND HIDING WHENEVER THERE'S TROUBLE! THINGS LIKE THAT CAN KEEP A FELLA REAL BUSY, CAN'T THEY, PETEY BOY?
20

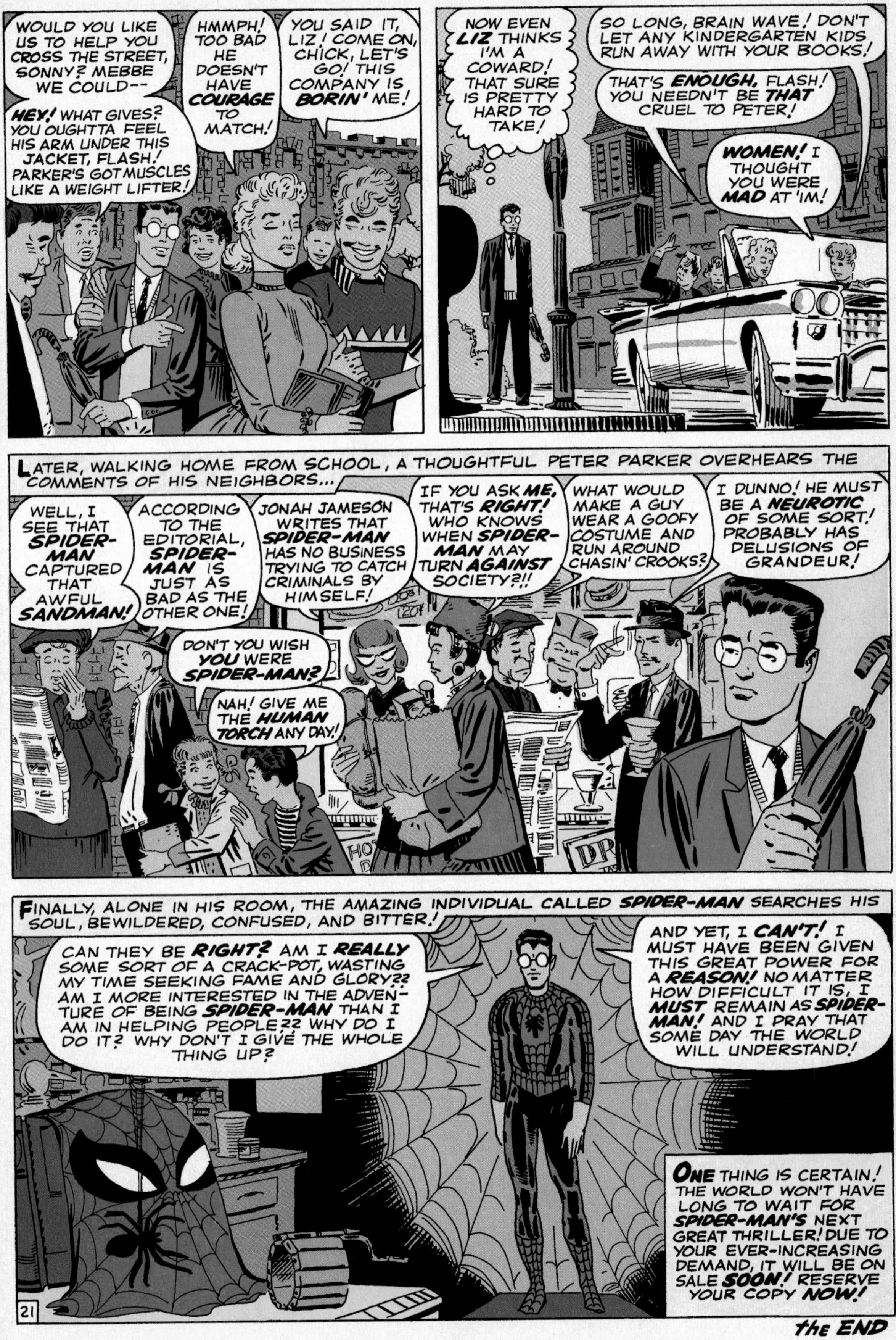
WOULD YOU LIKE US TO HELP YOU CROSS THE STREET, SONNY? MEBBE WE COULD--
HEY! WHAT GIVES? YOU OUGHTTA FEEL HIS ARM UNDER THIS JACKET, FLASH! PARKER'S GOT MUSCLES LIKE A WEIGHT LIFTER!
HMMPH! TOO BAD HE DOESN'T HAVE COURAGE TO MATCH!
YOU SAID IT, LIZ! COME ON, CHICK, LET'S GO! THIS COMPANY IS BORIN' ME!
NOW EVEN LIZ THINKS I'M A COWARD! THAT SURE IS PRETTY HARD TO TAKE!
SO LONG, BRAIN WAVE! DON'T LET ANY KINDERGARTEN KIDS RUN AWAY WITH YOUR BOOKS!
THAT'S ENOUGH, FLASH! YOU NEEDN'T BE THAT CRUEL TO PETER!
WOMEN! I THOUGHT YOU WERE MAD AT 'IM!
LATER, WALKING HOME FROM SCHOOL, A THOUGHTFUL PETER PARKER OVERHEARS THE COMMENTS OF HIS NEIGHBORS...
WELL, I SEE THAT SPIDER-MAN CAPTURED THAT AWFUL SANDMAN!
ACCORDING TO THE EDITORIAL, SPIDER-MAN IS JUST AS BAD AS THE OTHER ONE!
JONAH JAMESON WRITES THAT SPIDER-MAN HAS NO BUSINESS TRYING TO CATCH CRIMINALS BY HIMSELF!
IF YOU ASK ME, THAT'S RIGHT! WHO KNOWS WHEN SPIDER-MAN MAY TURN AGAINST SOCIETY?!!
WHAT WOULD MAKE A GUY WEAR A GOOFY COSTUME AND RUN AROUND CHASIN' CROOKS?
I DUNNO! HE MUST BE A NEUROTIC OF SOME SORT! PROBABLY HAS DELUSIONS OF GRANDEUR!
DON'T YOU WISH YOU WERE SPIDER-MAN?
NAH! GIVE ME THE HUMAN TORCH ANY DAY!
FINALLY, ALONE IN HIS ROOM, THE AMAZING INDIVIDUAL CALLED SPIDER-MAN SEARCHES HIS SOUL, BEWILDERED, CONFUSED, AND BITTER!
CAN THEY BE RIGHT? AM I REALLY SOME SORT OF A CRACK-POT, WASTING MY TIME SEEKING FAME AND GLORY?? AM I MORE INTERESTED IN THE ADVENTURE OF BEING SPIDER-MAN THAN I AM IN HELPING PEOPLE?? WHY DO I DO IT? WHY DON'T I GIVE THE WHOLE THING UP?
AND YET, I CAN'T! I MUST HAVE BEEN GIVEN THIS GREAT POWER FOR A REASON! NO MATTER HOW DIFFICULT IT IS, I MUST REMAIN AS SPIDER-MAN! AND I PRAY THAT SOME DAY THE WORLD WILL UNDERSTAND!
ONE THING IS CERTAIN! THE WORLD WON'T HAVE LONG TO WAIT FOR SPIDER-MAN'S NEXT GREAT THRILLER! DUE TO YOUR EVER-INCREASING DEMAND, IT WILL BE ON SALE SOON! RESERVE YOUR COPY NOW!
21
the END

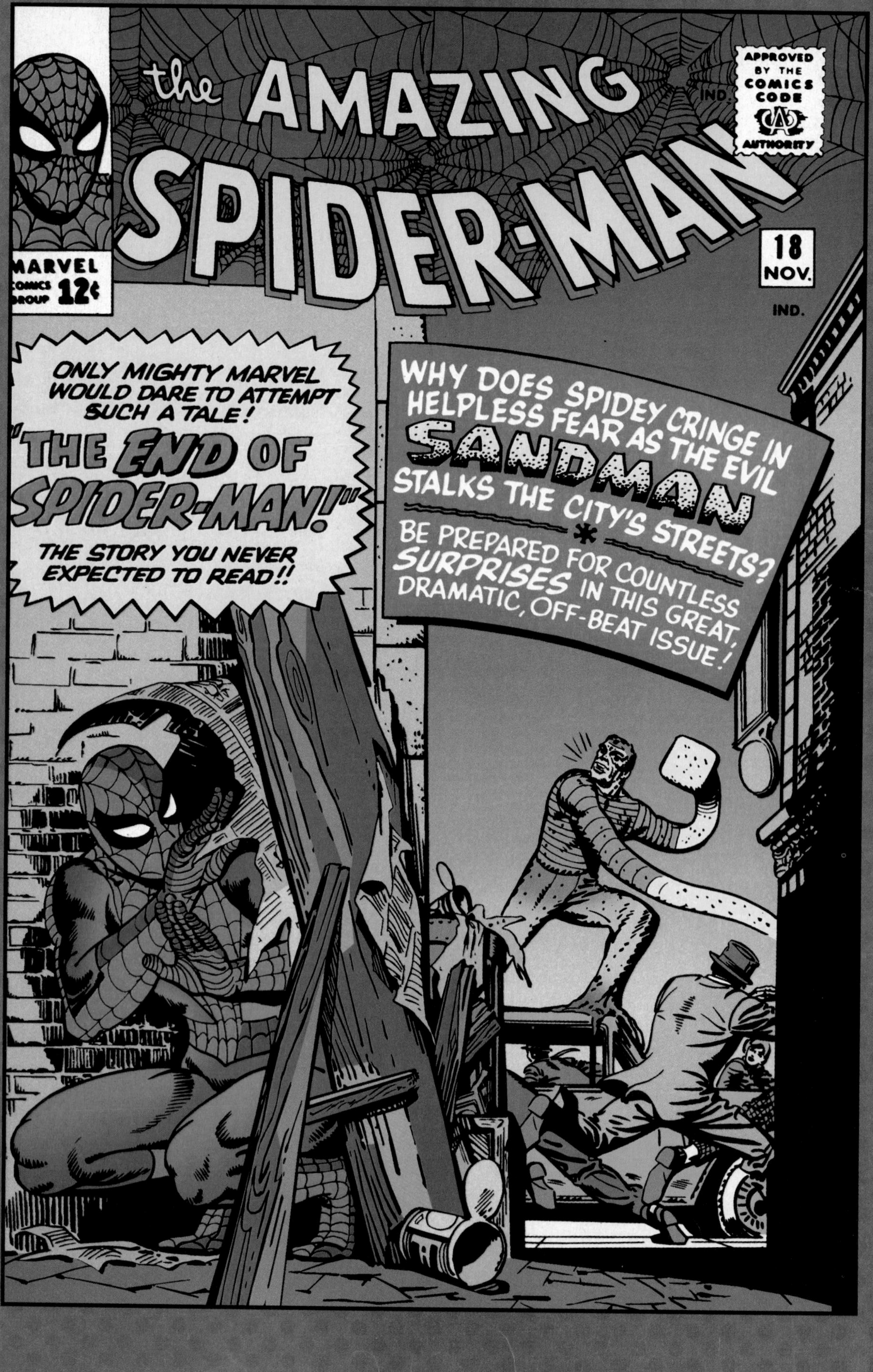
the AMAZING SPIDER-MAN
MARVEL COMICS GROUP 12¢
APPROVED BY THE COMICS CODE AUTHORITY
18 NOV.
IND.
ONLY MIGHTY MARVEL WOULD DARE TO ATTEMPT SUCH A TALE! "THE END OF SPIDER-MAN!" THE STORY YOU NEVER EXPECTED TO READ!!
WHY DOES SPIDEY CRINGE IN HELPLESS FEAR AS THE EVIL SANDMAN STALKS THE CITY'S STREETS?
BE PREPARED FOR COUNTLESS SURPRISES IN THIS GREAT, DRAMATIC, OFF-BEAT ISSUE!

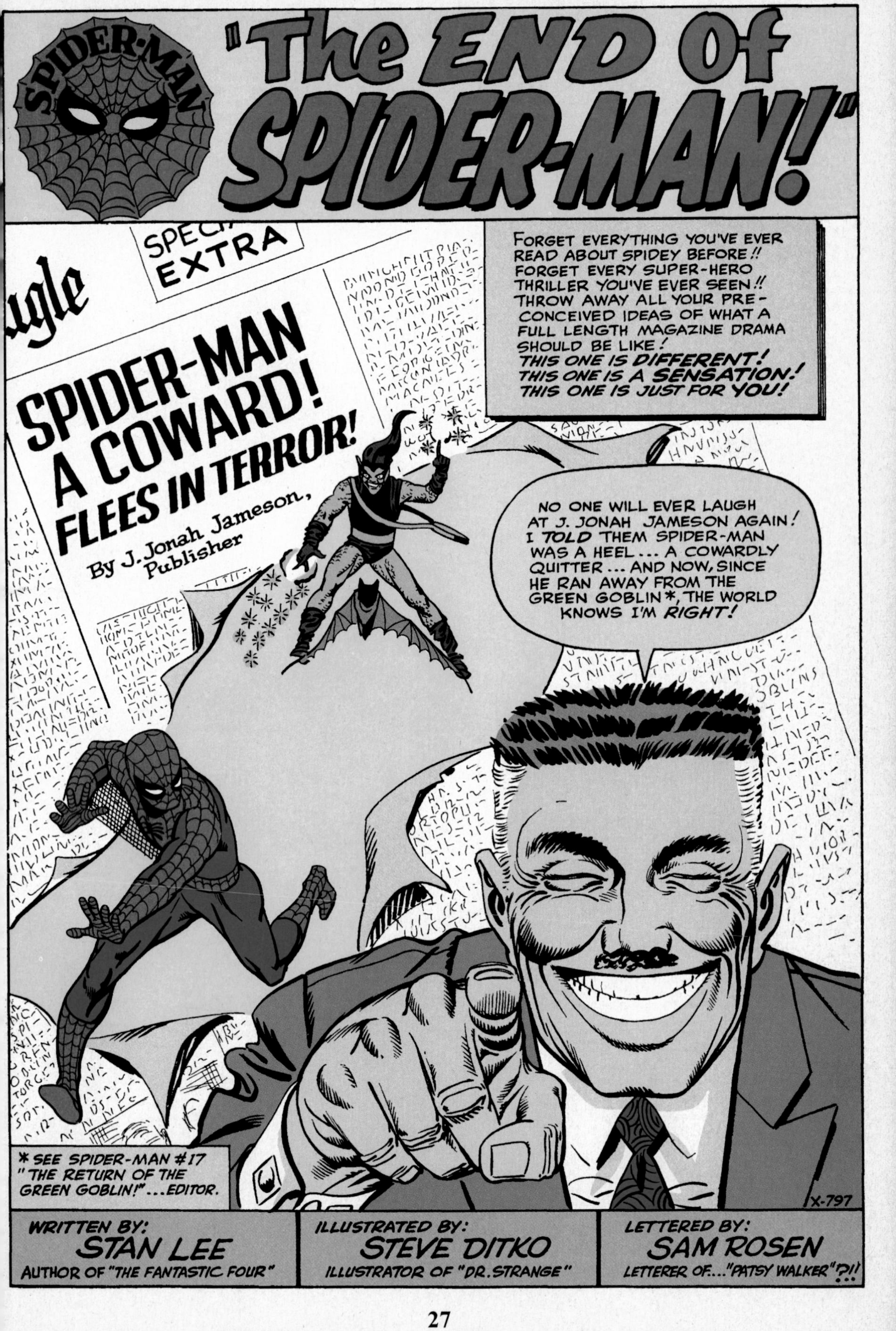
SPIDER-MAN
"The END of SPIDER-MAN!"
SPECI EXTRA
SPIDER-MAN A COWARD! FLEES IN TERROR!
By J. Jonah Jameson, Publisher
FORGET EVERYTHING YOU'VE EVER READ ABOUT SPIDEY BEFORE!! FORGET EVERY SUPER-HERO THRILLER YOU'VE EVER SEEN!! THROW AWAY ALL YOUR PRE-CONCEIVED IDEAS OF WHAT A FULL LENGTH MAGAZINE DRAMA SHOULD BE LIKE! THIS ONE IS DIFFERENT! THIS ONE IS A SENSATION! THIS ONE IS JUST FOR YOU!
NO ONE WILL EVER LAUGH AT J. JONAH JAMESON AGAIN! I TOLD THEM SPIDER-MAN WAS A HEEL... A COWARDLY QUITTER... AND NOW, SINCE HE RAN AWAY FROM THE GREEN GOBLIN*, THE WORLD KNOWS I'M RIGHT!
* SEE SPIDER-MAN #17 "THE RETURN OF THE GREEN GOBLIN!"... EDITOR.
X-797
WRITTEN BY: STAN LEE AUTHOR OF "THE FANTASTIC FOUR"
ILLUSTRATED BY: STEVE DITKO ILLUSTRATOR OF "DR. STRANGE"
LETTERED BY: SAM ROSEN LETTERER OF... "PATSY WALKER"?!!

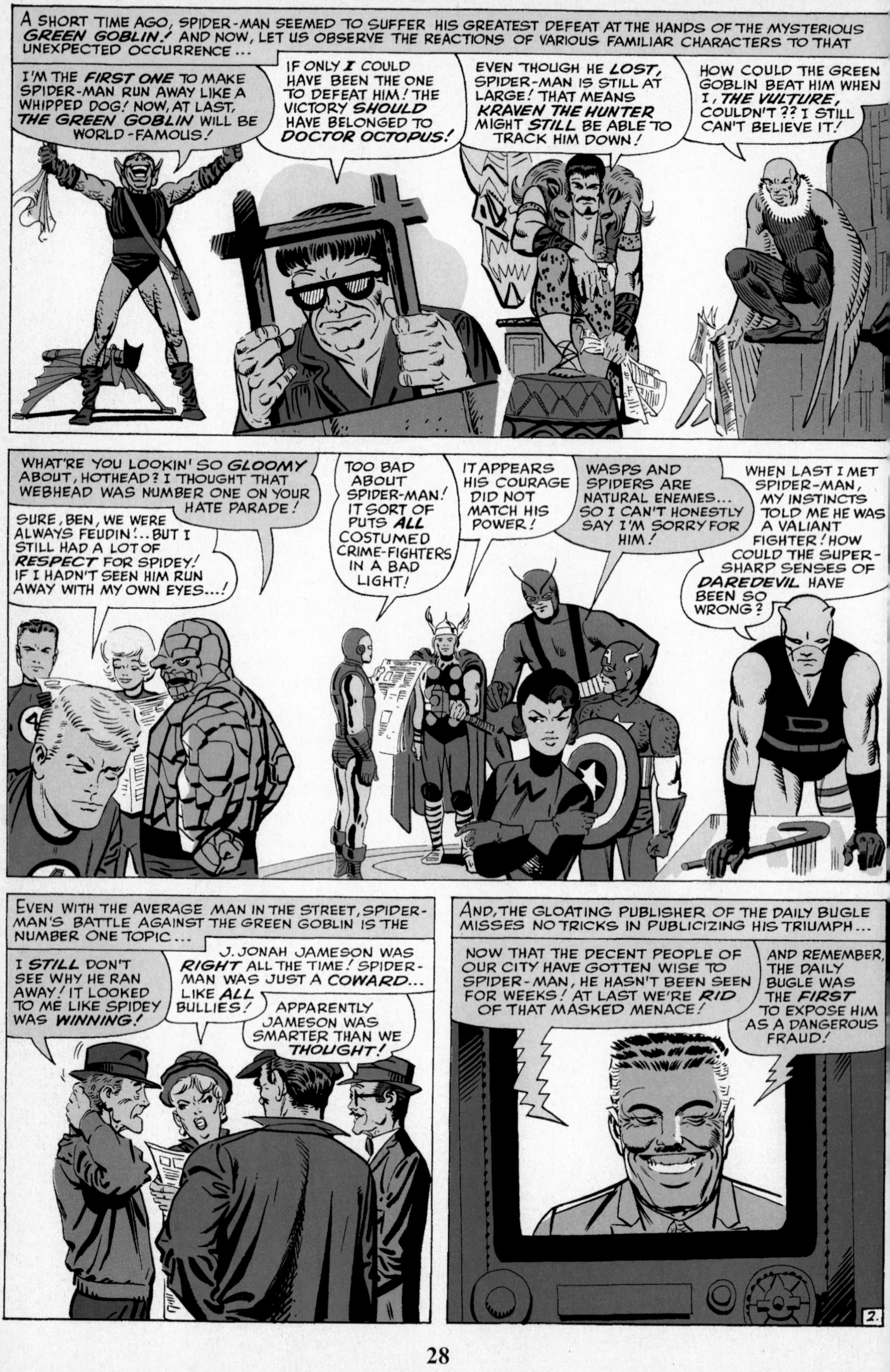

A SHORT TIME AGO, SPIDER-MAN SEEMED TO SUFFER HIS GREATEST DEFEAT AT THE HANDS OF THE MYSTERIOUS GREEN GOBLIN! AND NOW, LET US OBSERVE THE REACTIONS OF VARIOUS FAMILIAR CHARACTERS TO THAT UNEXPECTED OCCURRENCE...
I'M THE FIRST ONE TO MAKE SPIDER-MAN RUN AWAY LIKE A WHIPPED DOG! NOW, AT LAST, THE GREEN GOBLIN WILL BE WORLD-FAMOUS!
IF ONLY I COULD HAVE BEEN THE ONE TO DEFEAT HIM! THE VICTORY SHOULD HAVE BELONGED TO DOCTOR OCTOPUS!
EVEN THOUGH HE LOST, SPIDER-MAN IS STILL AT LARGE! THAT MEANS KRAVEN THE HUNTER MIGHT STILL BE ABLE TO TRACK HIM DOWN!
HOW COULD THE GREEN GOBLIN BEAT HIM WHEN I, THE VULTURE, COULDN'T?? I STILL CAN'T BELIEVE IT!
WHAT'RE YOU LOOKIN' SO GLOOMY ABOUT, HOTHEAD? I THOUGHT THAT WEBHEAD WAS NUMBER ONE ON YOUR HATE PARADE!
SURE, BEN, WE WERE ALWAYS FEUDIN'... BUT I STILL HAD A LOT OF RESPECT FOR SPIDEY! IF I HADN'T SEEN HIM RUN AWAY WITH MY OWN EYES...!
TOO BAD ABOUT SPIDER-MAN! IT SORT OF PUTS ALL COSTUMED CRIME-FIGHTERS IN A BAD LIGHT!
IT APPEARS HIS COURAGE DID NOT MATCH HIS POWER!
WASPS AND SPIDERS ARE NATURAL ENEMIES... SO I CAN'T HONESTLY SAY I'M SORRY FOR HIM!
WHEN LAST I MET SPIDER-MAN, MY INSTINCTS TOLD ME HE WAS A VALIANT FIGHTER! HOW COULD THE SUPER-SHARP SENSES OF DAREDEVIL HAVE BEEN SO WRONG?
EVEN WITH THE AVERAGE MAN IN THE STREET, SPIDER-MAN'S BATTLE AGAINST THE GREEN GOBLIN IS THE NUMBER ONE TOPIC...
I STILL DON'T SEE WHY HE RAN AWAY! IT LOOKED TO ME LIKE SPIDEY WAS WINNING!
J. JONAH JAMESON WAS RIGHT ALL THE TIME! SPIDER-MAN WAS JUST A COWARD... LIKE ALL BULLIES!
APPARENTLY JAMESON WAS SMARTER THAN WE THOUGHT!
AND, THE GLOATING PUBLISHER OF THE DAILY BUGLE MISSES NO TRICKS IN PUBLICIZING HIS TRIUMPH...
NOW THAT THE DECENT PEOPLE OF OUR CITY HAVE GOTTEN WISE TO SPIDER-MAN, HE HASN'T BEEN SEEN FOR WEEKS! AT LAST WE'RE RID OF THAT MASKED MENACE!
AND REMEMBER, THE DAILY BUGLE WAS THE FIRST TO EXPOSE HIM AS A DANGEROUS FRAUD!
2.

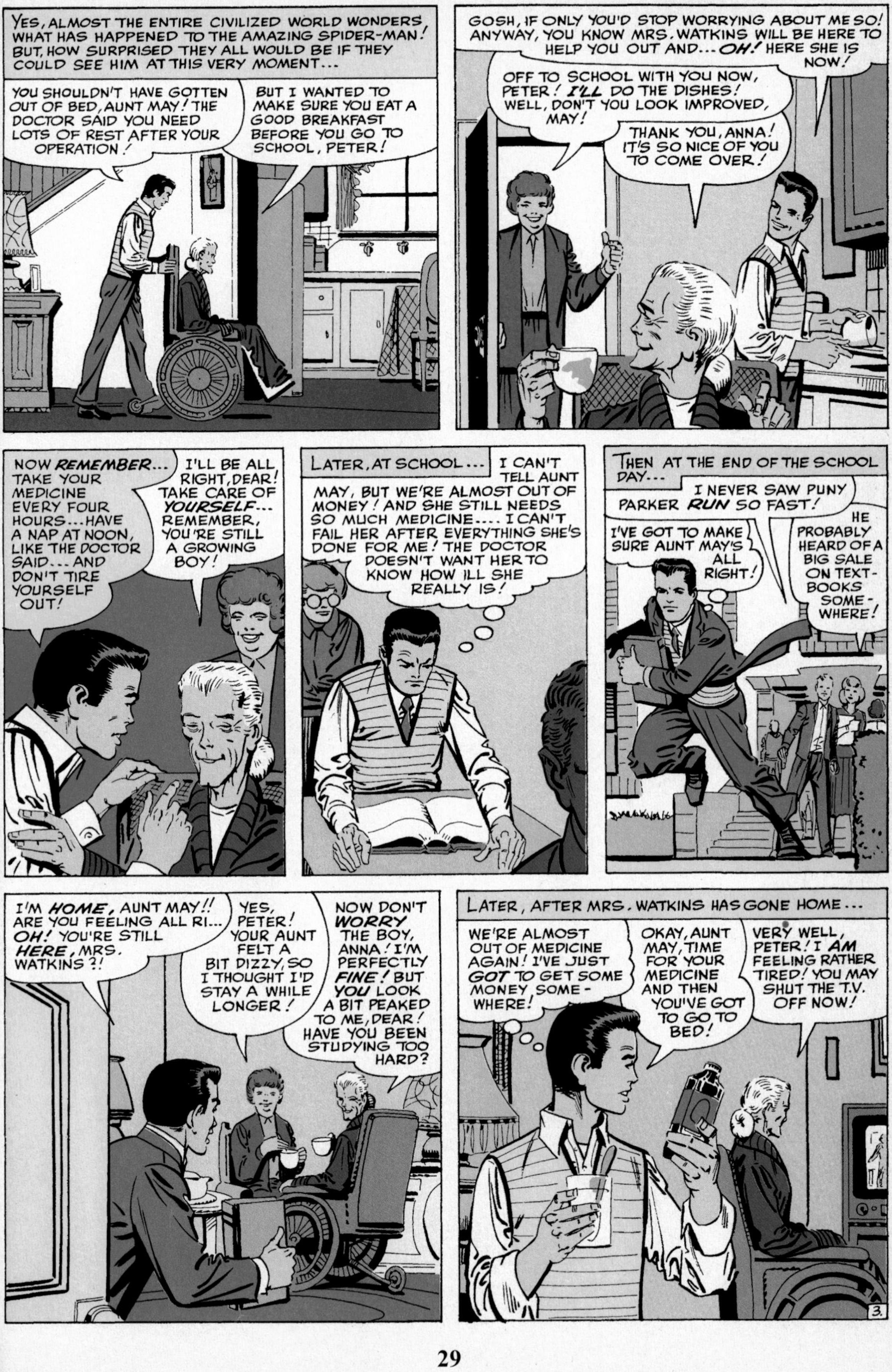

YES, ALMOST THE ENTIRE CIVILIZED WORLD WONDERS WHAT HAS HAPPENED TO THE AMAZING SPIDER-MAN! BUT, HOW SURPRISED THEY ALL WOULD BE IF THEY COULD SEE HIM AT THIS VERY MOMENT...
YOU SHOULDN'T HAVE GOTTEN OUT OF BED, AUNT MAY! THE DOCTOR SAID YOU NEED LOTS OF REST AFTER YOUR OPERATION!
BUT I WANTED TO MAKE SURE YOU EAT A GOOD BREAKFAST BEFORE YOU GO TO SCHOOL, PETER!
GOSH, IF ONLY YOU'D STOP WORRYING ABOUT ME SO! ANYWAY, YOU KNOW MRS. WATKINS WILL BE HERE TO HELP YOU OUT AND... OH! HERE SHE IS NOW!
OFF TO SCHOOL WITH YOU NOW, PETER! I'LL DO THE DISHES! WELL, DON'T YOU LOOK IMPROVED, MAY!
THANK YOU, ANNA! IT'S SO NICE OF YOU TO COME OVER!
NOW REMEMBER... TAKE YOUR MEDICINE EVERY FOUR HOURS... HAVE A NAP AT NOON, LIKE THE DOCTOR SAID... AND DON'T TIRE YOURSELF OUT!
I'LL BE ALL RIGHT, DEAR! TAKE CARE OF YOURSELF... REMEMBER, YOU'RE STILL A GROWING BOY!
LATER, AT SCHOOL...
I CAN'T TELL AUNT MAY, BUT WE'RE ALMOST OUT OF MONEY! AND SHE STILL NEEDS SO MUCH MEDICINE.... I CAN'T FAIL HER AFTER EVERYTHING SHE'S DONE FOR ME! THE DOCTOR DOESN'T WANT HER TO KNOW HOW ILL SHE REALLY IS!
THEN AT THE END OF THE SCHOOL DAY...
I NEVER SAW PUNY PARKER RUN SO FAST!
I'VE GOT TO MAKE SURE AUNT MAY'S ALL RIGHT!
HE PROBABLY HEARD OF A BIG SALE ON TEXT-BOOKS SOME-WHERE!
I'M HOME, AUNT MAY!! ARE YOU FEELING ALL RI... OH! YOU'RE STILL HERE, MRS. WATKINS?!
YES, PETER! YOUR AUNT FELT A BIT DIZZY, SO I THOUGHT I'D STAY A WHILE LONGER!
NOW DON'T WORRY THE BOY, ANNA! I'M PERFECTLY FINE! BUT YOU LOOK A BIT PEAKED TO ME, DEAR! HAVE YOU BEEN STUDYING TOO HARD?
LATER, AFTER MRS. WATKINS HAS GONE HOME...
WE'RE ALMOST OUT OF MEDICINE AGAIN! I'VE JUST GOT TO GET SOME MONEY SOME-WHERE!
OKAY, AUNT MAY, TIME FOR YOUR MEDICINE AND THEN YOU'VE GOT TO GO TO BED!
VERY WELL, PETER! I AM FEELING RATHER TIRED! YOU MAY SHUT THE T.V. OFF NOW!
3.

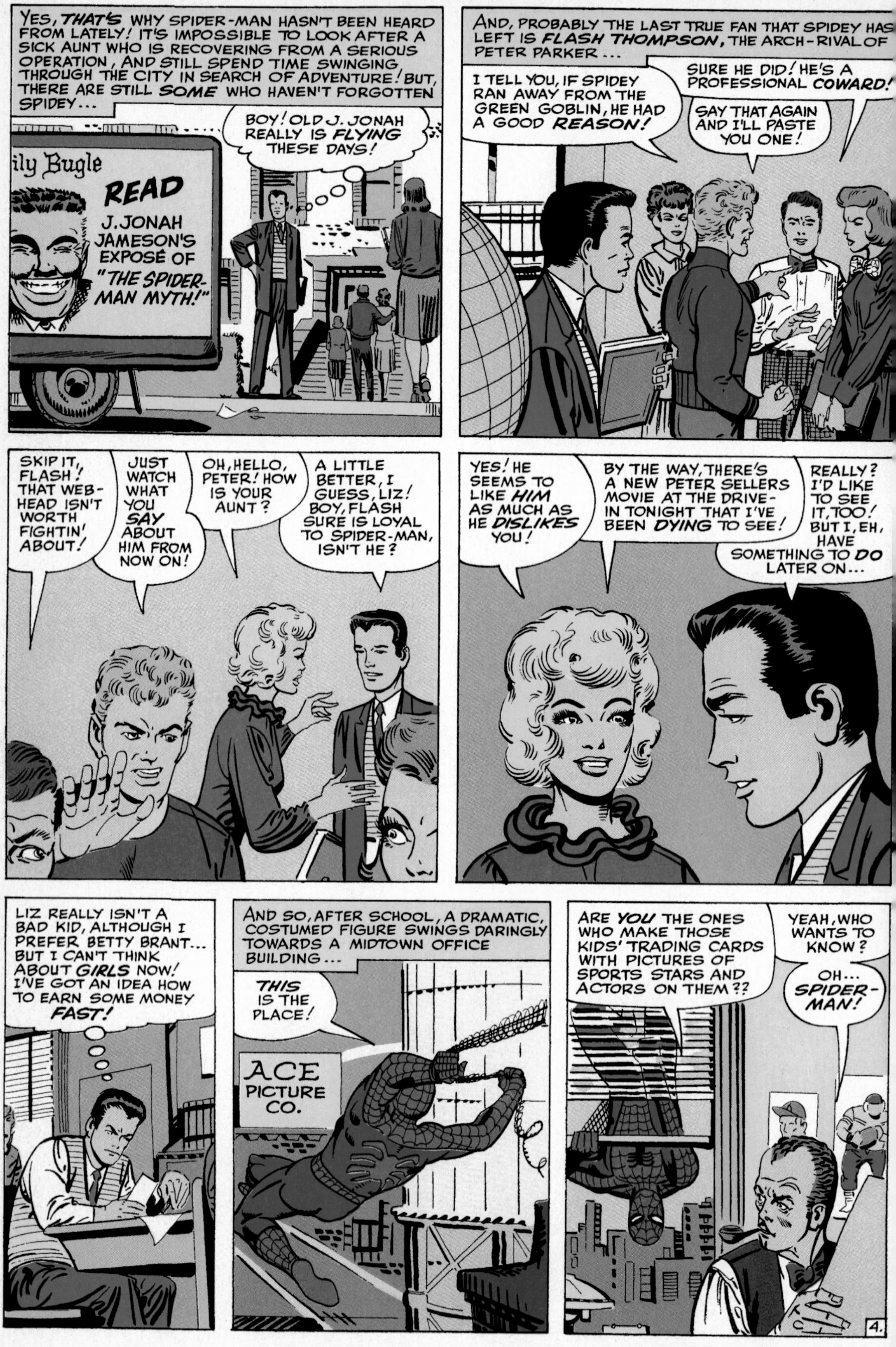

YES, THAT'S WHY SPIDER-MAN HASN'T BEEN HEARD FROM LATELY! IT'S IMPOSSIBLE TO LOOK AFTER A SICK AUNT WHO IS RECOVERING FROM A SERIOUS OPERATION, AND STILL SPEND TIME SWINGING THROUGH THE CITY IN SEARCH OF ADVENTURE! BUT, THERE ARE STILL SOME WHO HAVEN'T FORGOTTEN SPIDEY...
BOY! OLD J. JONAH REALLY IS FLYING THESE DAYS!
ily Bugle
READ J. JONAH JAMESON'S EXPOSÉ OF "THE SPIDER-MAN MYTH!"
AND, PROBABLY THE LAST TRUE FAN THAT SPIDEY HAS LEFT IS FLASH THOMPSON, THE ARCH-RIVAL OF PETER PARKER...
I TELL YOU, IF SPIDEY RAN AWAY FROM THE GREEN GOBLIN, HE HAD A GOOD REASON!
SURE HE DID! HE'S A PROFESSIONAL COWARD!
SAY THAT AGAIN AND I'LL PASTE YOU ONE!
SKIP IT, FLASH! THAT WEB-HEAD ISN'T WORTH FIGHTIN' ABOUT!
JUST WATCH WHAT YOU SAY ABOUT HIM FROM NOW ON!
OH, HELLO, PETER! HOW IS YOUR AUNT?
A LITTLE BETTER, I GUESS, LIZ! BOY, FLASH SURE IS LOYAL TO SPIDER-MAN, ISN'T HE?
YES! HE SEEMS TO LIKE HIM AS MUCH AS HE DISLIKES YOU!
BY THE WAY, THERE'S A NEW PETER SELLERS MOVIE AT THE DRIVE-IN TONIGHT THAT I'VE BEEN DYING TO SEE!
REALLY? I'D LIKE TO SEE IT, TOO! BUT I, EH, HAVE SOMETHING TO DO LATER ON...
LIZ REALLY ISN'T A BAD KID, ALTHOUGH I PREFER BETTY BRANT... BUT I CAN'T THINK ABOUT GIRLS NOW! I'VE GOT AN IDEA HOW TO EARN SOME MONEY FAST!
AND SO, AFTER SCHOOL, A DRAMATIC, COSTUMED FIGURE SWINGS DARINGLY TOWARDS A MIDTOWN OFFICE BUILDING...
THIS IS THE PLACE!
ACE PICTURE CO.
ARE YOU THE ONES WHO MAKE THOSE KIDS' TRADING CARDS WITH PICTURES OF SPORTS STARS AND ACTORS ON THEM??
YEAH, WHO WANTS TO KNOW?
OH... SPIDER-MAN!
4.

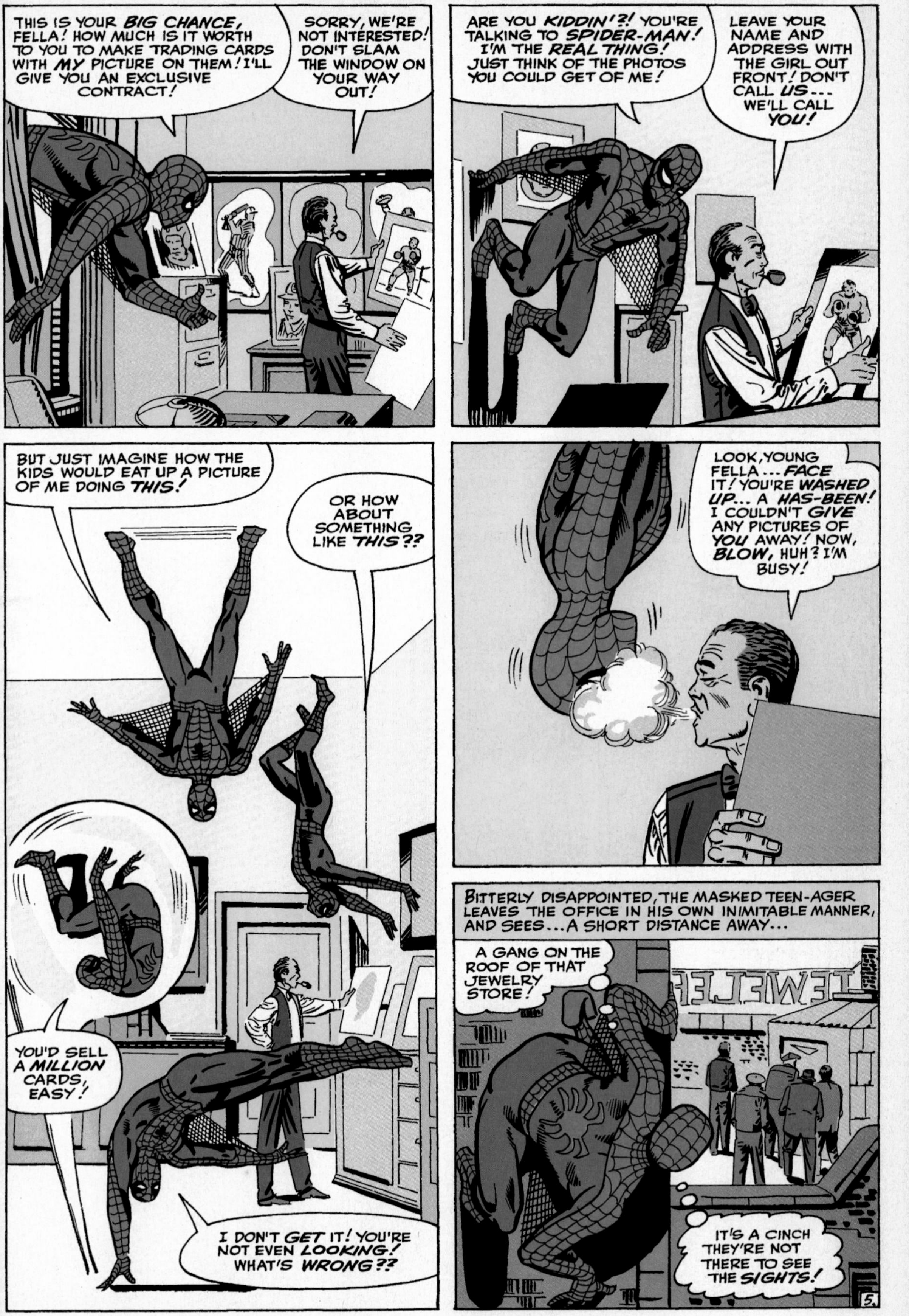
THIS IS YOUR BIG CHANCE, FELLA! HOW MUCH IS IT WORTH TO YOU TO MAKE TRADING CARDS WITH MY PICTURE ON THEM! I'LL GIVE YOU AN EXCLUSIVE CONTRACT!
SORRY, WE'RE NOT INTERESTED! DON'T SLAM THE WINDOW ON YOUR WAY OUT!
ARE YOU KIDDIN'?! YOU'RE TALKING TO SPIDER-MAN! I'M THE REAL THING! JUST THINK OF THE PHOTOS YOU COULD GET OF ME!
LEAVE YOUR NAME AND ADDRESS WITH THE GIRL OUT FRONT! DON'T CALL US... WE'LL CALL YOU!
BUT JUST IMAGINE HOW THE KIDS WOULD EAT UP A PICTURE OF ME DOING THIS!
OR HOW ABOUT SOMETHING LIKE THIS??
YOU'D SELL A MILLION CARDS, EASY!
I DON'T GET IT! YOU'RE NOT EVEN LOOKING! WHAT'S WRONG??
LOOK, YOUNG FELLA... FACE IT! YOU'RE WASHED UP... A HAS-BEEN! I COULDN'T GIVE ANY PICTURES OF YOU AWAY! NOW, BLOW, HUH? I'M BUSY!
BITTERLY DISAPPOINTED, THE MASKED TEEN-AGER LEAVES THE OFFICE IN HIS OWN INIMITABLE MANNER, AND SEES... A SHORT DISTANCE AWAY...
A GANG ON THE ROOF OF THAT JEWELRY STORE!
JEWELER
IT'S A CINCH THEY'RE NOT THERE TO SEE THE SIGHTS!
5.

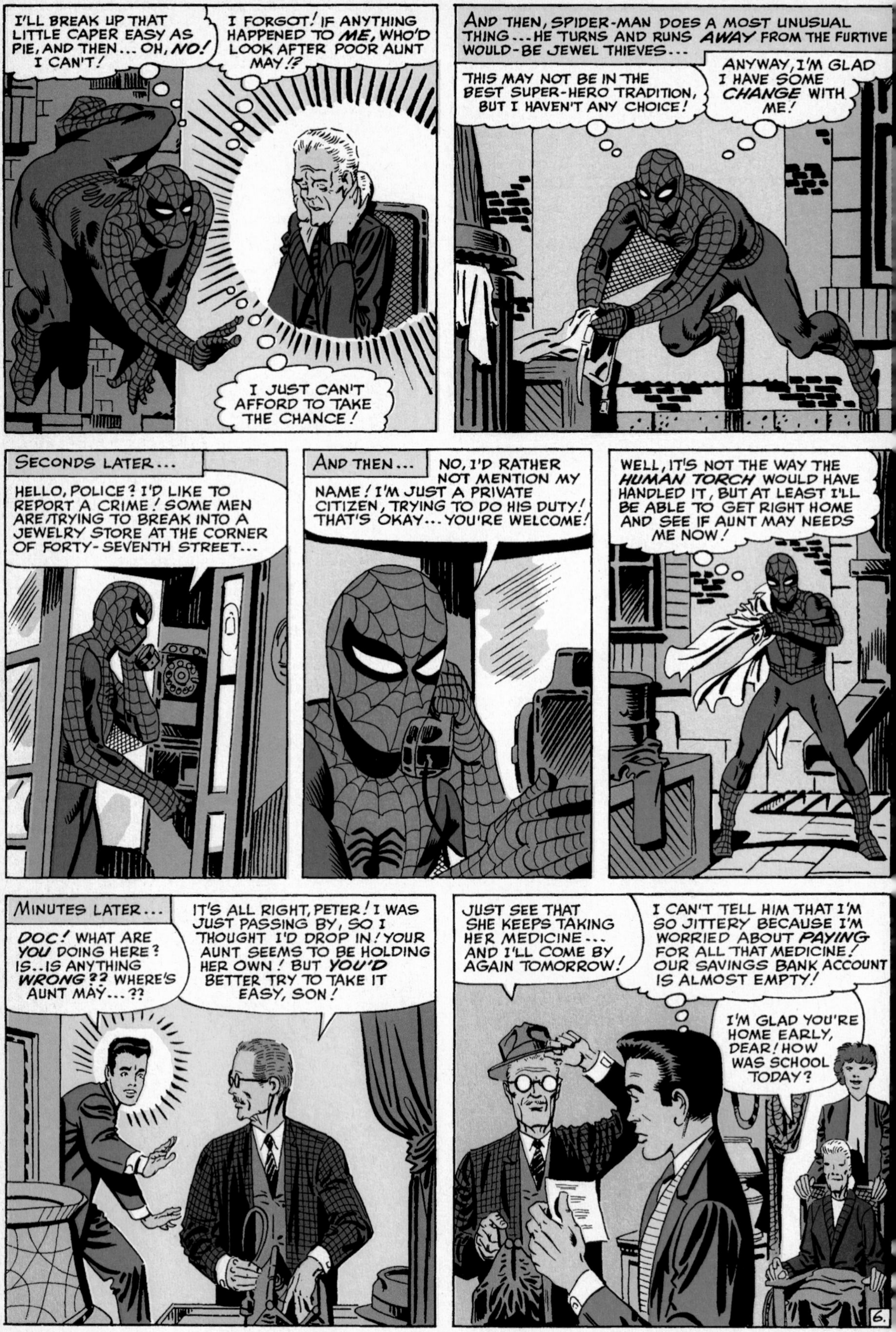
I'LL BREAK UP THAT LITTLE CAPER EASY AS PIE, AND THEN... OH, NO! I CAN'T!
I FORGOT! IF ANYTHING HAPPENED TO ME, WHO'D LOOK AFTER POOR AUNT MAY!?
I JUST CAN'T AFFORD TO TAKE THE CHANCE!
AND THEN, SPIDER-MAN DOES A MOST UNUSUAL THING... HE TURNS AND RUNS AWAY FROM THE FURTIVE WOULD-BE JEWEL THIEVES...
THIS MAY NOT BE IN THE BEST SUPER-HERO TRADITION, BUT I HAVEN'T ANY CHOICE!
ANYWAY, I'M GLAD I HAVE SOME CHANGE WITH ME!
SECONDS LATER...
HELLO, POLICE? I'D LIKE TO REPORT A CRIME! SOME MEN ARE TRYING TO BREAK INTO A JEWELRY STORE AT THE CORNER OF FORTY-SEVENTH STREET...
AND THEN...
NO, I'D RATHER NOT MENTION MY NAME! I'M JUST A PRIVATE CITIZEN, TRYING TO DO HIS DUTY! THAT'S OKAY... YOU'RE WELCOME!
WELL, IT'S NOT THE WAY THE HUMAN TORCH WOULD HAVE HANDLED IT, BUT AT LEAST I'LL BE ABLE TO GET RIGHT HOME AND SEE IF AUNT MAY NEEDS ME NOW!
MINUTES LATER...
DOC! WHAT ARE YOU DOING HERE? IS.. IS ANYTHING WRONG?? WHERE'S AUNT MAY...??
IT'S ALL RIGHT, PETER! I WAS JUST PASSING BY, SO I THOUGHT I'D DROP IN! YOUR AUNT SEEMS TO BE HOLDING HER OWN! BUT YOU'D BETTER TRY TO TAKE IT EASY, SON!
JUST SEE THAT SHE KEEPS TAKING HER MEDICINE... AND I'LL COME BY AGAIN TOMORROW!
I CAN'T TELL HIM THAT I'M SO JITTERY BECAUSE I'M WORRIED ABOUT PAYING FOR ALL THAT MEDICINE! OUR SAVINGS BANK ACCOUNT IS ALMOST EMPTY!
I'M GLAD YOU'RE HOME EARLY, DEAR! HOW WAS SCHOOL TODAY?
6.

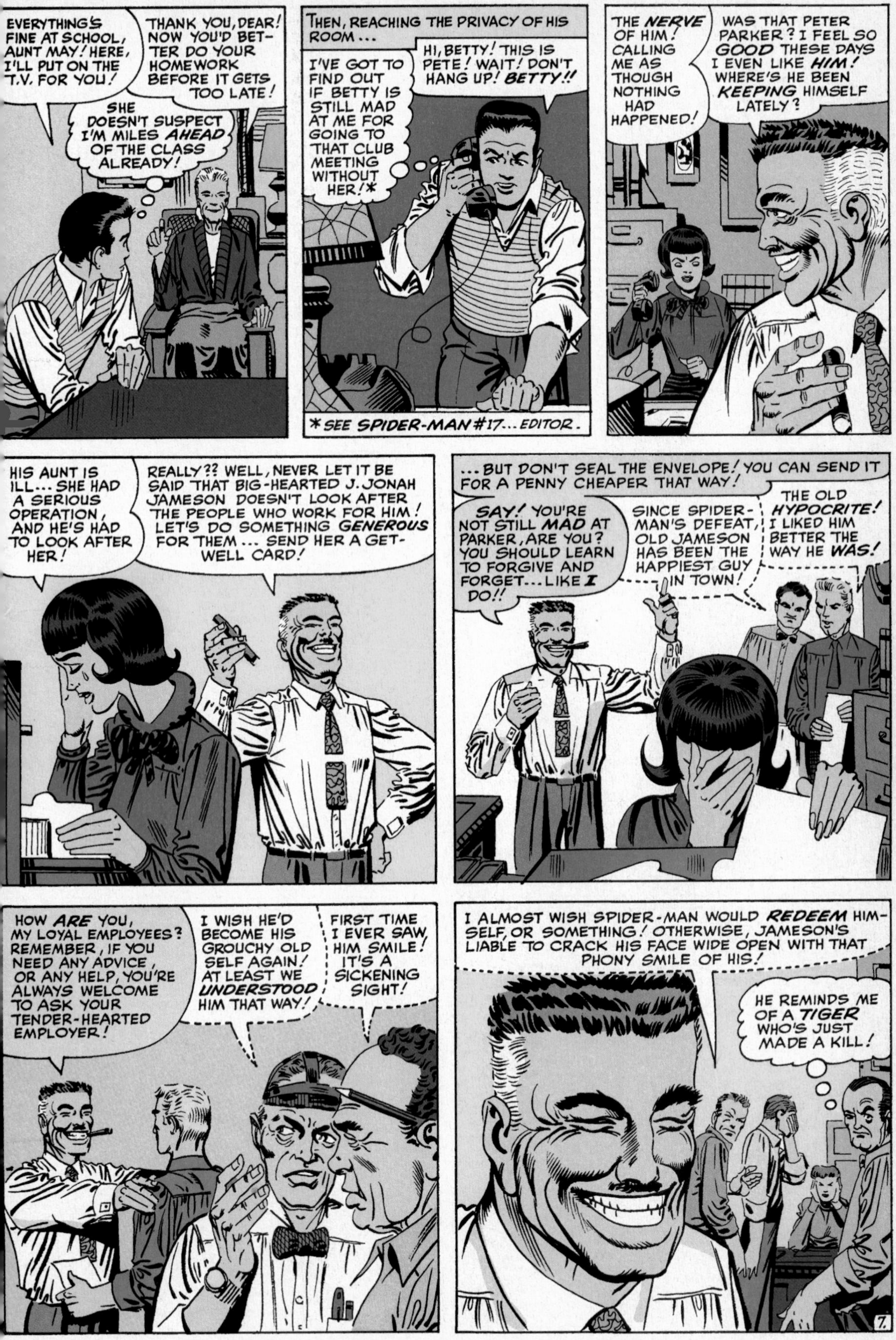
EVERYTHING'S FINE AT SCHOOL, AUNT MAY! HERE, I'LL PUT ON THE T.V. FOR YOU!
THANK YOU, DEAR! NOW YOU'D BETTER DO YOUR HOMEWORK BEFORE IT GETS TOO LATE!
SHE DOESN'T SUSPECT I'M MILES AHEAD OF THE CLASS ALREADY!
THEN, REACHING THE PRIVACY OF HIS ROOM...
I'VE GOT TO FIND OUT IF BETTY IS STILL MAD AT ME FOR GOING TO THAT CLUB MEETING WITHOUT HER!*
HI, BETTY! THIS IS PETE! WAIT! DON'T HANG UP! BETTY!!
*SEE SPIDER-MAN #17... EDITOR.
THE NERVE OF HIM! CALLING ME AS THOUGH NOTHING HAD HAPPENED!
WAS THAT PETER PARKER? I FEEL SO GOOD THESE DAYS I EVEN LIKE HIM! WHERE'S HE BEEN KEEPING HIMSELF LATELY?
HIS AUNT IS ILL... SHE HAD A SERIOUS OPERATION, AND HE'S HAD TO LOOK AFTER HER!
REALLY?? WELL, NEVER LET IT BE SAID THAT BIG-HEARTED J. JONAH JAMESON DOESN'T LOOK AFTER THE PEOPLE WHO WORK FOR HIM! LET'S DO SOMETHING GENEROUS FOR THEM... SEND HER A GET-WELL CARD!
...BUT DON'T SEAL THE ENVELOPE! YOU CAN SEND IT FOR A PENNY CHEAPER THAT WAY!
SAY! YOU'RE NOT STILL MAD AT PARKER, ARE YOU? YOU SHOULD LEARN TO FORGIVE AND FORGET... LIKE I DO!!
SINCE SPIDER-MAN'S DEFEAT, OLD JAMESON HAS BEEN THE HAPPIEST GUY IN TOWN!
THE OLD HYPOCRITE! I LIKED HIM BETTER THE WAY HE WAS!
HOW ARE YOU, MY LOYAL EMPLOYEES? REMEMBER, IF YOU NEED ANY ADVICE, OR ANY HELP, YOU'RE ALWAYS WELCOME TO ASK YOUR TENDER-HEARTED EMPLOYER!
I WISH HE'D BECOME HIS GROUCHY OLD SELF AGAIN! AT LEAST WE UNDERSTOOD HIM THAT WAY!
FIRST TIME I EVER SAW HIM SMILE! IT'S A SICKENING SIGHT!
I ALMOST WISH SPIDER-MAN WOULD REDEEM HIMSELF, OR SOMETHING! OTHERWISE, JAMESON'S LIABLE TO CRACK HIS FACE WIDE OPEN WITH THAT PHONY SMILE OF HIS!
HE REMINDS ME OF A TIGER WHO'S JUST MADE A KILL!
7.

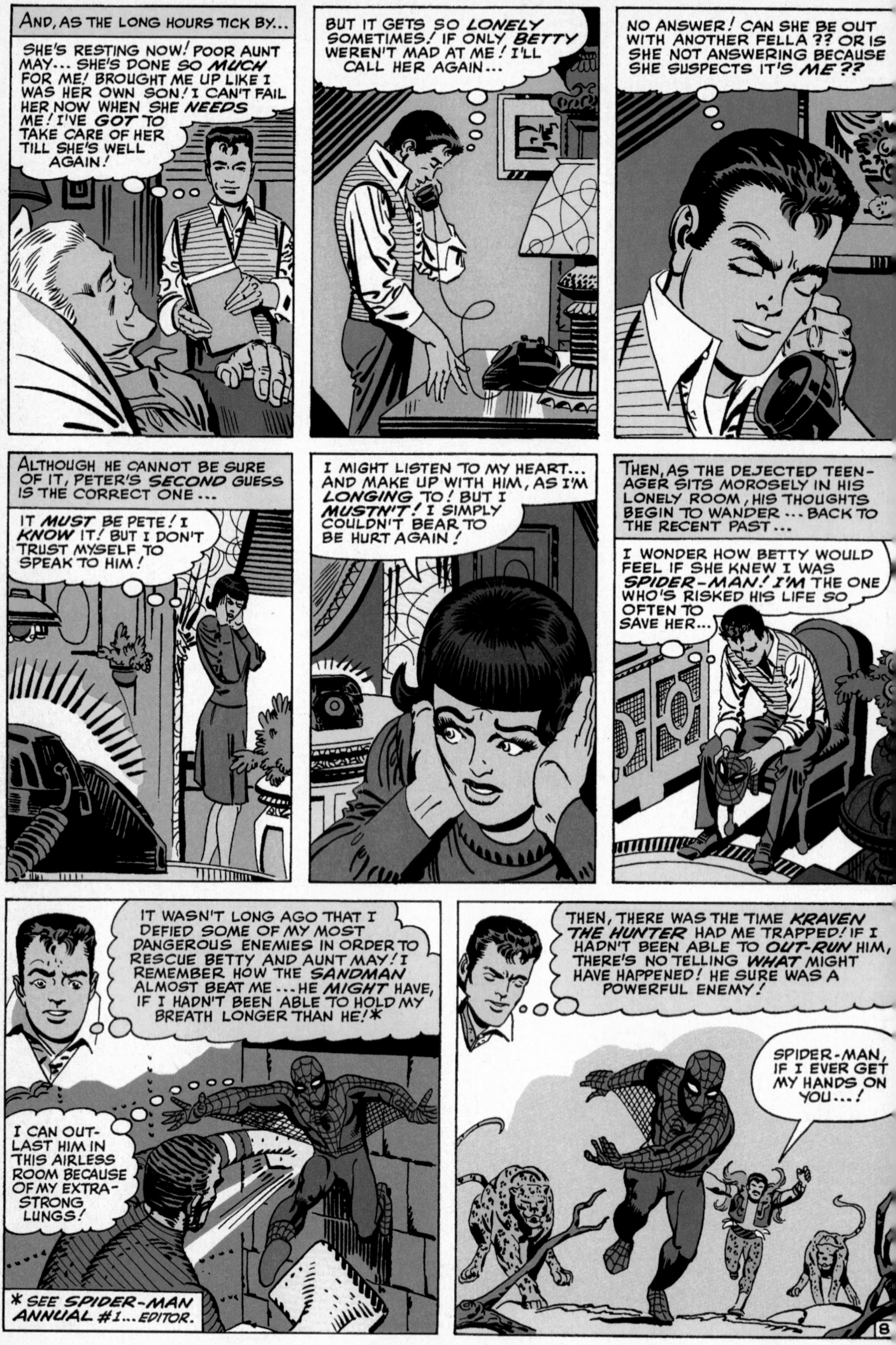
AND, AS THE LONG HOURS TICK BY...
SHE'S RESTING NOW! POOR AUNT MAY... SHE'S DONE SO MUCH FOR ME! BROUGHT ME UP LIKE I WAS HER OWN SON! I CAN'T FAIL HER NOW WHEN SHE NEEDS ME! I'VE GOT TO TAKE CARE OF HER TILL SHE'S WELL AGAIN!
BUT IT GETS SO LONELY SOMETIMES! IF ONLY BETTY WEREN'T MAD AT ME! I'LL CALL HER AGAIN...
NO ANSWER! CAN SHE BE OUT WITH ANOTHER FELLA ?? OR IS SHE NOT ANSWERING BECAUSE SHE SUSPECTS IT'S ME ??
ALTHOUGH HE CANNOT BE SURE OF IT, PETER'S SECOND GUESS IS THE CORRECT ONE...
IT MUST BE PETE! I KNOW IT! BUT I DON'T TRUST MYSELF TO SPEAK TO HIM!
I MIGHT LISTEN TO MY HEART... AND MAKE UP WITH HIM, AS I'M LONGING TO! BUT I MUSTN'T! I SIMPLY COULDN'T BEAR TO BE HURT AGAIN!
THEN, AS THE DEJECTED TEEN-AGER SITS MOROSELY IN HIS LONELY ROOM, HIS THOUGHTS BEGIN TO WANDER... BACK TO THE RECENT PAST...
I WONDER HOW BETTY WOULD FEEL IF SHE KNEW I WAS SPIDER-MAN! I'M THE ONE WHO'S RISKED HIS LIFE SO OFTEN TO SAVE HER...
IT WASN'T LONG AGO THAT I DEFIED SOME OF MY MOST DANGEROUS ENEMIES IN ORDER TO RESCUE BETTY AND AUNT MAY! I REMEMBER HOW THE SANDMAN ALMOST BEAT ME... HE MIGHT HAVE, IF I HADN'T BEEN ABLE TO HOLD MY BREATH LONGER THAN HE!*
I CAN OUT-LAST HIM IN THIS AIRLESS ROOM BECAUSE OF MY EXTRA-STRONG LUNGS!
* SEE SPIDER-MAN ANNUAL #1... EDITOR.
THEN, THERE WAS THE TIME KRAVEN THE HUNTER HAD ME TRAPPED! IF I HADN'T BEEN ABLE TO OUT-RUN HIM, THERE'S NO TELLING WHAT MIGHT HAVE HAPPENED! HE SURE WAS A POWERFUL ENEMY!
SPIDER-MAN, IF I EVER GET MY HANDS ON YOU...!
8

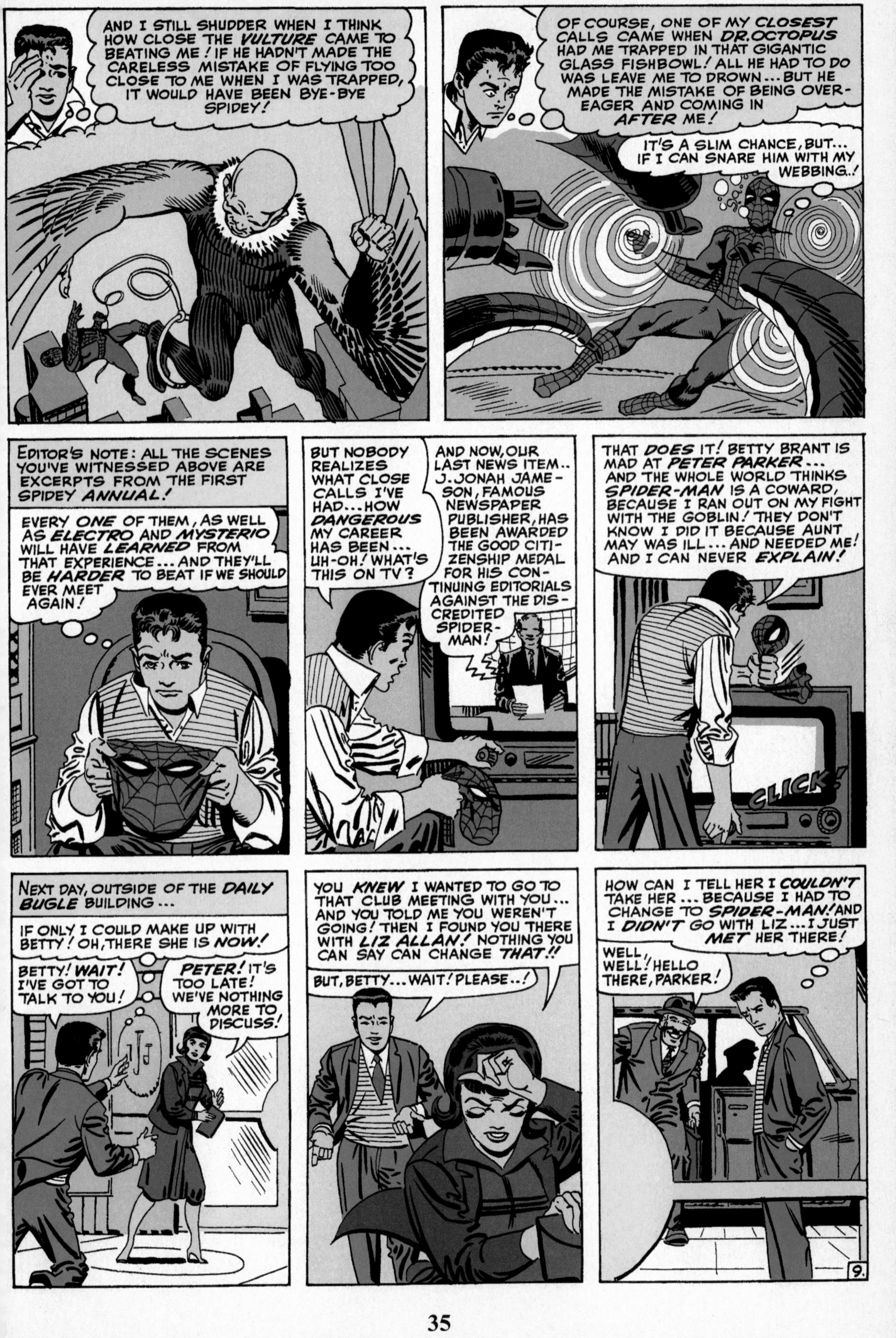

AND I STILL SHUDDER WHEN I THINK HOW CLOSE THE VULTURE CAME TO BEATING ME! IF HE HADN'T MADE THE CARELESS MISTAKE OF FLYING TOO CLOSE TO ME WHEN I WAS TRAPPED, IT WOULD HAVE BEEN BYE-BYE SPIDEY!
OF COURSE, ONE OF MY CLOSEST CALLS CAME WHEN DR. OCTOPUS HAD ME TRAPPED IN THAT GIGANTIC GLASS FISHBOWL! ALL HE HAD TO DO WAS LEAVE ME TO DROWN... BUT HE MADE THE MISTAKE OF BEING OVER-EAGER AND COMING IN AFTER ME!
IT'S A SLIM CHANCE, BUT... IF I CAN SNARE HIM WITH MY WEBBING..!
EDITOR'S NOTE: ALL THE SCENES YOU'VE WITNESSED ABOVE ARE EXCERPTS FROM THE FIRST SPIDEY ANNUAL!
EVERY ONE OF THEM, AS WELL AS ELECTRO AND MYSTERIO WILL HAVE LEARNED FROM THAT EXPERIENCE... AND THEY'LL BE HARDER TO BEAT IF WE SHOULD EVER MEET AGAIN!
BUT NOBODY REALIZES WHAT CLOSE CALLS I'VE HAD... HOW DANGEROUS MY CAREER HAS BEEN... UH-OH! WHAT'S THIS ON TV?
AND NOW, OUR LAST NEWS ITEM.. J. JONAH JAMESON, FAMOUS NEWSPAPER PUBLISHER, HAS BEEN AWARDED THE GOOD CITIZENSHIP MEDAL FOR HIS CONTINUING EDITORIALS AGAINST THE DISCREDITED SPIDER-MAN!
THAT DOES IT! BETTY BRANT IS MAD AT PETER PARKER... AND THE WHOLE WORLD THINKS SPIDER-MAN IS A COWARD, BECAUSE I RAN OUT ON MY FIGHT WITH THE GOBLIN! THEY DON'T KNOW I DID IT BECAUSE AUNT MAY WAS ILL... AND NEEDED ME! AND I CAN NEVER EXPLAIN!
CLICK!
NEXT DAY, OUTSIDE OF THE DAILY BUGLE BUILDING...
IF ONLY I COULD MAKE UP WITH BETTY! OH, THERE SHE IS NOW!
BETTY! WAIT! I'VE GOT TO TALK TO YOU!
PETER! IT'S TOO LATE! WE'VE NOTHING MORE TO DISCUSS!
YOU KNEW I WANTED TO GO TO THAT CLUB MEETING WITH YOU... AND YOU TOLD ME YOU WEREN'T GOING! THEN I FOUND YOU THERE WITH LIZ ALLAN! NOTHING YOU CAN SAY CAN CHANGE THAT!!
BUT, BETTY... WAIT! PLEASE..!
HOW CAN I TELL HER I COULDN'T TAKE HER... BECAUSE I HAD TO CHANGE TO SPIDER-MAN! AND I DIDN'T GO WITH LIZ... I JUST MET HER THERE!
WELL, WELL! HELLO THERE, PARKER!
9.

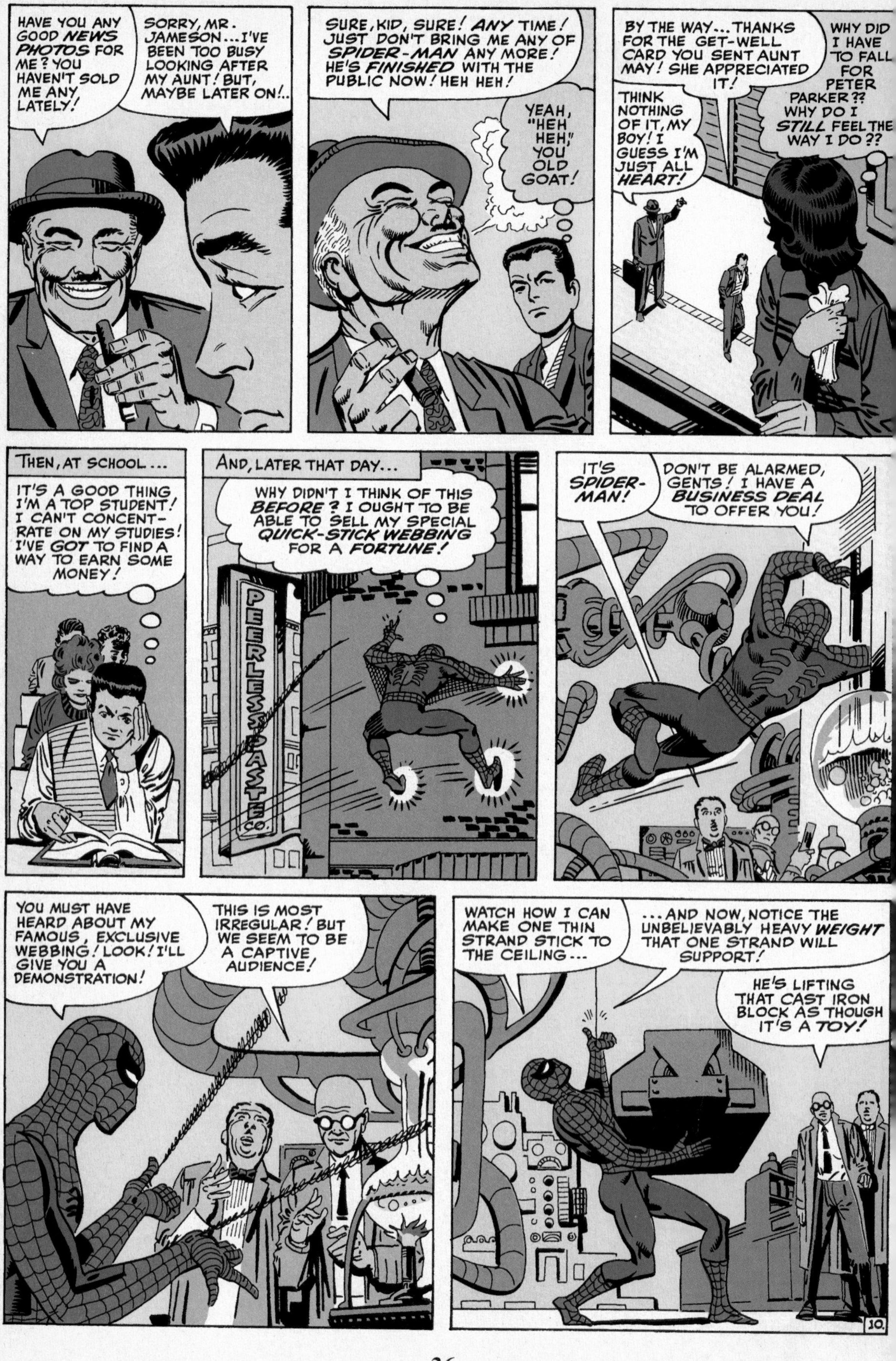

HAVE YOU ANY GOOD NEWS PHOTOS FOR ME? YOU HAVEN'T SOLD ME ANY LATELY!
SORRY, MR. JAMESON...I'VE BEEN TOO BUSY LOOKING AFTER MY AUNT! BUT, MAYBE LATER ON!..
SURE, KID, SURE! ANY TIME! JUST DON'T BRING ME ANY OF SPIDER-MAN ANY MORE! HE'S FINISHED WITH THE PUBLIC NOW! HEH HEH!
YEAH, "HEH HEH," YOU OLD GOAT!
BY THE WAY... THANKS FOR THE GET-WELL CARD YOU SENT AUNT MAY! SHE APPRECIATED IT!
THINK NOTHING OF IT, MY BOY! I GUESS I'M JUST ALL HEART!
WHY DID I HAVE TO FALL FOR PETER PARKER?? WHY DO I STILL FEEL THE WAY I DO??
THEN, AT SCHOOL...
IT'S A GOOD THING I'M A TOP STUDENT! I CAN'T CONCENTRATE ON MY STUDIES! I'VE GOT TO FIND A WAY TO EARN SOME MONEY!
AND, LATER THAT DAY...
WHY DIDN'T I THINK OF THIS BEFORE? I OUGHT TO BE ABLE TO SELL MY SPECIAL QUICK-STICK WEBBING FOR A FORTUNE!
PEERLESS PASTE CO.
IT'S SPIDER-MAN!
DON'T BE ALARMED, GENTS! I HAVE A BUSINESS DEAL TO OFFER YOU!
YOU MUST HAVE HEARD ABOUT MY FAMOUS, EXCLUSIVE WEBBING! LOOK! I'LL GIVE YOU A DEMONSTRATION!
THIS IS MOST IRREGULAR! BUT WE SEEM TO BE A CAPTIVE AUDIENCE!
WATCH HOW I CAN MAKE ONE THIN STRAND STICK TO THE CEILING...
...AND NOW, NOTICE THE UNBELIEVABLY HEAVY WEIGHT THAT ONE STRAND WILL SUPPORT!
HE'S LIFTING THAT CAST IRON BLOCK AS THOUGH IT'S A TOY!
10.

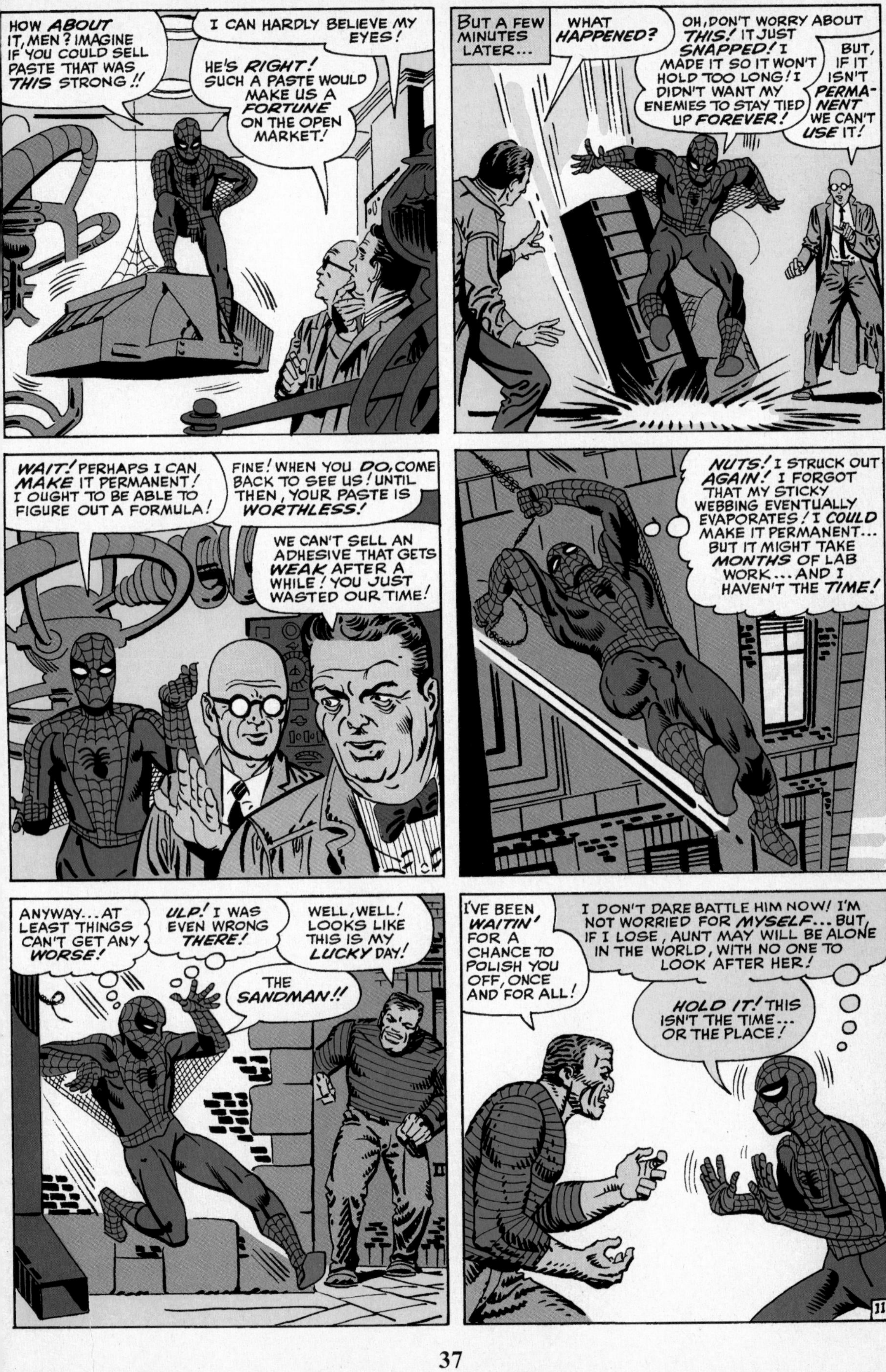
HOW ABOUT IT, MEN? IMAGINE IF YOU COULD SELL PASTE THAT WAS THIS STRONG!!
I CAN HARDLY BELIEVE MY EYES!
HE'S RIGHT! SUCH A PASTE WOULD MAKE US A FORTUNE ON THE OPEN MARKET!
BUT A FEW MINUTES LATER...
WHAT HAPPENED?
OH, DON'T WORRY ABOUT THIS! IT JUST SNAPPED! I MADE IT SO IT WON'T HOLD TOO LONG! I DIDN'T WANT MY ENEMIES TO STAY TIED UP FOREVER!
BUT, IF IT ISN'T PERMANENT WE CAN'T USE IT!
WAIT! PERHAPS I CAN MAKE IT PERMANENT! I OUGHT TO BE ABLE TO FIGURE OUT A FORMULA!
FINE! WHEN YOU DO, COME BACK TO SEE US! UNTIL THEN, YOUR PASTE IS WORTHLESS!
WE CAN'T SELL AN ADHESIVE THAT GETS WEAK AFTER A WHILE! YOU JUST WASTED OUR TIME!
NUTS! I STRUCK OUT AGAIN! I FORGOT THAT MY STICKY WEBBING EVENTUALLY EVAPORATES! I COULD MAKE IT PERMANENT... BUT IT MIGHT TAKE MONTHS OF LAB WORK... AND I HAVEN'T THE TIME!
ANYWAY... AT LEAST THINGS CAN'T GET ANY WORSE!
ULP! I WAS EVEN WRONG THERE!
WELL, WELL! LOOKS LIKE THIS IS MY LUCKY DAY!
THE SANDMAN!!
I'VE BEEN WAITIN' FOR A CHANCE TO POLISH YOU OFF, ONCE AND FOR ALL!
I DON'T DARE BATTLE HIM NOW! I'M NOT WORRIED FOR MYSELF... BUT, IF I LOSE, AUNT MAY WILL BE ALONE IN THE WORLD, WITH NO ONE TO LOOK AFTER HER!
HOLD IT! THIS ISN'T THE TIME... OR THE PLACE!
11.

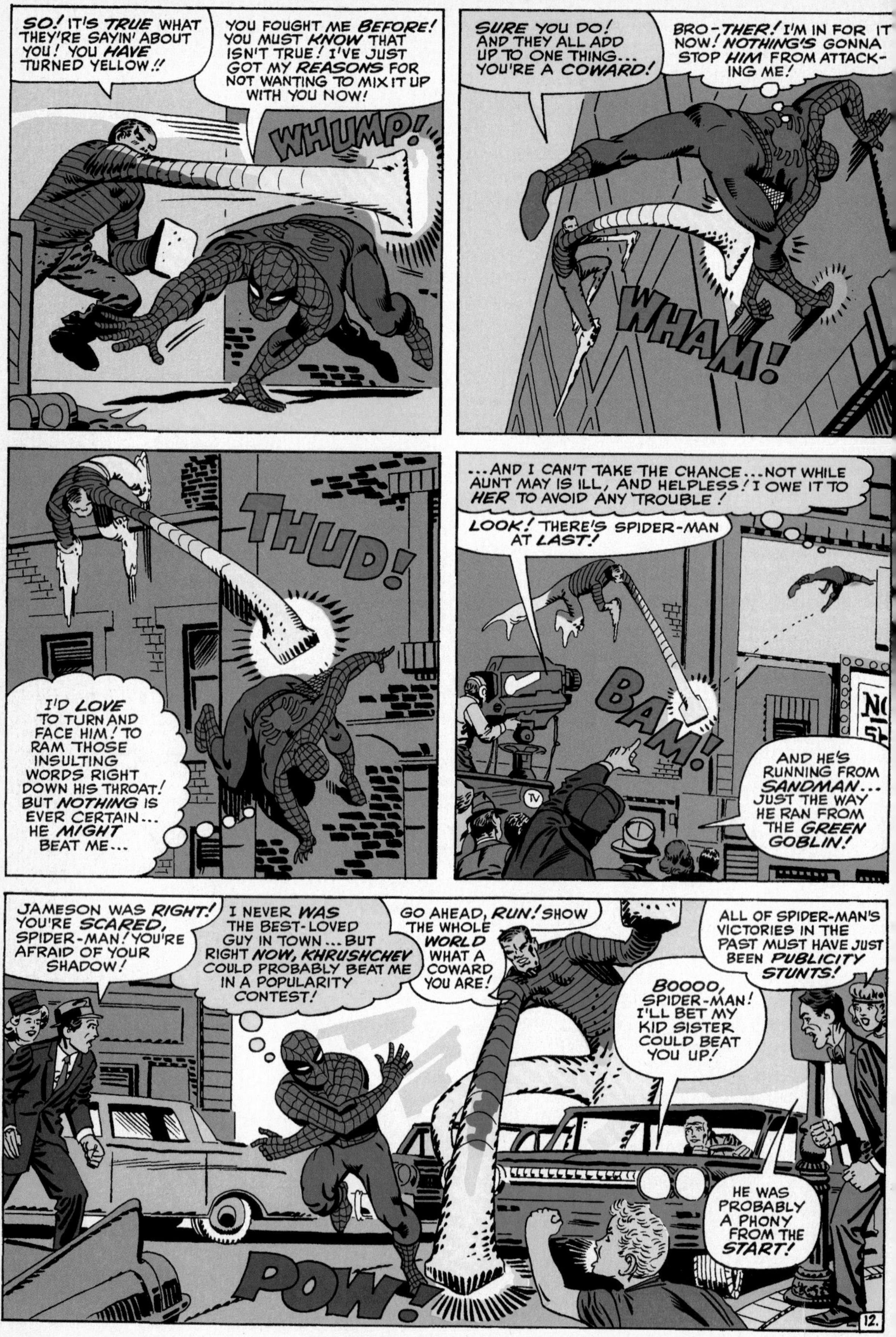
SO! IT'S TRUE WHAT THEY'RE SAYIN' ABOUT YOU! YOU HAVE TURNED YELLOW!!
YOU FOUGHT ME BEFORE! YOU MUST KNOW THAT ISN'T TRUE! I'VE JUST GOT MY REASONS FOR NOT WANTING TO MIX IT UP WITH YOU NOW!
WHUMP!
SURE YOU DO! AND THEY ALL ADD UP TO ONE THING... YOU'RE A COWARD!
BRO-THER! I'M IN FOR IT NOW! NOTHING'S GONNA STOP HIM FROM ATTACKING ME!
WHAM!
THUD!
I'D LOVE TO TURN AND FACE HIM! TO RAM THOSE INSULTING WORDS RIGHT DOWN HIS THROAT! BUT NOTHING IS EVER CERTAIN... HE MIGHT BEAT ME...
...AND I CAN'T TAKE THE CHANCE...NOT WHILE AUNT MAY IS ILL, AND HELPLESS! I OWE IT TO HER TO AVOID ANY TROUBLE!
LOOK! THERE'S SPIDER-MAN AT LAST!
BAM!
TV
AND HE'S RUNNING FROM SANDMAN... JUST THE WAY HE RAN FROM THE GREEN GOBLIN!
JAMESON WAS RIGHT! YOU'RE SCARED, SPIDER-MAN! YOU'RE AFRAID OF YOUR SHADOW!
I NEVER WAS THE BEST-LOVED GUY IN TOWN... BUT RIGHT NOW, KHRUSHCHEV COULD PROBABLY BEAT ME IN A POPULARITY CONTEST!
GO AHEAD, RUN! SHOW THE WHOLE WORLD WHAT A COWARD YOU ARE!
ALL OF SPIDER-MAN'S VICTORIES IN THE PAST MUST HAVE JUST BEEN PUBLICITY STUNTS!
BOOOO, SPIDER-MAN! I'LL BET MY KID SISTER COULD BEAT YOU UP!
HE WAS PROBABLY A PHONY FROM THE START!
POW!
12.

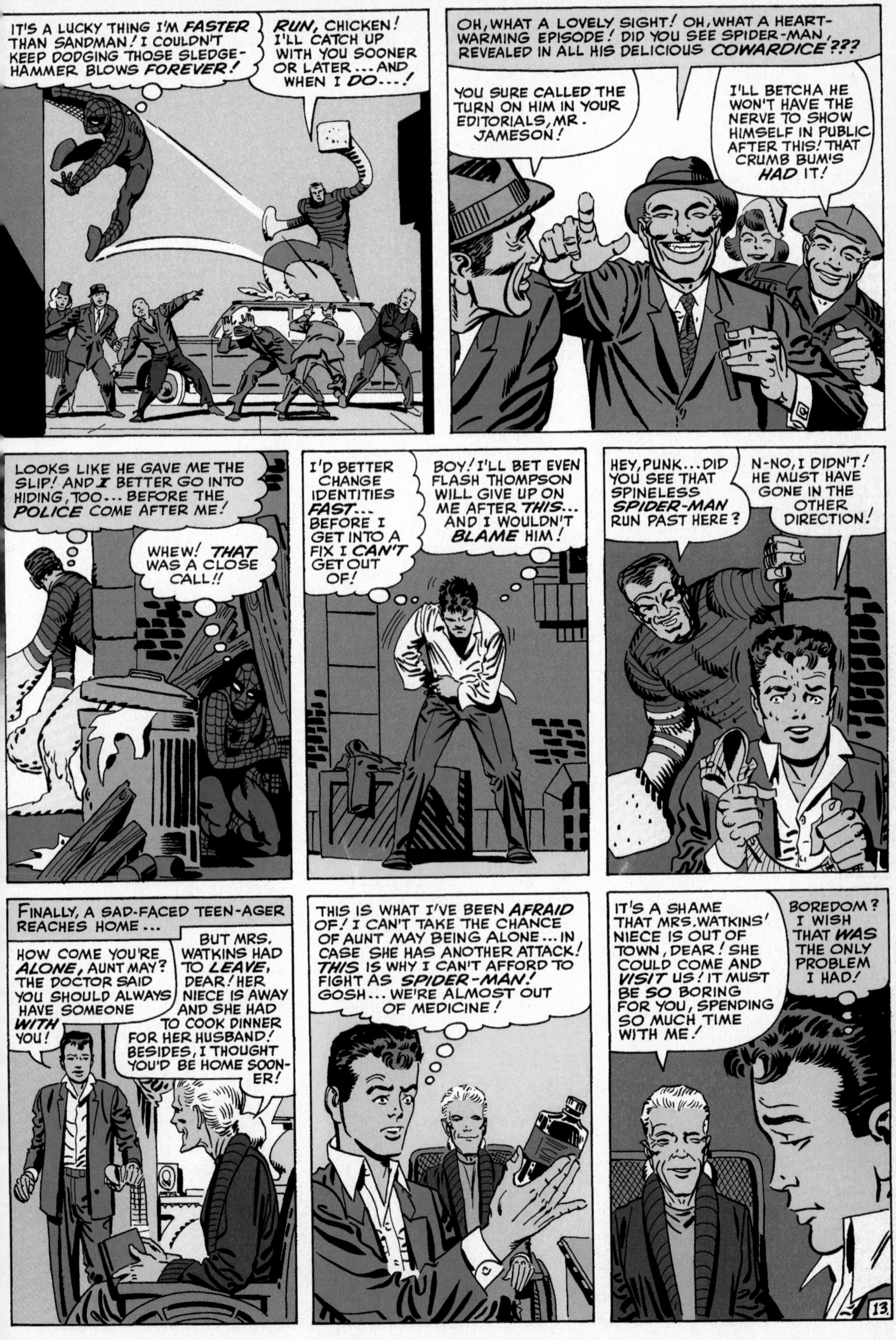
IT'S A LUCKY THING I'M FASTER THAN SANDMAN! I COULDN'T KEEP DODGING THOSE SLEDGE-HAMMER BLOWS FOREVER!
RUN, CHICKEN! I'LL CATCH UP WITH YOU SOONER OR LATER... AND WHEN I DO...!
OH, WHAT A LOVELY SIGHT! OH, WHAT A HEART-WARMING EPISODE! DID YOU SEE SPIDER-MAN, REVEALED IN ALL HIS DELICIOUS COWARDICE???
YOU SURE CALLED THE TURN ON HIM IN YOUR EDITORIALS, MR. JAMESON!
I'LL BETCHA HE WON'T HAVE THE NERVE TO SHOW HIMSELF IN PUBLIC AFTER THIS! THAT CRUMB BUM'S HAD IT!
LOOKS LIKE HE GAVE ME THE SLIP! AND I BETTER GO INTO HIDING, TOO... BEFORE THE POLICE COME AFTER ME!
WHEW! THAT WAS A CLOSE CALL!!
I'D BETTER CHANGE IDENTITIES FAST... BEFORE I GET INTO A FIX I CAN'T GET OUT OF!
BOY! I'LL BET EVEN FLASH THOMPSON WILL GIVE UP ON ME AFTER THIS... AND I WOULDN'T BLAME HIM!
HEY, PUNK... DID YOU SEE THAT SPINELESS SPIDER-MAN RUN PAST HERE?
N-NO, I DIDN'T! HE MUST HAVE GONE IN THE OTHER DIRECTION!
FINALLY, A SAD-FACED TEEN-AGER REACHES HOME...
HOW COME YOU'RE ALONE, AUNT MAY? THE DOCTOR SAID YOU SHOULD ALWAYS HAVE SOMEONE WITH YOU!
BUT MRS. WATKINS HAD TO LEAVE, DEAR! HER NIECE IS AWAY AND SHE HAD TO COOK DINNER FOR HER HUSBAND! BESIDES, I THOUGHT YOU'D BE HOME SOONER!
THIS IS WHAT I'VE BEEN AFRAID OF! I CAN'T TAKE THE CHANCE OF AUNT MAY BEING ALONE... IN CASE SHE HAS ANOTHER ATTACK! THIS IS WHY I CAN'T AFFORD TO FIGHT AS SPIDER-MAN! GOSH... WE'RE ALMOST OUT OF MEDICINE!
IT'S A SHAME THAT MRS. WATKINS' NIECE IS OUT OF TOWN, DEAR! SHE COULD COME AND VISIT US! IT MUST BE SO BORING FOR YOU, SPENDING SO MUCH TIME WITH ME!
BOREDOM? I WISH THAT WAS THE ONLY PROBLEM I HAD!
13.

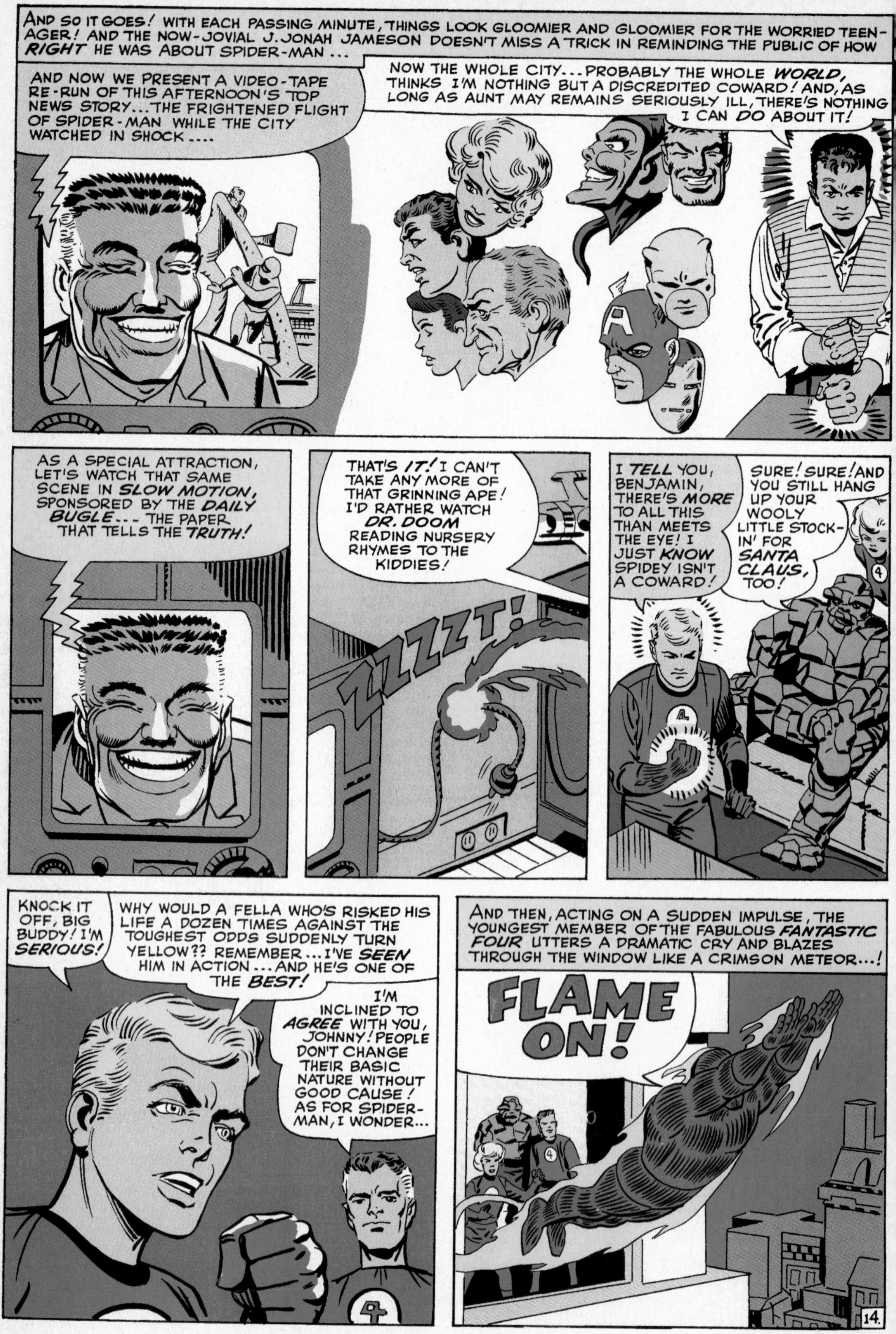
AND SO IT GOES! WITH EACH PASSING MINUTE, THINGS LOOK GLOOMIER AND GLOOMIER FOR THE WORRIED TEEN-AGER! AND THE NOW-JOVIAL J. JONAH JAMESON DOESN'T MISS A TRICK IN REMINDING THE PUBLIC OF HOW RIGHT HE WAS ABOUT SPIDER-MAN ...
AND NOW WE PRESENT A VIDEO-TAPE RE-RUN OF THIS AFTERNOON'S TOP NEWS STORY...THE FRIGHTENED FLIGHT OF SPIDER-MAN WHILE THE CITY WATCHED IN SHOCK....
NOW THE WHOLE CITY...PROBABLY THE WHOLE WORLD, THINKS I'M NOTHING BUT A DISCREDITED COWARD! AND, AS LONG AS AUNT MAY REMAINS SERIOUSLY ILL, THERE'S NOTHING I CAN DO ABOUT IT!
AS A SPECIAL ATTRACTION, LET'S WATCH THAT SAME SCENE IN SLOW MOTION, SPONSORED BY THE DAILY BUGLE... THE PAPER THAT TELLS THE TRUTH!
THAT'S IT! I CAN'T TAKE ANY MORE OF THAT GRINNING APE! I'D RATHER WATCH DR. DOOM READING NURSERY RHYMES TO THE KIDDIES!
ZZZZZT!
I TELL YOU, BENJAMIN, THERE'S MORE TO ALL THIS THAN MEETS THE EYE! I JUST KNOW SPIDEY ISN'T A COWARD!
SURE! SURE! AND YOU STILL HANG UP YOUR WOOLY LITTLE STOCK-IN' FOR SANTA CLAUS, TOO!
KNOCK IT OFF, BIG BUDDY! I'M SERIOUS!
WHY WOULD A FELLA WHO'S RISKED HIS LIFE A DOZEN TIMES AGAINST THE TOUGHEST ODDS SUDDENLY TURN YELLOW?? REMEMBER...I'VE SEEN HIM IN ACTION...AND HE'S ONE OF THE BEST!
I'M INCLINED TO AGREE WITH YOU, JOHNNY! PEOPLE DON'T CHANGE THEIR BASIC NATURE WITHOUT GOOD CAUSE! AS FOR SPIDER-MAN, I WONDER...
AND THEN, ACTING ON A SUDDEN IMPULSE, THE YOUNGEST MEMBER OF THE FABULOUS FANTASTIC FOUR UTTERS A DRAMATIC CRY AND BLAZES THROUGH THE WINDOW LIKE A CRIMSON METEOR...!
FLAME ON!
14.

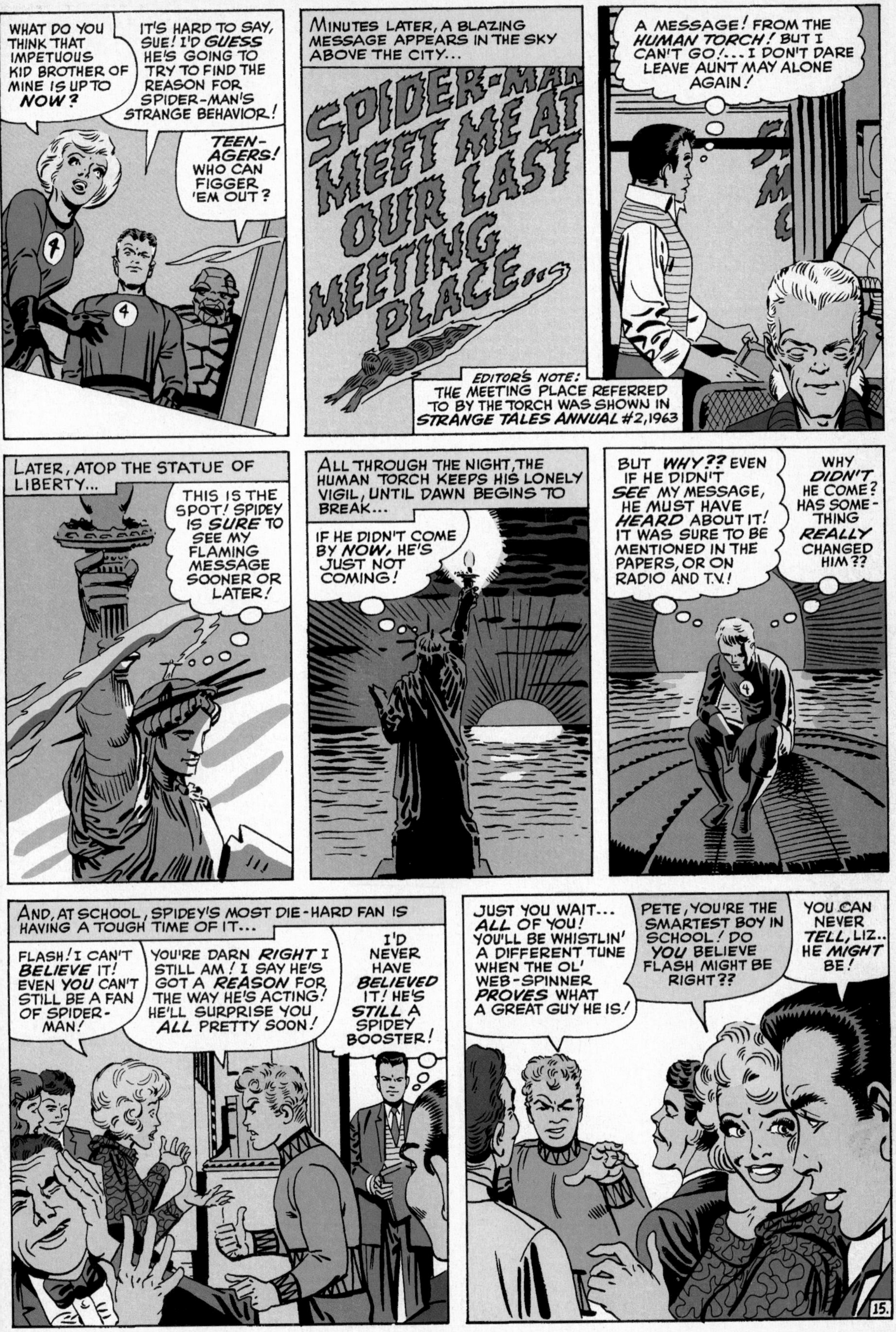
WHAT DO YOU THINK THAT IMPETUOUS KID BROTHER OF MINE IS UP TO NOW?
IT'S HARD TO SAY, SUE! I'D GUESS HE'S GOING TO TRY TO FIND THE REASON FOR SPIDER-MAN'S STRANGE BEHAVIOR!
TEEN-AGERS! WHO CAN FIGGER 'EM OUT?
MINUTES LATER, A BLAZING MESSAGE APPEARS IN THE SKY ABOVE THE CITY...
SPIDER-MAN MEET ME AT OUR LAST MEETING PLACE...
EDITOR'S NOTE: THE MEETING PLACE REFERRED TO BY THE TORCH WAS SHOWN IN STRANGE TALES ANNUAL #2, 1963
A MESSAGE! FROM THE HUMAN TORCH! BUT I CAN'T GO!... I DON'T DARE LEAVE AUNT MAY ALONE AGAIN!
LATER, ATOP THE STATUE OF LIBERTY...
THIS IS THE SPOT! SPIDEY IS SURE TO SEE MY FLAMING MESSAGE SOONER OR LATER!
ALL THROUGH THE NIGHT, THE HUMAN TORCH KEEPS HIS LONELY VIGIL, UNTIL DAWN BEGINS TO BREAK...
IF HE DIDN'T COME BY NOW, HE'S JUST NOT COMING!
BUT WHY?? EVEN IF HE DIDN'T SEE MY MESSAGE, HE MUST HAVE HEARD ABOUT IT! IT WAS SURE TO BE MENTIONED IN THE PAPERS, OR ON RADIO AND T.V.!
WHY DIDN'T HE COME? HAS SOME-THING REALLY CHANGED HIM??
AND, AT SCHOOL, SPIDEY'S MOST DIE-HARD FAN IS HAVING A TOUGH TIME OF IT...
FLASH! I CAN'T BELIEVE IT! EVEN YOU CAN'T STILL BE A FAN OF SPIDER-MAN!
YOU'RE DARN RIGHT I STILL AM! I SAY HE'S GOT A REASON FOR THE WAY HE'S ACTING! HE'LL SURPRISE YOU ALL PRETTY SOON!
I'D NEVER HAVE BELIEVED IT! HE'S STILL A SPIDEY BOOSTER!
JUST YOU WAIT... ALL OF YOU! YOU'LL BE WHISTLIN' A DIFFERENT TUNE WHEN THE OL' WEB-SPINNER PROVES WHAT A GREAT GUY HE IS!
PETE, YOU'RE THE SMARTEST BOY IN SCHOOL! DO YOU BELIEVE FLASH MIGHT BE RIGHT??
YOU CAN NEVER TELL, LIZ.. HE MIGHT BE!
15.

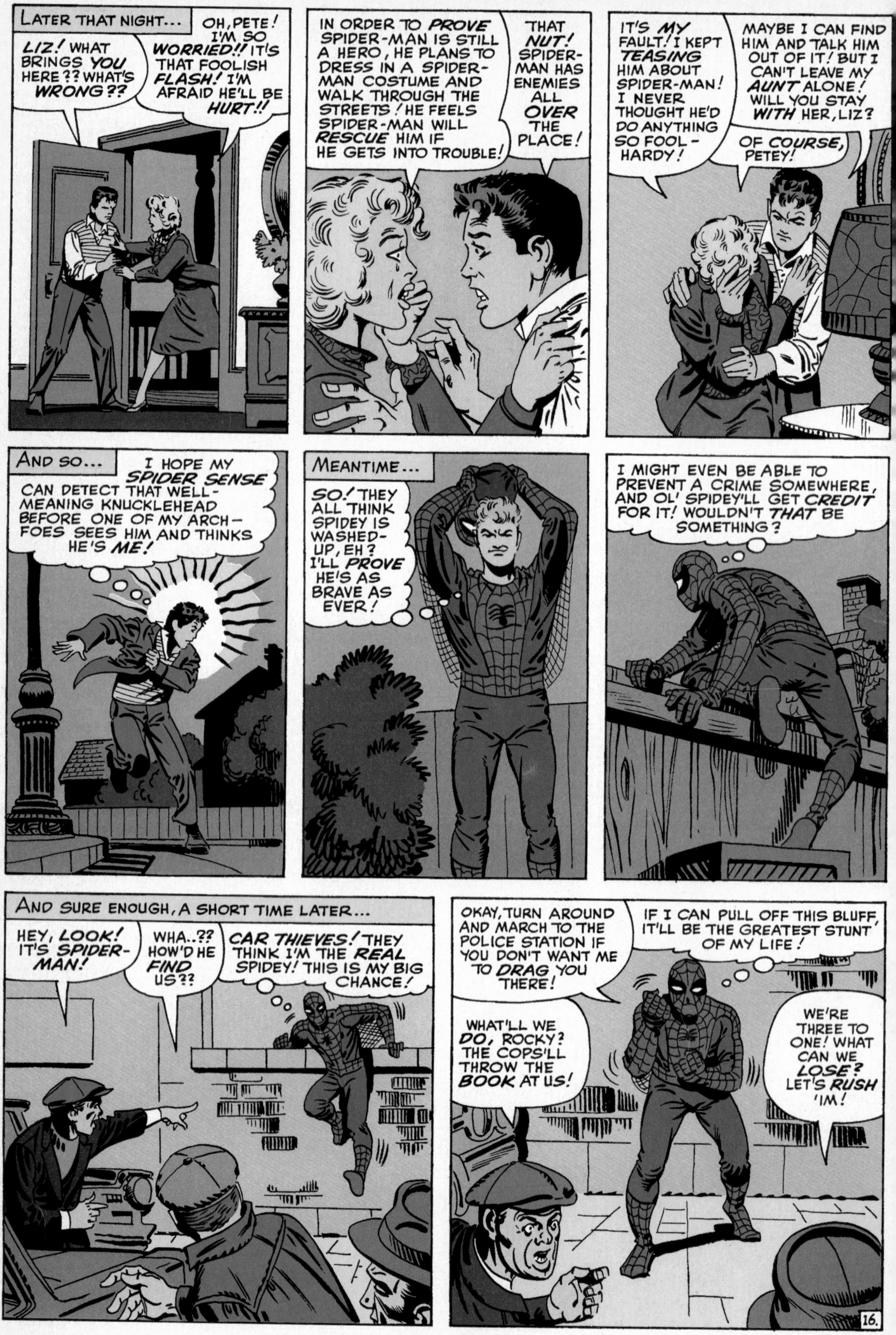
LATER THAT NIGHT...
LIZ! WHAT BRINGS YOU HERE?? WHAT'S WRONG??
OH, PETE! I'M SO WORRIED!! IT'S THAT FOOLISH FLASH! I'M AFRAID HE'LL BE HURT!!
IN ORDER TO PROVE SPIDER-MAN IS STILL A HERO, HE PLANS TO DRESS IN A SPIDER-MAN COSTUME AND WALK THROUGH THE STREETS! HE FEELS SPIDER-MAN WILL RESCUE HIM IF HE GETS INTO TROUBLE!
THAT NUT! SPIDER-MAN HAS ENEMIES ALL OVER THE PLACE!
IT'S MY FAULT! I KEPT TEASING HIM ABOUT SPIDER-MAN! I NEVER THOUGHT HE'D DO ANYTHING SO FOOL-HARDY!
MAYBE I CAN FIND HIM AND TALK HIM OUT OF IT! BUT I CAN'T LEAVE MY AUNT ALONE! WILL YOU STAY WITH HER, LIZ?
OF COURSE, PETEY!
AND SO...
I HOPE MY SPIDER SENSE CAN DETECT THAT WELL-MEANING KNUCKLEHEAD BEFORE ONE OF MY ARCH-FOES SEES HIM AND THINKS HE'S ME!
MEANTIME...
SO! THEY ALL THINK SPIDEY IS WASHED-UP, EH? I'LL PROVE HE'S AS BRAVE AS EVER!
I MIGHT EVEN BE ABLE TO PREVENT A CRIME SOMEWHERE, AND OL' SPIDEY'LL GET CREDIT FOR IT! WOULDN'T THAT BE SOMETHING?
AND SURE ENOUGH, A SHORT TIME LATER...
HEY, LOOK! IT'S SPIDER-MAN!
WHA..?? HOW'D HE FIND US??
CAR THIEVES! THEY THINK I'M THE REAL SPIDEY! THIS IS MY BIG CHANCE!
OKAY, TURN AROUND AND MARCH TO THE POLICE STATION IF YOU DON'T WANT ME TO DRAG YOU THERE!
IF I CAN PULL OFF THIS BLUFF, IT'LL BE THE GREATEST STUNT OF MY LIFE!
WHAT'LL WE DO, ROCKY? THE COPS'LL THROW THE BOOK AT US!
WE'RE THREE TO ONE! WHAT CAN WE LOSE? LET'S RUSH 'IM!
16.

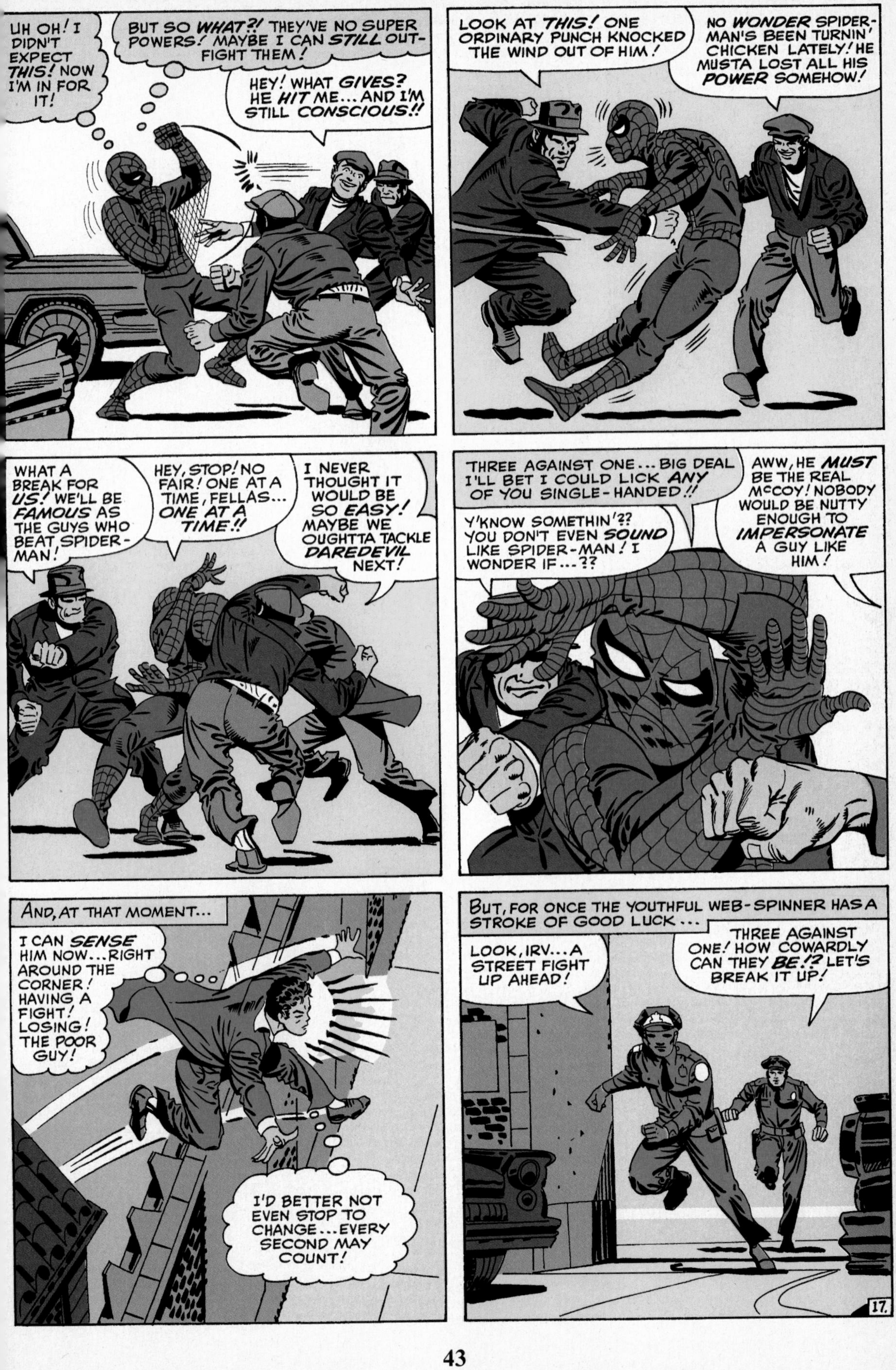
UH OH! I DIDN'T EXPECT THIS! NOW I'M IN FOR IT!
BUT SO WHAT?! THEY'VE NO SUPER POWERS! MAYBE I CAN STILL OUT-FIGHT THEM!
HEY! WHAT GIVES? HE HIT ME... AND I'M STILL CONSCIOUS!!
LOOK AT THIS! ONE ORDINARY PUNCH KNOCKED THE WIND OUT OF HIM!
NO WONDER SPIDER-MAN'S BEEN TURNIN' CHICKEN LATELY! HE MUSTA LOST ALL HIS POWER SOMEHOW!
WHAT A BREAK FOR US! WE'LL BE FAMOUS AS THE GUYS WHO BEAT SPIDER-MAN!
HEY, STOP! NO FAIR! ONE AT A TIME, FELLAS... ONE AT A TIME!!
I NEVER THOUGHT IT WOULD BE SO EASY! MAYBE WE OUGHTTA TACKLE DAREDEVIL NEXT!
THREE AGAINST ONE... BIG DEAL I'LL BET I COULD LICK ANY OF YOU SINGLE-HANDED!!
Y'KNOW SOMETHIN'?? YOU DON'T EVEN SOUND LIKE SPIDER-MAN! I WONDER IF...??
AWW, HE MUST BE THE REAL McCOY! NOBODY WOULD BE NUTTY ENOUGH TO IMPERSONATE A GUY LIKE HIM!
AND, AT THAT MOMENT...
I CAN SENSE HIM NOW... RIGHT AROUND THE CORNER! HAVING A FIGHT! LOSING! THE POOR GUY!
I'D BETTER NOT EVEN STOP TO CHANGE... EVERY SECOND MAY COUNT!
BUT, FOR ONCE THE YOUTHFUL WEB-SPINNER HAS A STROKE OF GOOD LUCK...
LOOK, IRV... A STREET FIGHT UP AHEAD!
THREE AGAINST ONE! HOW COWARDLY CAN THEY BE!? LET'S BREAK IT UP!
17.

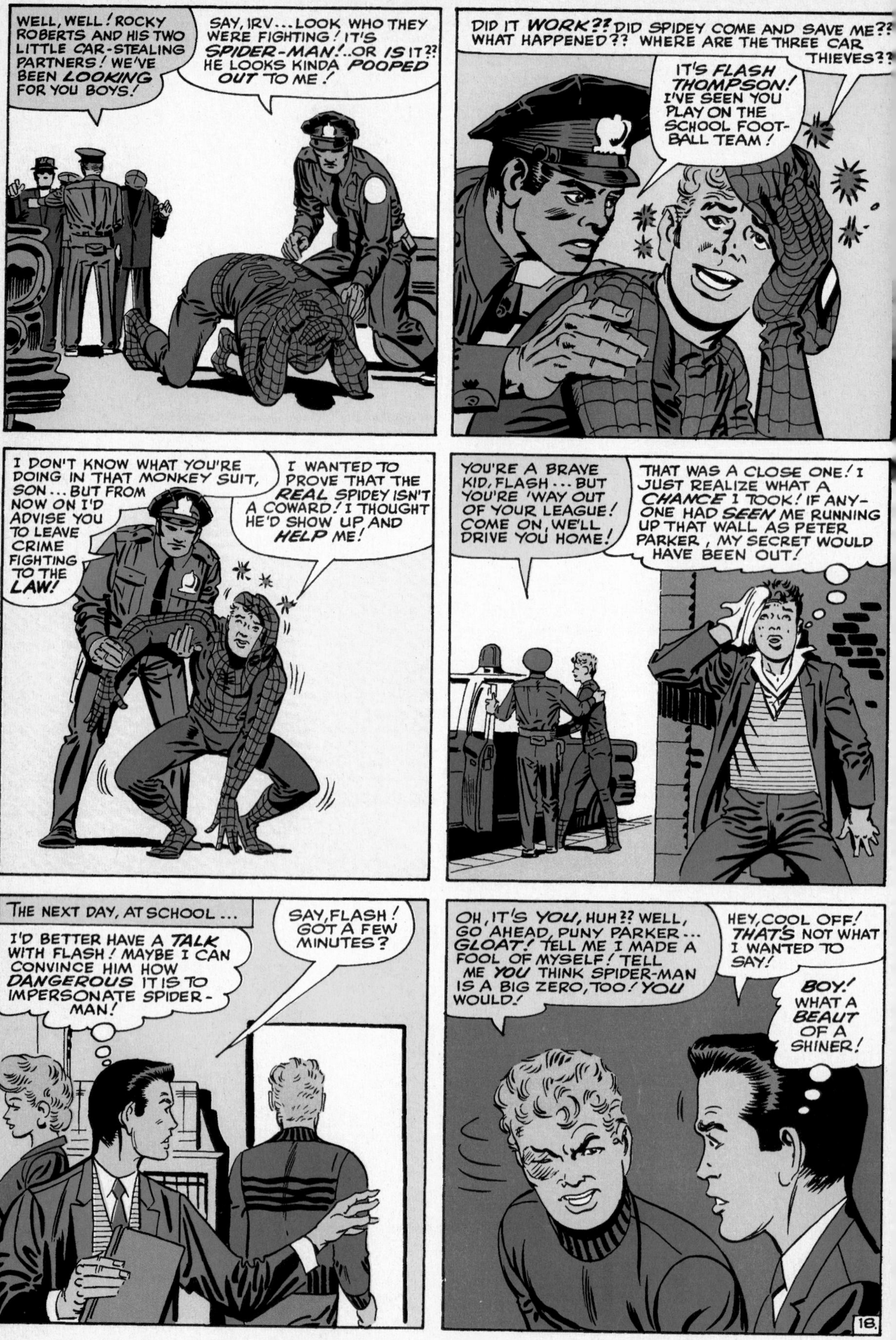
WELL, WELL! ROCKY ROBERTS AND HIS TWO LITTLE CAR-STEALING PARTNERS! WE'VE BEEN LOOKING FOR YOU BOYS!
SAY, IRV... LOOK WHO THEY WERE FIGHTING! IT'S SPIDER-MAN!..OR IS IT?? HE LOOKS KINDA POOPED OUT TO ME!
DID IT WORK?? DID SPIDEY COME AND SAVE ME?? WHAT HAPPENED?? WHERE ARE THE THREE CAR THIEVES??
IT'S FLASH THOMPSON! I'VE SEEN YOU PLAY ON THE SCHOOL FOOT-BALL TEAM!
I DON'T KNOW WHAT YOU'RE DOING IN THAT MONKEY SUIT, SON... BUT FROM NOW ON I'D ADVISE YOU TO LEAVE CRIME FIGHTING TO THE LAW!
I WANTED TO PROVE THAT THE REAL SPIDEY ISN'T A COWARD! I THOUGHT HE'D SHOW UP AND HELP ME!
YOU'RE A BRAVE KID, FLASH... BUT YOU'RE 'WAY OUT OF YOUR LEAGUE! COME ON, WE'LL DRIVE YOU HOME!
THAT WAS A CLOSE ONE! I JUST REALIZE WHAT A CHANCE I TOOK! IF ANY-ONE HAD SEEN ME RUNNING UP THAT WALL AS PETER PARKER, MY SECRET WOULD HAVE BEEN OUT!
THE NEXT DAY, AT SCHOOL...
I'D BETTER HAVE A TALK WITH FLASH! MAYBE I CAN CONVINCE HIM HOW DANGEROUS IT IS TO IMPERSONATE SPIDER-MAN!
SAY, FLASH! GOT A FEW MINUTES?
OH, IT'S YOU, HUH?? WELL, GO AHEAD, PUNY PARKER... GLOAT! TELL ME I MADE A FOOL OF MYSELF! TELL ME YOU THINK SPIDER-MAN IS A BIG ZERO, TOO! YOU WOULD!
HEY, COOL OFF! THAT'S NOT WHAT I WANTED TO SAY!
BOY! WHAT A BEAUT OF A SHINER!
18.

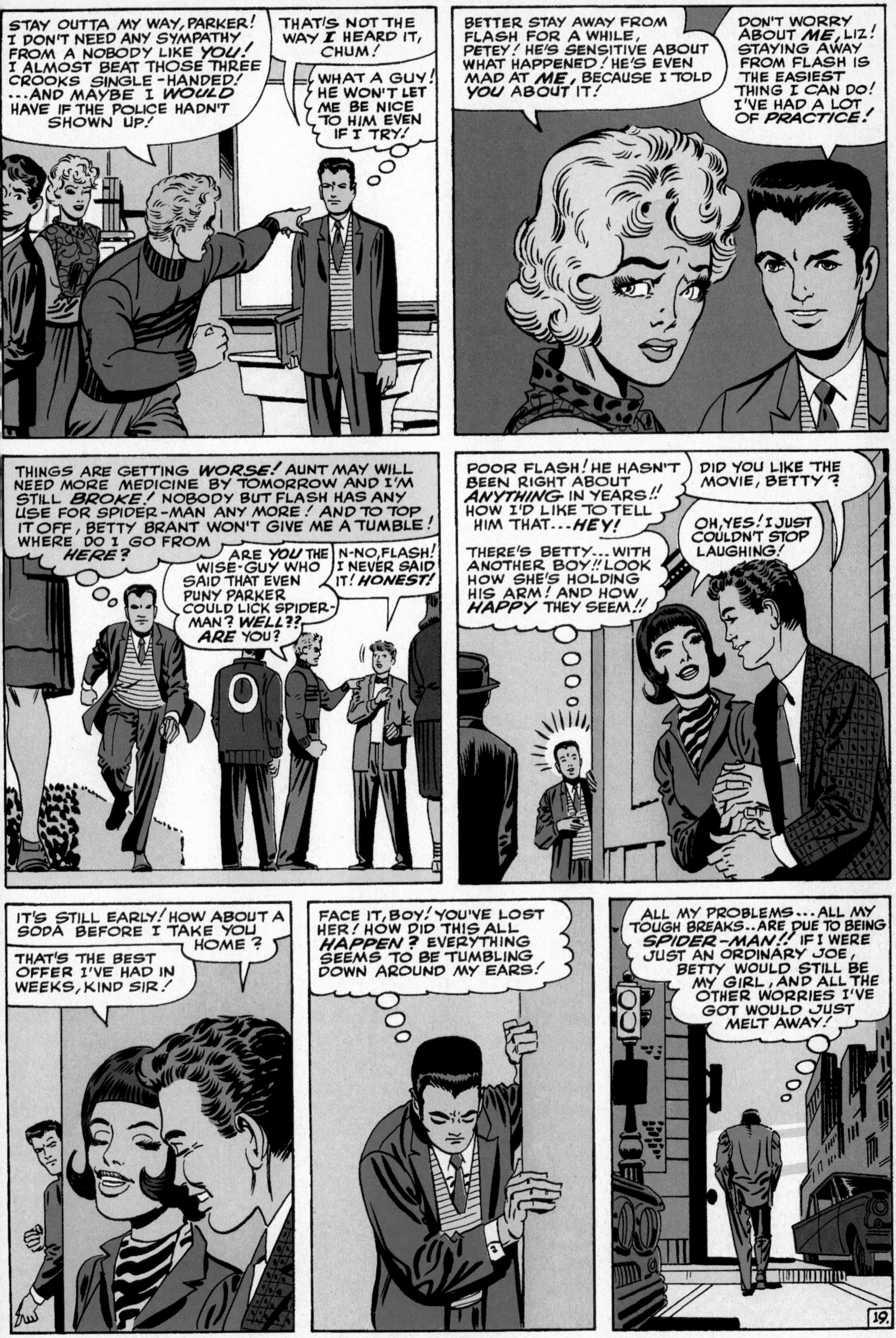
STAY OUTTA MY WAY, PARKER! I DON'T NEED ANY SYMPATHY FROM A NOBODY LIKE YOU! I ALMOST BEAT THOSE THREE CROOKS SINGLE-HANDED! ...AND MAYBE I WOULD HAVE IF THE POLICE HADN'T SHOWN UP!
THAT'S NOT THE WAY I HEARD IT, CHUM!
WHAT A GUY! HE WON'T LET ME BE NICE TO HIM EVEN IF I TRY!
BETTER STAY AWAY FROM FLASH FOR A WHILE, PETEY! HE'S SENSITIVE ABOUT WHAT HAPPENED! HE'S EVEN MAD AT ME, BECAUSE I TOLD YOU ABOUT IT!
DON'T WORRY ABOUT ME, LIZ! STAYING AWAY FROM FLASH IS THE EASIEST THING I CAN DO! I'VE HAD A LOT OF PRACTICE!
THINGS ARE GETTING WORSE! AUNT MAY WILL NEED MORE MEDICINE BY TOMORROW AND I'M STILL BROKE! NOBODY BUT FLASH HAS ANY USE FOR SPIDER-MAN ANY MORE! AND TO TOP IT OFF, BETTY BRANT WON'T GIVE ME A TUMBLE! WHERE DO I GO FROM HERE?
ARE YOU THE WISE-GUY WHO SAID THAT EVEN PUNY PARKER COULD LICK SPIDER-MAN? WELL?? ARE YOU?
N-NO, FLASH! I NEVER SAID IT! HONEST!
POOR FLASH! HE HASN'T BEEN RIGHT ABOUT ANYTHING IN YEARS!! HOW I'D LIKE TO TELL HIM THAT... HEY!
THERE'S BETTY... WITH ANOTHER BOY!! LOOK HOW SHE'S HOLDING HIS ARM! AND HOW HAPPY THEY SEEM!!
DID YOU LIKE THE MOVIE, BETTY?
OH, YES! I JUST COULDN'T STOP LAUGHING!
IT'S STILL EARLY! HOW ABOUT A SODA BEFORE I TAKE YOU HOME?
THAT'S THE BEST OFFER I'VE HAD IN WEEKS, KIND SIR!
FACE IT, BOY! YOU'VE LOST HER! HOW DID THIS ALL HAPPEN? EVERYTHING SEEMS TO BE TUMBLING DOWN AROUND MY EARS!
ALL MY PROBLEMS... ALL MY TOUGH BREAKS.. ARE DUE TO BEING SPIDER-MAN!! IF I WERE JUST AN ORDINARY JOE, BETTY WOULD STILL BE MY GIRL, AND ALL THE OTHER WORRIES I'VE GOT WOULD JUST MELT AWAY!
19.

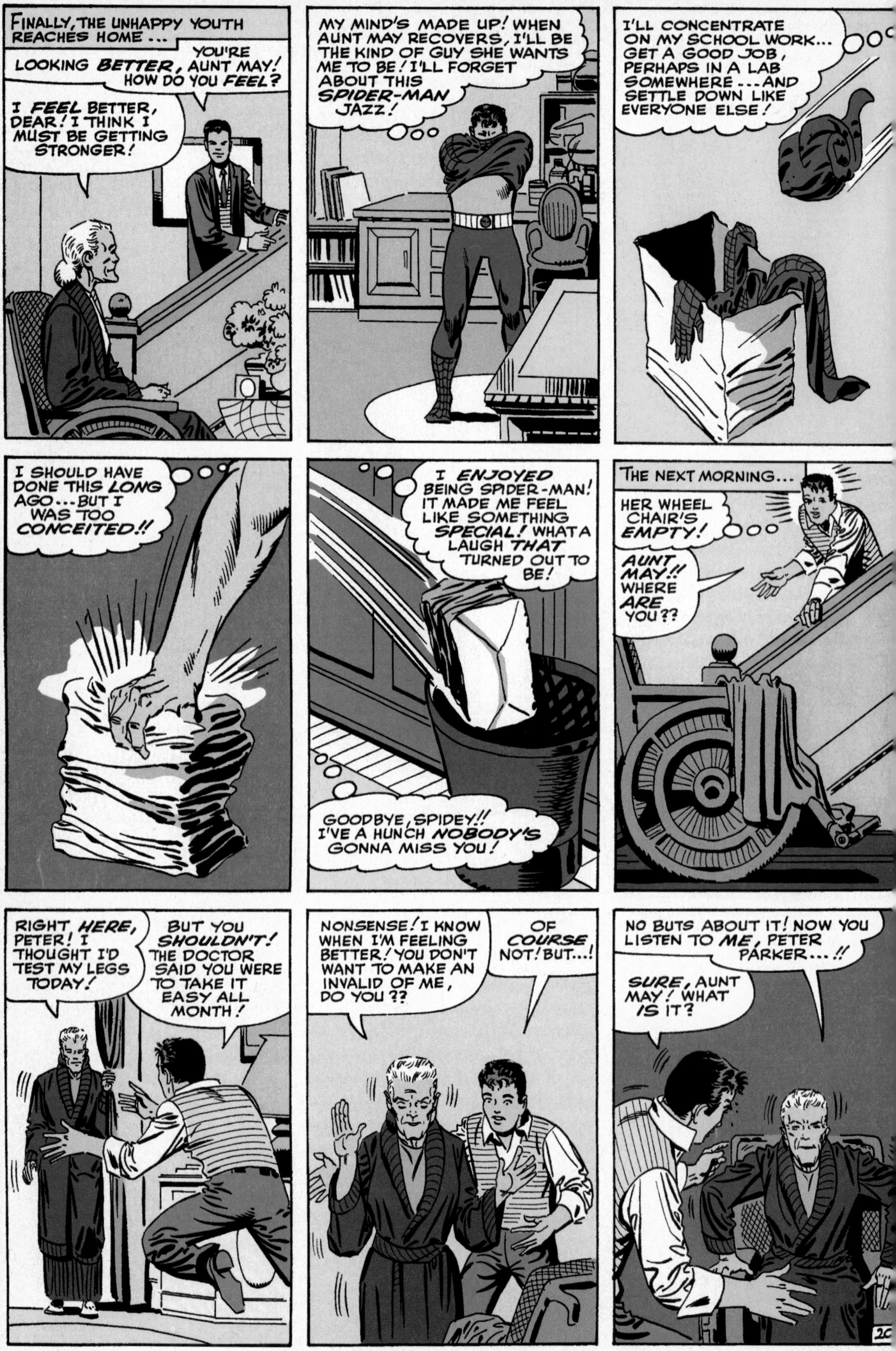
FINALLY, THE UNHAPPY YOUTH REACHES HOME ...
YOU'RE LOOKING BETTER, AUNT MAY! HOW DO YOU FEEL?
I FEEL BETTER, DEAR! I THINK I MUST BE GETTING STRONGER!
MY MIND'S MADE UP! WHEN AUNT MAY RECOVERS, I'LL BE THE KIND OF GUY SHE WANTS ME TO BE! I'LL FORGET ABOUT THIS SPIDER-MAN JAZZ!
I'LL CONCENTRATE ON MY SCHOOL WORK... GET A GOOD JOB, PERHAPS IN A LAB SOMEWHERE ... AND SETTLE DOWN LIKE EVERYONE ELSE!
I SHOULD HAVE DONE THIS LONG AGO... BUT I WAS TOO CONCEITED!!
I ENJOYED BEING SPIDER-MAN! IT MADE ME FEEL LIKE SOMETHING SPECIAL! WHAT A LAUGH THAT TURNED OUT TO BE!
GOODBYE, SPIDEY!! I'VE A HUNCH NOBODY'S GONNA MISS YOU!
THE NEXT MORNING...
HER WHEEL CHAIR'S EMPTY!
AUNT MAY!! WHERE ARE YOU??
RIGHT HERE, PETER! I THOUGHT I'D TEST MY LEGS TODAY!
BUT YOU SHOULDN'T! THE DOCTOR SAID YOU WERE TO TAKE IT EASY ALL MONTH!
NONSENSE! I KNOW WHEN I'M FEELING BETTER! YOU DON'T WANT TO MAKE AN INVALID OF ME, DO YOU??
OF COURSE NOT! BUT...!
NO BUTS ABOUT IT! NOW YOU LISTEN TO ME, PETER PARKER...!!
SURE, AUNT MAY! WHAT IS IT?

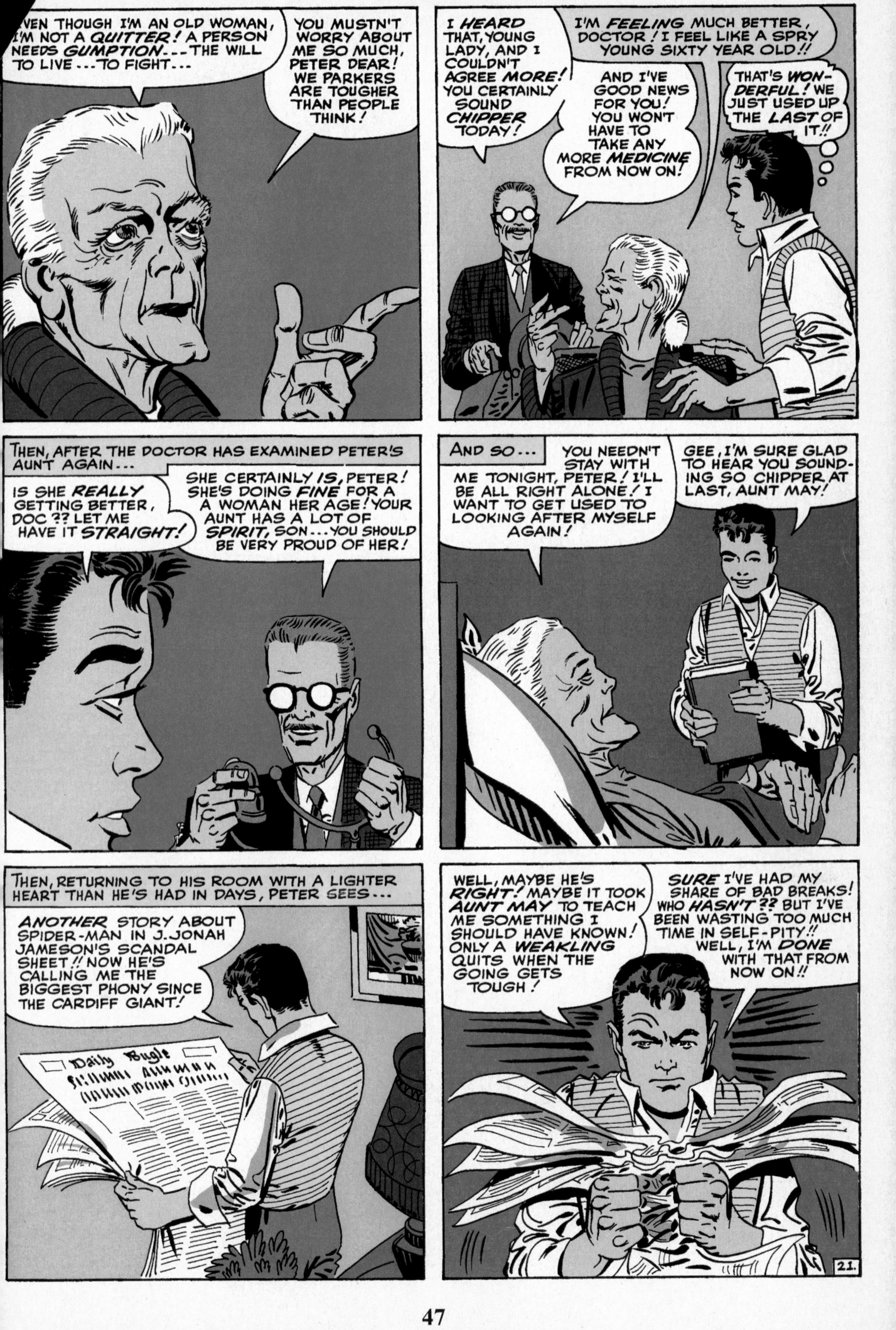
EVEN THOUGH I'M AN OLD WOMAN, I'M NOT A QUITTER! A PERSON NEEDS GUMPTION--- THE WILL TO LIVE --- TO FIGHT---
YOU MUSTN'T WORRY ABOUT ME SO MUCH, PETER DEAR! WE PARKERS ARE TOUGHER THAN PEOPLE THINK!
I'M FEELING MUCH BETTER, DOCTOR! I FEEL LIKE A SPRY YOUNG SIXTY YEAR OLD!!
I HEARD THAT, YOUNG LADY, AND I COULDN'T AGREE MORE! YOU CERTAINLY SOUND CHIPPER TODAY!
AND I'VE GOOD NEWS FOR YOU! YOU WON'T HAVE TO TAKE ANY MORE MEDICINE FROM NOW ON!
THAT'S WONDERFUL! WE JUST USED UP THE LAST OF IT!!
THEN, AFTER THE DOCTOR HAS EXAMINED PETER'S AUNT AGAIN...
IS SHE REALLY GETTING BETTER, DOC ?? LET ME HAVE IT STRAIGHT!
SHE CERTAINLY IS, PETER! SHE'S DOING FINE FOR A WOMAN HER AGE! YOUR AUNT HAS A LOT OF SPIRIT, SON... YOU SHOULD BE VERY PROUD OF HER!
AND SO...
YOU NEEDN'T STAY WITH ME TONIGHT, PETER! I'LL BE ALL RIGHT ALONE! I WANT TO GET USED TO LOOKING AFTER MYSELF AGAIN!
GEE, I'M SURE GLAD TO HEAR YOU SOUNDING SO CHIPPER AT LAST, AUNT MAY!
THEN, RETURNING TO HIS ROOM WITH A LIGHTER HEART THAN HE'S HAD IN DAYS, PETER SEES...
ANOTHER STORY ABOUT SPIDER-MAN IN J. JONAH JAMESON'S SCANDAL SHEET!! NOW HE'S CALLING ME THE BIGGEST PHONY SINCE THE CARDIFF GIANT!
Daily Bugle
WELL, MAYBE HE'S RIGHT! MAYBE IT TOOK AUNT MAY TO TEACH ME SOMETHING I SHOULD HAVE KNOWN! ONLY A WEAKLING QUITS WHEN THE GOING GETS TOUGH!
SURE I'VE HAD MY SHARE OF BAD BREAKS! WHO HASN'T ?? BUT I'VE BEEN WASTING TOO MUCH TIME IN SELF-PITY!! WELL, I'M DONE WITH THAT FROM NOW ON!!
21.

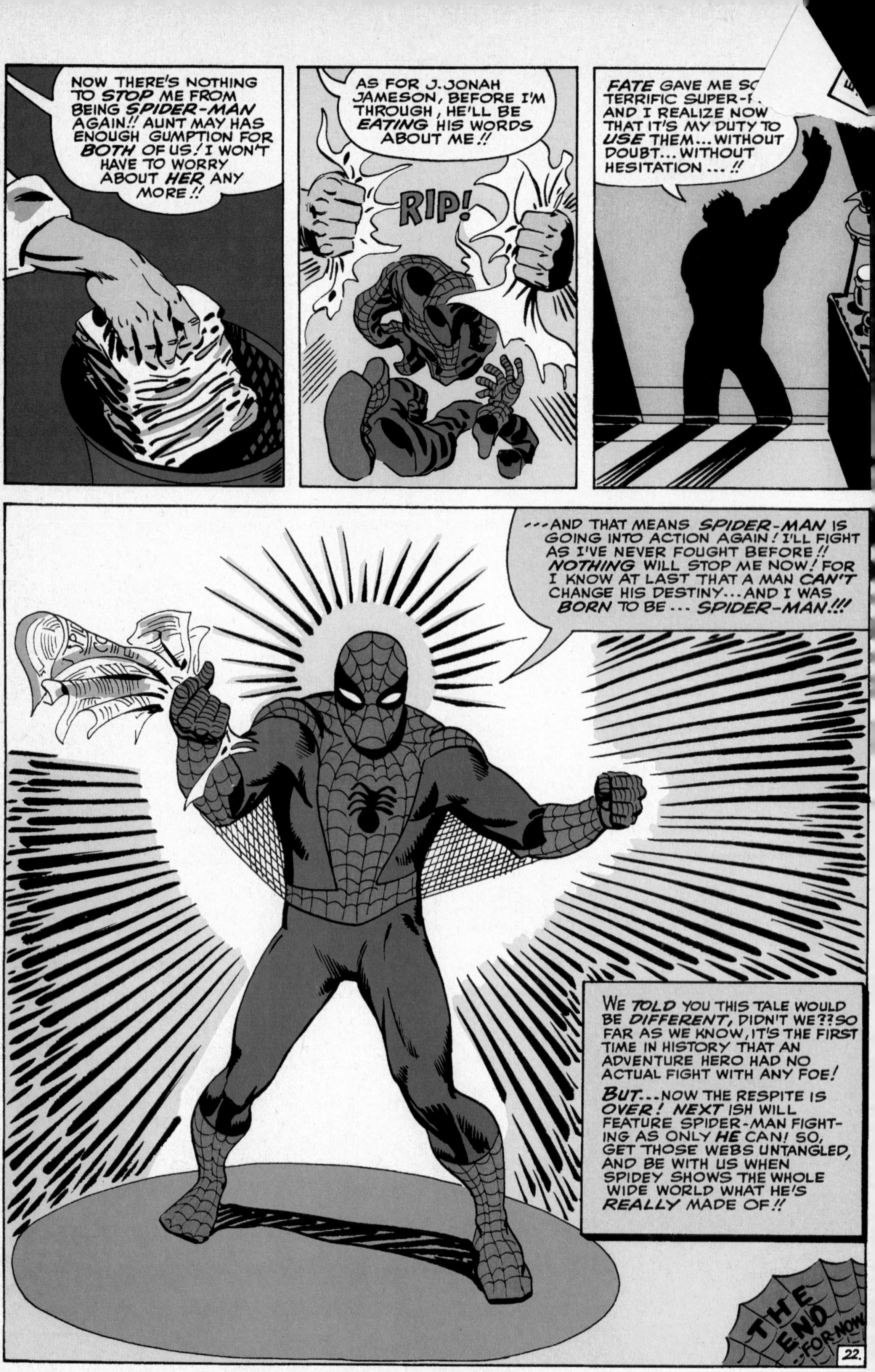

NOW THERE'S NOTHING TO STOP ME FROM BEING SPIDER-MAN AGAIN!! AUNT MAY HAS ENOUGH GUMPTION FOR BOTH OF US! I WON'T HAVE TO WORRY ABOUT HER ANY MORE!!
AS FOR J. JONAH JAMESON, BEFORE I'M THROUGH, HE'LL BE EATING HIS WORDS ABOUT ME!!
RIP!
FATE GAVE ME SO TERRIFIC SUPER-P AND I REALIZE NOW THAT IT'S MY DUTY TO USE THEM... WITHOUT DOUBT... WITHOUT HESITATION...!!
...AND THAT MEANS SPIDER-MAN IS GOING INTO ACTION AGAIN! I'LL FIGHT AS I'VE NEVER FOUGHT BEFORE!! NOTHING WILL STOP ME NOW! FOR I KNOW AT LAST THAT A MAN CAN'T CHANGE HIS DESTINY... AND I WAS BORN TO BE... SPIDER-MAN!!!
WE TOLD YOU THIS TALE WOULD BE DIFFERENT, DIDN'T WE?? SO FAR AS WE KNOW, IT'S THE FIRST TIME IN HISTORY THAT AN ADVENTURE HERO HAD NO ACTUAL FIGHT WITH ANY FOE!
BUT... NOW THE RESPITE IS OVER! NEXT ISH WILL FEATURE SPIDER-MAN FIGHTING AS ONLY HE CAN! SO, GET THOSE WEBS UNTANGLED, AND BE WITH US WHEN SPIDEY SHOWS THE WHOLE WIDE WORLD WHAT HE'S REALLY MADE OF!!
THE END ...FOR NOW
22.

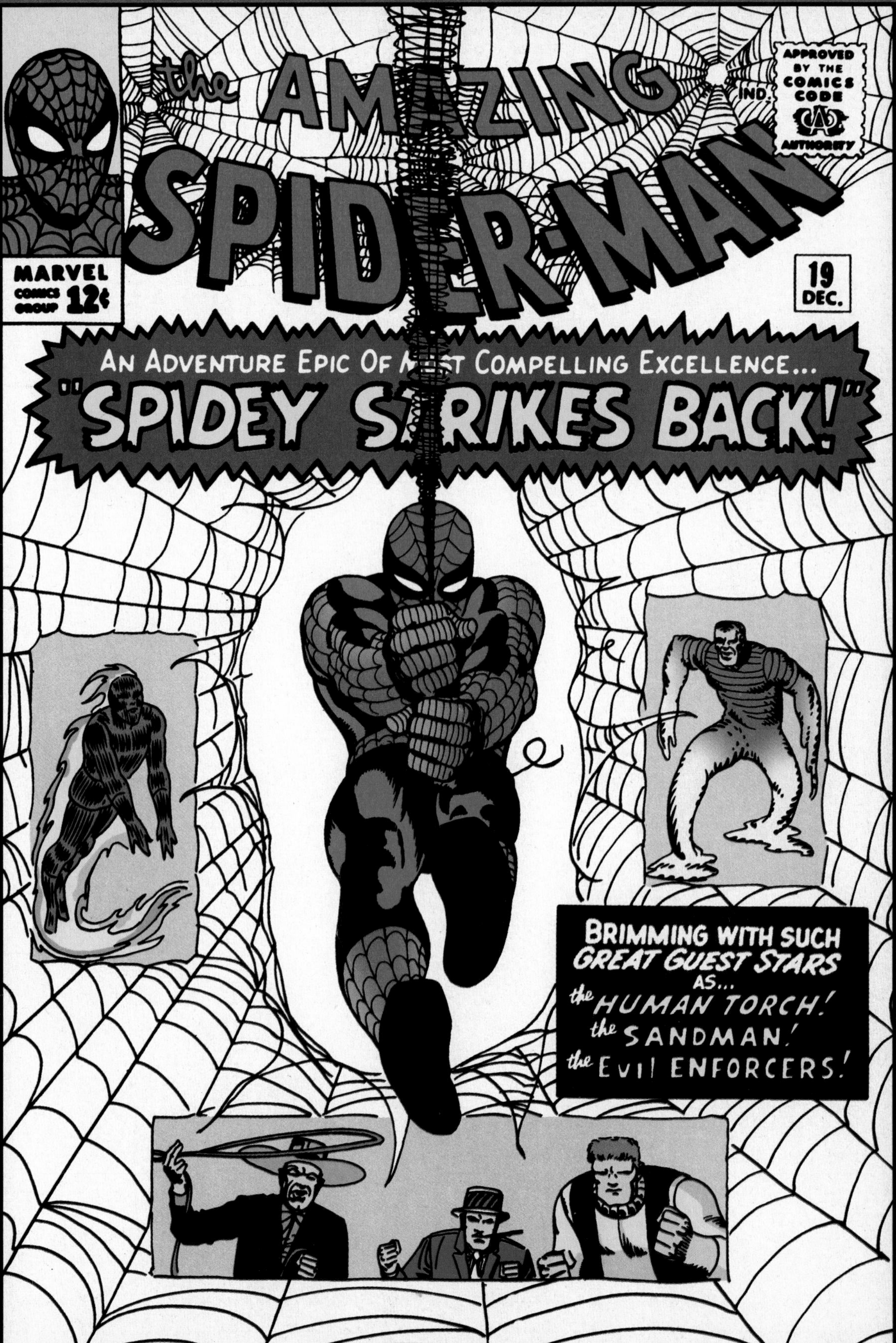
the AMAZING SPIDER-MAN
IND.
APPROVED BY THE COMICS CODE AUTHORITY
MARVEL COMICS GROUP 12¢
19 DEC.
AN ADVENTURE EPIC OF MOST COMPELLING EXCELLENCE...
"SPIDEY STRIKES BACK!"
BRIMMING WITH SUCH GREAT GUEST STARS AS...
the HUMAN TORCH!
the SANDMAN!
the EVIL ENFORCERS!

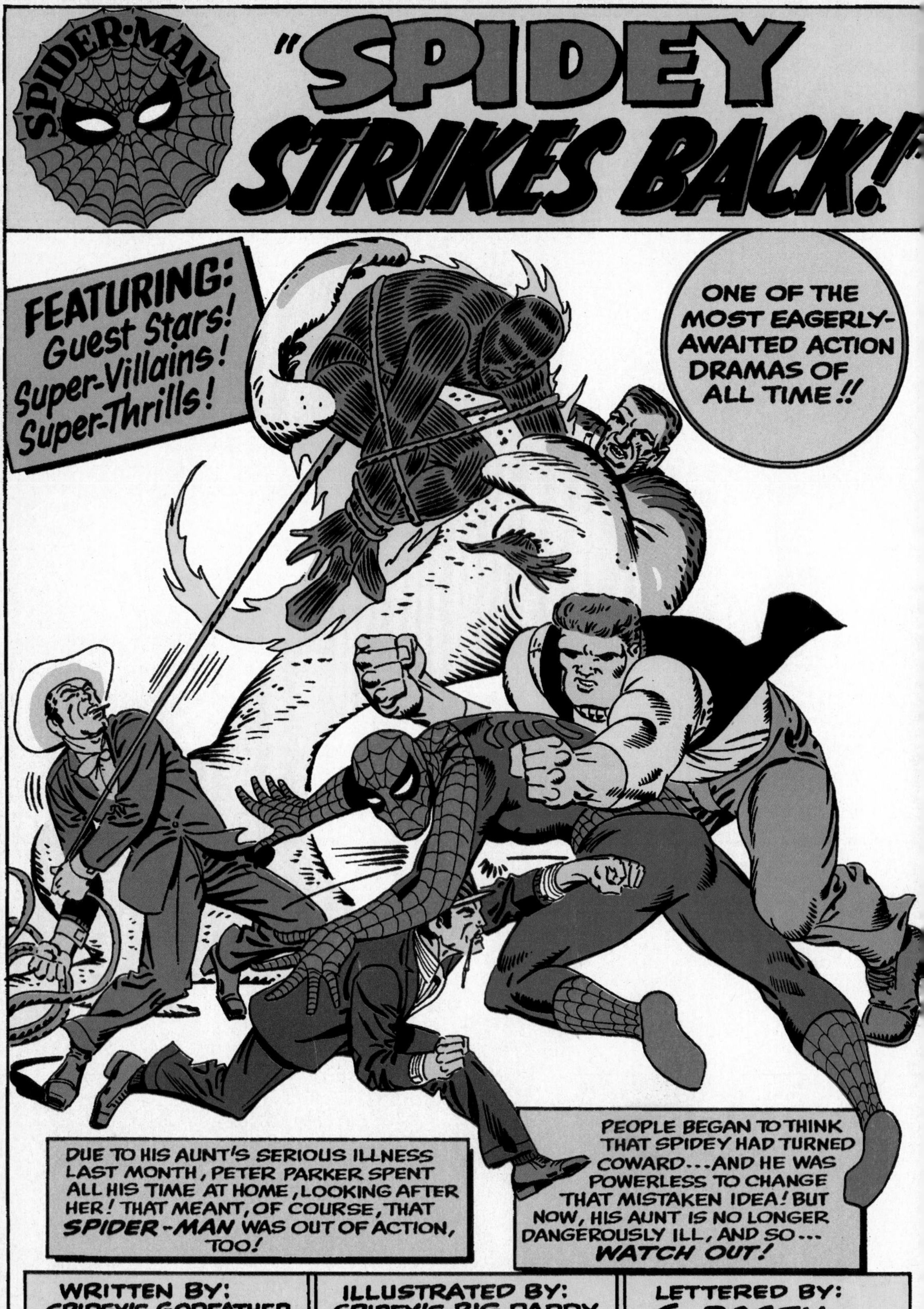

SPIDER-MAN
"SPIDEY STRIKES BACK!"
FEATURING: Guest Stars! Super-Villains! Super-Thrills!
ONE OF THE MOST EAGERLY-AWAITED ACTION DRAMAS OF ALL TIME!!
DUE TO HIS AUNT'S SERIOUS ILLNESS LAST MONTH, PETER PARKER SPENT ALL HIS TIME AT HOME, LOOKING AFTER HER! THAT MEANT, OF COURSE, THAT SPIDER-MAN WAS OUT OF ACTION, TOO!
PEOPLE BEGAN TO THINK THAT SPIDEY HAD TURNED COWARD... AND HE WAS POWERLESS TO CHANGE THAT MISTAKEN IDEA! BUT NOW, HIS AUNT IS NO LONGER DANGEROUSLY ILL, AND SO... WATCH OUT!
WRITTEN BY: SPIDEY'S GODFATHER, STAN LEE
ILLUSTRATED BY: SPIDEY'S BIG DADDY, STEVE DITKO
LETTERED BY: S. ROSEN (SPIDEY'S SECOND COUSIN ON HIS UNCLE'S SIDE!)
X-816

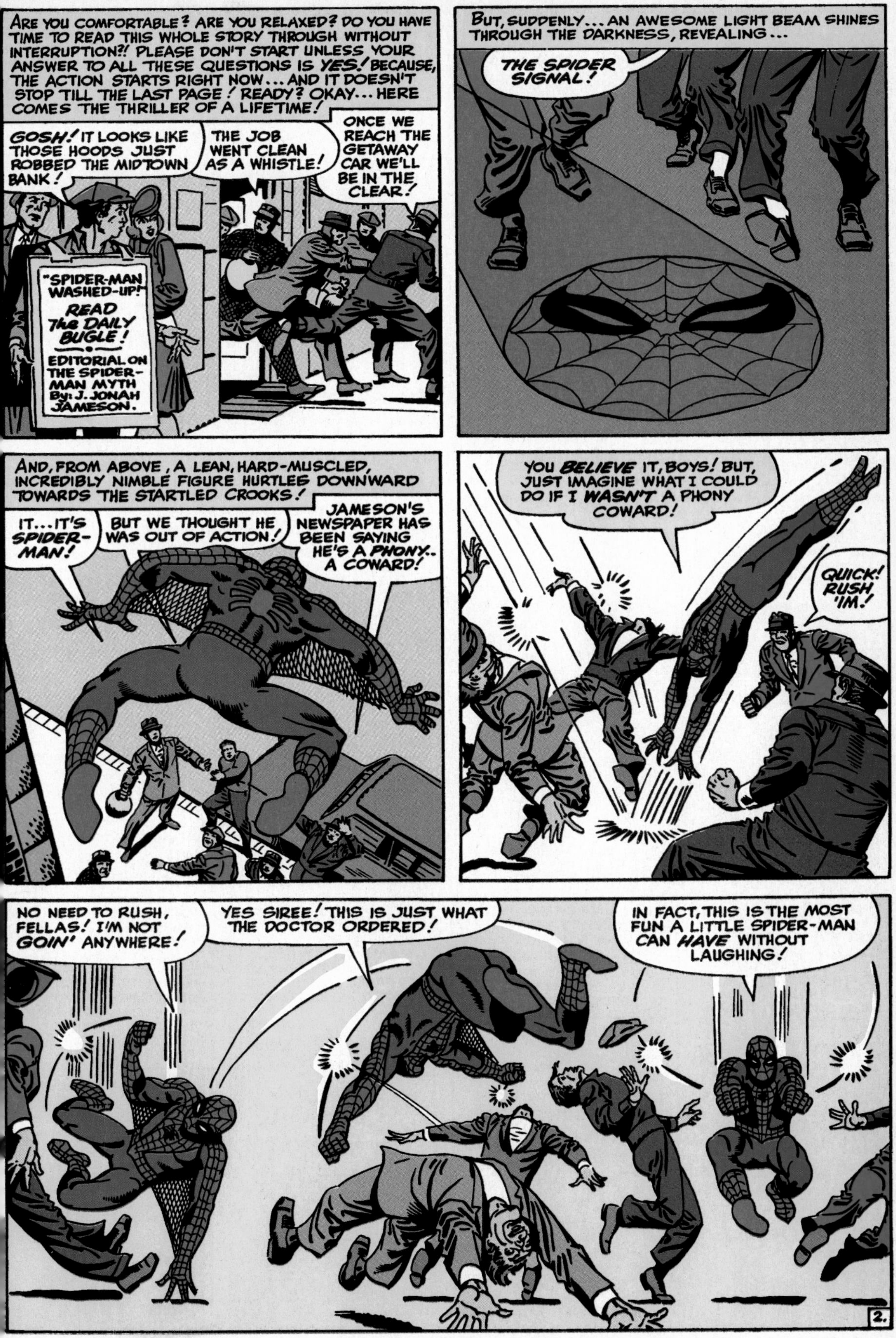

ARE YOU COMFORTABLE? ARE YOU RELAXED? DO YOU HAVE TIME TO READ THIS WHOLE STORY THROUGH WITHOUT INTERRUPTION?! PLEASE DON'T START UNLESS YOUR ANSWER TO ALL THESE QUESTIONS IS YES! BECAUSE, THE ACTION STARTS RIGHT NOW... AND IT DOESN'T STOP TILL THE LAST PAGE! READY? OKAY... HERE COMES THE THRILLER OF A LIFETIME!
GOSH! IT LOOKS LIKE THOSE HOODS JUST ROBBED THE MIDTOWN BANK!
THE JOB WENT CLEAN AS A WHISTLE!
ONCE WE REACH THE GETAWAY CAR WE'LL BE IN THE CLEAR!
"SPIDER-MAN WASHED-UP!" READ the DAILY BUGLE! EDITORIAL ON THE SPIDER-MAN MYTH By: J. JONAH JAMESON.
BUT, SUDDENLY... AN AWESOME LIGHT BEAM SHINES THROUGH THE DARKNESS, REVEALING...
THE SPIDER SIGNAL!
AND, FROM ABOVE, A LEAN, HARD-MUSCLED, INCREDIBLY NIMBLE FIGURE HURTLES DOWNWARD TOWARDS THE STARTLED CROOKS!
IT... IT'S SPIDER-MAN!
BUT WE THOUGHT HE WAS OUT OF ACTION!
JAMESON'S NEWSPAPER HAS BEEN SAYING HE'S A PHONY.. A COWARD!
YOU BELIEVE IT, BOYS! BUT, JUST IMAGINE WHAT I COULD DO IF I WASN'T A PHONY COWARD!
QUICK! RUSH 'IM!
NO NEED TO RUSH, FELLAS! I'M NOT GOIN' ANYWHERE!
YES SIREE! THIS IS JUST WHAT THE DOCTOR ORDERED!
IN FACT, THIS IS THE MOST FUN A LITTLE SPIDER-MAN CAN HAVE WITHOUT LAUGHING!
2.

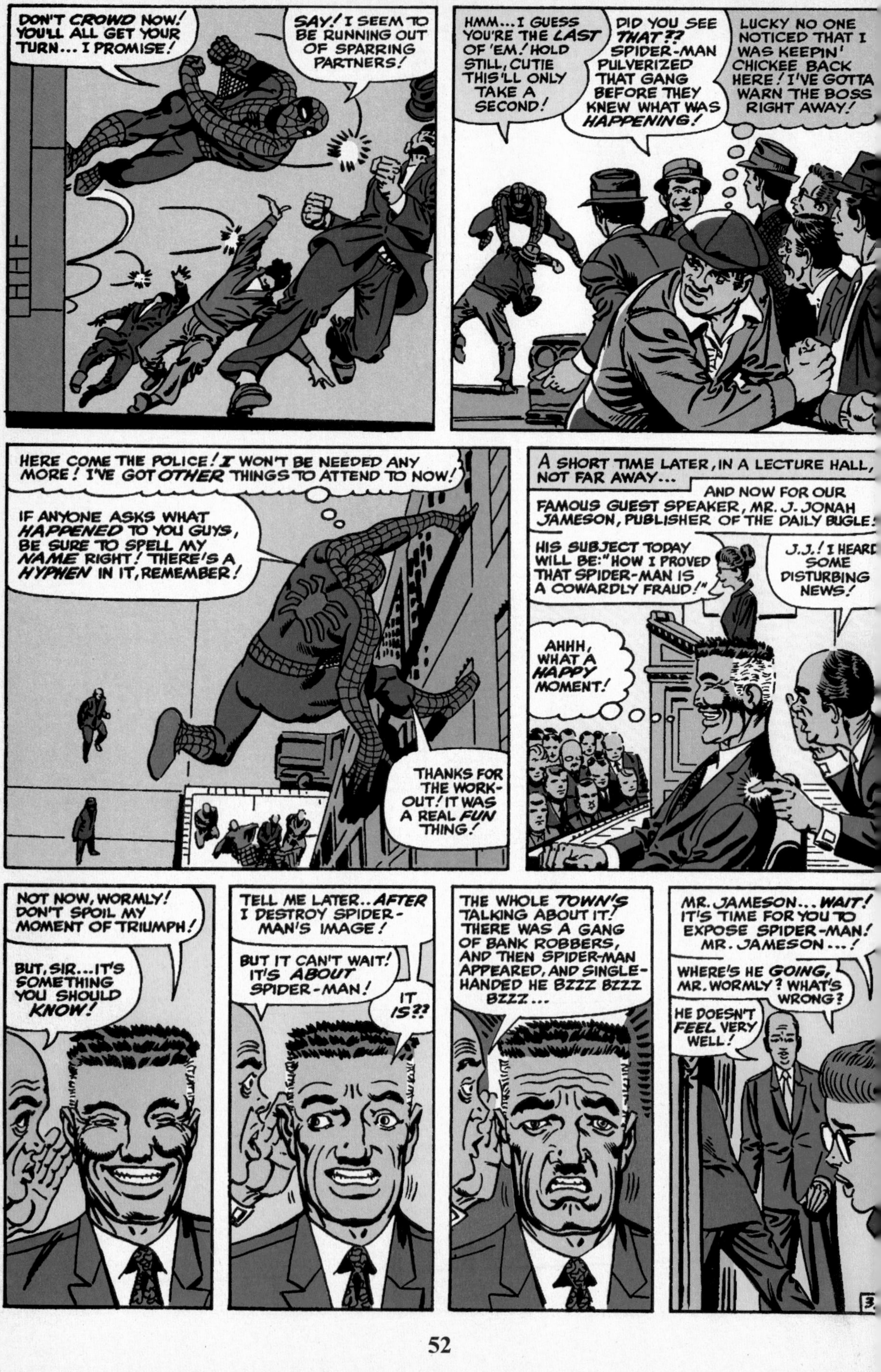
DON'T CROWD NOW! YOU'LL ALL GET YOUR TURN... I PROMISE!
SAY! I SEEM TO BE RUNNING OUT OF SPARRING PARTNERS!
HMM... I GUESS YOU'RE THE LAST OF 'EM! HOLD STILL, CUTIE THIS'LL ONLY TAKE A SECOND!
DID YOU SEE THAT?? SPIDER-MAN PULVERIZED THAT GANG BEFORE THEY KNEW WHAT WAS HAPPENING!
LUCKY NO ONE NOTICED THAT I WAS KEEPIN' CHICKEE BACK HERE! I'VE GOTTA WARN THE BOSS RIGHT AWAY!
HERE COME THE POLICE! I WON'T BE NEEDED ANY MORE! I'VE GOT OTHER THINGS TO ATTEND TO NOW!
IF ANYONE ASKS WHAT HAPPENED TO YOU GUYS, BE SURE TO SPELL MY NAME RIGHT! THERE'S A HYPHEN IN IT, REMEMBER!
THANKS FOR THE WORK-OUT! IT WAS A REAL FUN THING!
A SHORT TIME LATER, IN A LECTURE HALL, NOT FAR AWAY...
AND NOW FOR OUR FAMOUS GUEST SPEAKER, MR. J. JONAH JAMESON, PUBLISHER OF THE DAILY BUGLE!
HIS SUBJECT TODAY WILL BE: "HOW I PROVED THAT SPIDER-MAN IS A COWARDLY FRAUD!"
J.J.! I HEARD SOME DISTURBING NEWS!
AHHH, WHAT A HAPPY MOMENT!
NOT NOW, WORMLY! DON'T SPOIL MY MOMENT OF TRIUMPH!
BUT, SIR... IT'S SOMETHING YOU SHOULD KNOW!
TELL ME LATER... AFTER I DESTROY SPIDER-MAN'S IMAGE!
BUT IT CAN'T WAIT! IT'S ABOUT SPIDER-MAN!
IT IS??
THE WHOLE TOWN'S TALKING ABOUT IT! THERE WAS A GANG OF BANK ROBBERS, AND THEN SPIDER-MAN APPEARED, AND SINGLE-HANDED HE BZZZ BZZZ BZZZ...
MR. JAMESON... WAIT! IT'S TIME FOR YOU TO EXPOSE SPIDER-MAN! MR. JAMESON...!
WHERE'S HE GOING, MR. WORMLY? WHAT'S WRONG?
HE DOESN'T FEEL VERY WELL!

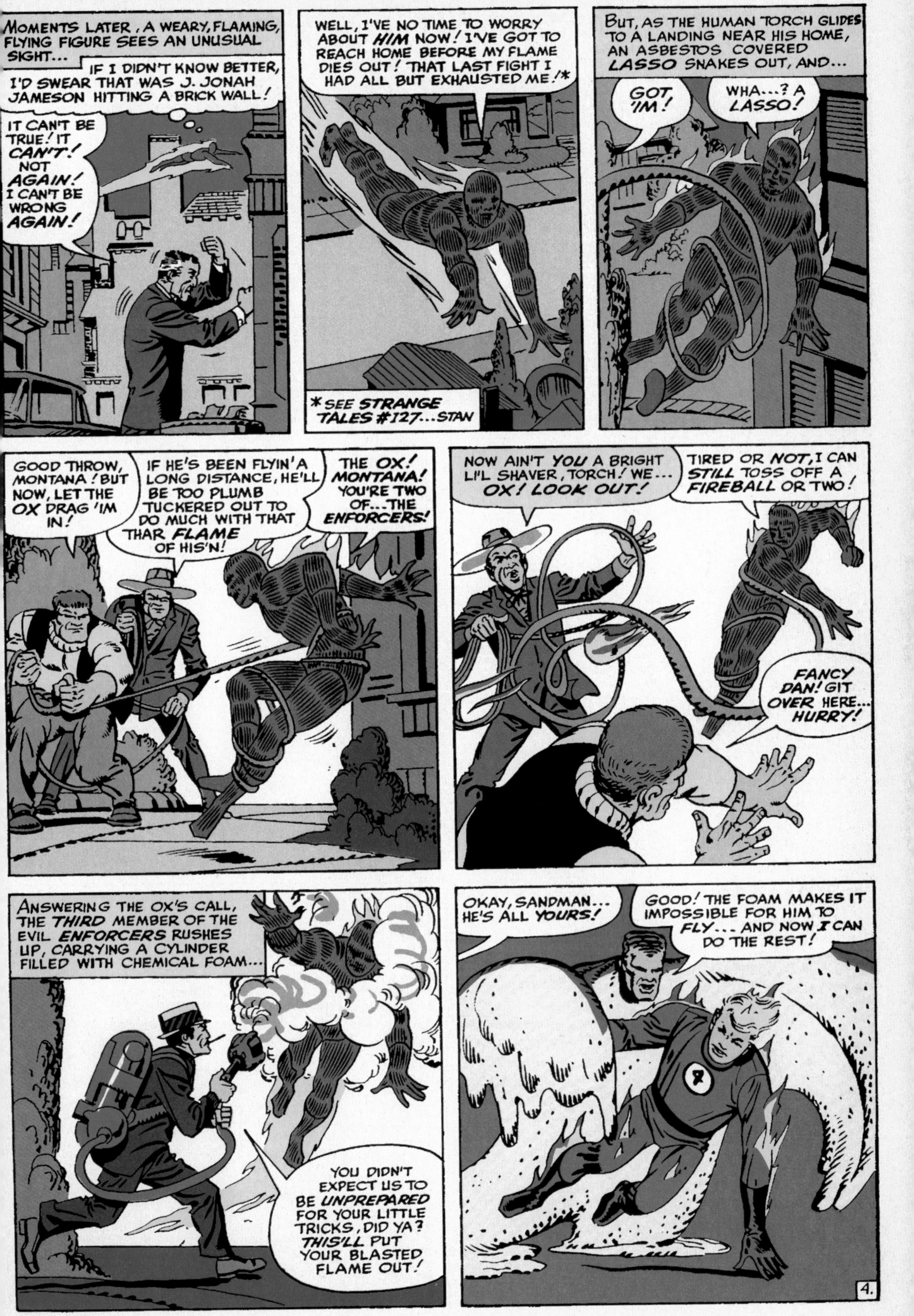

MOMENTS LATER, A WEARY, FLAMING, FLYING FIGURE SEES AN UNUSUAL SIGHT...
IF I DIDN'T KNOW BETTER, I'D SWEAR THAT WAS J. JONAH JAMESON HITTING A BRICK WALL!
IT CAN'T BE TRUE! IT CAN'T! NOT AGAIN! I CAN'T BE WRONG AGAIN!
WELL, I'VE NO TIME TO WORRY ABOUT HIM NOW! I'VE GOT TO REACH HOME BEFORE MY FLAME DIES OUT! THAT LAST FIGHT I HAD ALL BUT EXHAUSTED ME!*
*SEE STRANGE TALES #127...STAN
BUT, AS THE HUMAN TORCH GLIDES TO A LANDING NEAR HIS HOME, AN ASBESTOS COVERED LASSO SNAKES OUT, AND...
GOT 'IM!
WHA...? A LASSO!
GOOD THROW, MONTANA! BUT NOW, LET THE OX DRAG 'IM IN!
IF HE'S BEEN FLYIN' A LONG DISTANCE, HE'LL BE TOO PLUMB TUCKERED OUT TO DO MUCH WITH THAT THAR FLAME OF HIS'N!
THE OX! MONTANA! YOU'RE TWO OF... THE ENFORCERS!
NOW AIN'T YOU A BRIGHT LI'L SHAVER, TORCH! WE... OX! LOOK OUT!
TIRED OR NOT, I CAN STILL TOSS OFF A FIREBALL OR TWO!
FANCY DAN! GIT OVER HERE... HURRY!
ANSWERING THE OX'S CALL, THE THIRD MEMBER OF THE EVIL ENFORCERS RUSHES UP, CARRYING A CYLINDER FILLED WITH CHEMICAL FOAM...
YOU DIDN'T EXPECT US TO BE UNPREPARED FOR YOUR LITTLE TRICKS, DID YA? THIS'LL PUT YOUR BLASTED FLAME OUT!
OKAY, SANDMAN... HE'S ALL YOURS!
GOOD! THE FOAM MAKES IT IMPOSSIBLE FOR HIM TO FLY... AND NOW I CAN DO THE REST!
4.

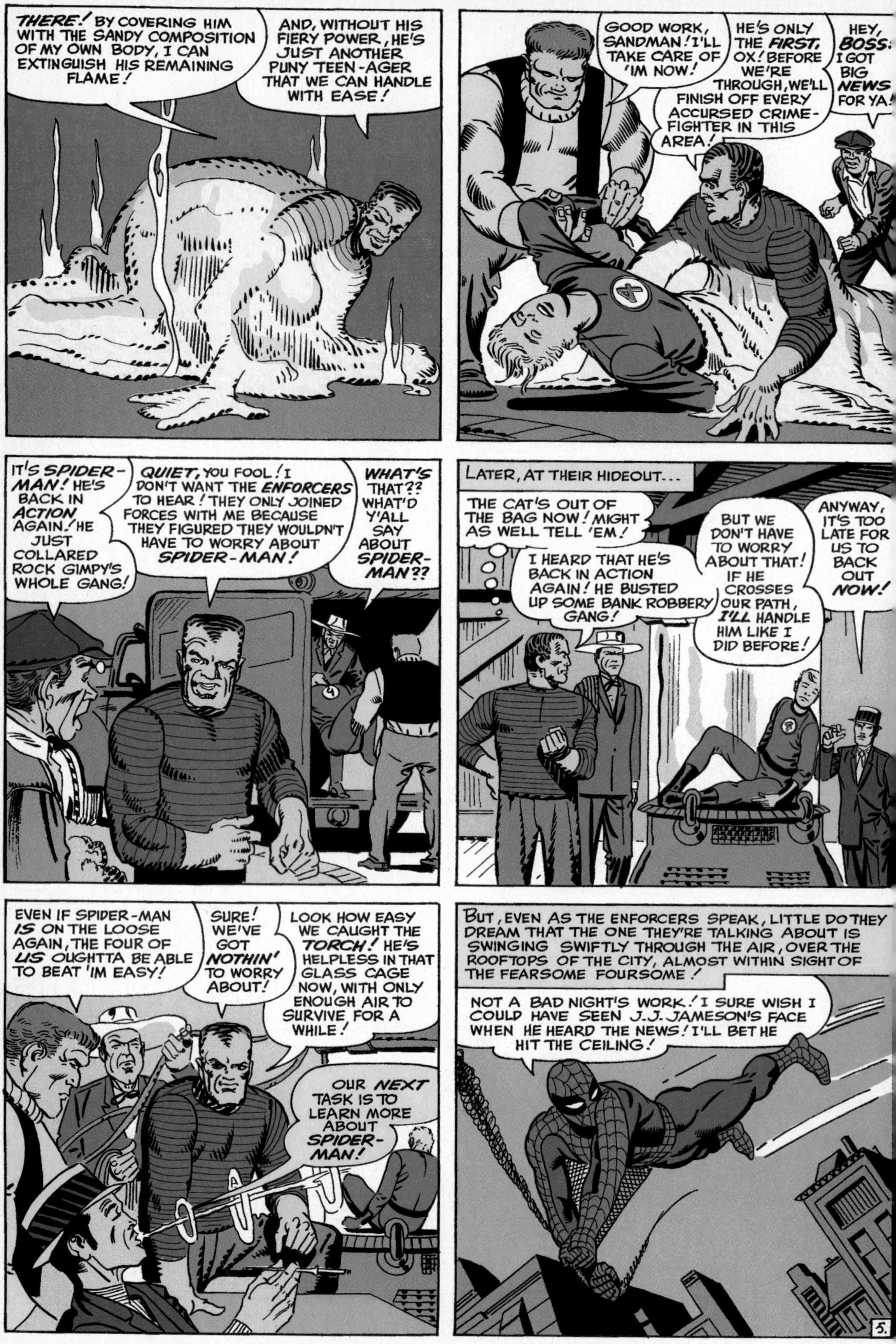
THERE! BY COVERING HIM WITH THE SANDY COMPOSITION OF MY OWN BODY, I CAN EXTINGUISH HIS REMAINING FLAME!
AND, WITHOUT HIS FIERY POWER, HE'S JUST ANOTHER PUNY TEEN-AGER THAT WE CAN HANDLE WITH EASE!
GOOD WORK, SANDMAN! I'LL TAKE CARE OF 'IM NOW!
HE'S ONLY THE FIRST, OX! BEFORE WE'RE THROUGH, WE'LL FINISH OFF EVERY ACCURSED CRIME-FIGHTER IN THIS AREA!
HEY, BOSS! I GOT BIG NEWS FOR YA!
IT'S SPIDER-MAN! HE'S BACK IN ACTION AGAIN! HE JUST COLLARED ROCK GIMPY'S WHOLE GANG!
QUIET, YOU FOOL! I DON'T WANT THE ENFORCERS TO HEAR! THEY ONLY JOINED FORCES WITH ME BECAUSE THEY FIGURED THEY WOULDN'T HAVE TO WORRY ABOUT SPIDER-MAN!
WHAT'S THAT?? WHAT'D Y'ALL SAY ABOUT SPIDER-MAN??
LATER, AT THEIR HIDEOUT...
THE CAT'S OUT OF THE BAG NOW! MIGHT AS WELL TELL 'EM!
I HEARD THAT HE'S BACK IN ACTION AGAIN! HE BUSTED UP SOME BANK ROBBERY GANG!
BUT WE DON'T HAVE TO WORRY ABOUT THAT! IF HE CROSSES OUR PATH, I'LL HANDLE HIM LIKE I DID BEFORE!
ANYWAY, IT'S TOO LATE FOR US TO BACK OUT NOW!
EVEN IF SPIDER-MAN IS ON THE LOOSE AGAIN, THE FOUR OF US OUGHTTA BE ABLE TO BEAT 'IM EASY!
SURE! WE'VE GOT NOTHIN' TO WORRY ABOUT!
LOOK HOW EASY WE CAUGHT THE TORCH! HE'S HELPLESS IN THAT GLASS CAGE NOW, WITH ONLY ENOUGH AIR TO SURVIVE FOR A WHILE!
OUR NEXT TASK IS TO LEARN MORE ABOUT SPIDER-MAN!
BUT, EVEN AS THE ENFORCERS SPEAK, LITTLE DO THEY DREAM THAT THE ONE THEY'RE TALKING ABOUT IS SWINGING SWIFTLY THROUGH THE AIR, OVER THE ROOFTOPS OF THE CITY, ALMOST WITHIN SIGHT OF THE FEARSOME FOURSOME!
NOT A BAD NIGHT'S WORK! I SURE WISH I COULD HAVE SEEN J.J. JAMESON'S FACE WHEN HE HEARD THE NEWS! I'LL BET HE HIT THE CEILING!
5.

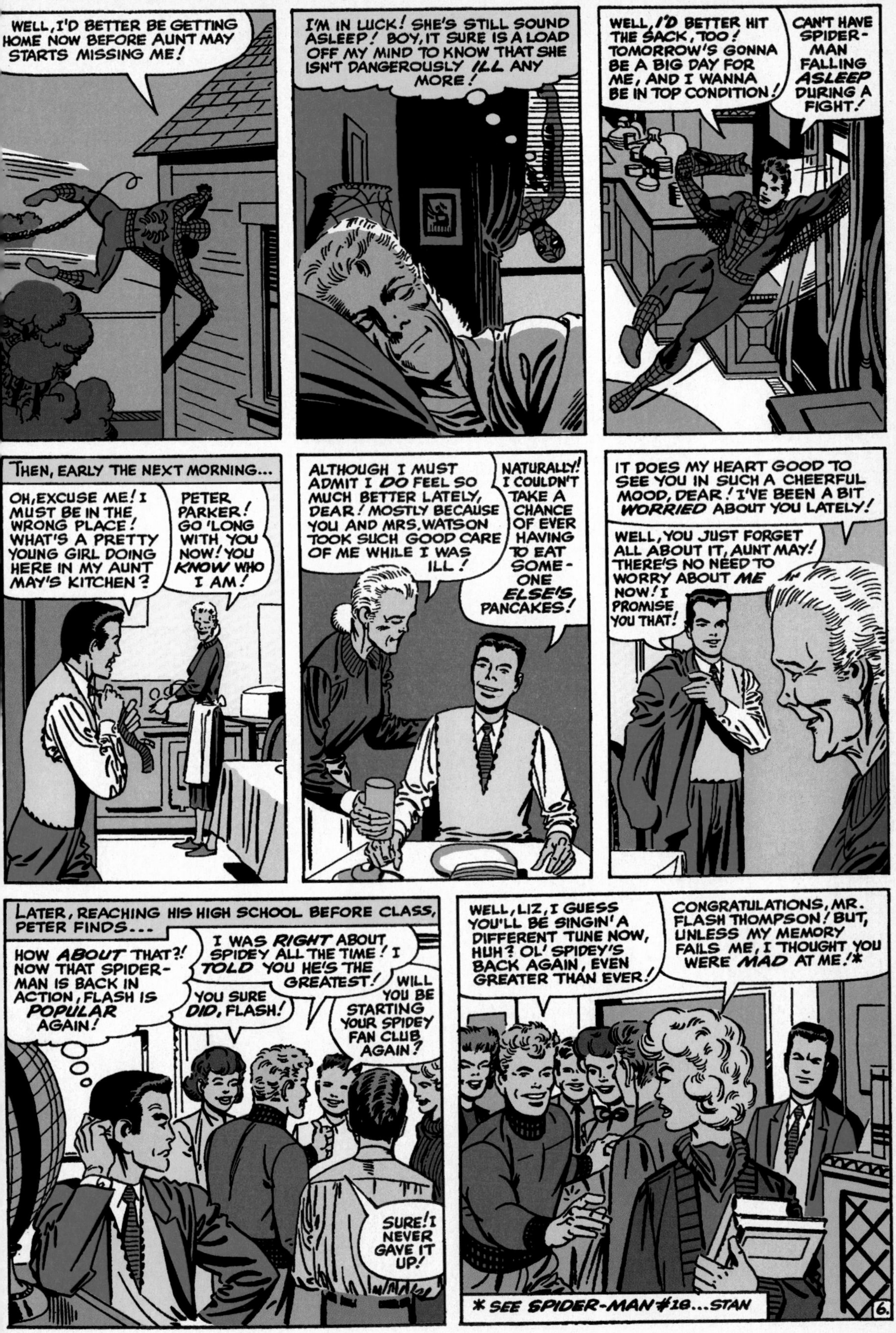
WELL, I'D BETTER BE GETTING HOME NOW BEFORE AUNT MAY STARTS MISSING ME!
I'M IN LUCK! SHE'S STILL SOUND ASLEEP! BOY, IT SURE IS A LOAD OFF MY MIND TO KNOW THAT SHE ISN'T DANGEROUSLY ILL ANY MORE!
WELL, I'D BETTER HIT THE SACK, TOO! TOMORROW'S GONNA BE A BIG DAY FOR ME, AND I WANNA BE IN TOP CONDITION!
CAN'T HAVE SPIDER-MAN FALLING ASLEEP DURING A FIGHT!
THEN, EARLY THE NEXT MORNING...
OH, EXCUSE ME! I MUST BE IN THE WRONG PLACE! WHAT'S A PRETTY YOUNG GIRL DOING HERE IN MY AUNT MAY'S KITCHEN?
PETER PARKER! GO 'LONG WITH YOU NOW! YOU KNOW WHO I AM!
ALTHOUGH I MUST ADMIT I DO FEEL SO MUCH BETTER LATELY, DEAR! MOSTLY BECAUSE YOU AND MRS. WATSON TOOK SUCH GOOD CARE OF ME WHILE I WAS ILL!
NATURALLY! I COULDN'T TAKE A CHANCE OF EVER HAVING TO EAT SOME-ONE ELSE'S PANCAKES!
IT DOES MY HEART GOOD TO SEE YOU IN SUCH A CHEERFUL MOOD, DEAR! I'VE BEEN A BIT WORRIED ABOUT YOU LATELY!
WELL, YOU JUST FORGET ALL ABOUT IT, AUNT MAY! THERE'S NO NEED TO WORRY ABOUT ME NOW! I PROMISE YOU THAT!
LATER, REACHING HIS HIGH SCHOOL BEFORE CLASS, PETER FINDS...
HOW ABOUT THAT?! NOW THAT SPIDER-MAN IS BACK IN ACTION, FLASH IS POPULAR AGAIN!
I WAS RIGHT ABOUT SPIDEY ALL THE TIME! I TOLD YOU HE'S THE GREATEST!
YOU SURE DID, FLASH!
WILL YOU BE STARTING YOUR SPIDEY FAN CLUB AGAIN?
SURE! I NEVER GAVE IT UP!
WELL, LIZ, I GUESS YOU'LL BE SINGIN' A DIFFERENT TUNE NOW, HUH? OL' SPIDEY'S BACK AGAIN, EVEN GREATER THAN EVER!
CONGRATULATIONS, MR. FLASH THOMPSON! BUT, UNLESS MY MEMORY FAILS ME, I THOUGHT YOU WERE MAD AT ME!*
* SEE SPIDER-MAN #18... STAN
6.

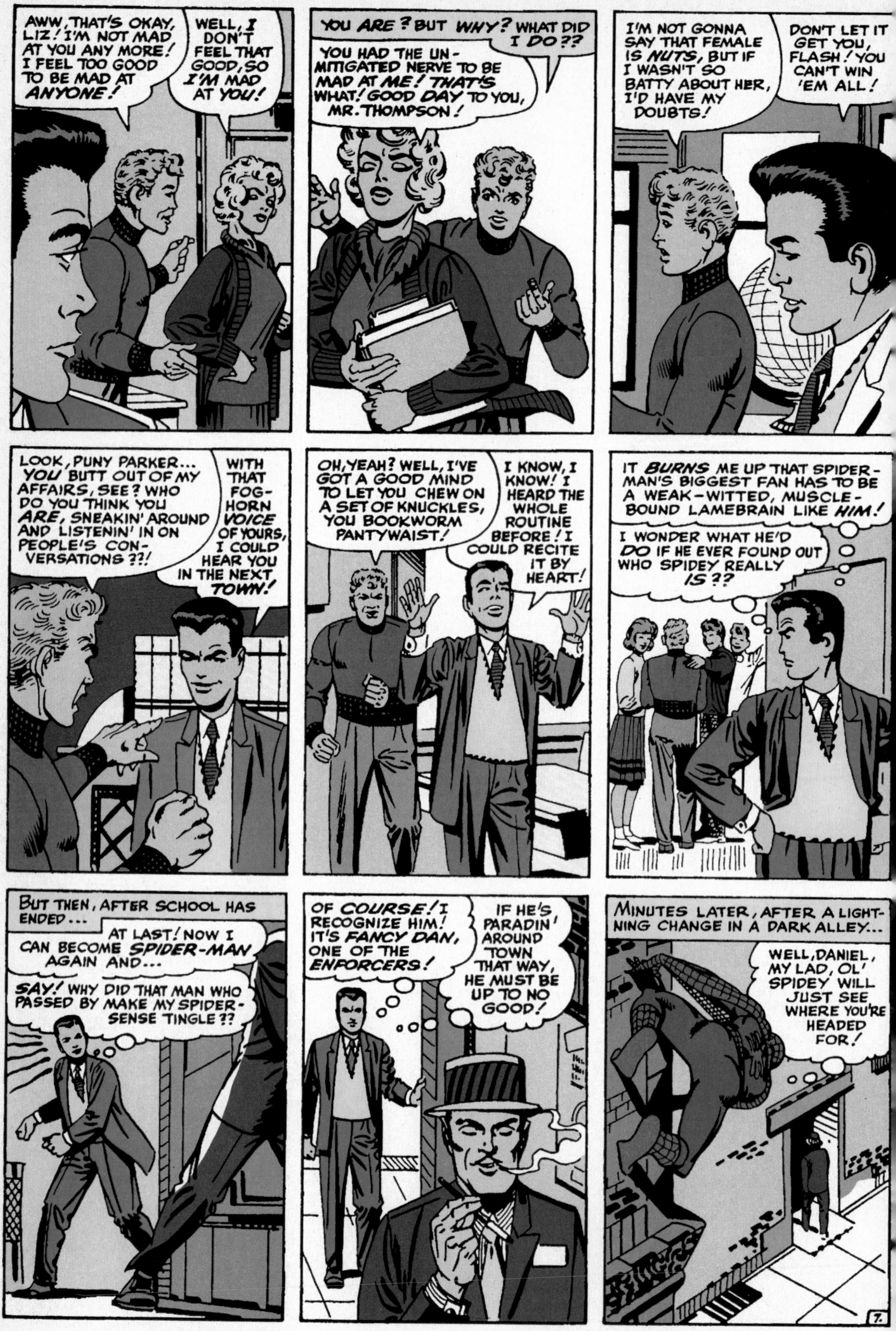

AWW, THAT'S OKAY, LIZ! I'M NOT MAD AT YOU ANY MORE! I FEEL TOO GOOD TO BE MAD AT ANYONE!
WELL, I DON'T FEEL THAT GOOD, SO I'M MAD AT YOU!
YOU ARE? BUT WHY? WHAT DID I DO??
YOU HAD THE UN-MITIGATED NERVE TO BE MAD AT ME! THAT'S WHAT! GOOD DAY TO YOU, MR. THOMPSON!
I'M NOT GONNA SAY THAT FEMALE IS NUTS, BUT IF I WASN'T SO BATTY ABOUT HER, I'D HAVE MY DOUBTS!
DON'T LET IT GET YOU, FLASH! YOU CAN'T WIN 'EM ALL!
LOOK, PUNY PARKER... YOU BUTT OUT OF MY AFFAIRS, SEE? WHO DO YOU THINK YOU ARE, SNEAKIN' AROUND AND LISTENIN' IN ON PEOPLE'S CON-VERSATIONS??!
WITH THAT FOG-HORN VOICE OF YOURS, I COULD HEAR YOU IN THE NEXT TOWN!
OH, YEAH? WELL, I'VE GOT A GOOD MIND TO LET YOU CHEW ON A SET OF KNUCKLES, YOU BOOKWORM PANTYWAIST!
I KNOW, I KNOW! I HEARD THE WHOLE ROUTINE BEFORE! I COULD RECITE IT BY HEART!
IT BURNS ME UP THAT SPIDER-MAN'S BIGGEST FAN HAS TO BE A WEAK-WITTED, MUSCLE-BOUND LAMEBRAIN LIKE HIM!
I WONDER WHAT HE'D DO IF HE EVER FOUND OUT WHO SPIDEY REALLY IS??
BUT THEN, AFTER SCHOOL HAS ENDED...
AT LAST! NOW I CAN BECOME SPIDER-MAN AGAIN AND...
SAY! WHY DID THAT MAN WHO PASSED BY MAKE MY SPIDER-SENSE TINGLE??
OF COURSE! I RECOGNIZE HIM! IT'S FANCY DAN, ONE OF THE ENFORCERS!
IF HE'S PARADIN' AROUND TOWN THAT WAY, HE MUST BE UP TO NO GOOD!
MINUTES LATER, AFTER A LIGHT-NING CHANGE IN A DARK ALLEY...
WELL, DANIEL, MY LAD, OL' SPIDEY WILL JUST SEE WHERE YOU'RE HEADED FOR!
7.

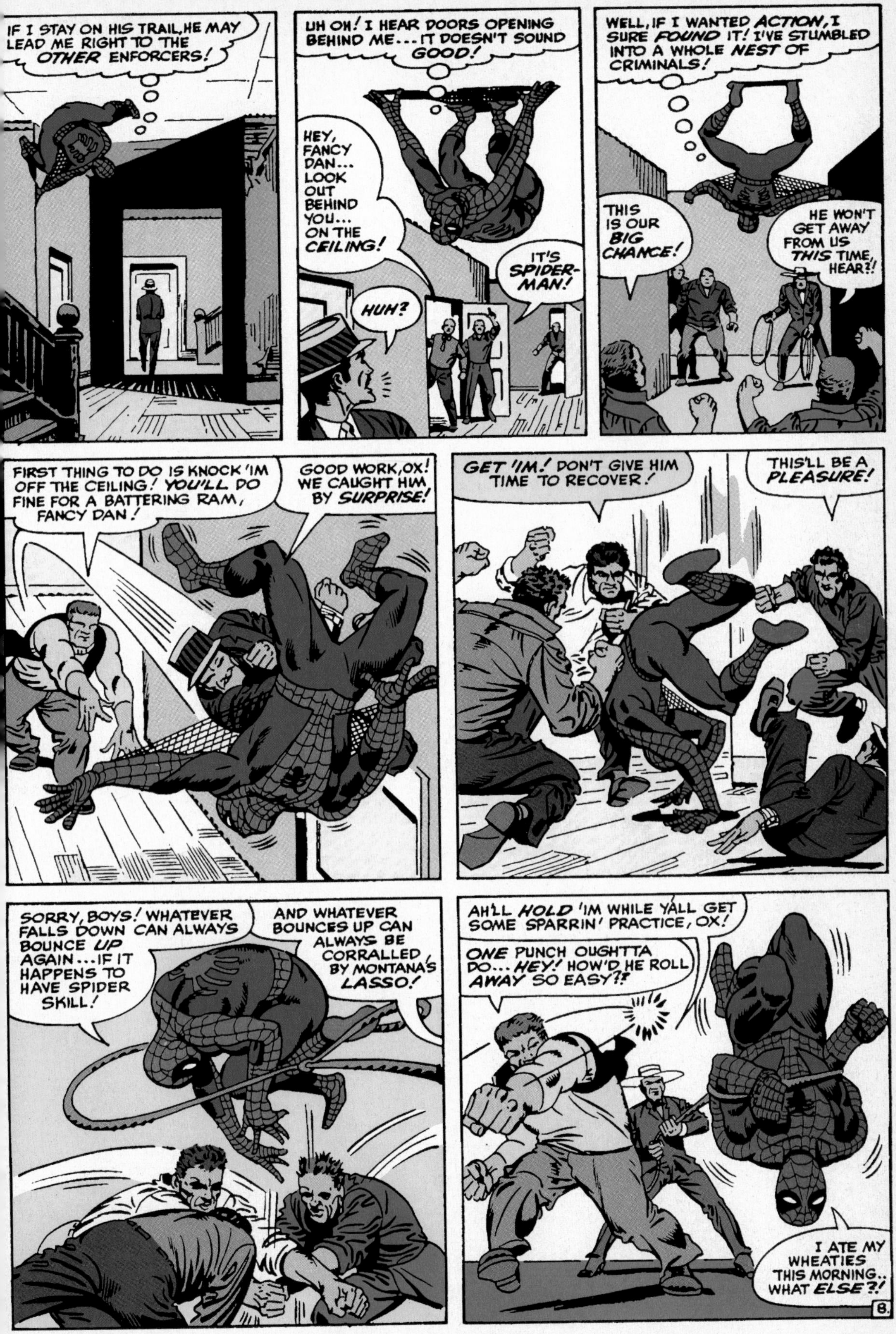

IF I STAY ON HIS TRAIL, HE MAY LEAD ME RIGHT TO THE OTHER ENFORCERS!
UH OH! I HEAR DOORS OPENING BEHIND ME... IT DOESN'T SOUND GOOD!
HEY, FANCY DAN... LOOK OUT BEHIND YOU... ON THE CEILING!
HUH?
IT'S SPIDER-MAN!
WELL, IF I WANTED ACTION, I SURE FOUND IT! I'VE STUMBLED INTO A WHOLE NEST OF CRIMINALS!
THIS IS OUR BIG CHANCE!
HE WON'T GET AWAY FROM US THIS TIME, HEAR?!
FIRST THING TO DO IS KNOCK 'IM OFF THE CEILING! YOU'LL DO FINE FOR A BATTERING RAM, FANCY DAN!
GOOD WORK, OX! WE CAUGHT HIM BY SURPRISE!
GET 'IM! DON'T GIVE HIM TIME TO RECOVER!
THIS'LL BE A PLEASURE!
SORRY, BOYS! WHATEVER FALLS DOWN CAN ALWAYS BOUNCE UP AGAIN... IF IT HAPPENS TO HAVE SPIDER SKILL!
AND WHATEVER BOUNCES UP CAN ALWAYS BE CORRALLED BY MONTANA'S LASSO!
AH'LL HOLD 'IM WHILE YALL GET SOME SPARRIN' PRACTICE, OX!
ONE PUNCH OUGHTTA DO... HEY! HOW'D HE ROLL AWAY SO EASY?!
I ATE MY WHEATIES THIS MORNING.. WHAT ELSE?!
8.

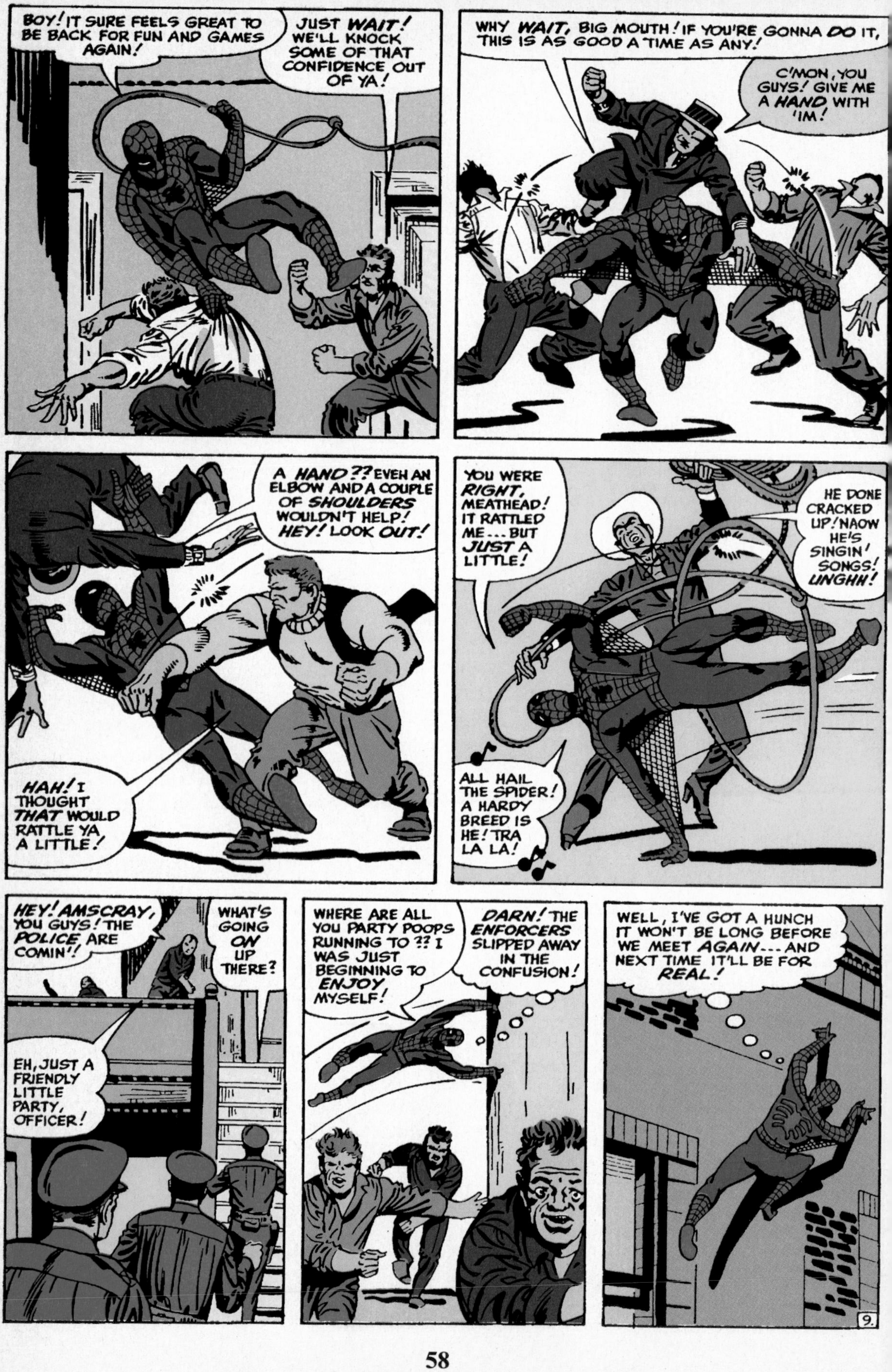
BOY! IT SURE FEELS GREAT TO BE BACK FOR FUN AND GAMES AGAIN!
JUST WAIT! WE'LL KNOCK SOME OF THAT CONFIDENCE OUT OF YA!
WHY WAIT, BIG MOUTH! IF YOU'RE GONNA DO IT, THIS IS AS GOOD A TIME AS ANY!
C'MON, YOU GUYS! GIVE ME A HAND WITH 'IM!
A HAND?? EVEN AN ELBOW AND A COUPLE OF SHOULDERS WOULDN'T HELP! HEY! LOOK OUT!
HAH! I THOUGHT THAT WOULD RATTLE YA A LITTLE!
YOU WERE RIGHT, MEATHEAD! IT RATTLED ME... BUT JUST A LITTLE!
HE DONE CRACKED UP! NAOW HE'S SINGIN' SONGS! UNGHH!
ALL HAIL THE SPIDER! A HARDY BREED IS HE! TRA LA LA!
HEY! AMSCRAY, YOU GUYS! THE POLICE ARE COMIN'!
WHAT'S GOING ON UP THERE?
EH, JUST A FRIENDLY LITTLE PARTY, OFFICER!
WHERE ARE ALL YOU PARTY POOPS RUNNING TO ?? I WAS JUST BEGINNING TO ENJOY MYSELF!
DARN! THE ENFORCERS SLIPPED AWAY IN THE CONFUSION!
WELL, I'VE GOT A HUNCH IT WON'T BE LONG BEFORE WE MEET AGAIN... AND NEXT TIME IT'LL BE FOR REAL!
9.

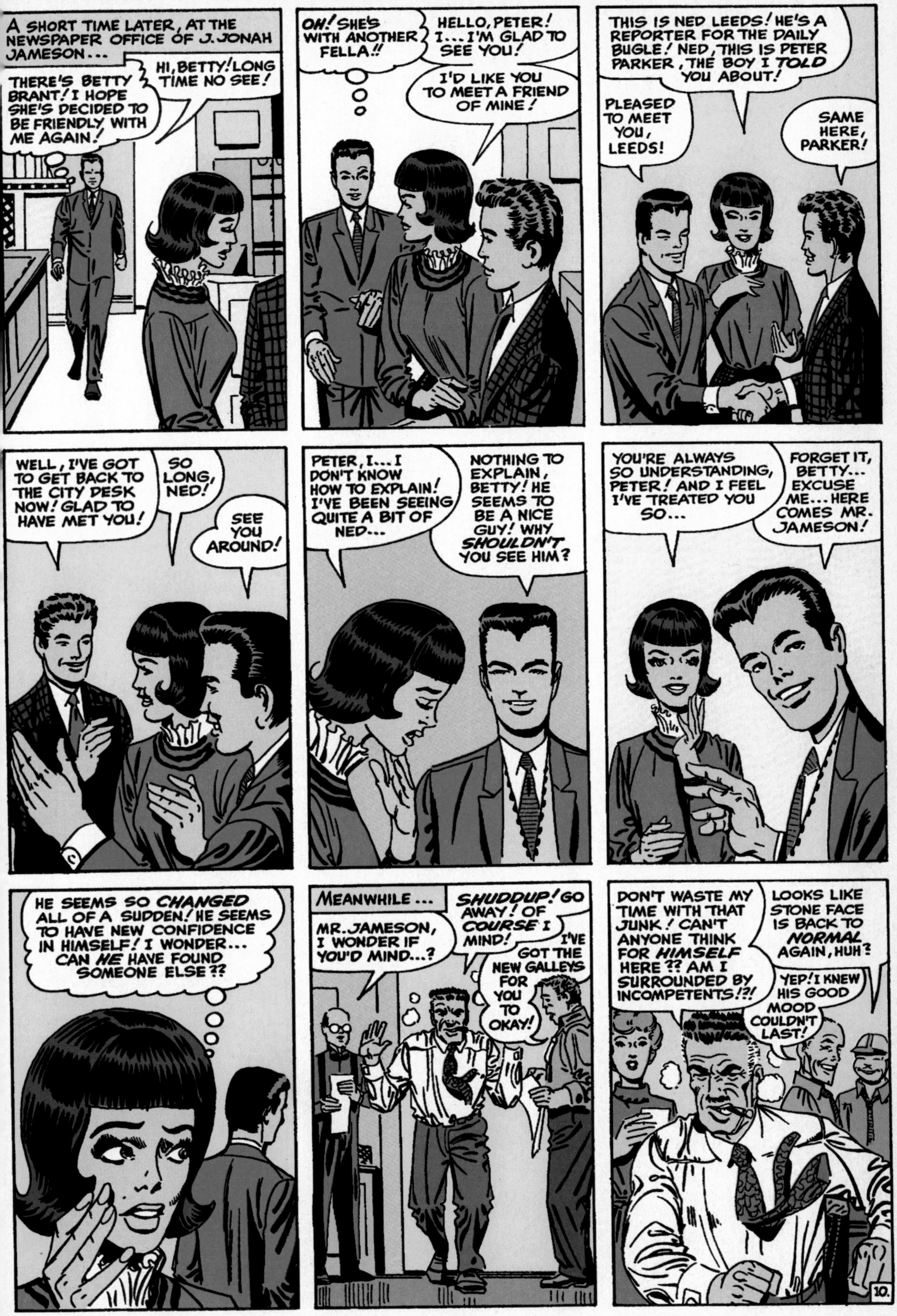
A SHORT TIME LATER, AT THE NEWSPAPER OFFICE OF J. JONAH JAMESON...
THERE'S BETTY BRANT! I HOPE SHE'S DECIDED TO BE FRIENDLY WITH ME AGAIN!
HI, BETTY! LONG TIME NO SEE!
OH! SHE'S WITH ANOTHER FELLA!!
HELLO, PETER! I... I'M GLAD TO SEE YOU!
I'D LIKE YOU TO MEET A FRIEND OF MINE!
THIS IS NED LEEDS! HE'S A REPORTER FOR THE DAILY BUGLE! NED, THIS IS PETER PARKER, THE BOY I TOLD YOU ABOUT!
PLEASED TO MEET YOU, LEEDS!
SAME HERE, PARKER!
WELL, I'VE GOT TO GET BACK TO THE CITY DESK NOW! GLAD TO HAVE MET YOU!
SO LONG, NED!
SEE YOU AROUND!
PETER, I... I DON'T KNOW HOW TO EXPLAIN! I'VE BEEN SEEING QUITE A BIT OF NED...
NOTHING TO EXPLAIN, BETTY! HE SEEMS TO BE A NICE GUY! WHY SHOULDN'T YOU SEE HIM?
YOU'RE ALWAYS SO UNDERSTANDING, PETER! AND I FEEL I'VE TREATED YOU SO...
FORGET IT, BETTY... EXCUSE ME... HERE COMES MR. JAMESON!
HE SEEMS SO CHANGED ALL OF A SUDDEN! HE SEEMS TO HAVE NEW CONFIDENCE IN HIMSELF! I WONDER... CAN HE HAVE FOUND SOMEONE ELSE??
MEANWHILE...
MR. JAMESON, I WONDER IF YOU'D MIND...?
SHUDDUP! GO AWAY! OF COURSE I MIND!
I'VE GOT THE NEW GALLEYS FOR YOU TO OKAY!
DON'T WASTE MY TIME WITH THAT JUNK! CAN'T ANYONE THINK FOR HIMSELF HERE?? AM I SURROUNDED BY INCOMPETENTS!?!
LOOKS LIKE STONE FACE IS BACK TO NORMAL AGAIN, HUH?
YEP! I KNEW HIS GOOD MOOD COULDN'T LAST!
10.

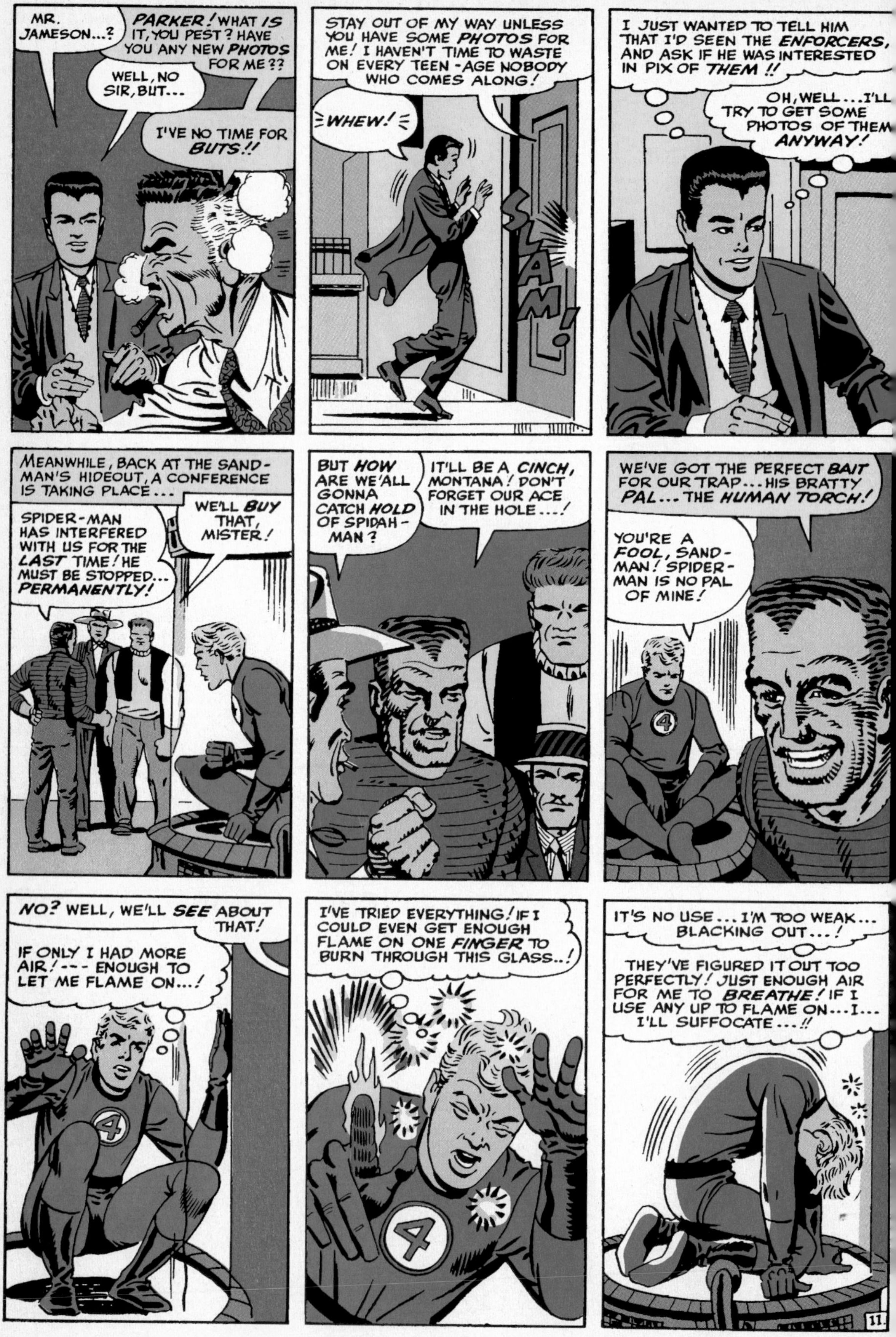
MR. JAMESON...?
PARKER! WHAT IS IT, YOU PEST? HAVE YOU ANY NEW PHOTOS FOR ME??
WELL, NO SIR, BUT...
I'VE NO TIME FOR BUTS!!
STAY OUT OF MY WAY UNLESS YOU HAVE SOME PHOTOS FOR ME! I HAVEN'T TIME TO WASTE ON EVERY TEEN-AGE NOBODY WHO COMES ALONG!
WHEW!
SLAM!
I JUST WANTED TO TELL HIM THAT I'D SEEN THE ENFORCERS, AND ASK IF HE WAS INTERESTED IN PIX OF THEM!!
OH, WELL...I'LL TRY TO GET SOME PHOTOS OF THEM ANYWAY!
MEANWHILE, BACK AT THE SAND-MAN'S HIDEOUT, A CONFERENCE IS TAKING PLACE...
SPIDER-MAN HAS INTERFERED WITH US FOR THE LAST TIME! HE MUST BE STOPPED... PERMANENTLY!
WE'LL BUY THAT, MISTER!
BUT HOW ARE WE'ALL GONNA CATCH HOLD OF SPIDAH-MAN?
IT'LL BE A CINCH, MONTANA! DON'T FORGET OUR ACE IN THE HOLE...!
WE'VE GOT THE PERFECT BAIT FOR OUR TRAP...HIS BRATTY PAL... THE HUMAN TORCH!
YOU'RE A FOOL, SAND-MAN! SPIDER-MAN IS NO PAL OF MINE!
NO? WELL, WE'LL SEE ABOUT THAT!
IF ONLY I HAD MORE AIR!--- ENOUGH TO LET ME FLAME ON...!
I'VE TRIED EVERYTHING! IF I COULD EVEN GET ENOUGH FLAME ON ONE FINGER TO BURN THROUGH THIS GLASS..!
IT'S NO USE... I'M TOO WEAK... BLACKING OUT...!
THEY'VE FIGURED IT OUT TOO PERFECTLY! JUST ENOUGH AIR FOR ME TO BREATHE! IF I USE ANY UP TO FLAME ON...I... I'LL SUFFOCATE...!!
11.

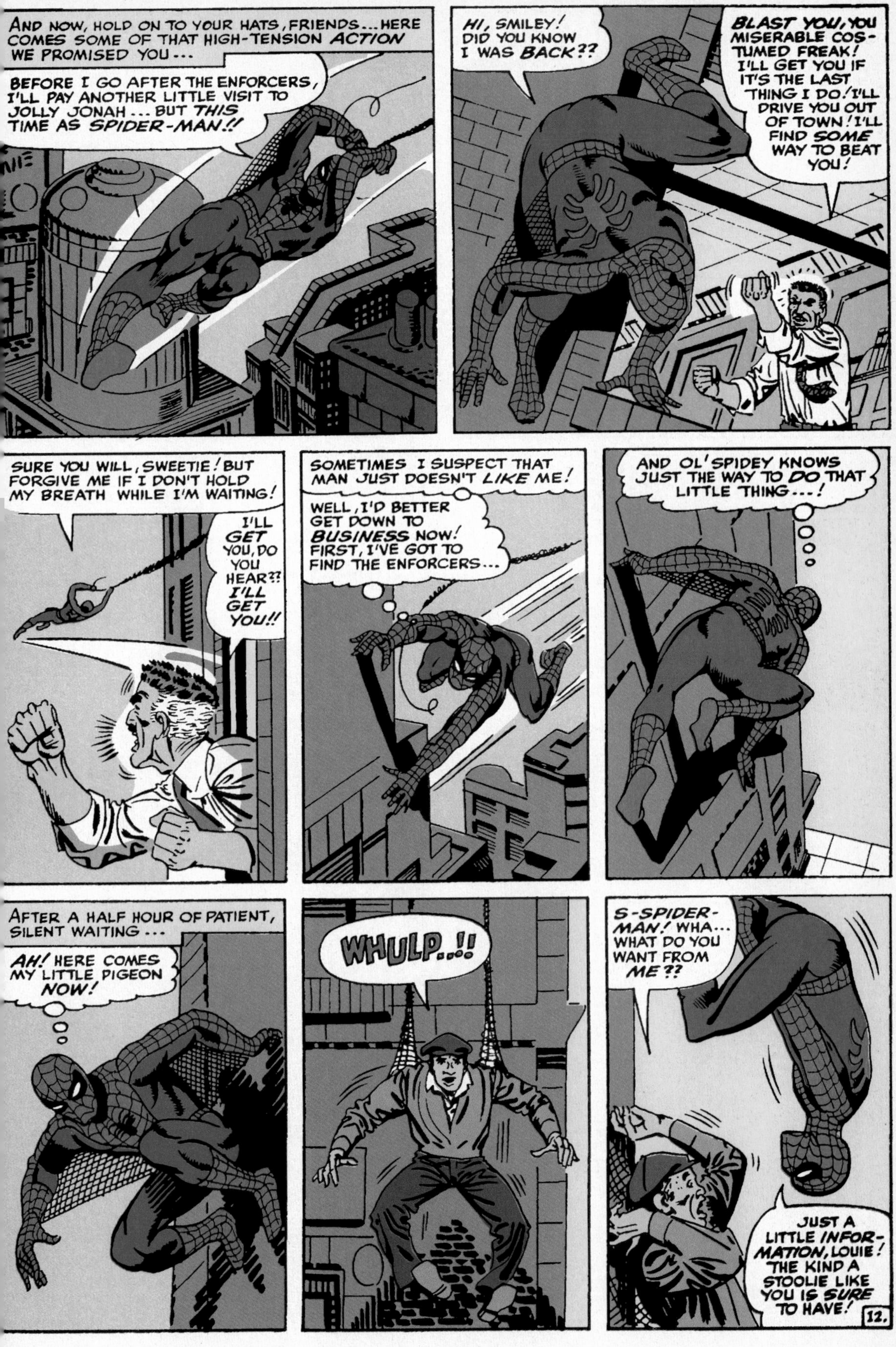

AND NOW, HOLD ON TO YOUR HATS, FRIENDS... HERE COMES SOME OF THAT HIGH-TENSION ACTION WE PROMISED YOU...
BEFORE I GO AFTER THE ENFORCERS, I'LL PAY ANOTHER LITTLE VISIT TO JOLLY JONAH... BUT THIS TIME AS SPIDER-MAN!!
HI, SMILEY! DID YOU KNOW I WAS BACK??
BLAST YOU, YOU MISERABLE COS-TUMED FREAK! I'LL GET YOU IF IT'S THE LAST THING I DO! I'LL DRIVE YOU OUT OF TOWN! I'LL FIND SOME WAY TO BEAT YOU!
SURE YOU WILL, SWEETIE! BUT FORGIVE ME IF I DON'T HOLD MY BREATH WHILE I'M WAITING!
I'LL GET YOU, DO YOU HEAR?? I'LL GET YOU!!
SOMETIMES I SUSPECT THAT MAN JUST DOESN'T LIKE ME!
WELL, I'D BETTER GET DOWN TO BUSINESS NOW! FIRST, I'VE GOT TO FIND THE ENFORCERS...
AND OL' SPIDEY KNOWS JUST THE WAY TO DO THAT LITTLE THING...!
AFTER A HALF HOUR OF PATIENT, SILENT WAITING...
AH! HERE COMES MY LITTLE PIGEON NOW!
WHULP..!!
S-SPIDER-MAN! WHA... WHAT DO YOU WANT FROM ME??
JUST A LITTLE INFORMATION, LOUIE! THE KIND A STOOLIE LIKE YOU IS SURE TO HAVE!
12.

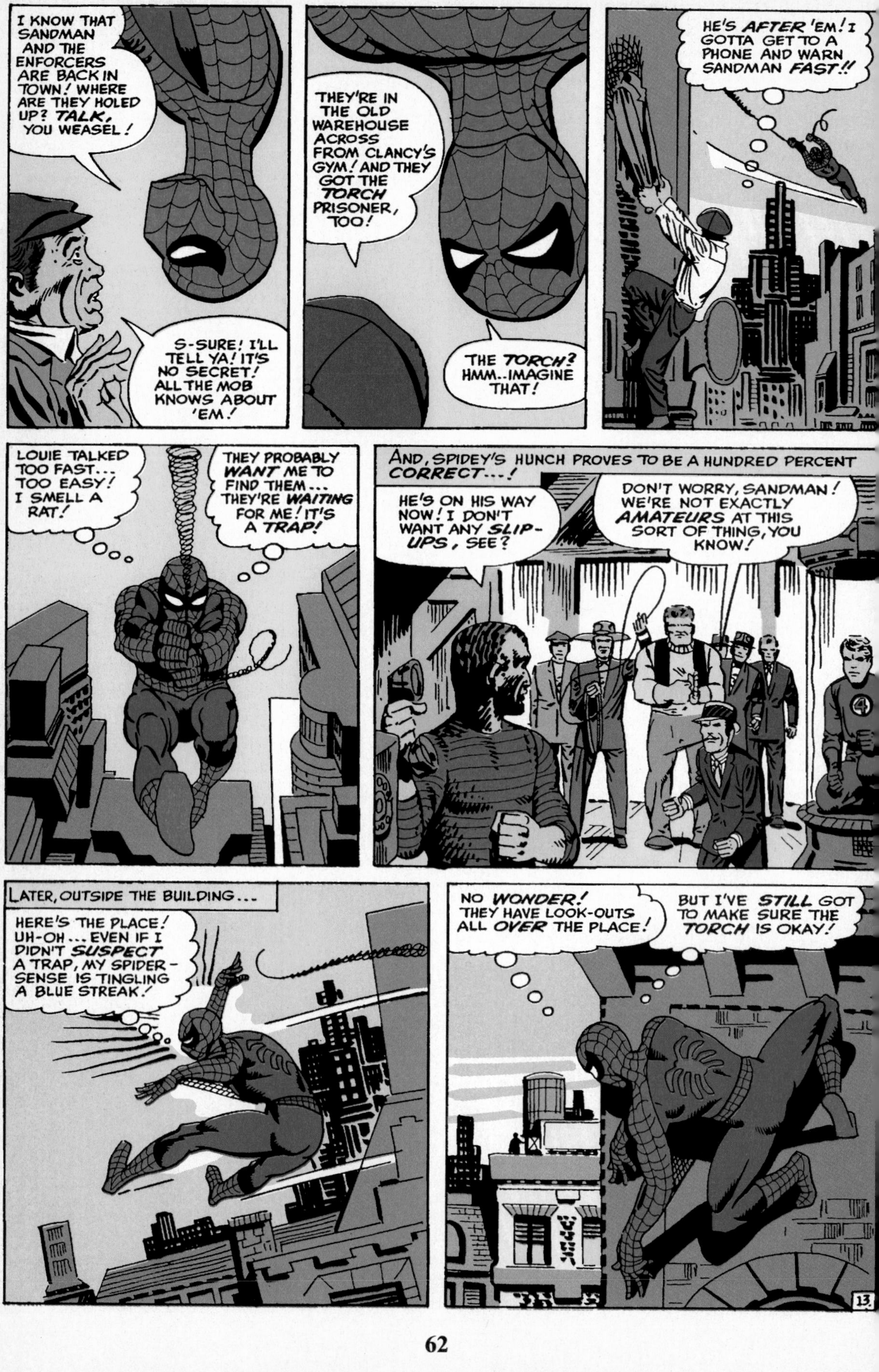
I KNOW THAT SANDMAN AND THE ENFORCERS ARE BACK IN TOWN! WHERE ARE THEY HOLED UP? TALK, YOU WEASEL!
S-SURE! I'LL TELL YA! IT'S NO SECRET! ALL THE MOB KNOWS ABOUT 'EM!
THEY'RE IN THE OLD WAREHOUSE ACROSS FROM CLANCY'S GYM! AND THEY GOT THE TORCH PRISONER, TOO!
THE TORCH? HMM..IMAGINE THAT!
HE'S AFTER 'EM! I GOTTA GET TO A PHONE AND WARN SANDMAN FAST!!
LOUIE TALKED TOO FAST... TOO EASY! I SMELL A RAT!
THEY PROBABLY WANT ME TO FIND THEM... THEY'RE WAITING FOR ME! IT'S A TRAP!
AND, SPIDEY'S HUNCH PROVES TO BE A HUNDRED PERCENT CORRECT...!
HE'S ON HIS WAY NOW! I DON'T WANT ANY SLIP-UPS, SEE?
DON'T WORRY, SANDMAN! WE'RE NOT EXACTLY AMATEURS AT THIS SORT OF THING, YOU KNOW!
LATER, OUTSIDE THE BUILDING...
HERE'S THE PLACE! UH-OH... EVEN IF I DIDN'T SUSPECT A TRAP, MY SPIDER-SENSE IS TINGLING A BLUE STREAK!
NO WONDER! THEY HAVE LOOK-OUTS ALL OVER THE PLACE!
BUT I'VE STILL GOT TO MAKE SURE THE TORCH IS OKAY!
13

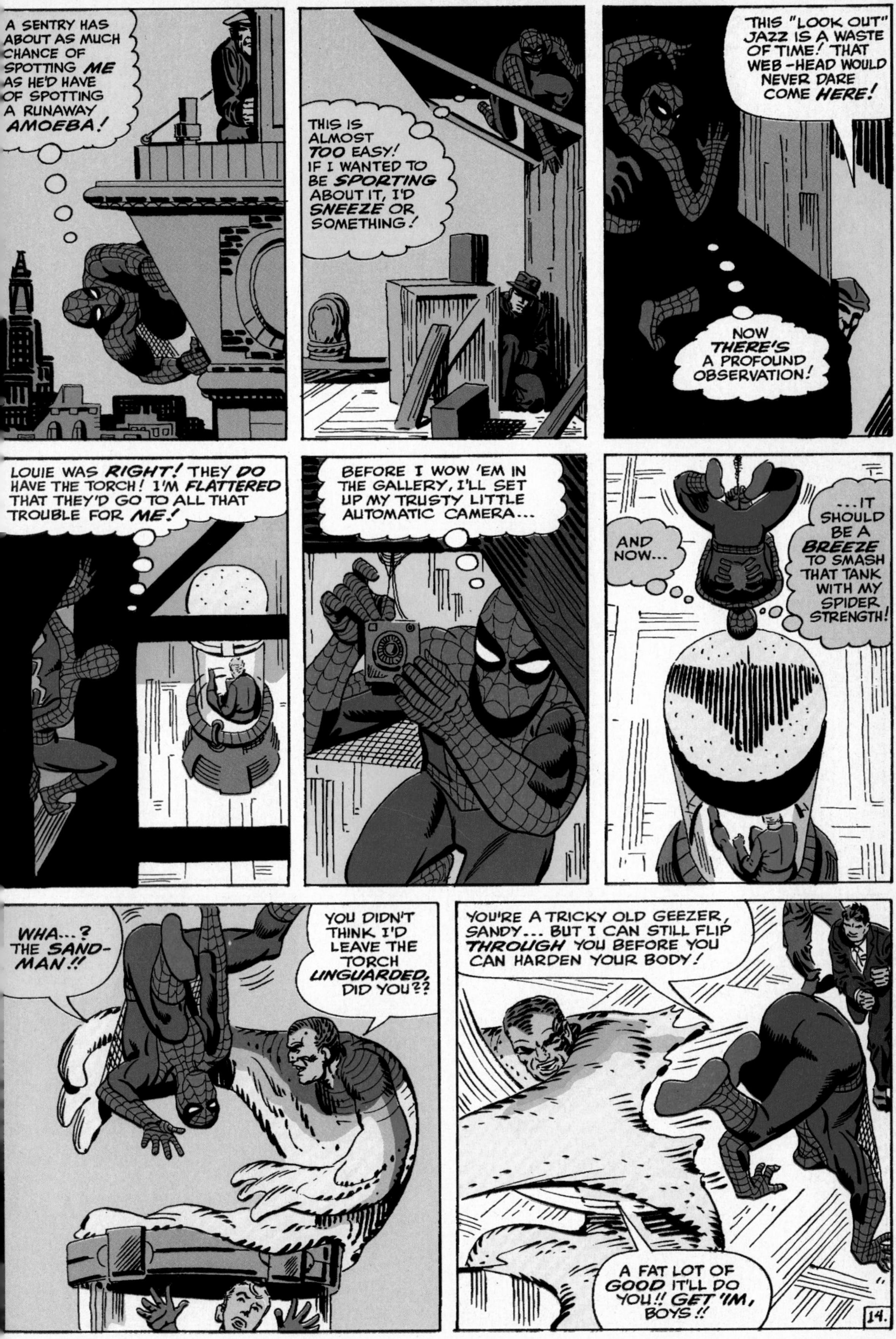
A SENTRY HAS ABOUT AS MUCH CHANCE OF SPOTTING ME AS HE'D HAVE OF SPOTTING A RUNAWAY AMOEBA!
THIS IS ALMOST TOO EASY! IF I WANTED TO BE SPORTING ABOUT IT, I'D SNEEZE OR SOMETHING!
THIS "LOOK OUT" JAZZ IS A WASTE OF TIME! THAT WEB-HEAD WOULD NEVER DARE COME HERE!
NOW THERE'S A PROFOUND OBSERVATION!
LOUIE WAS RIGHT! THEY DO HAVE THE TORCH! I'M FLATTERED THAT THEY'D GO TO ALL THAT TROUBLE FOR ME!
BEFORE I WOW 'EM IN THE GALLERY, I'LL SET UP MY TRUSTY LITTLE AUTOMATIC CAMERA...
AND NOW...
...IT SHOULD BE A BREEZE TO SMASH THAT TANK WITH MY SPIDER STRENGTH!
WHA...? THE SANDMAN!!
YOU DIDN'T THINK I'D LEAVE THE TORCH UNGUARDED, DID YOU??
YOU'RE A TRICKY OLD GEEZER, SANDY... BUT I CAN STILL FLIP THROUGH YOU BEFORE YOU CAN HARDEN YOUR BODY!
A FAT LOT OF GOOD IT'LL DO YOU!! GET 'IM, BOYS!!
14.

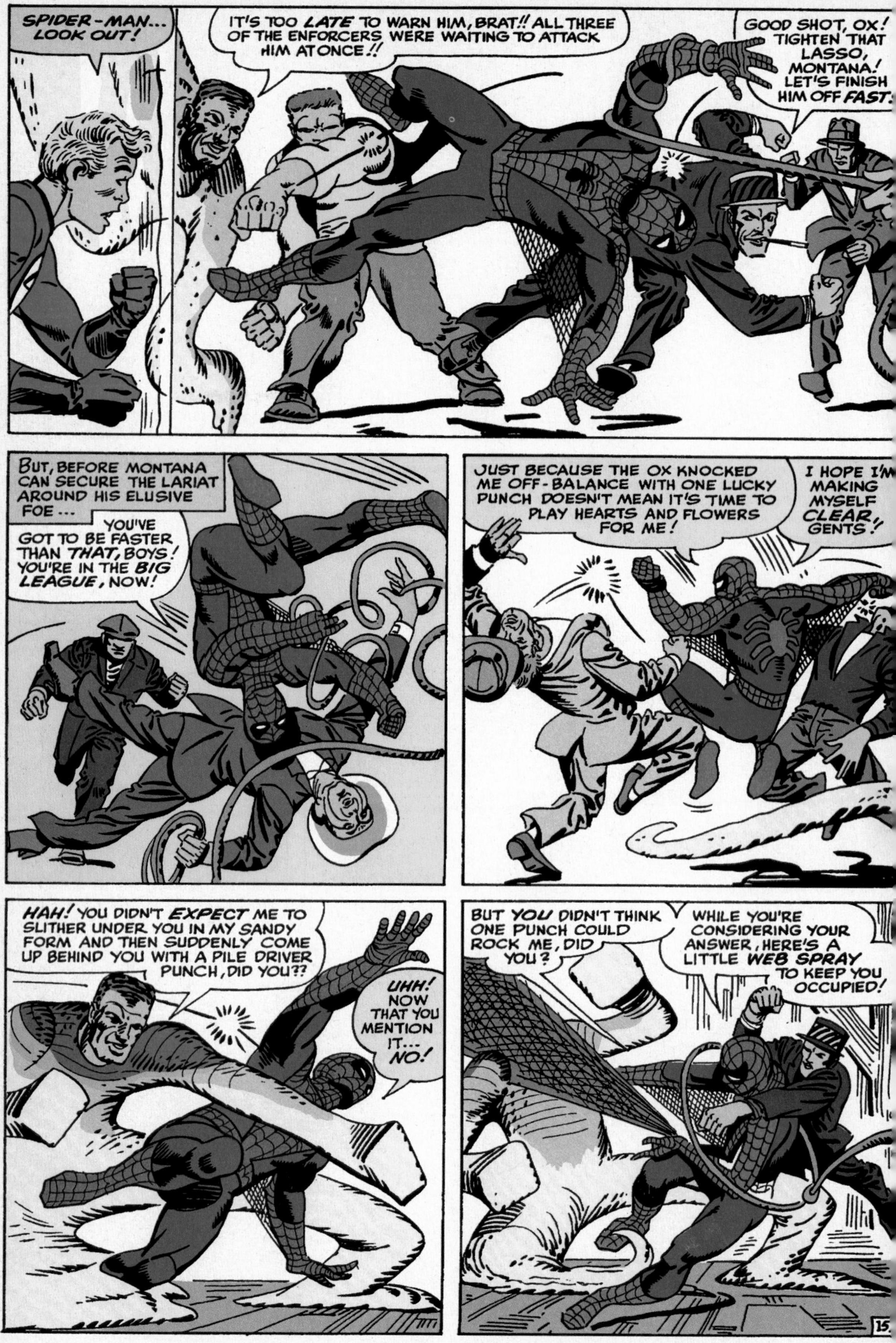
SPIDER-MAN... LOOK OUT!
IT'S TOO LATE TO WARN HIM, BRAT!! ALL THREE OF THE ENFORCERS WERE WAITING TO ATTACK HIM AT ONCE!!
GOOD SHOT, OX! TIGHTEN THAT LASSO, MONTANA! LET'S FINISH HIM OFF FAST!
BUT, BEFORE MONTANA CAN SECURE THE LARIAT AROUND HIS ELUSIVE FOE...
YOU'VE GOT TO BE FASTER THAN THAT, BOYS! YOU'RE IN THE BIG LEAGUE, NOW!
JUST BECAUSE THE OX KNOCKED ME OFF-BALANCE WITH ONE LUCKY PUNCH DOESN'T MEAN IT'S TIME TO PLAY HEARTS AND FLOWERS FOR ME!
I HOPE I'M MAKING MYSELF CLEAR, GENTS!
HAH! YOU DIDN'T EXPECT ME TO SLITHER UNDER YOU IN MY SANDY FORM AND THEN SUDDENLY COME UP BEHIND YOU WITH A PILE DRIVER PUNCH, DID YOU??
UHH! NOW THAT YOU MENTION IT... NO!
BUT YOU DIDN'T THINK ONE PUNCH COULD ROCK ME, DID YOU?
WHILE YOU'RE CONSIDERING YOUR ANSWER, HERE'S A LITTLE WEB SPRAY TO KEEP YOU OCCUPIED!
15

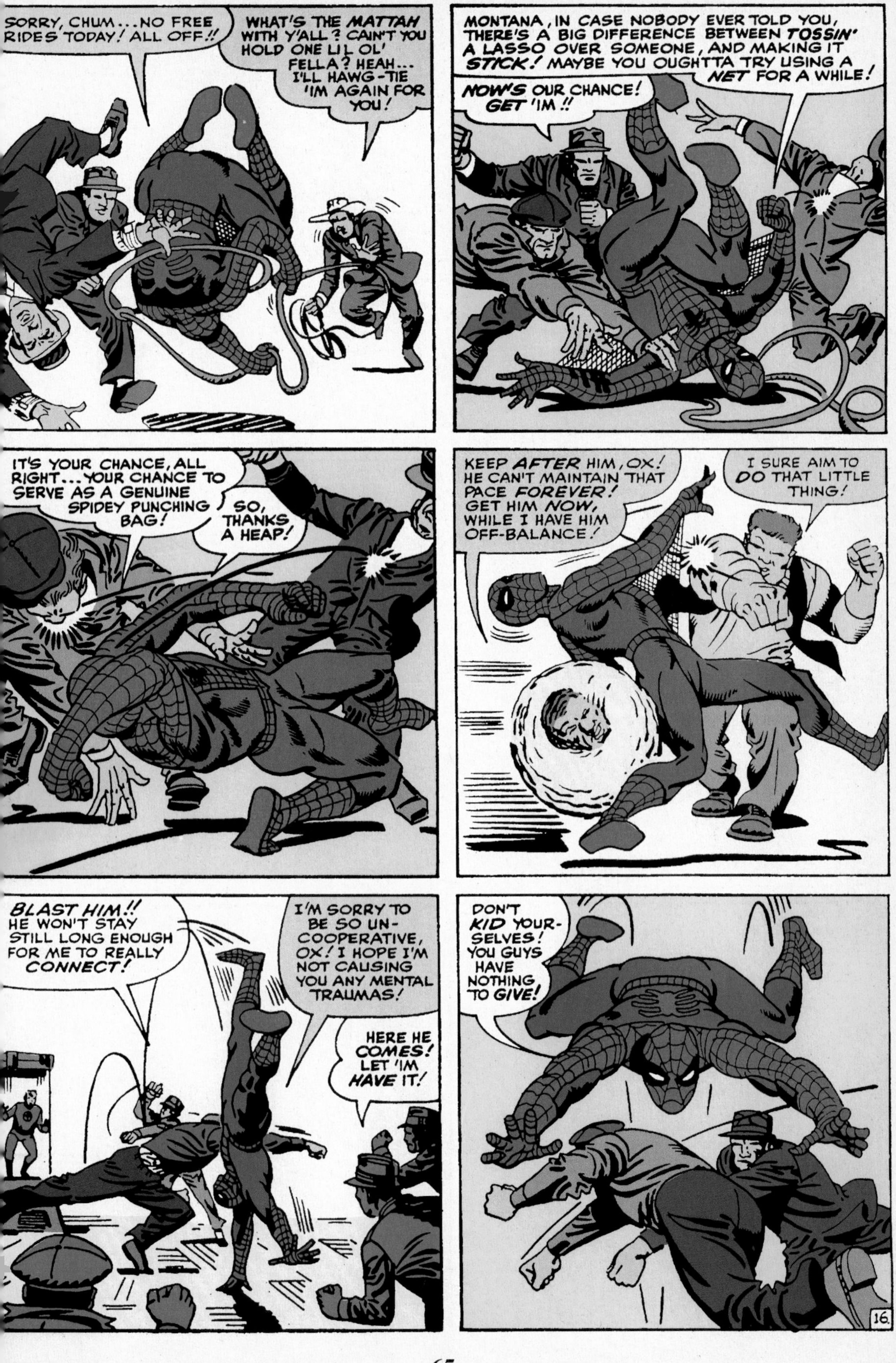
SORRY, CHUM... NO FREE RIDES TODAY! ALL OFF!!
WHAT'S THE MATTAH WITH Y'ALL? CAIN'T YOU HOLD ONE LIL OL' FELLA? HEAH... I'LL HAWG-TIE 'IM AGAIN FOR YOU!
MONTANA, IN CASE NOBODY EVER TOLD YOU, THERE'S A BIG DIFFERENCE BETWEEN TOSSIN' A LASSO OVER SOMEONE, AND MAKING IT STICK! MAYBE YOU OUGHTTA TRY USING A NET FOR A WHILE!
NOW'S OUR CHANCE! GET 'IM!!
IT'S YOUR CHANCE, ALL RIGHT... YOUR CHANCE TO SERVE AS A GENUINE SPIDEY PUNCHING BAG!
SO, THANKS A HEAP!
KEEP AFTER HIM, OX! HE CAN'T MAINTAIN THAT PACE FOREVER! GET HIM NOW, WHILE I HAVE HIM OFF-BALANCE!
I SURE AIM TO DO THAT LITTLE THING!
BLAST HIM!! HE WON'T STAY STILL LONG ENOUGH FOR ME TO REALLY CONNECT!
I'M SORRY TO BE SO UN-COOPERATIVE, OX! I HOPE I'M NOT CAUSING YOU ANY MENTAL TRAUMAS!
HERE HE COMES! LET 'IM HAVE IT!
DON'T KID YOUR-SELVES! YOU GUYS HAVE NOTHING TO GIVE!
16.

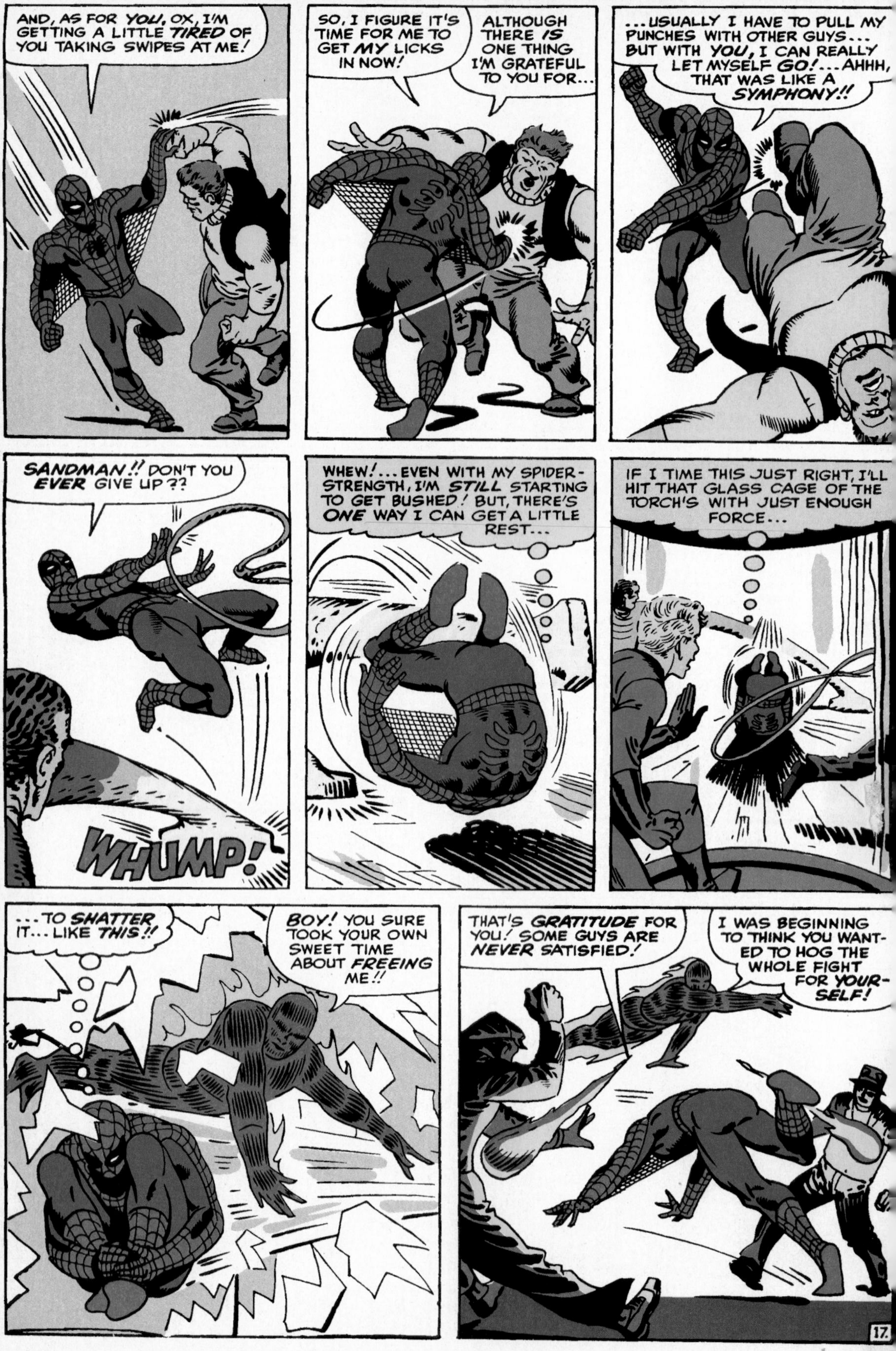
AND, AS FOR YOU, OX, I'M GETTING A LITTLE TIRED OF YOU TAKING SWIPES AT ME!
SO, I FIGURE IT'S TIME FOR ME TO GET MY LICKS IN NOW!
ALTHOUGH THERE IS ONE THING I'M GRATEFUL TO YOU FOR...
...USUALLY I HAVE TO PULL MY PUNCHES WITH OTHER GUYS... BUT WITH YOU, I CAN REALLY LET MYSELF GO!...AHHH, THAT WAS LIKE A SYMPHONY!!
SANDMAN!! DON'T YOU EVER GIVE UP??
WHUMP!
WHEW!... EVEN WITH MY SPIDER-STRENGTH, I'M STILL STARTING TO GET BUSHED! BUT, THERE'S ONE WAY I CAN GET A LITTLE REST...
IF I TIME THIS JUST RIGHT, I'LL HIT THAT GLASS CAGE OF THE TORCH'S WITH JUST ENOUGH FORCE...
...TO SHATTER IT... LIKE THIS!!
BOY! YOU SURE TOOK YOUR OWN SWEET TIME ABOUT FREEING ME!!
THAT'S GRATITUDE FOR YOU! SOME GUYS ARE NEVER SATISFIED!
I WAS BEGINNING TO THINK YOU WANTED TO HOG THE WHOLE FIGHT FOR YOURSELF!
17.

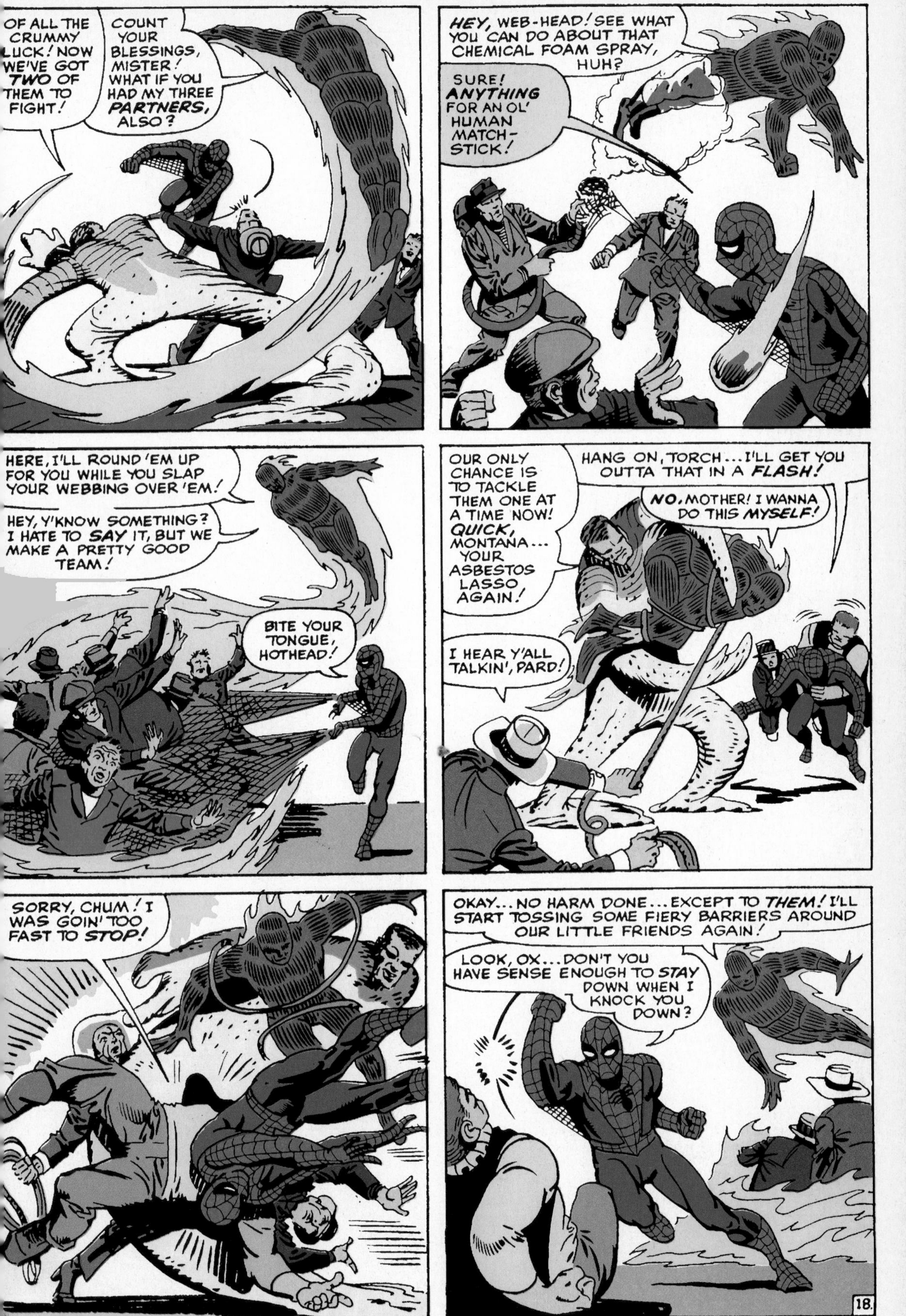

OF ALL THE CRUMMY LUCK! NOW WE'VE GOT TWO OF THEM TO FIGHT!
COUNT YOUR BLESSINGS, MISTER! WHAT IF YOU HAD MY THREE PARTNERS, ALSO?
HEY, WEB-HEAD! SEE WHAT YOU CAN DO ABOUT THAT CHEMICAL FOAM SPRAY, HUH?
SURE! ANYTHING FOR AN OL' HUMAN MATCH-STICK!
HERE, I'LL ROUND 'EM UP FOR YOU WHILE YOU SLAP YOUR WEBBING OVER 'EM!
HEY, Y'KNOW SOMETHING? I HATE TO SAY IT, BUT WE MAKE A PRETTY GOOD TEAM!
BITE YOUR TONGUE, HOTHEAD!
OUR ONLY CHANCE IS TO TACKLE THEM ONE AT A TIME NOW! QUICK, MONTANA... YOUR ASBESTOS LASSO AGAIN!
I HEAR Y'ALL TALKIN', PARD!
HANG ON, TORCH... I'LL GET YOU OUTTA THAT IN A FLASH!
NO, MOTHER! I WANNA DO THIS MYSELF!
SORRY, CHUM! I WAS GOIN' TOO FAST TO STOP!
OKAY... NO HARM DONE... EXCEPT TO THEM! I'LL START TOSSING SOME FIERY BARRIERS AROUND OUR LITTLE FRIENDS AGAIN!
LOOK, OX... DON'T YOU HAVE SENSE ENOUGH TO STAY DOWN WHEN I KNOCK YOU DOWN?
18.

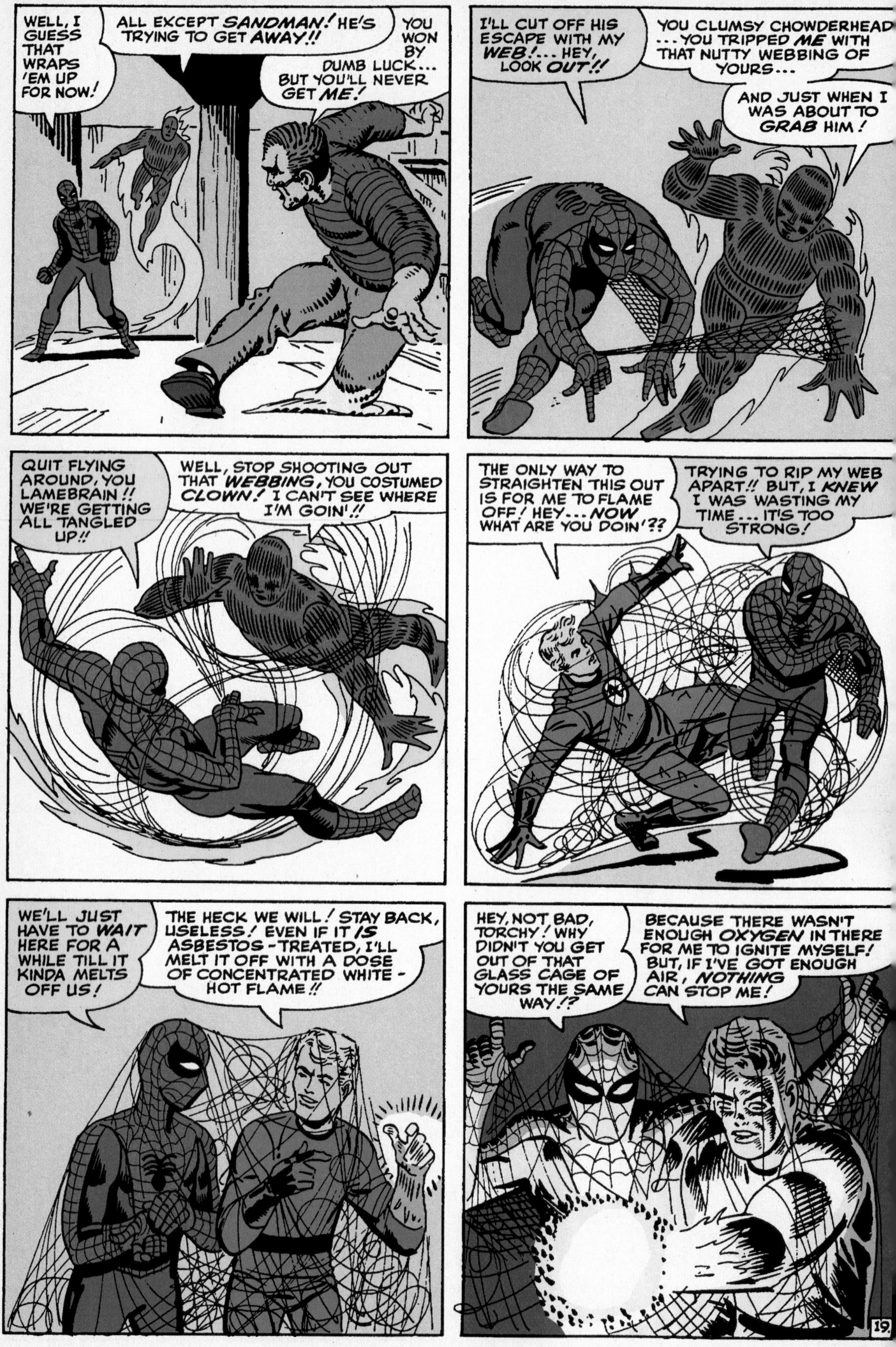
WELL, I GUESS THAT WRAPS 'EM UP FOR NOW!
ALL EXCEPT SANDMAN! HE'S TRYING TO GET AWAY!!
YOU WON BY DUMB LUCK... BUT YOU'LL NEVER GET ME!
I'LL CUT OFF HIS ESCAPE WITH MY WEB!... HEY, LOOK OUT!!
YOU CLUMSY CHOWDERHEAD ...YOU TRIPPED ME WITH THAT NUTTY WEBBING OF YOURS...
AND JUST WHEN I WAS ABOUT TO GRAB HIM!
QUIT FLYING AROUND, YOU LAMEBRAIN!! WE'RE GETTING ALL TANGLED UP!!
WELL, STOP SHOOTING OUT THAT WEBBING, YOU COSTUMED CLOWN! I CAN'T SEE WHERE I'M GOIN'!!
THE ONLY WAY TO STRAIGHTEN THIS OUT IS FOR ME TO FLAME OFF! HEY... NOW WHAT ARE YOU DOIN'??
TRYING TO RIP MY WEB APART!! BUT, I KNEW I WAS WASTING MY TIME... IT'S TOO STRONG!
WE'LL JUST HAVE TO WAIT HERE FOR A WHILE TILL IT KINDA MELTS OFF US!
THE HECK WE WILL! STAY BACK, USELESS! EVEN IF IT IS ASBESTOS-TREATED, I'LL MELT IT OFF WITH A DOSE OF CONCENTRATED WHITE-HOT FLAME!!
HEY, NOT BAD, TORCHY! WHY DIDN'T YOU GET OUT OF THAT GLASS CAGE OF YOURS THE SAME WAY!?
BECAUSE THERE WASN'T ENOUGH OXYGEN IN THERE FOR ME TO IGNITE MYSELF! BUT, IF I'VE GOT ENOUGH AIR, NOTHING CAN STOP ME!
19

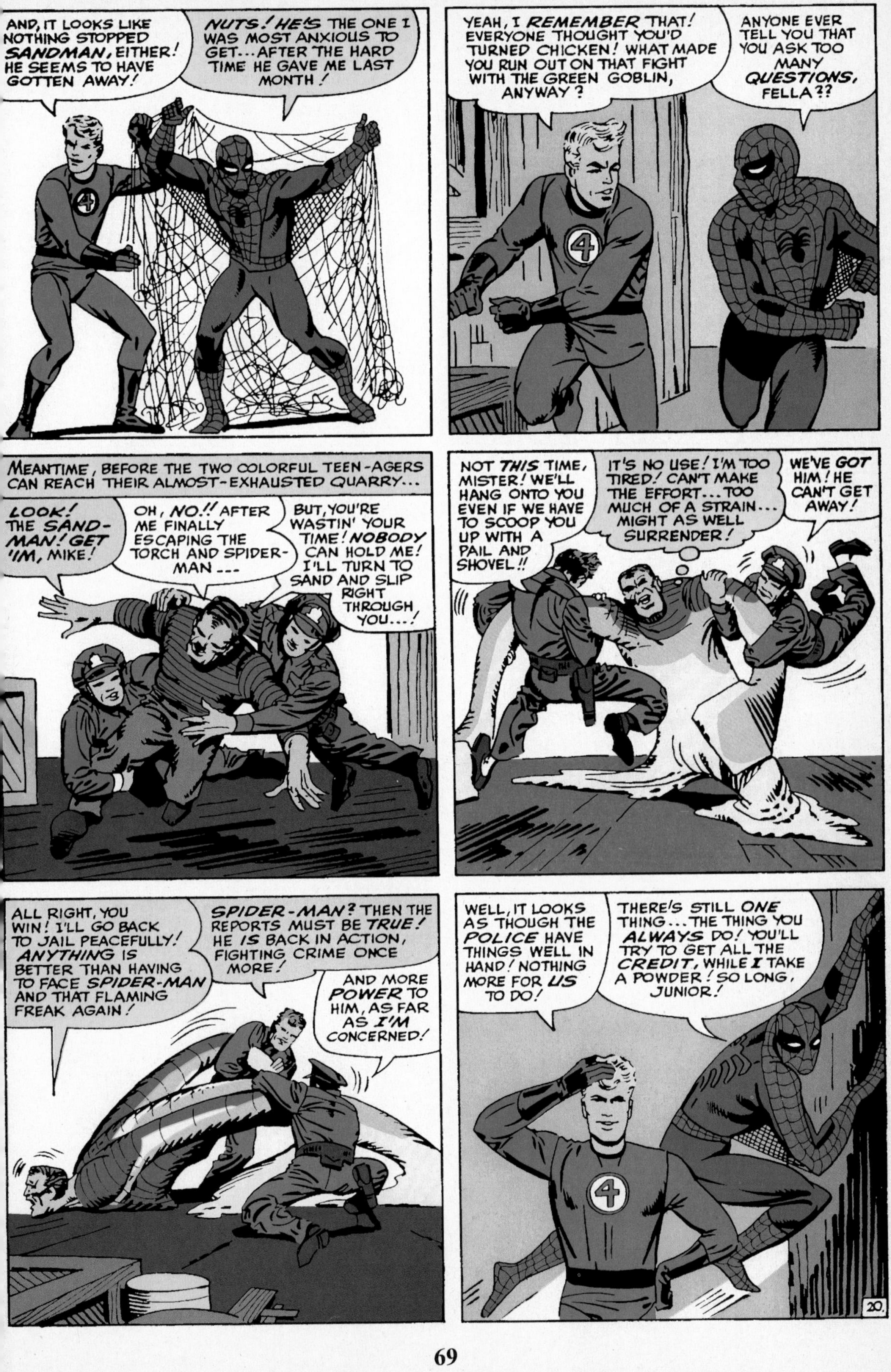
AND, IT LOOKS LIKE NOTHING STOPPED SANDMAN, EITHER! HE SEEMS TO HAVE GOTTEN AWAY!
NUTS! HE'S THE ONE I WAS MOST ANXIOUS TO GET... AFTER THE HARD TIME HE GAVE ME LAST MONTH!
YEAH, I REMEMBER THAT! EVERYONE THOUGHT YOU'D TURNED CHICKEN! WHAT MADE YOU RUN OUT ON THAT FIGHT WITH THE GREEN GOBLIN, ANYWAY?
ANYONE EVER TELL YOU THAT YOU ASK TOO MANY QUESTIONS, FELLA??
MEANTIME, BEFORE THE TWO COLORFUL TEEN-AGERS CAN REACH THEIR ALMOST-EXHAUSTED QUARRY...
LOOK! THE SAND-MAN! GET 'IM, MIKE!
OH, NO!! AFTER ME FINALLY ESCAPING THE TORCH AND SPIDER-MAN ---
BUT, YOU'RE WASTIN' YOUR TIME! NOBODY CAN HOLD ME! I'LL TURN TO SAND AND SLIP RIGHT THROUGH YOU...!
NOT THIS TIME, MISTER! WE'LL HANG ONTO YOU EVEN IF WE HAVE TO SCOOP YOU UP WITH A PAIL AND SHOVEL!!
IT'S NO USE! I'M TOO TIRED! CAN'T MAKE THE EFFORT... TOO MUCH OF A STRAIN... MIGHT AS WELL SURRENDER!
WE'VE GOT HIM! HE CAN'T GET AWAY!
ALL RIGHT, YOU WIN! I'LL GO BACK TO JAIL PEACEFULLY! ANYTHING IS BETTER THAN HAVING TO FACE SPIDER-MAN AND THAT FLAMING FREAK AGAIN!
SPIDER-MAN? THEN THE REPORTS MUST BE TRUE! HE IS BACK IN ACTION, FIGHTING CRIME ONCE MORE!
AND MORE POWER TO HIM, AS FAR AS I'M CONCERNED!
WELL, IT LOOKS AS THOUGH THE POLICE HAVE THINGS WELL IN HAND! NOTHING MORE FOR US TO DO!
THERE'S STILL ONE THING... THE THING YOU ALWAYS DO! YOU'LL TRY TO GET ALL THE CREDIT, WHILE I TAKE A POWDER! SO LONG, JUNIOR!
20.

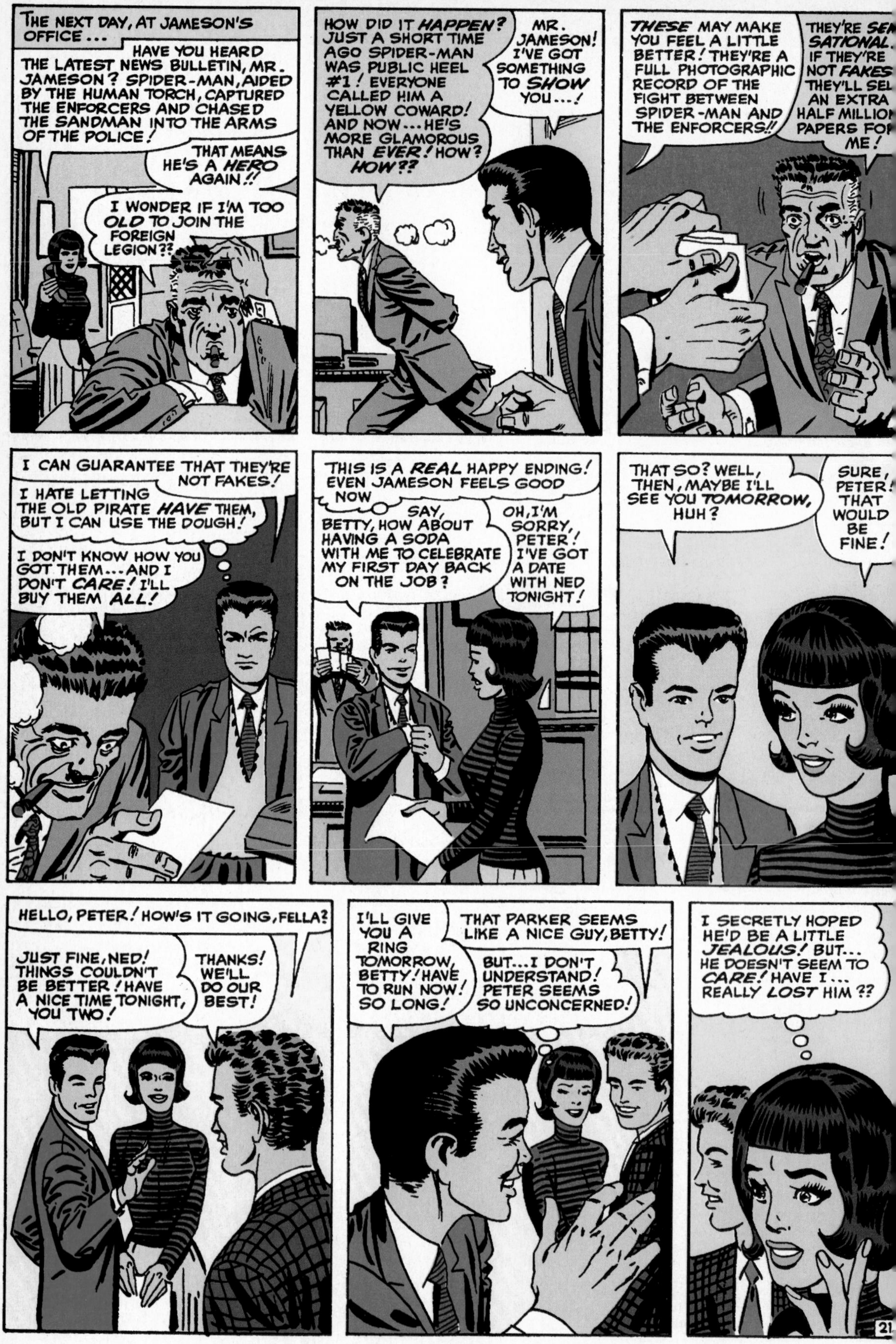
THE NEXT DAY, AT JAMESON'S OFFICE...
HAVE YOU HEARD THE LATEST NEWS BULLETIN, MR. JAMESON? SPIDER-MAN, AIDED BY THE HUMAN TORCH, CAPTURED THE ENFORCERS AND CHASED THE SANDMAN INTO THE ARMS OF THE POLICE!
THAT MEANS HE'S A HERO AGAIN!!
I WONDER IF I'M TOO OLD TO JOIN THE FOREIGN LEGION??
HOW DID IT HAPPEN? JUST A SHORT TIME AGO SPIDER-MAN WAS PUBLIC HEEL #1! EVERYONE CALLED HIM A YELLOW COWARD! AND NOW... HE'S MORE GLAMOROUS THAN EVER! HOW? HOW??
MR. JAMESON! I'VE GOT SOMETHING TO SHOW YOU...!
THESE MAY MAKE YOU FEEL A LITTLE BETTER! THEY'RE A FULL PHOTOGRAPHIC RECORD OF THE FIGHT BETWEEN SPIDER-MAN AND THE ENFORCERS!!
THEY'RE SEN SATIONAL. IF THEY'RE NOT FAKES THEY'LL SEL AN EXTRA HALF MILLIO PAPERS FO ME!
I CAN GUARANTEE THAT THEY'RE NOT FAKES!
I HATE LETTING THE OLD PIRATE HAVE THEM, BUT I CAN USE THE DOUGH!
I DON'T KNOW HOW YOU GOT THEM... AND I DON'T CARE! I'LL BUY THEM ALL!
THIS IS A REAL HAPPY ENDING! EVEN JAMESON FEELS GOOD NOW
SAY, BETTY, HOW ABOUT HAVING A SODA WITH ME TO CELEBRATE MY FIRST DAY BACK ON THE JOB?
OH, I'M SORRY, PETER! I'VE GOT A DATE WITH NED TONIGHT!
THAT SO? WELL, THEN, MAYBE I'LL SEE YOU TOMORROW, HUH?
SURE, PETER! THAT WOULD BE FINE!
HELLO, PETER! HOW'S IT GOING, FELLA?
JUST FINE, NED! THINGS COULDN'T BE BETTER! HAVE A NICE TIME TONIGHT, YOU TWO!
THANKS! WE'LL DO OUR BEST!
I'LL GIVE YOU A RING TOMORROW, BETTY! HAVE TO RUN NOW! SO LONG!
THAT PARKER SEEMS LIKE A NICE GUY, BETTY!
BUT... I DON'T UNDERSTAND! PETER SEEMS SO UNCONCERNED!
I SECRETLY HOPED HE'D BE A LITTLE JEALOUS! BUT... HE DOESN'T SEEM TO CARE! HAVE I... REALLY LOST HIM??
21

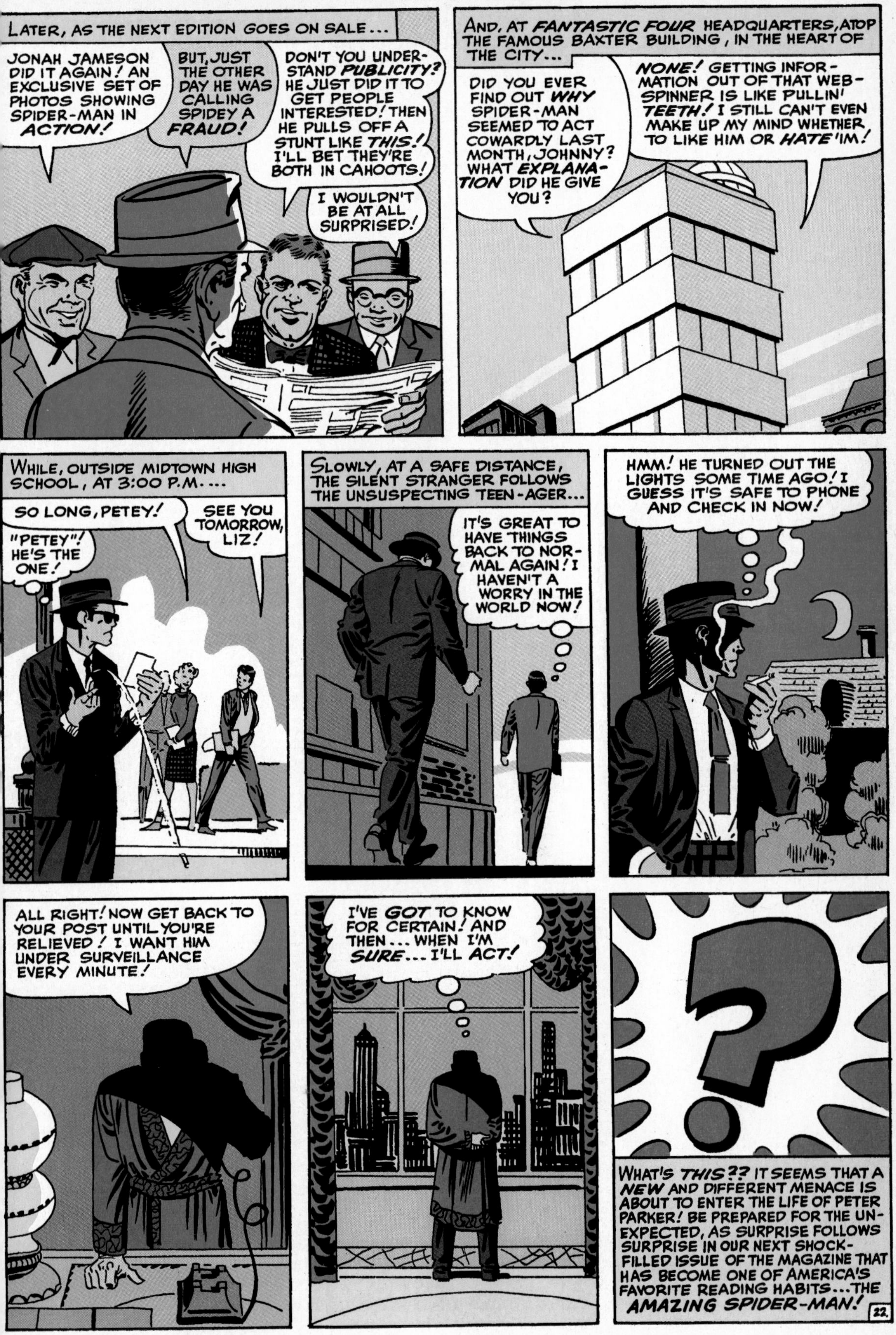
LATER, AS THE NEXT EDITION GOES ON SALE...
JONAH JAMESON DID IT AGAIN! AN EXCLUSIVE SET OF PHOTOS SHOWING SPIDER-MAN IN ACTION!
BUT, JUST THE OTHER DAY HE WAS CALLING SPIDEY A FRAUD!
DON'T YOU UNDERSTAND PUBLICITY? HE JUST DID IT TO GET PEOPLE INTERESTED! THEN HE PULLS OFF A STUNT LIKE THIS! I'LL BET THEY'RE BOTH IN CAHOOTS!
I WOULDN'T BE AT ALL SURPRISED!
AND, AT FANTASTIC FOUR HEADQUARTERS, ATOP THE FAMOUS BAXTER BUILDING, IN THE HEART OF THE CITY...
DID YOU EVER FIND OUT WHY SPIDER-MAN SEEMED TO ACT COWARDLY LAST MONTH, JOHNNY? WHAT EXPLANATION DID HE GIVE YOU?
NONE! GETTING INFORMATION OUT OF THAT WEB-SPINNER IS LIKE PULLIN' TEETH! I STILL CAN'T EVEN MAKE UP MY MIND WHETHER TO LIKE HIM OR HATE 'IM!
WHILE, OUTSIDE MIDTOWN HIGH SCHOOL, AT 3:00 P.M....
SO LONG, PETEY!
SEE YOU TOMORROW, LIZ!
"PETEY"! HE'S THE ONE!
SLOWLY, AT A SAFE DISTANCE, THE SILENT STRANGER FOLLOWS THE UNSUSPECTING TEEN-AGER...
IT'S GREAT TO HAVE THINGS BACK TO NORMAL AGAIN! I HAVEN'T A WORRY IN THE WORLD NOW!
HMM! HE TURNED OUT THE LIGHTS SOME TIME AGO! I GUESS IT'S SAFE TO PHONE AND CHECK IN NOW!
ALL RIGHT! NOW GET BACK TO YOUR POST UNTIL YOU'RE RELIEVED! I WANT HIM UNDER SURVEILLANCE EVERY MINUTE!
I'VE GOT TO KNOW FOR CERTAIN! AND THEN... WHEN I'M SURE... I'LL ACT!
?
WHAT'S THIS?? IT SEEMS THAT A NEW AND DIFFERENT MENACE IS ABOUT TO ENTER THE LIFE OF PETER PARKER! BE PREPARED FOR THE UNEXPECTED, AS SURPRISE FOLLOWS SURPRISE IN OUR NEXT SHOCK-FILLED ISSUE OF THE MAGAZINE THAT HAS BECOME ONE OF AMERICA'S FAVORITE READING HABITS... THE AMAZING SPIDER-MAN!
22.

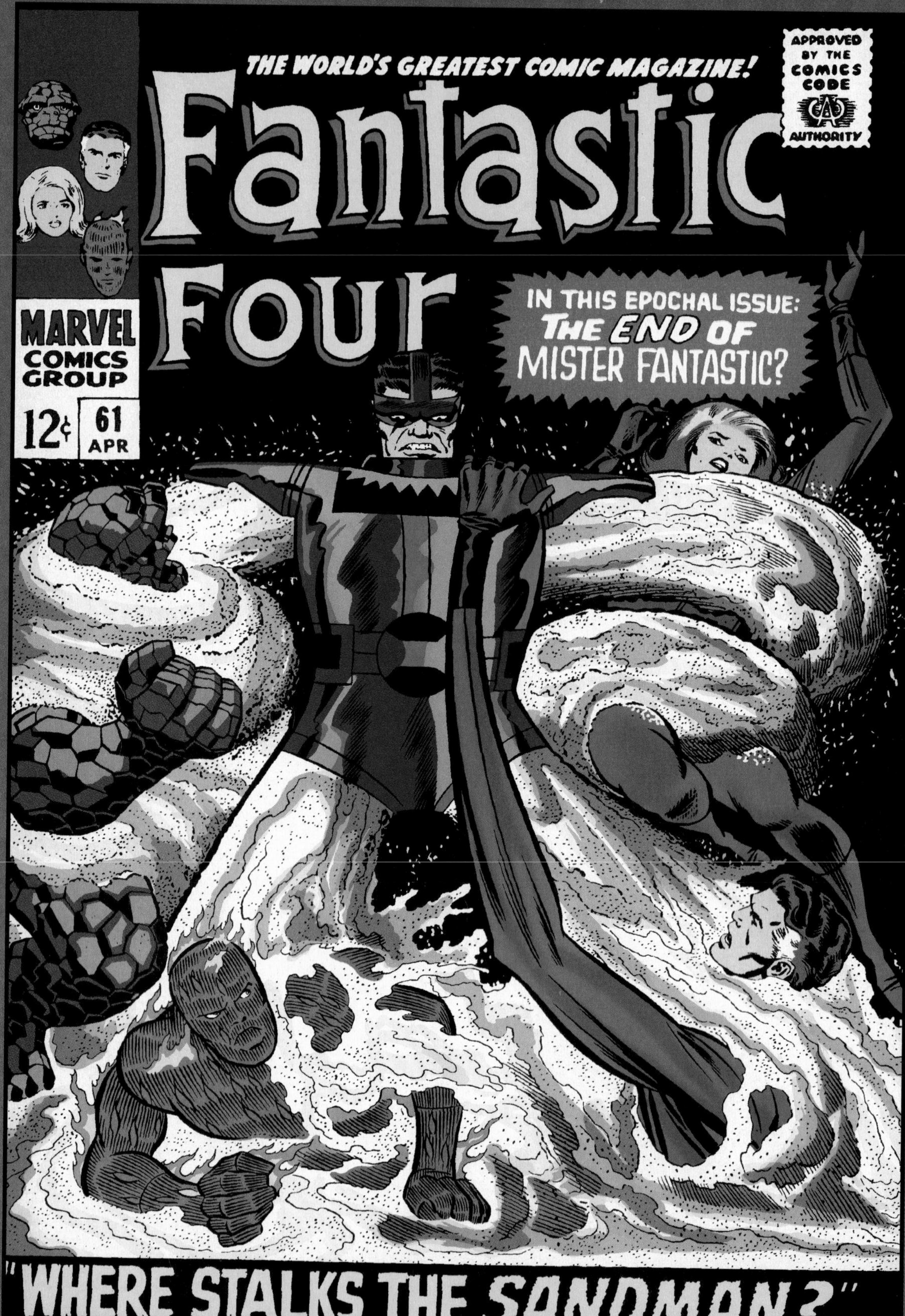
THE WORLD'S GREATEST COMIC MAGAZINE!
APPROVED BY THE COMICS CODE AUTHORITY
Fantastic Four
MARVEL COMICS GROUP
12¢ 61 APR
IN THIS EPOCHAL ISSUE: THE END OF MISTER FANTASTIC?
"WHERE STALKS THE SANDMAN?"

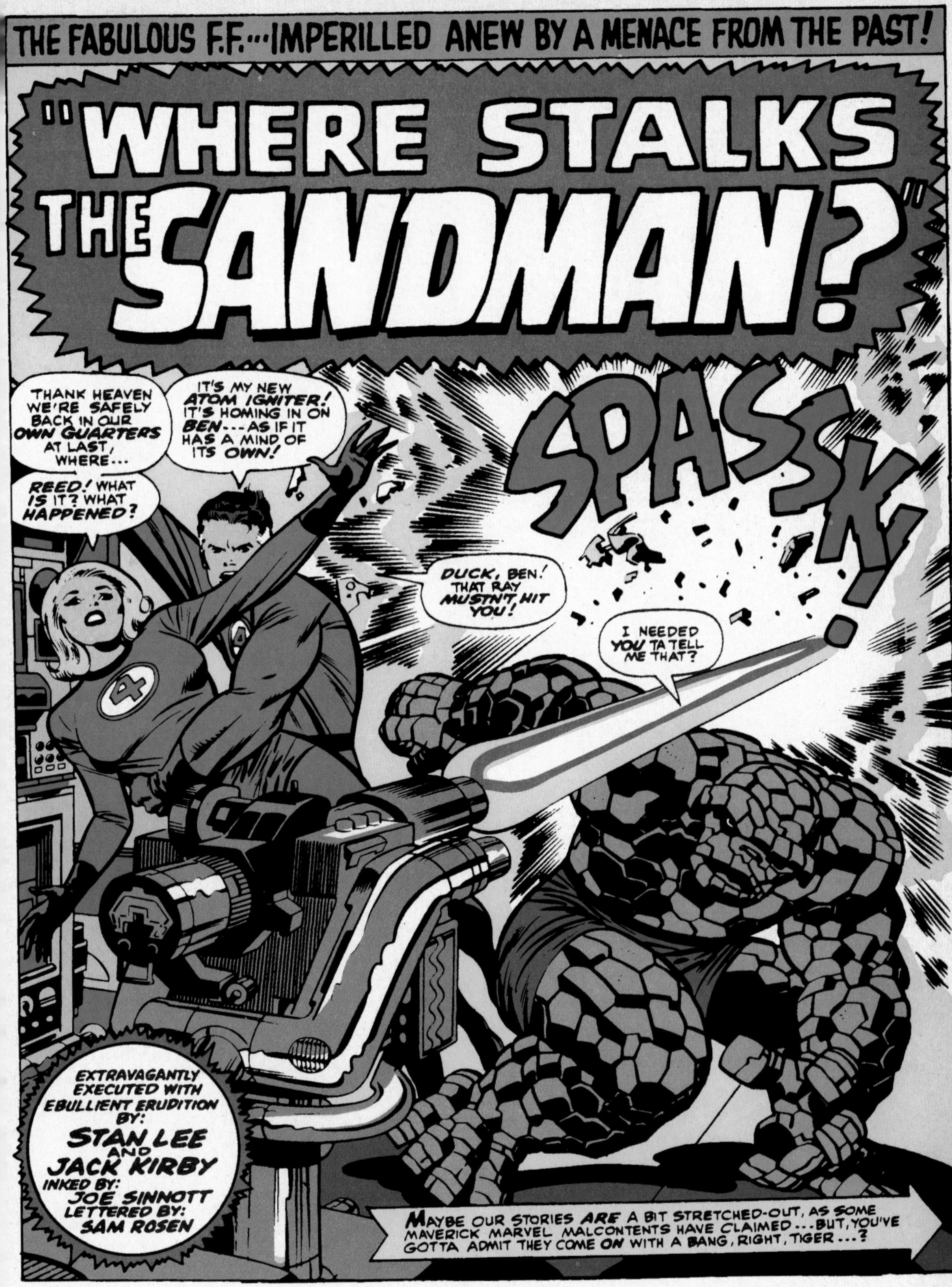
THE FABULOUS F.F.···IMPERILLED ANEW BY A MENACE FROM THE PAST!
"WHERE STALKS THE SANDMAN?"
THANK HEAVEN WE'RE SAFELY BACK IN OUR OWN QUARTERS AT LAST, WHERE...
REED! WHAT IS IT? WHAT HAPPENED?
IT'S MY NEW ATOM IGNITER! IT'S HOMING IN ON BEN---AS IF IT HAS A MIND OF ITS OWN!
SPASSK!
DUCK, BEN! THAT RAY MUSTN'T HIT YOU!
I NEEDED YOU TA TELL ME THAT?
EXTRAVAGANTLY EXECUTED WITH EBULLIENT ERUDITION BY: STAN LEE AND JACK KIRBY INKED BY: JOE SINNOTT LETTERED BY: SAM ROSEN
MAYBE OUR STORIES ARE A BIT STRETCHED-OUT, AS SOME MAVERICK MARVEL MALCONTENTS HAVE CLAIMED...BUT, YOU'VE GOTTA ADMIT THEY COME ON WITH A BANG, RIGHT, TIGER...?

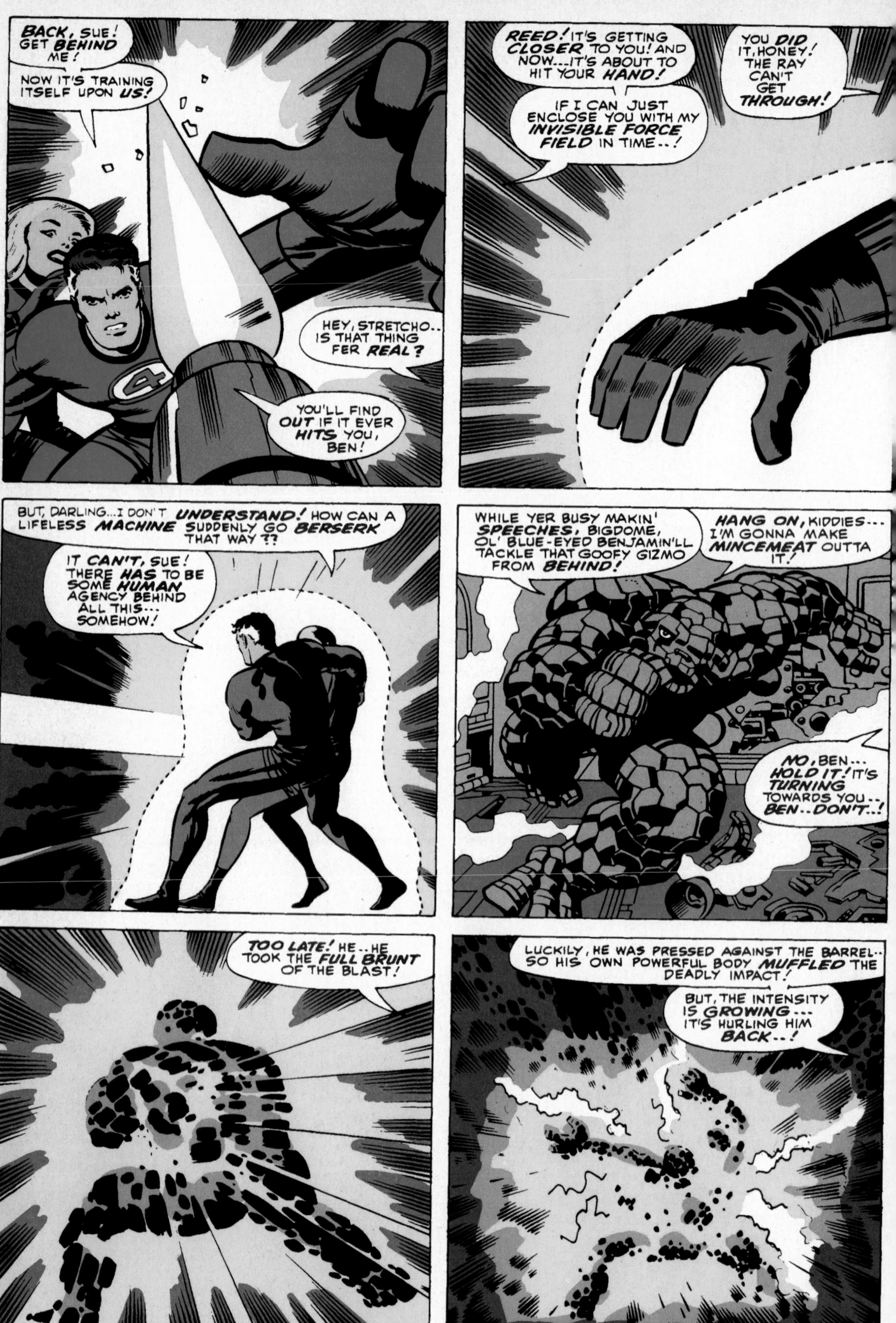
BACK, SUE! GET BEHIND ME!
NOW IT'S TRAINING ITSELF UPON US!
HEY, STRETCHO.. IS THAT THING FER REAL?
YOU'LL FIND OUT IF IT EVER HITS YOU, BEN!
REED! IT'S GETTING CLOSER TO YOU! AND NOW...IT'S ABOUT TO HIT YOUR HAND!
IF I CAN JUST ENCLOSE YOU WITH MY INVISIBLE FORCE FIELD IN TIME..!
YOU DID IT, HONEY! THE RAY CAN'T GET THROUGH!
BUT, DARLING...I DON'T UNDERSTAND! HOW CAN A LIFELESS MACHINE SUDDENLY GO BERSERK THAT WAY ??
IT CAN'T, SUE! THERE HAS TO BE SOME HUMAN AGENCY BEHIND ALL THIS... SOMEHOW!
WHILE YER BUSY MAKIN' SPEECHES, BIGDOME, OL' BLUE-EYED BENJAMIN'LL TACKLE THAT GOOFY GIZMO FROM BEHIND!
HANG ON, KIDDIES... I'M GONNA MAKE MINCEMEAT OUTTA IT!
NO, BEN... HOLD IT! IT'S TURNING TOWARDS YOU.. BEN..DON'T..!
TOO LATE! HE..HE TOOK THE FULL BRUNT OF THE BLAST!
LUCKILY, HE WAS PRESSED AGAINST THE BARREL.. SO HIS OWN POWERFUL BODY MUFFLED THE DEADLY IMPACT!
BUT, THE INTENSITY IS GROWING... IT'S HURLING HIM BACK..!

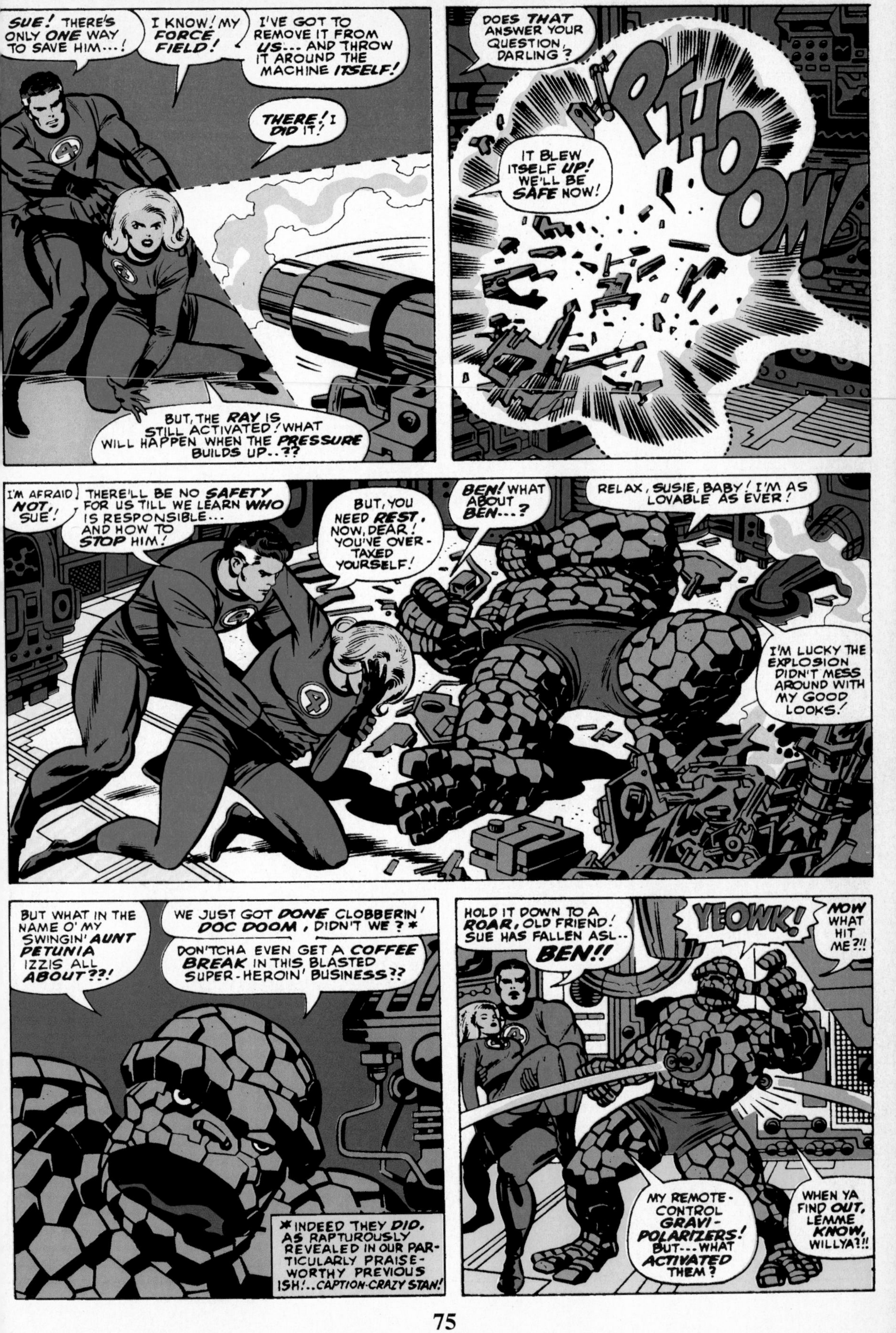
SUE! THERE'S ONLY ONE WAY TO SAVE HIM...!
I KNOW! MY FORCE FIELD!
I'VE GOT TO REMOVE IT FROM US... AND THROW IT AROUND THE MACHINE ITSELF!
THERE! I DID IT!
BUT, THE RAY IS STILL ACTIVATED! WHAT WILL HAPPEN WHEN THE PRESSURE BUILDS UP..??
DOES THAT ANSWER YOUR QUESTION, DARLING?
PTHOOOM!
IT BLEW ITSELF UP! WE'LL BE SAFE NOW!
I'M AFRAID NOT, SUE!
THERE'LL BE NO SAFETY FOR US TILL WE LEARN WHO IS RESPONSIBLE... AND HOW TO STOP HIM!
BUT, YOU NEED REST, NOW, DEAR! YOU'VE OVER-TAXED YOURSELF!
BEN! WHAT ABOUT BEN...?
RELAX, SUSIE, BABY! I'M AS LOVABLE AS EVER!
I'M LUCKY THE EXPLOSION DIDN'T MESS AROUND WITH MY GOOD LOOKS!
BUT WHAT IN THE NAME O' MY SWINGIN' AUNT PETUNIA IZZIS ALL ABOUT??!
WE JUST GOT DONE CLOBBERIN' DOC DOOM, DIDN'T WE?*
DON'TCHA EVEN GET A COFFEE BREAK IN THIS BLASTED SUPER-HEROIN' BUSINESS??
*INDEED THEY DID, AS RAPTUROUSLY REVEALED IN OUR PARTICULARLY PRAISE-WORTHY PREVIOUS ISH!..CAPTION-CRAZY STAN!
HOLD IT DOWN TO A ROAR, OLD FRIEND! SUE HAS FALLEN ASL.. BEN!!
YEOWK!
NOW WHAT HIT ME?!!
MY REMOTE-CONTROL GRAVI-POLARIZERS! BUT... WHAT ACTIVATED THEM?
WHEN YA FIND OUT, LEMME KNOW, WILLYA?!!

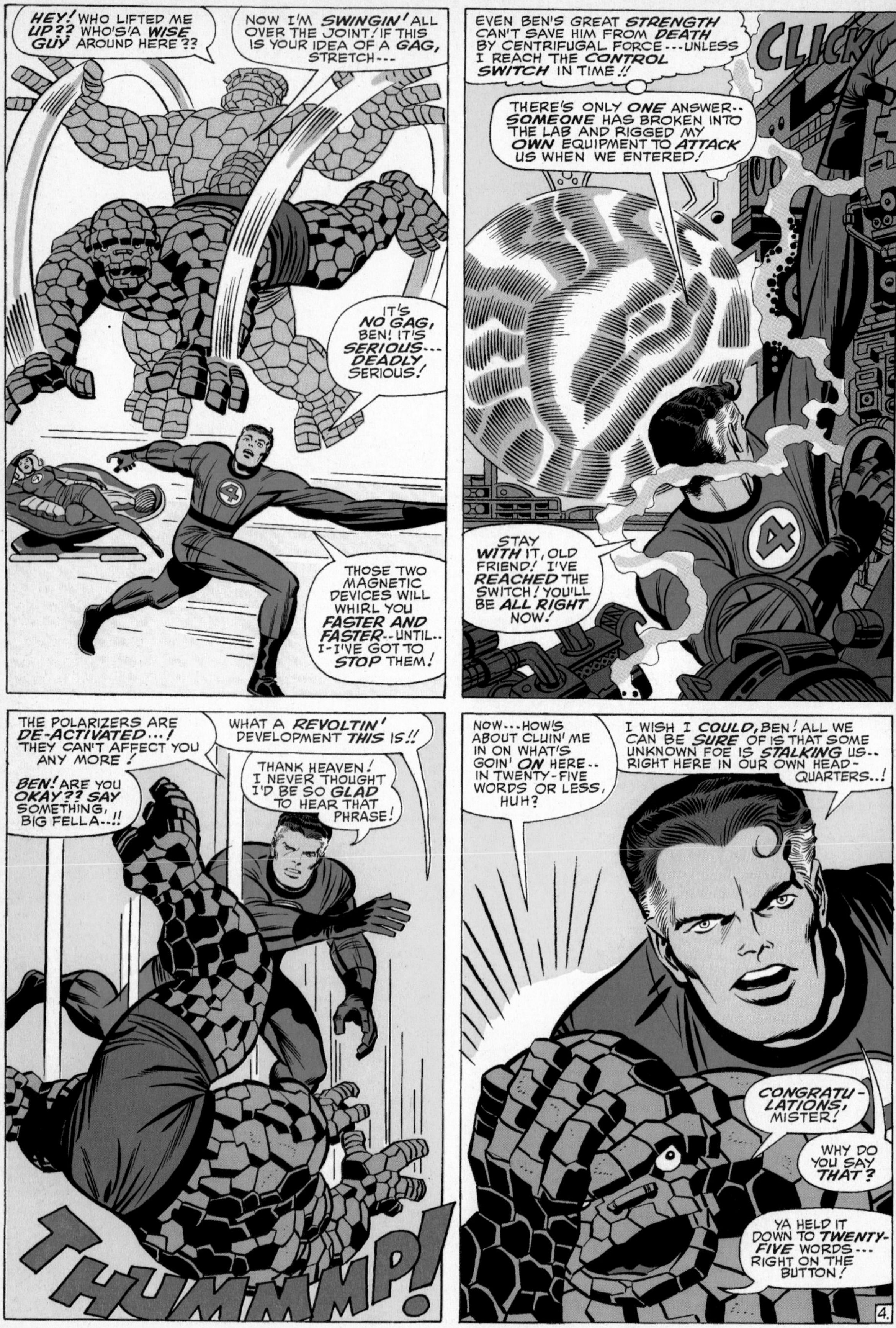
HEY! WHO LIFTED ME UP?? WHO'S A WISE GUY AROUND HERE??
NOW I'M SWINGIN' ALL OVER THE JOINT! IF THIS IS YOUR IDEA OF A GAG, STRETCH---
IT'S NO GAG, BEN! IT'S SERIOUS--- DEADLY SERIOUS!
THOSE TWO MAGNETIC DEVICES WILL WHIRL YOU FASTER AND FASTER--UNTIL-- I-I'VE GOT TO STOP THEM!
EVEN BEN'S GREAT STRENGTH CAN'T SAVE HIM FROM DEATH BY CENTRIFUGAL FORCE---UNLESS I REACH THE CONTROL SWITCH IN TIME!!
CLICK
THERE'S ONLY ONE ANSWER-- SOMEONE HAS BROKEN INTO THE LAB AND RIGGED MY OWN EQUIPMENT TO ATTACK US WHEN WE ENTERED!
STAY WITH IT, OLD FRIEND! I'VE REACHED THE SWITCH! YOU'LL BE ALL RIGHT NOW!
THE POLARIZERS ARE DE-ACTIVATED...! THEY CAN'T AFFECT YOU ANY MORE!
BEN! ARE YOU OKAY?? SAY SOMETHING, BIG FELLA--!!
WHAT A REVOLTIN' DEVELOPMENT THIS IS!!
THANK HEAVEN! I NEVER THOUGHT I'D BE SO GLAD TO HEAR THAT PHRASE!
THUMMMMP!
NOW---HOW'S ABOUT CLUIN' ME IN ON WHAT'S GOIN' ON HERE-- IN TWENTY-FIVE WORDS OR LESS, HUH?
I WISH I COULD, BEN! ALL WE CAN BE SURE OF IS THAT SOME UNKNOWN FOE IS STALKING US-- RIGHT HERE IN OUR OWN HEAD-QUARTERS--!
CONGRATU-LATIONS, MISTER!
WHY DO YOU SAY THAT?
YA HELD IT DOWN TO TWENTY-FIVE WORDS--- RIGHT ON THE BUTTON!
4.

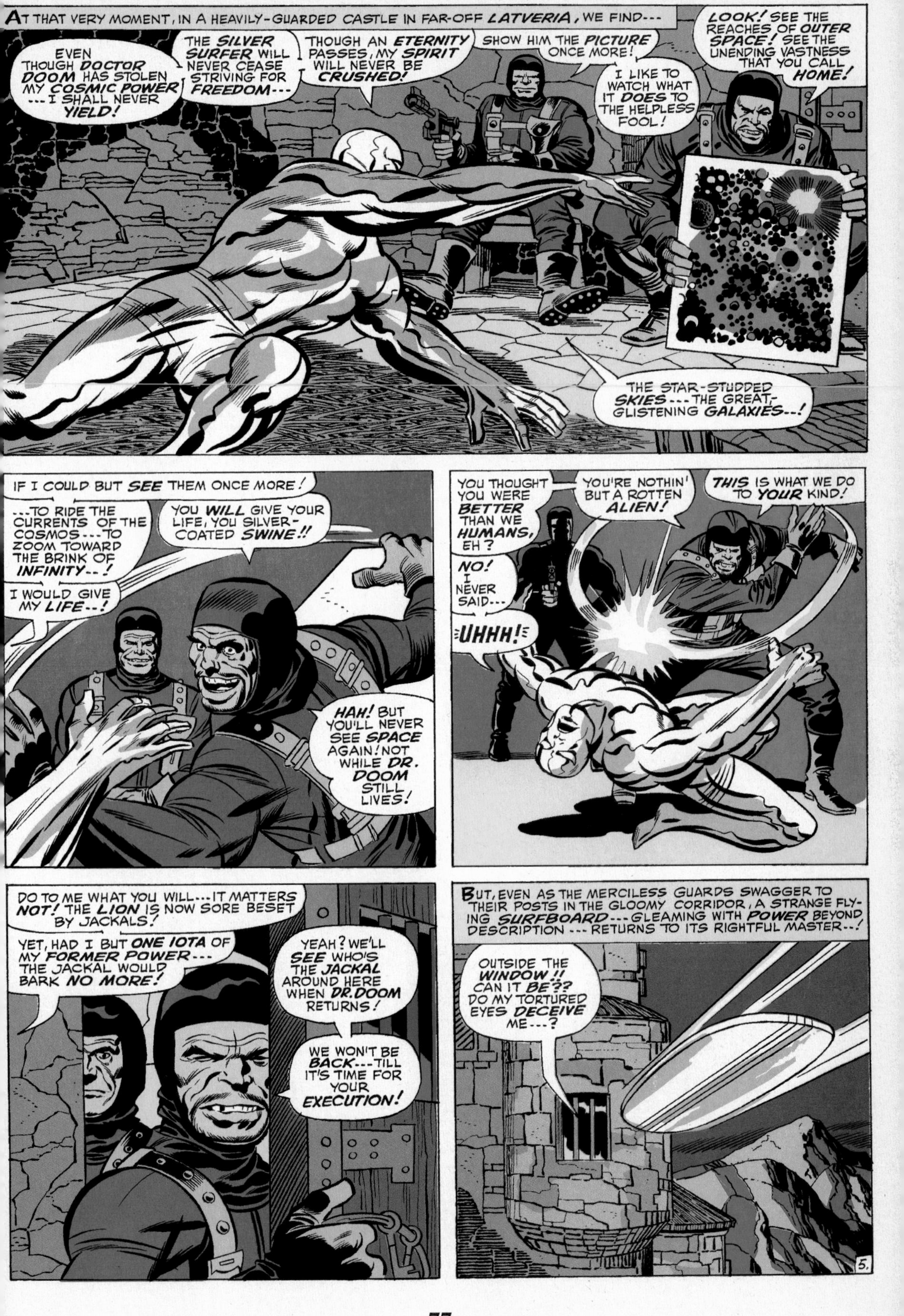
AT THAT VERY MOMENT, IN A HEAVILY-GUARDED CASTLE IN FAR-OFF LATVERIA, WE FIND---
EVEN THOUGH DOCTOR DOOM HAS STOLEN MY COSMIC POWER --- I SHALL NEVER YIELD!
THE SILVER SURFER WILL NEVER CEASE STRIVING FOR FREEDOM---
THOUGH AN ETERNITY PASSES, MY SPIRIT WILL NEVER BE CRUSHED!
SHOW HIM THE PICTURE ONCE MORE!
I LIKE TO WATCH WHAT IT DOES TO THE HELPLESS FOOL!
LOOK! SEE THE REACHES OF OUTER SPACE! SEE THE UNENDING VASTNESS THAT YOU CALL HOME!
THE STAR-STUDDED SKIES --- THE GREAT, GLISTENING GALAXIES--!
IF I COULD BUT SEE THEM ONCE MORE!
--TO RIDE THE CURRENTS OF THE COSMOS---TO ZOOM TOWARD THE BRINK OF INFINITY--!
I WOULD GIVE MY LIFE--!
YOU WILL GIVE YOUR LIFE, YOU SILVER-COATED SWINE!!
HAH! BUT YOU'LL NEVER SEE SPACE AGAIN! NOT WHILE DR. DOOM STILL LIVES!
YOU THOUGHT YOU WERE BETTER THAN WE HUMANS, EH?
YOU'RE NOTHIN' BUT A ROTTEN ALIEN!
THIS IS WHAT WE DO TO YOUR KIND!
NO! I NEVER SAID---
UHHH!
DO TO ME WHAT YOU WILL---IT MATTERS NOT! THE LION IS NOW SORE BESET BY JACKALS!
YET, HAD I BUT ONE IOTA OF MY FORMER POWER--- THE JACKAL WOULD BARK NO MORE!
YEAH? WE'LL SEE WHO'S THE JACKAL AROUND HERE WHEN DR. DOOM RETURNS!
WE WON'T BE BACK---TILL IT'S TIME FOR YOUR EXECUTION!
BUT, EVEN AS THE MERCILESS GUARDS SWAGGER TO THEIR POSTS IN THE GLOOMY CORRIDOR, A STRANGE FLYING SURFBOARD---GLEAMING WITH POWER BEYOND DESCRIPTION --- RETURNS TO ITS RIGHTFUL MASTER--!
OUTSIDE THE WINDOW!! CAN IT BE?? DO MY TORTURED EYES DECEIVE ME---?
5.

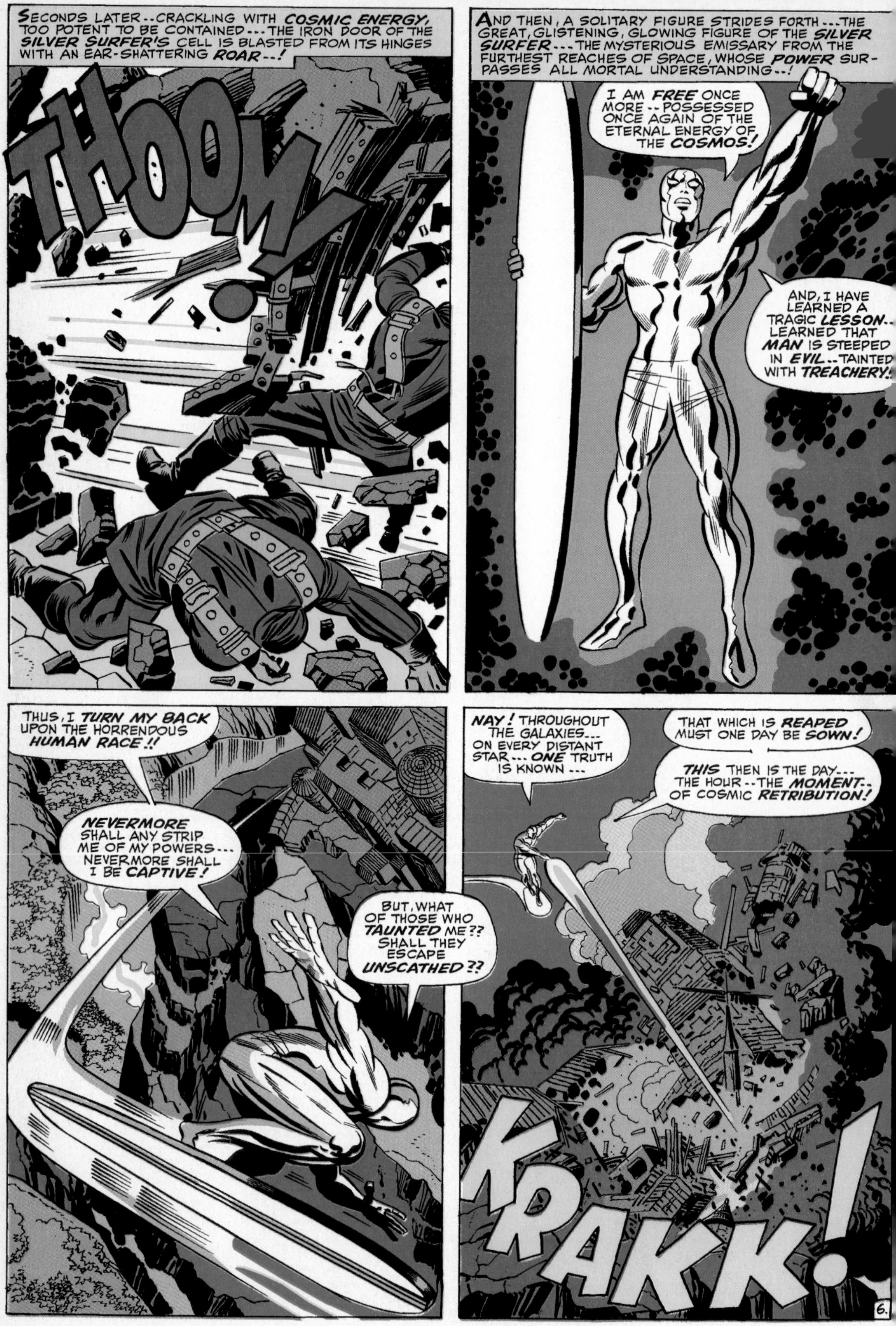
SECONDS LATER--CRACKLING WITH COSMIC ENERGY, TOO POTENT TO BE CONTAINED--- THE IRON DOOR OF THE SILVER SURFER'S CELL IS BLASTED FROM ITS HINGES WITH AN EAR-SHATTERING ROAR--!
THOOM
AND THEN, A SOLITARY FIGURE STRIDES FORTH---THE GREAT, GLISTENING, GLOWING FIGURE OF THE SILVER SURFER---THE MYSTERIOUS EMISSARY FROM THE FURTHEST REACHES OF SPACE, WHOSE POWER SURPASSES ALL MORTAL UNDERSTANDING--!
I AM FREE ONCE MORE--POSSESSED ONCE AGAIN OF THE ETERNAL ENERGY OF THE COSMOS!
AND, I HAVE LEARNED A TRAGIC LESSON-- LEARNED THAT MAN IS STEEPED IN EVIL--TAINTED WITH TREACHERY!
THUS, I TURN MY BACK UPON THE HORRENDOUS HUMAN RACE!!
NEVERMORE SHALL ANY STRIP ME OF MY POWERS--- NEVERMORE SHALL I BE CAPTIVE!
BUT, WHAT OF THOSE WHO TAUNTED ME?? SHALL THEY ESCAPE UNSCATHED??
NAY! THROUGHOUT THE GALAXIES--- ON EVERY DISTANT STAR--- ONE TRUTH IS KNOWN ---
THAT WHICH IS REAPED MUST ONE DAY BE SOWN!
THIS THEN IS THE DAY--- THE HOUR--THE MOMENT-- OF COSMIC RETRIBUTION!
KRAKK!
6.

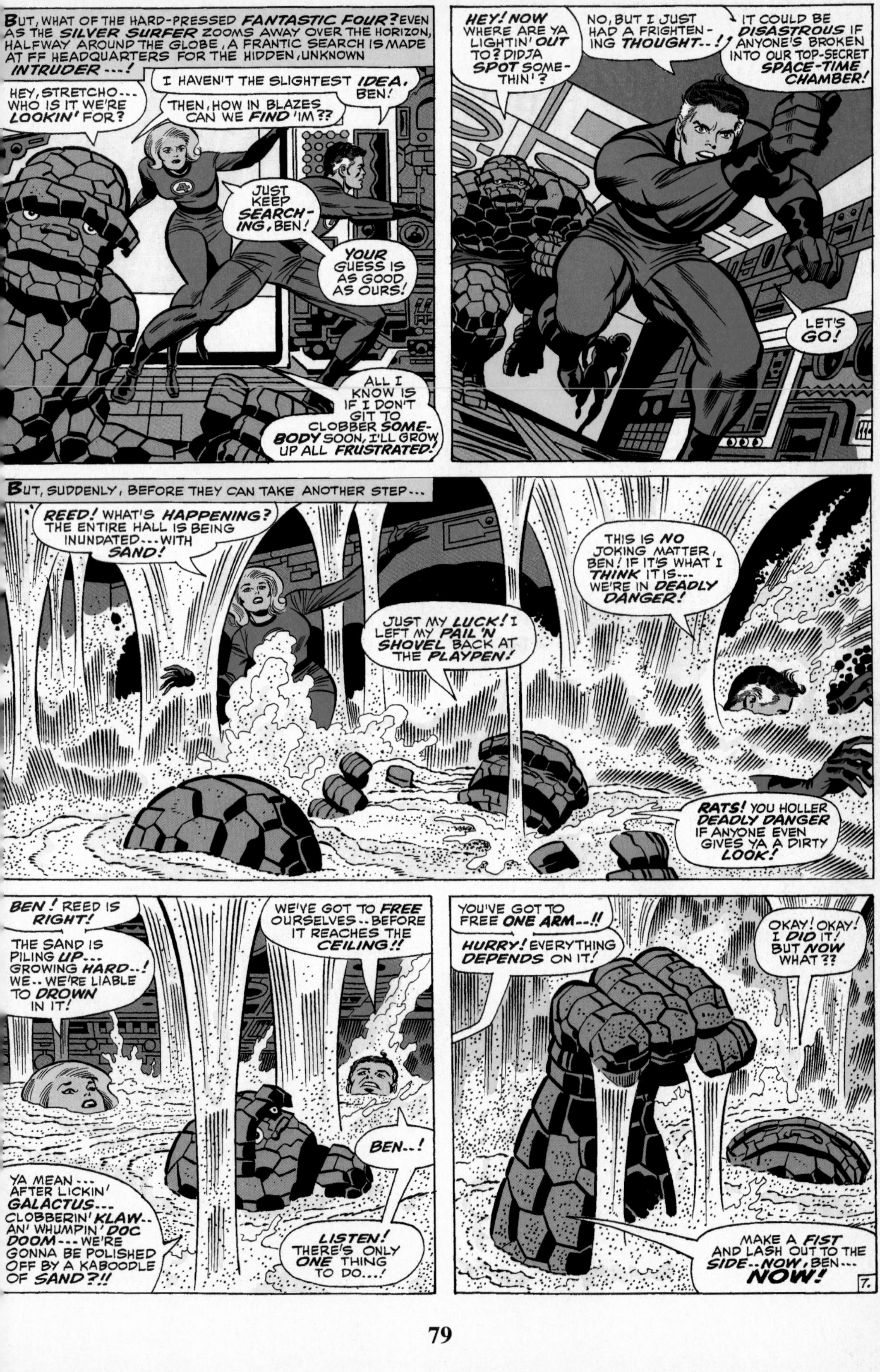
BUT, WHAT OF THE HARD-PRESSED FANTASTIC FOUR? EVEN AS THE SILVER SURFER ZOOMS AWAY OVER THE HORIZON, HALFWAY AROUND THE GLOBE, A FRANTIC SEARCH IS MADE AT FF HEADQUARTERS FOR THE HIDDEN, UNKNOWN INTRUDER---!
HEY, STRETCHO--- WHO IS IT WE'RE LOOKIN' FOR?
I HAVEN'T THE SLIGHTEST IDEA, BEN!
THEN, HOW IN BLAZES CAN WE FIND 'IM??
JUST KEEP SEARCHING, BEN!
YOUR GUESS IS AS GOOD AS OURS!
ALL I KNOW IS IF I DON'T GIT TO CLOBBER SOMEBODY SOON, I'LL GROW UP ALL FRUSTRATED!
HEY! NOW WHERE ARE YA LIGHTIN' OUT TO? DIDJA SPOT SOMETHIN'?
NO, BUT I JUST HAD A FRIGHTENING THOUGHT--!
IT COULD BE DISASTROUS IF ANYONE'S BROKEN INTO OUR TOP-SECRET SPACE-TIME CHAMBER!
LET'S GO!
BUT, SUDDENLY, BEFORE THEY CAN TAKE ANOTHER STEP---
REED! WHAT'S HAPPENING? THE ENTIRE HALL IS BEING INUNDATED---WITH SAND!
JUST MY LUCK! I LEFT MY PAIL 'N SHOVEL BACK AT THE PLAYPEN!
THIS IS NO JOKING MATTER, BEN! IF IT'S WHAT I THINK IT IS--- WE'RE IN DEADLY DANGER!
RATS! YOU HOLLER DEADLY DANGER IF ANYONE EVEN GIVES YA A DIRTY LOOK!
BEN! REED IS RIGHT!
THE SAND IS PILING UP--- GROWING HARD--! WE--WE'RE LIABLE TO DROWN IN IT!
WE'VE GOT TO FREE OURSELVES---BEFORE IT REACHES THE CEILING!!
BEN--!
YA MEAN--- AFTER LICKIN' GALACTUS--- CLOBBERIN' KLAW-- AN' WHUMPIN' DOC DOOM---WE'RE GONNA BE POLISHED OFF BY A KABOODLE OF SAND?!!
LISTEN! THERE'S ONLY ONE THING TO DO---!
YOU'VE GOT TO FREE ONE ARM--!!
HURRY! EVERYTHING DEPENDS ON IT!
OKAY! OKAY! I DID IT! BUT NOW WHAT??
MAKE A FIST AND LASH OUT TO THE SIDE--NOW, BEN--- NOW!
7.

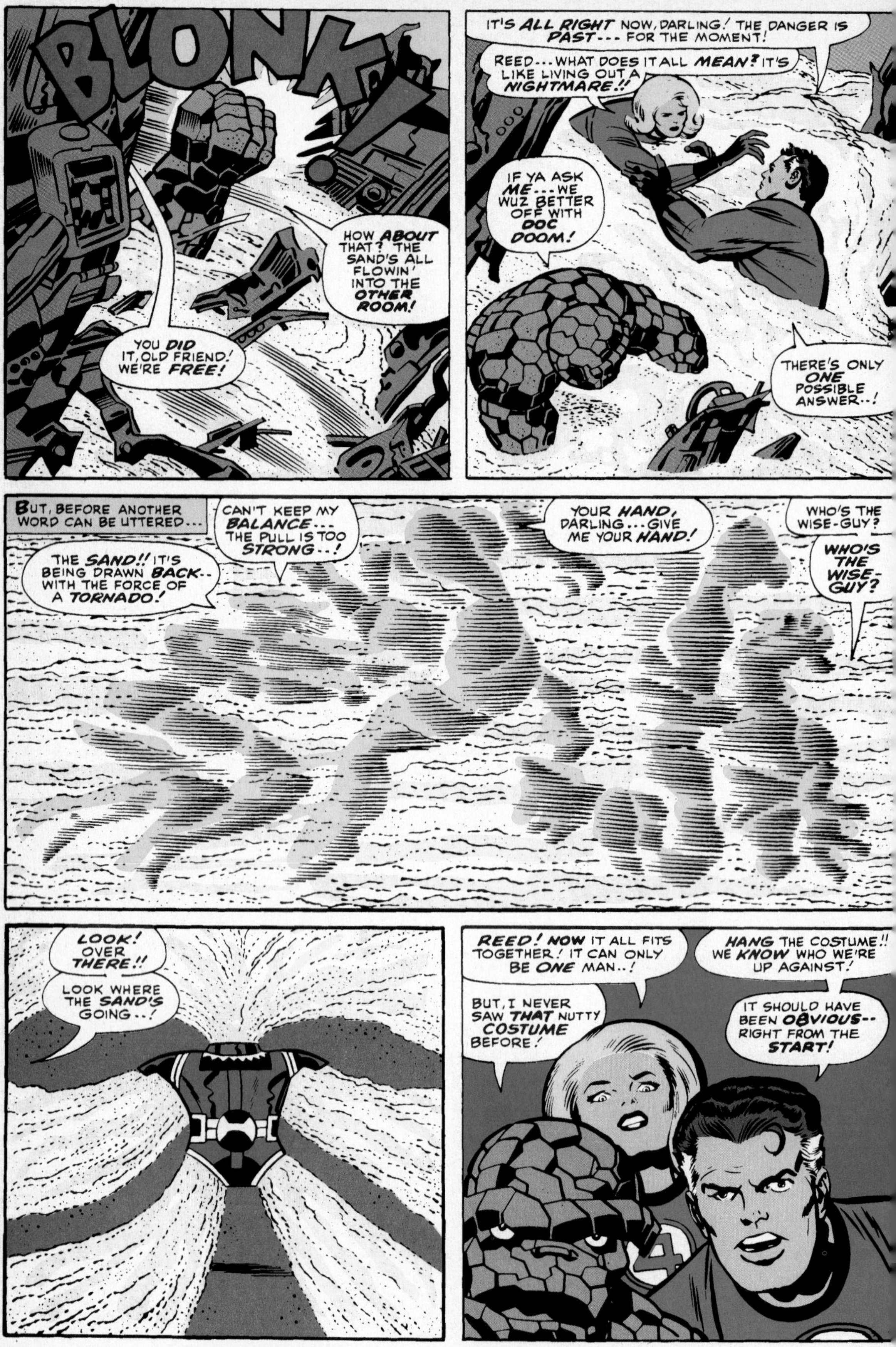
BLONK
HOW ABOUT THAT? THE SAND'S ALL FLOWIN' INTO THE OTHER ROOM!
YOU DID IT, OLD FRIEND! WE'RE FREE!
IT'S ALL RIGHT NOW, DARLING! THE DANGER IS PAST--- FOR THE MOMENT!
REED--- WHAT DOES IT ALL MEAN? IT'S LIKE LIVING OUT A NIGHTMARE!!
IF YA ASK ME--- WE WUZ BETTER OFF WITH DOC DOOM!
THERE'S ONLY ONE POSSIBLE ANSWER--!
BUT, BEFORE ANOTHER WORD CAN BE UTTERED...
THE SAND!! IT'S BEING DRAWN BACK-- WITH THE FORCE OF A TORNADO!
CAN'T KEEP MY BALANCE--- THE PULL IS TOO STRONG--!
YOUR HAND, DARLING--- GIVE ME YOUR HAND!
WHO'S THE WISE-GUY?
WHO'S THE WISE-GUY?
LOOK! OVER THERE!!
LOOK WHERE THE SAND'S GOING--!
REED! NOW IT ALL FITS TOGETHER! IT CAN ONLY BE ONE MAN--!
BUT, I NEVER SAW THAT NUTTY COSTUME BEFORE!
HANG THE COSTUME!! WE KNOW WHO WE'RE UP AGAINST!
IT SHOULD HAVE BEEN OBVIOUS-- RIGHT FROM THE START!

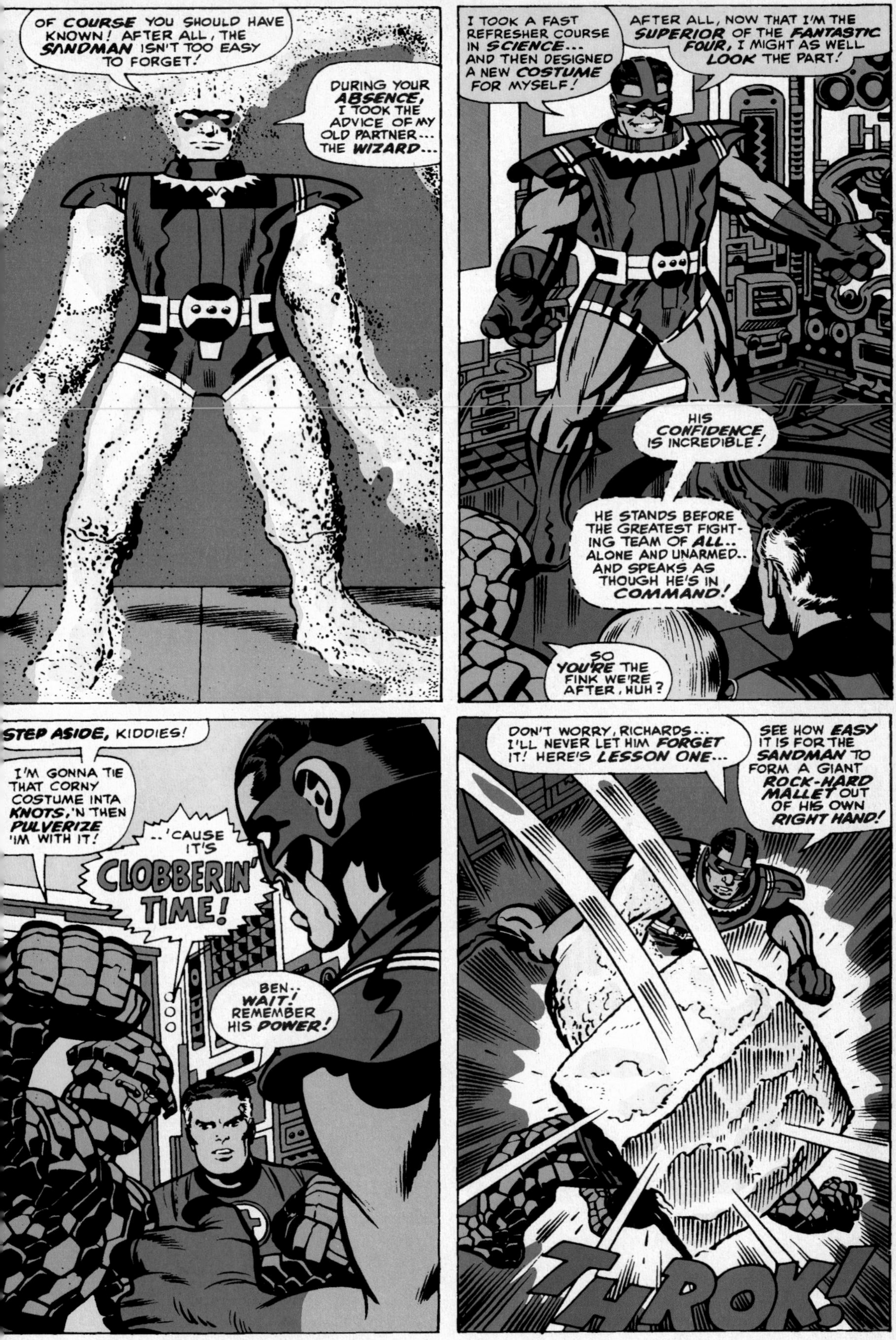
OF COURSE YOU SHOULD HAVE KNOWN! AFTER ALL, THE SANDMAN ISN'T TOO EASY TO FORGET!
DURING YOUR ABSENCE, I TOOK THE ADVICE OF MY OLD PARTNER--- THE WIZARD...
I TOOK A FAST REFRESHER COURSE IN SCIENCE... AND THEN DESIGNED A NEW COSTUME FOR MYSELF!
AFTER ALL, NOW THAT I'M THE SUPERIOR OF THE FANTASTIC FOUR, I MIGHT AS WELL LOOK THE PART!
HIS CONFIDENCE IS INCREDIBLE!
HE STANDS BEFORE THE GREATEST FIGHTING TEAM OF ALL.. ALONE AND UNARMED.. AND SPEAKS AS THOUGH HE'S IN COMMAND!
SO YOU'RE THE FINK WE'RE AFTER, HUH?
STEP ASIDE, KIDDIES!
I'M GONNA TIE THAT CORNY COSTUME INTA KNOTS, 'N THEN PULVERIZE 'IM WITH IT!
..'CAUSE IT'S
CLOBBERIN' TIME!
BEN.. WAIT! REMEMBER HIS POWER!
DON'T WORRY, RICHARDS... I'LL NEVER LET HIM FORGET IT! HERE'S LESSON ONE...
SEE HOW EASY IT IS FOR THE SANDMAN TO FORM A GIANT ROCK-HARD MALLET OUT OF HIS OWN RIGHT HAND!
THROK!

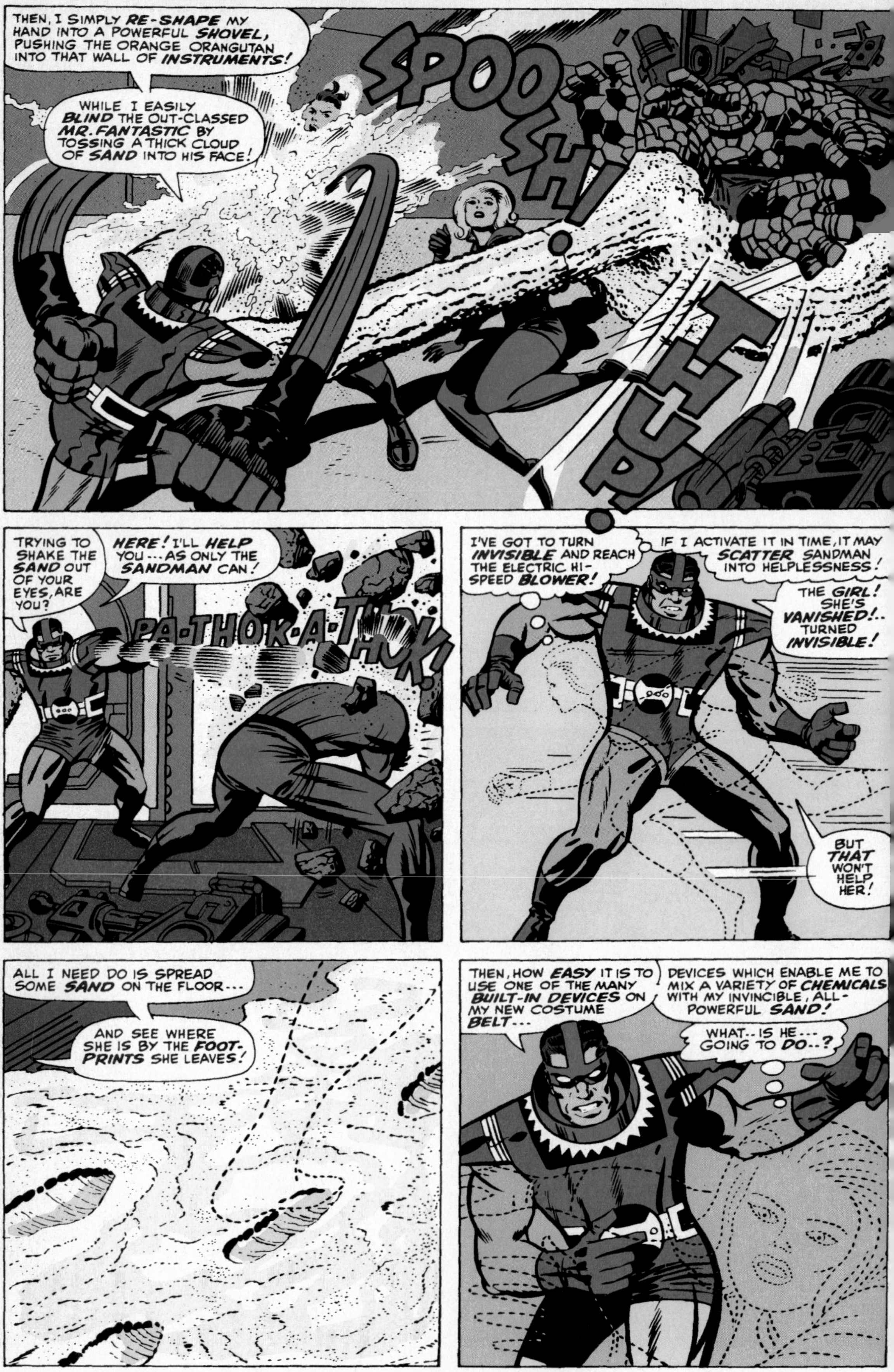
THEN, I SIMPLY RE-SHAPE MY HAND INTO A POWERFUL SHOVEL, PUSHING THE ORANGE ORANGUTAN INTO THAT WALL OF INSTRUMENTS!
WHILE I EASILY BLIND THE OUT-CLASSED MR. FANTASTIC BY TOSSING A THICK CLOUD OF SAND INTO HIS FACE!
SPOOSH!
THUP!
TRYING TO SHAKE THE SAND OUT OF YOUR EYES, ARE YOU?
HERE! I'LL HELP YOU... AS ONLY THE SANDMAN CAN!
PA-THOK-A-THOK!
I'VE GOT TO TURN INVISIBLE AND REACH THE ELECTRIC HI-SPEED BLOWER!
IF I ACTIVATE IT IN TIME, IT MAY SCATTER SANDMAN INTO HELPLESSNESS!
THE GIRL! SHE'S VANISHED!.. TURNED INVISIBLE!
BUT THAT WON'T HELP HER!
ALL I NEED DO IS SPREAD SOME SAND ON THE FLOOR...
AND SEE WHERE SHE IS BY THE FOOT-PRINTS SHE LEAVES!
THEN, HOW EASY IT IS TO USE ONE OF THE MANY BUILT-IN DEVICES ON MY NEW COSTUME BELT...
DEVICES WHICH ENABLE ME TO MIX A VARIETY OF CHEMICALS WITH MY INVINCIBLE, ALL-POWERFUL SAND!
WHAT-- IS HE... GOING TO DO--?

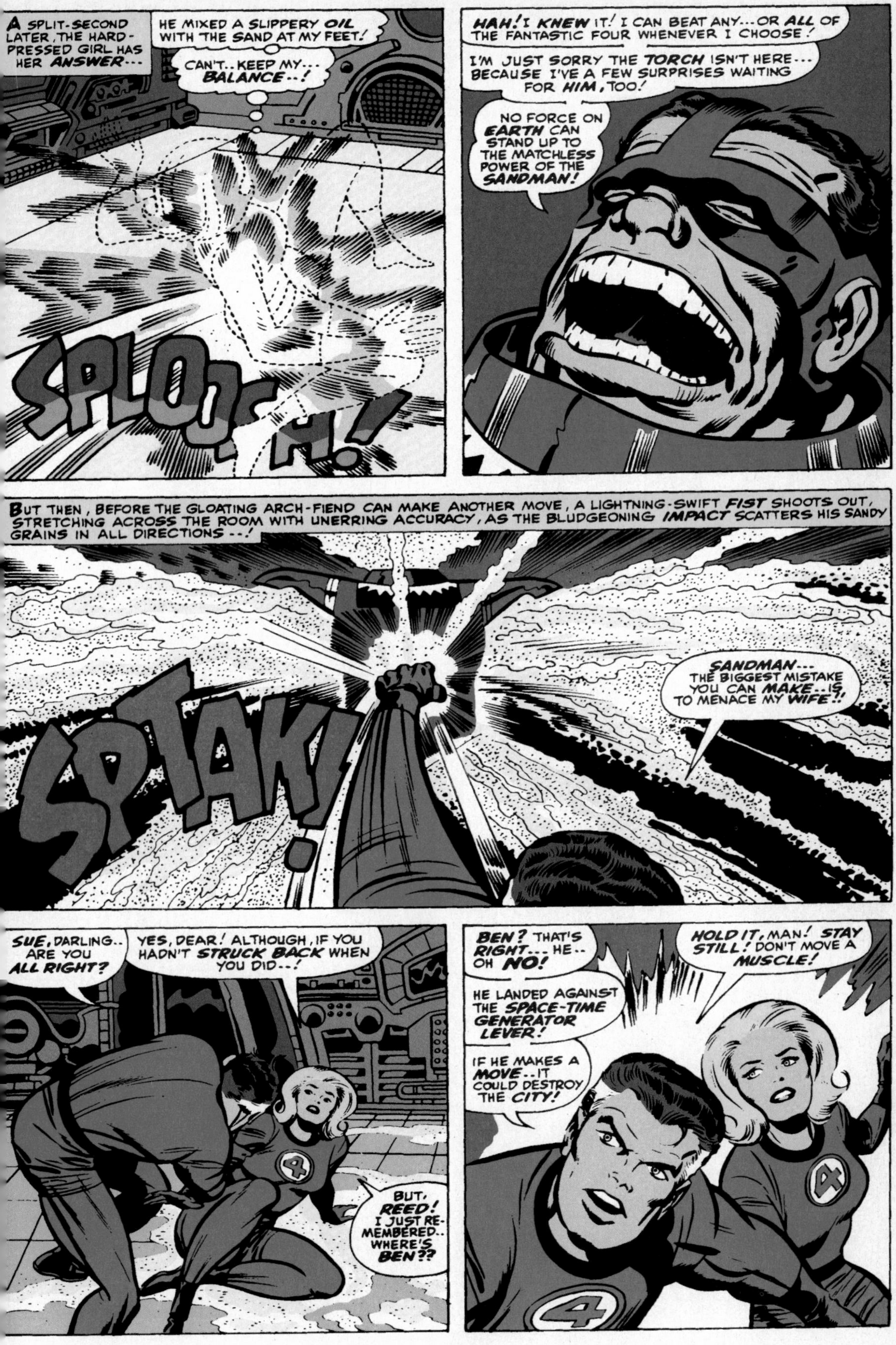
A SPLIT-SECOND LATER, THE HARD-PRESSED GIRL HAS HER ANSWER...
HE MIXED A SLIPPERY OIL WITH THE SAND AT MY FEET!
CAN'T.. KEEP MY... BALANCE--!
SPLOOSH!
HAH! I KNEW IT! I CAN BEAT ANY...OR ALL OF THE FANTASTIC FOUR WHENEVER I CHOOSE!
I'M JUST SORRY THE TORCH ISN'T HERE... BECAUSE I'VE A FEW SURPRISES WAITING FOR HIM, TOO!
NO FORCE ON EARTH CAN STAND UP TO THE MATCHLESS POWER OF THE SANDMAN!
BUT THEN, BEFORE THE GLOATING ARCH-FIEND CAN MAKE ANOTHER MOVE, A LIGHTNING-SWIFT FIST SHOOTS OUT, STRETCHING ACROSS THE ROOM WITH UNERRING ACCURACY, AS THE BLUDGEONING IMPACT SCATTERS HIS SANDY GRAINS IN ALL DIRECTIONS--!
SPTAK!
SANDMAN... THE BIGGEST MISTAKE YOU CAN MAKE.. IS TO MENACE MY WIFE?!
SUE, DARLING.. ARE YOU ALL RIGHT?
YES, DEAR! ALTHOUGH, IF YOU HADN'T STRUCK BACK WHEN YOU DID--!
BUT, REED! I JUST REMEMBERED.. WHERE'S BEN??
BEN? THAT'S RIGHT... HE.. OH NO!
HE LANDED AGAINST THE SPACE-TIME GENERATOR LEVER!
IF HE MAKES A MOVE.. IT COULD DESTROY THE CITY!
HOLD IT, MAN! STAY STILL! DON'T MOVE A MUSCLE!

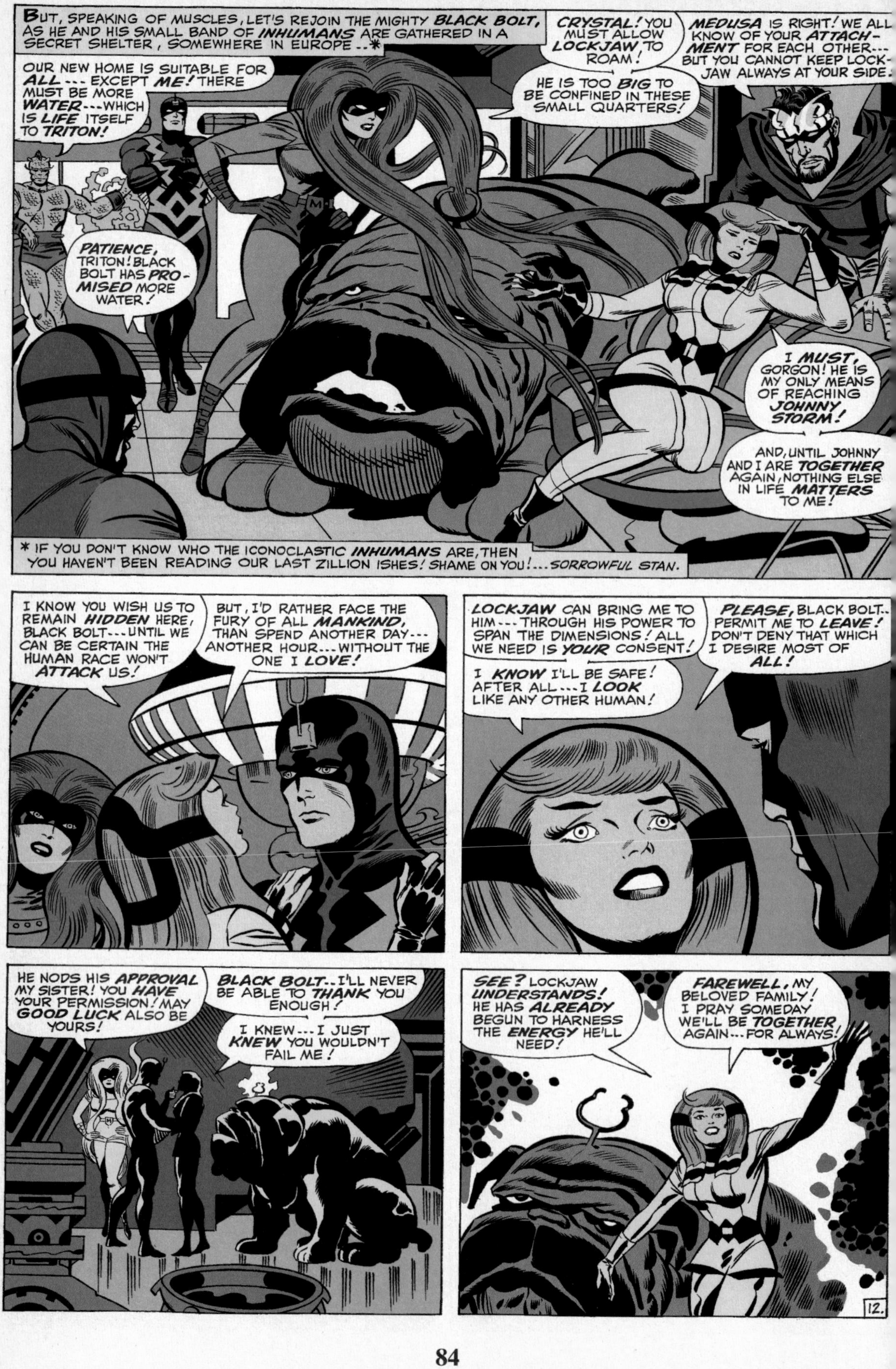

BUT, SPEAKING OF MUSCLES, LET'S REJOIN THE MIGHTY BLACK BOLT, AS HE AND HIS SMALL BAND OF INHUMANS ARE GATHERED IN A SECRET SHELTER, SOMEWHERE IN EUROPE..*
OUR NEW HOME IS SUITABLE FOR ALL... EXCEPT ME! THERE MUST BE MORE WATER...WHICH IS LIFE ITSELF TO TRITON!
CRYSTAL! YOU MUST ALLOW LOCKJAW TO ROAM!
HE IS TOO BIG TO BE CONFINED IN THESE SMALL QUARTERS!
MEDUSA IS RIGHT! WE ALL KNOW OF YOUR ATTACHMENT FOR EACH OTHER... BUT YOU CANNOT KEEP LOCKJAW ALWAYS AT YOUR SIDE!
PATIENCE, TRITON! BLACK BOLT HAS PROMISED MORE WATER!
I MUST, GORGON! HE IS MY ONLY MEANS OF REACHING JOHNNY STORM!
AND, UNTIL JOHNNY AND I ARE TOGETHER AGAIN, NOTHING ELSE IN LIFE MATTERS TO ME!
* IF YOU DON'T KNOW WHO THE ICONOCLASTIC INHUMANS ARE, THEN YOU HAVEN'T BEEN READING OUR LAST ZILLION ISHES! SHAME ON YOU!... SORROWFUL STAN.
I KNOW YOU WISH US TO REMAIN HIDDEN HERE, BLACK BOLT... UNTIL WE CAN BE CERTAIN THE HUMAN RACE WON'T ATTACK US!
BUT, I'D RATHER FACE THE FURY OF ALL MANKIND, THAN SPEND ANOTHER DAY... ANOTHER HOUR... WITHOUT THE ONE I LOVE!
LOCKJAW CAN BRING ME TO HIM... THROUGH HIS POWER TO SPAN THE DIMENSIONS! ALL WE NEED IS YOUR CONSENT!
I KNOW I'LL BE SAFE! AFTER ALL... I LOOK LIKE ANY OTHER HUMAN!
PLEASE, BLACK BOLT.. PERMIT ME TO LEAVE! DON'T DENY THAT WHICH I DESIRE MOST OF ALL!
HE NODS HIS APPROVAL MY SISTER! YOU HAVE YOUR PERMISSION! MAY GOOD LUCK ALSO BE YOURS!
BLACK BOLT.. I'LL NEVER BE ABLE TO THANK YOU ENOUGH!
I KNEW... I JUST KNEW YOU WOULDN'T FAIL ME!
SEE? LOCKJAW UNDERSTANDS! HE HAS ALREADY BEGUN TO HARNESS THE ENERGY HE'LL NEED!
FAREWELL, MY BELOVED FAMILY! I PRAY SOMEDAY WE'LL BE TOGETHER AGAIN... FOR ALWAYS!
12.

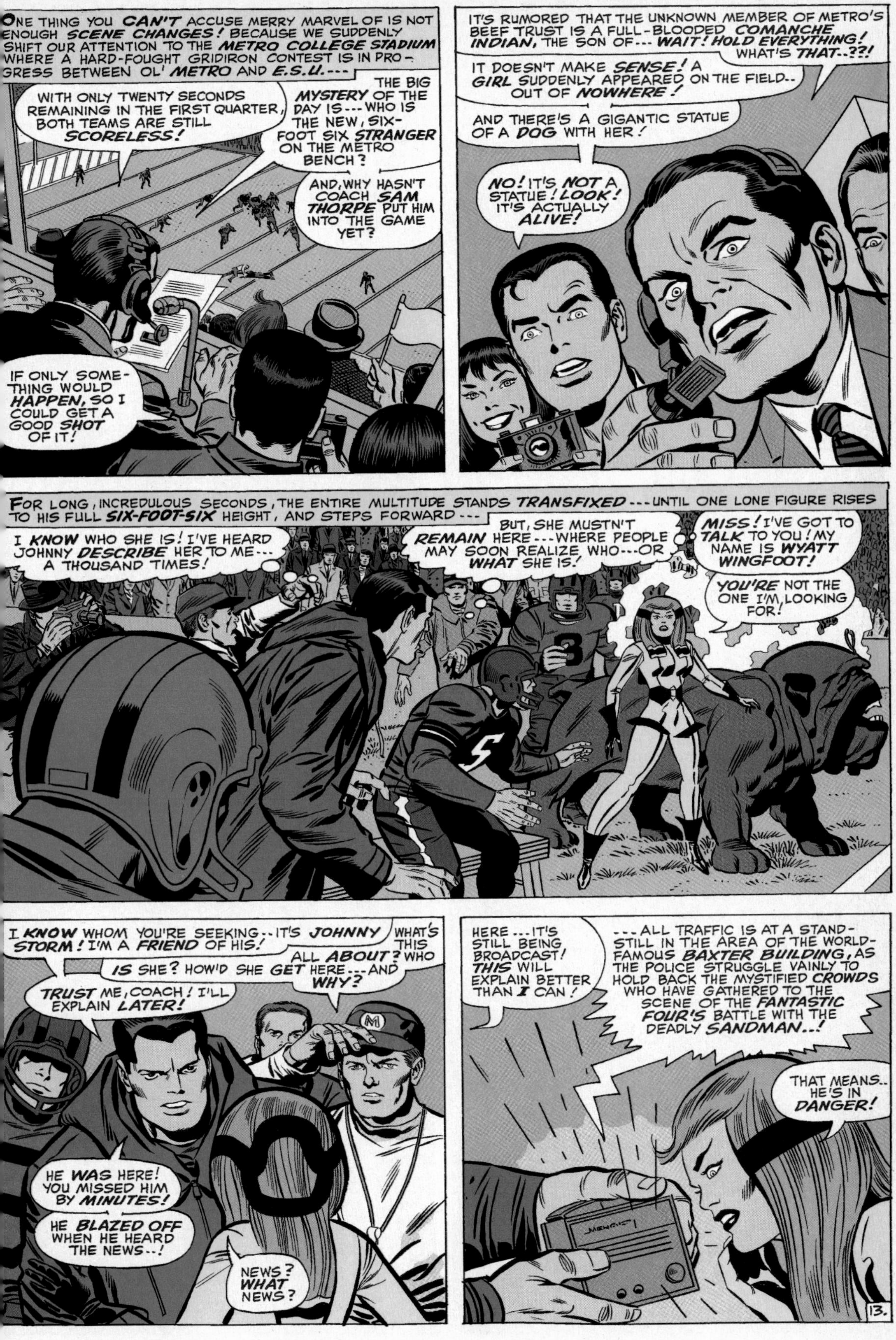
ONE THING YOU CAN'T ACCUSE MERRY MARVEL OF IS NOT ENOUGH SCENE CHANGES! BECAUSE WE SUDDENLY SHIFT OUR ATTENTION TO THE METRO COLLEGE STADIUM WHERE A HARD-FOUGHT GRIDIRON CONTEST IS IN PROGRESS BETWEEN OL' METRO AND E.S.U.---
WITH ONLY TWENTY SECONDS REMAINING IN THE FIRST QUARTER, BOTH TEAMS ARE STILL SCORELESS!
THE BIG MYSTERY OF THE DAY IS---WHO IS THE NEW, SIX-FOOT SIX STRANGER ON THE METRO BENCH?
AND, WHY HASN'T COACH SAM THORPE PUT HIM INTO THE GAME YET?
IF ONLY SOMETHING WOULD HAPPEN, SO I COULD GET A GOOD SHOT OF IT!
IT'S RUMORED THAT THE UNKNOWN MEMBER OF METRO'S BEEF TRUST IS A FULL-BLOODED COMANCHE INDIAN, THE SON OF--- WAIT! HOLD EVERYTHING! WHAT'S THAT-??!
IT DOESN'T MAKE SENSE! A GIRL SUDDENLY APPEARED ON THE FIELD.. OUT OF NOWHERE!
AND THERE'S A GIGANTIC STATUE OF A DOG WITH HER!
NO! IT'S NOT A STATUE! LOOK! IT'S ACTUALLY ALIVE!
FOR LONG, INCREDULOUS SECONDS, THE ENTIRE MULTITUDE STANDS TRANSFIXED---UNTIL ONE LONE FIGURE RISES TO HIS FULL SIX-FOOT-SIX HEIGHT, AND STEPS FORWARD---
I KNOW WHO SHE IS! I'VE HEARD JOHNNY DESCRIBE HER TO ME--- A THOUSAND TIMES!
BUT, SHE MUSTN'T REMAIN HERE---WHERE PEOPLE MAY SOON REALIZE WHO---OR WHAT SHE IS!
MISS! I'VE GOT TO TALK TO YOU! MY NAME IS WYATT WINGFOOT!
YOU'RE NOT THE ONE I'M LOOKING FOR!
I KNOW WHOM YOU'RE SEEKING--IT'S JOHNNY STORM! I'M A FRIEND OF HIS!
WHAT'S THIS ALL ABOUT? WHO IS SHE? HOW'D SHE GET HERE---AND WHY?
TRUST ME, COACH! I'LL EXPLAIN LATER!
HE WAS HERE! YOU MISSED HIM BY MINUTES!
HE BLAZED OFF WHEN HE HEARD THE NEWS--!
NEWS? WHAT NEWS?
HERE---IT'S STILL BEING BROADCAST! THIS WILL EXPLAIN BETTER THAN I CAN!
---ALL TRAFFIC IS AT A STANDSTILL IN THE AREA OF THE WORLD-FAMOUS BAXTER BUILDING, AS THE POLICE STRUGGLE VAINLY TO HOLD BACK THE MYSTIFIED CROWDS WHO HAVE GATHERED TO THE SCENE OF THE FANTASTIC FOUR'S BATTLE WITH THE DEADLY SANDMAN--!
THAT MEANS.. HE'S IN DANGER!
13.

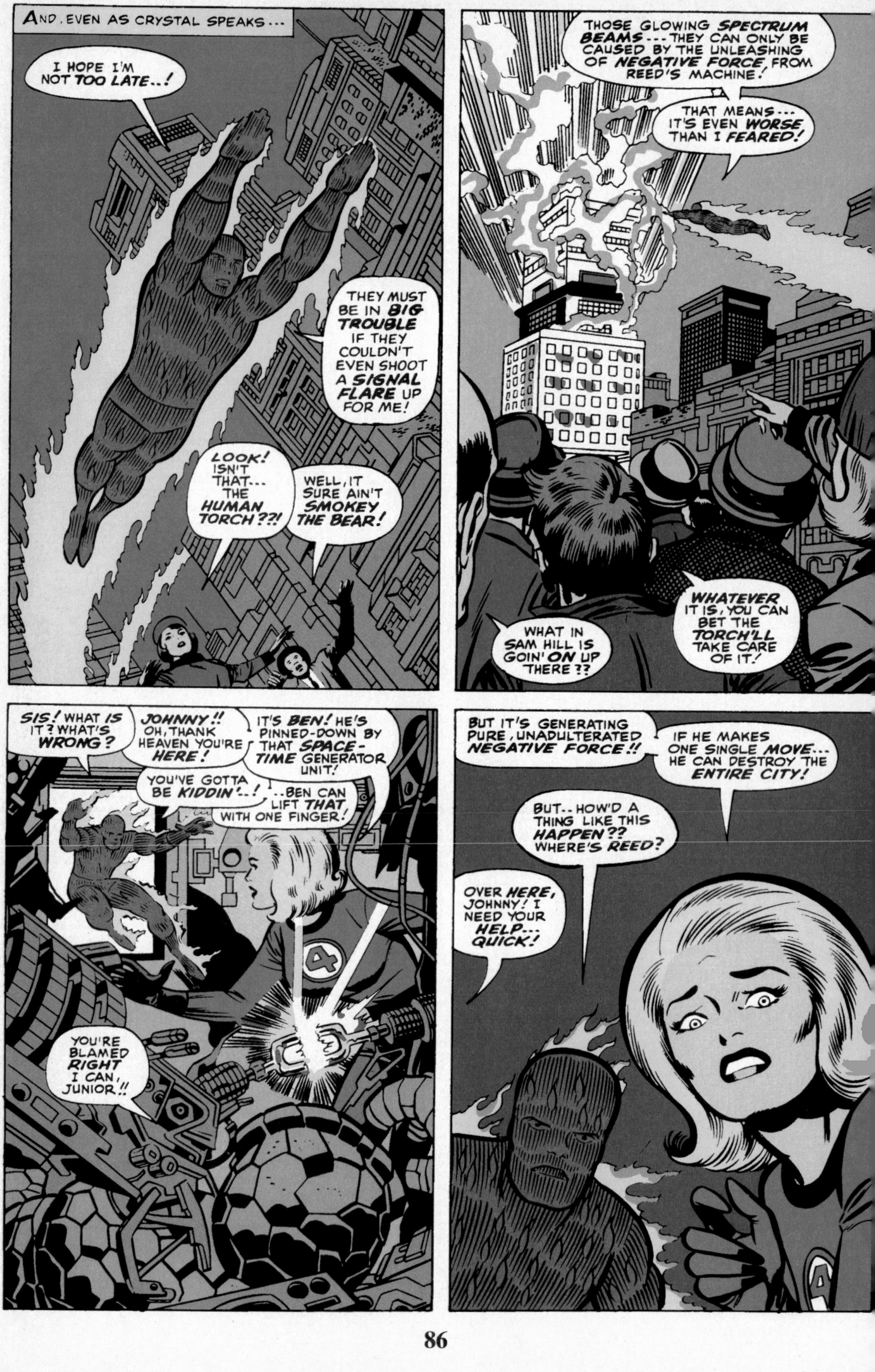
AND, EVEN AS CRYSTAL SPEAKS...
I HOPE I'M NOT TOO LATE..!
THEY MUST BE IN BIG TROUBLE IF THEY COULDN'T EVEN SHOOT A SIGNAL FLARE UP FOR ME!
LOOK! ISN'T THAT... THE HUMAN TORCH??!
WELL, IT SURE AIN'T SMOKEY THE BEAR!
THOSE GLOWING SPECTRUM BEAMS--- THEY CAN ONLY BE CAUSED BY THE UNLEASHING OF NEGATIVE FORCE, FROM REED'S MACHINE!
THAT MEANS... IT'S EVEN WORSE THAN I FEARED!
WHAT IN SAM HILL IS GOIN' ON UP THERE??
WHATEVER IT IS, YOU CAN BET THE TORCH'LL TAKE CARE OF IT!
SIS! WHAT IS IT? WHAT'S WRONG?
JOHNNY!! OH, THANK HEAVEN YOU'RE HERE!
IT'S BEN! HE'S PINNED-DOWN BY THAT SPACE-TIME GENERATOR UNIT!
YOU'VE GOTTA BE KIDDIN'..!
..BEN CAN LIFT THAT WITH ONE FINGER!
YOU'RE BLAMED RIGHT I CAN, JUNIOR!!
BUT IT'S GENERATING PURE, UNADULTERATED NEGATIVE FORCE!!
IF HE MAKES ONE SINGLE MOVE... HE CAN DESTROY THE ENTIRE CITY!
BUT.. HOW'D A THING LIKE THIS HAPPEN?? WHERE'S REED?
OVER HERE, JOHNNY! I NEED YOUR HELP... QUICK!

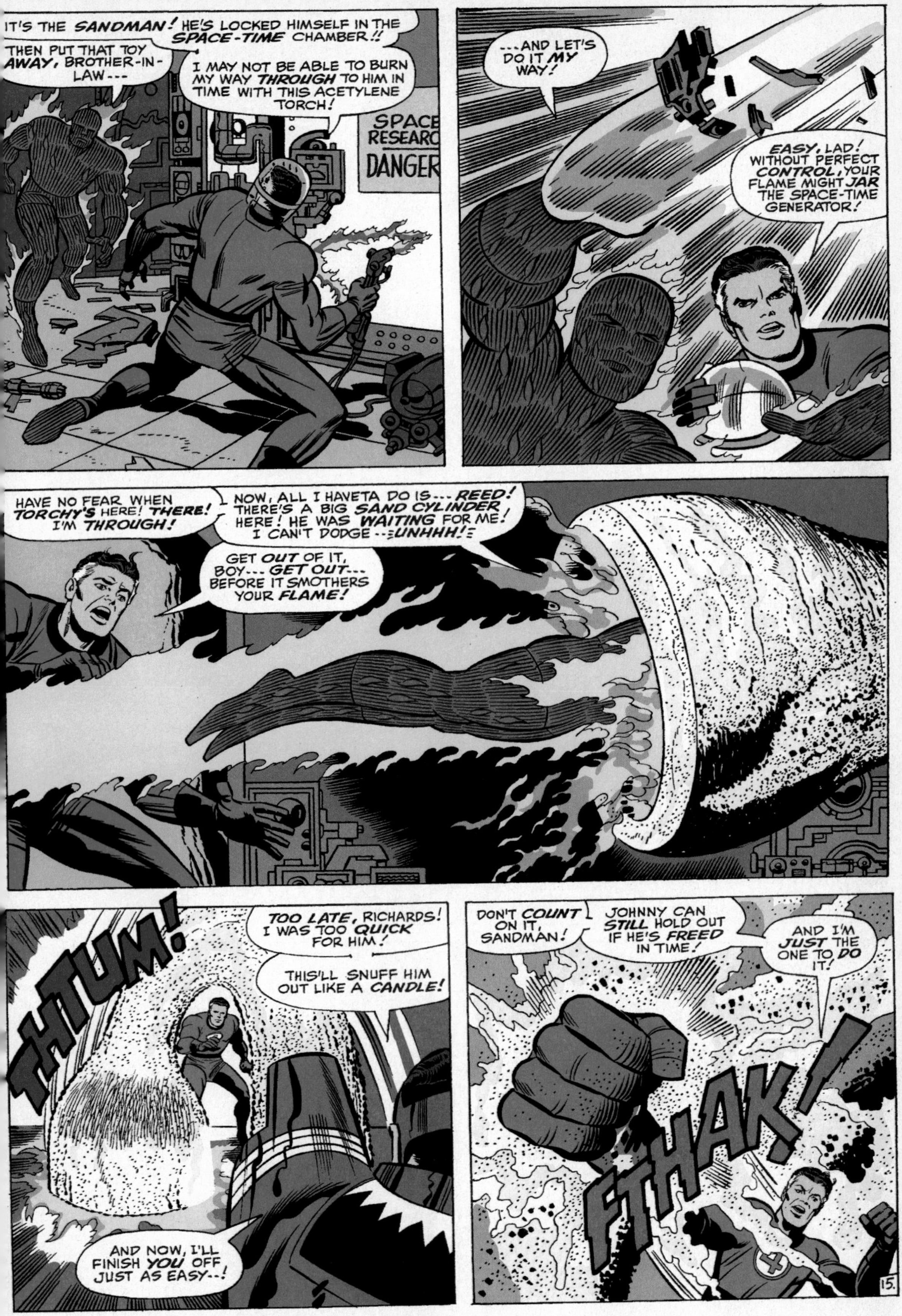
IT'S THE SANDMAN! HE'S LOCKED HIMSELF IN THE SPACE-TIME CHAMBER!!
THEN PUT THAT TOY AWAY, BROTHER-IN-LAW---
I MAY NOT BE ABLE TO BURN MY WAY THROUGH TO HIM IN TIME WITH THIS ACETYLENE TORCH!
SPACE RESEARC
DANGER
---AND LET'S DO IT MY WAY!
EASY, LAD! WITHOUT PERFECT CONTROL, YOUR FLAME MIGHT JAR THE SPACE-TIME GENERATOR!
HAVE NO FEAR WHEN TORCHY'S HERE! THERE! I'M THROUGH!
NOW, ALL I HAVETA DO IS... REED! THERE'S A BIG SAND CYLINDER HERE! HE WAS WAITING FOR ME! I CAN'T DODGE --UNHHH!
GET OUT OF IT, BOY... GET OUT... BEFORE IT SMOTHERS YOUR FLAME!
THTUM!
TOO LATE, RICHARDS! I WAS TOO QUICK FOR HIM!
THIS'LL SNUFF HIM OUT LIKE A CANDLE!
AND NOW, I'LL FINISH YOU OFF JUST AS EASY--!
DON'T COUNT ON IT, SANDMAN!
JOHNNY CAN STILL HOLD OUT IF HE'S FREED IN TIME!
AND I'M JUST THE ONE TO DO IT!
FTHAK!
15.

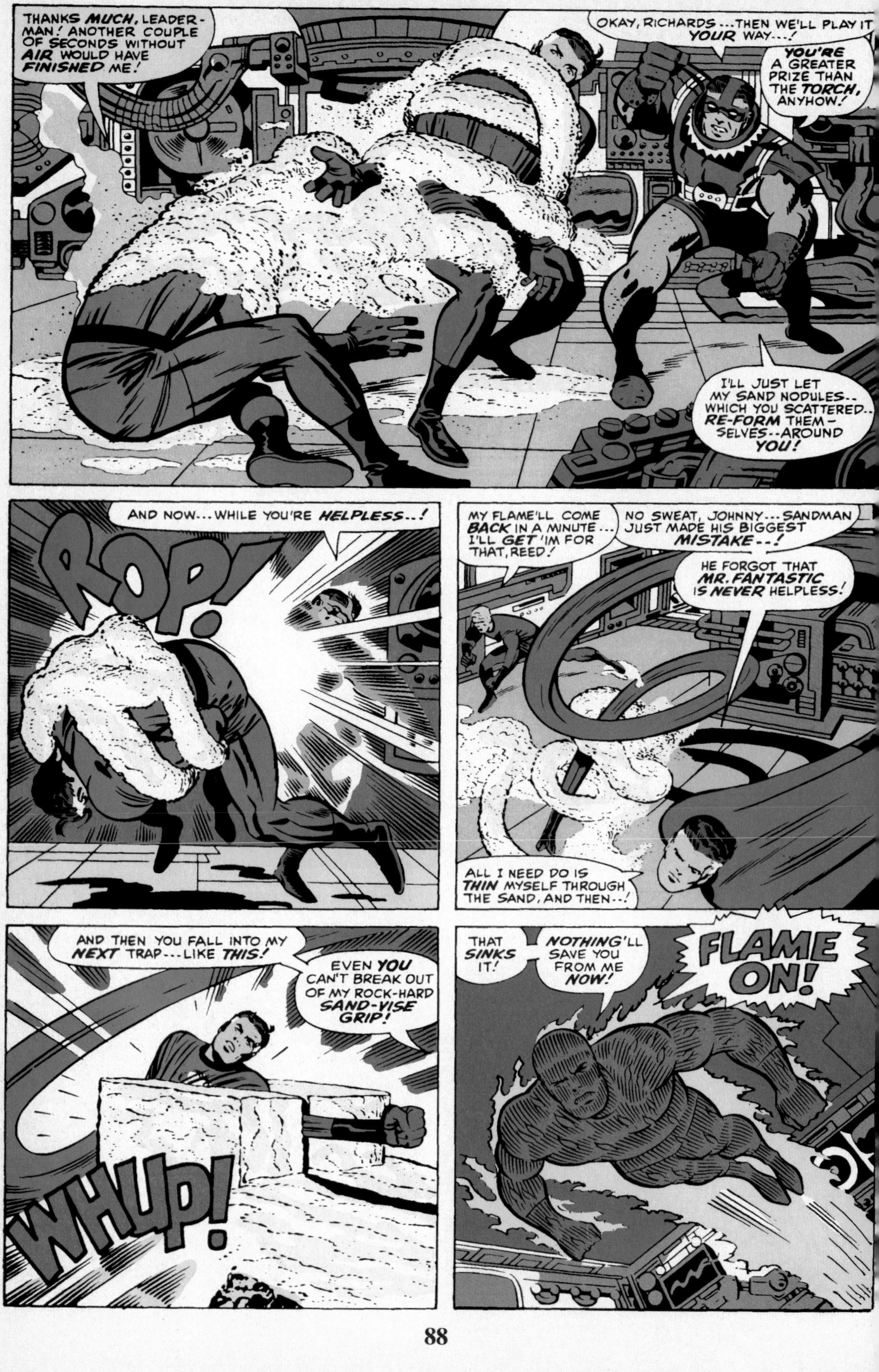
THANKS MUCH, LEADER-MAN! ANOTHER COUPLE OF SECONDS WITHOUT AIR WOULD HAVE FINISHED ME!
OKAY, RICHARDS...THEN WE'LL PLAY IT YOUR WAY...!
YOU'RE A GREATER PRIZE THAN THE TORCH, ANYHOW!
I'LL JUST LET MY SAND NODULES.. WHICH YOU SCATTERED.. RE-FORM THEM-SELVES--AROUND YOU!
AND NOW...WHILE YOU'RE HELPLESS..!
ROP!
MY FLAME'LL COME BACK IN A MINUTE... I'LL GET 'IM FOR THAT, REED!
NO SWEAT, JOHNNY...SANDMAN JUST MADE HIS BIGGEST MISTAKE--!
HE FORGOT THAT MR. FANTASTIC IS NEVER HELPLESS!
ALL I NEED DO IS THIN MYSELF THROUGH THE SAND, AND THEN--!
AND THEN YOU FALL INTO MY NEXT TRAP...LIKE THIS!
EVEN YOU CAN'T BREAK OUT OF MY ROCK-HARD SAND-VISE GRIP!
WHUP!
THAT SINKS IT!
NOTHING'LL SAVE YOU FROM ME NOW!
FLAME ON!

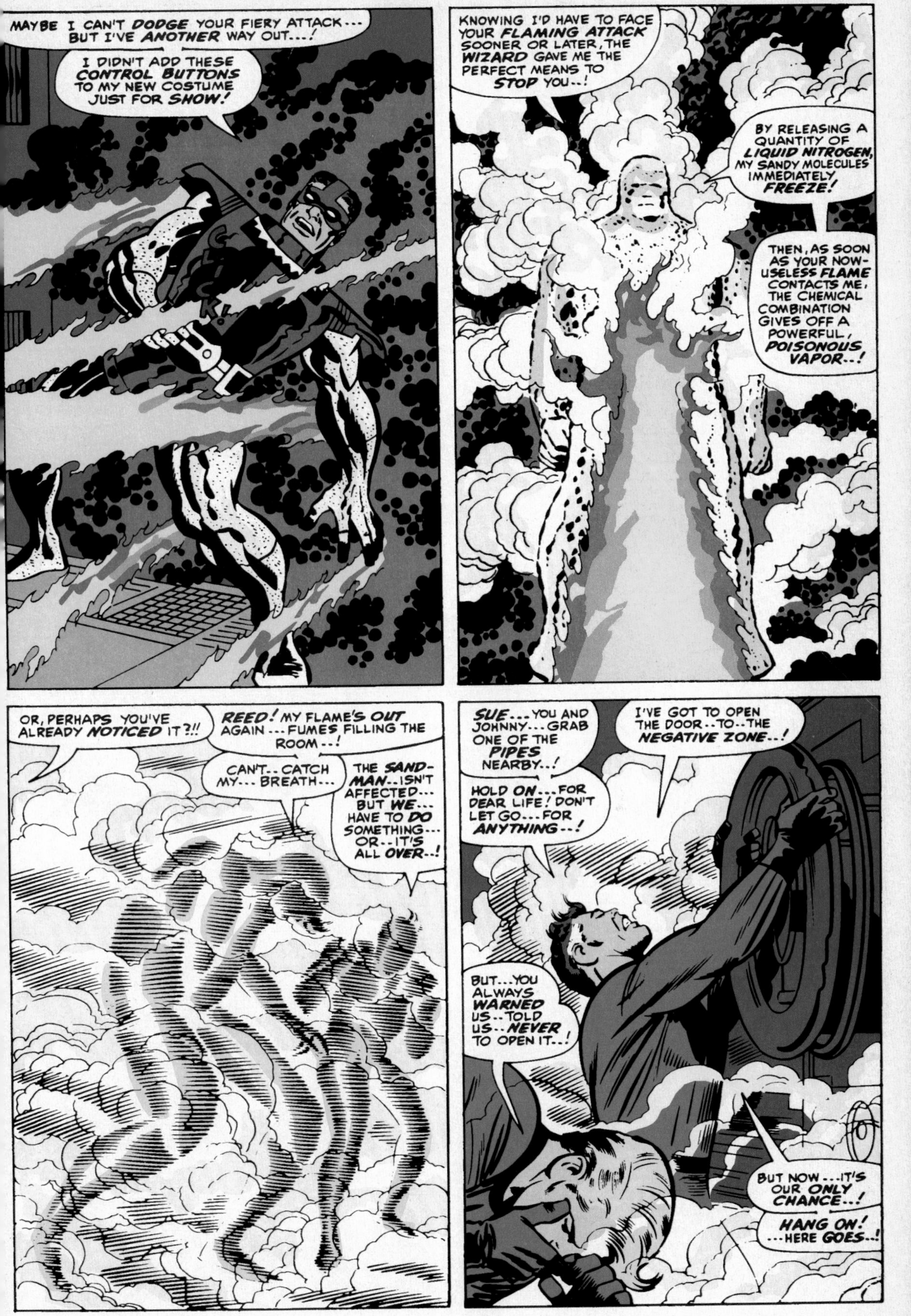
MAYBE I CAN'T DODGE YOUR FIERY ATTACK... BUT I'VE ANOTHER WAY OUT...!
I DIDN'T ADD THESE CONTROL BUTTONS TO MY NEW COSTUME JUST FOR SHOW!
KNOWING I'D HAVE TO FACE YOUR FLAMING ATTACK SOONER OR LATER, THE WIZARD GAVE ME THE PERFECT MEANS TO STOP YOU...!
BY RELEASING A QUANTITY OF LIQUID NITROGEN, MY SANDY MOLECULES IMMEDIATELY FREEZE!
THEN, AS SOON AS YOUR NOW-USELESS FLAME CONTACTS ME, THE CHEMICAL COMBINATION GIVES OFF A POWERFUL, POISONOUS VAPOR..!
OR, PERHAPS YOU'VE ALREADY NOTICED IT?!!
REED! MY FLAME'S OUT AGAIN... FUMES FILLING THE ROOM..!
CAN'T.. CATCH MY... BREATH...
THE SAND-MAN..ISN'T AFFECTED... BUT WE... HAVE TO DO SOMETHING... OR..IT'S ALL OVER..!
SUE... YOU AND JOHNNY.. GRAB ONE OF THE PIPES NEARBY..!
HOLD ON... FOR DEAR LIFE! DON'T LET GO... FOR ANYTHING..!
I'VE GOT TO OPEN THE DOOR..TO..THE NEGATIVE ZONE..!
BUT...YOU ALWAYS WARNED US..TOLD US..NEVER TO OPEN IT..!
BUT NOW...IT'S OUR ONLY CHANCE..!
HANG ON! ...HERE GOES..!

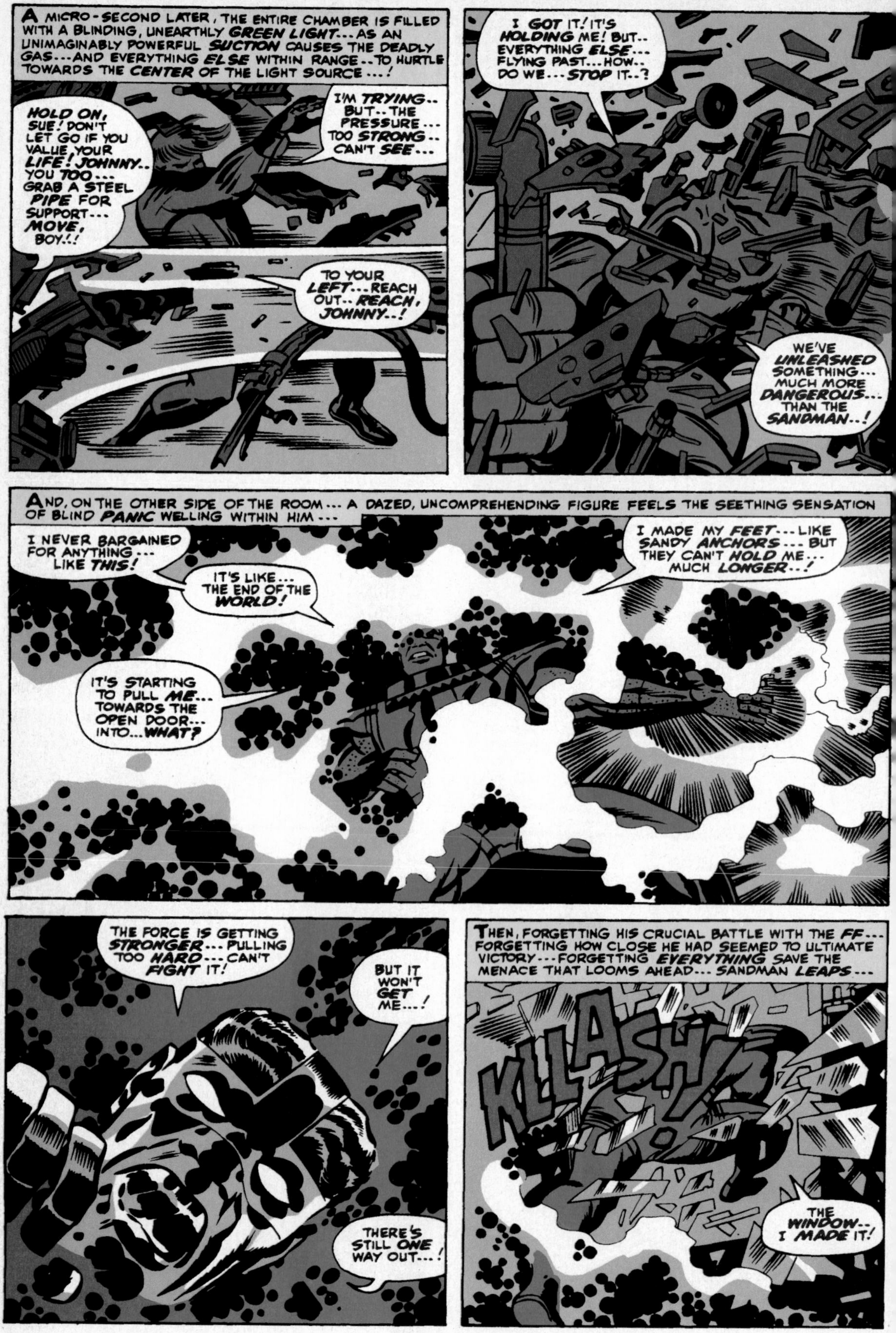
A MICRO-SECOND LATER, THE ENTIRE CHAMBER IS FILLED WITH A BLINDING, UNEARTHLY GREEN LIGHT... AS AN UNIMAGINABLY POWERFUL SUCTION CAUSES THE DEADLY GAS... AND EVERYTHING ELSE WITHIN RANGE -- TO HURTLE TOWARDS THE CENTER OF THE LIGHT SOURCE...!
HOLD ON, SUE! DON'T LET GO IF YOU VALUE YOUR LIFE! JOHNNY.. YOU TOO... GRAB A STEEL PIPE FOR SUPPORT... MOVE, BOY!!
I'M TRYING.. BUT.. THE PRESSURE... TOO STRONG... CAN'T SEE...
TO YOUR LEFT... REACH OUT.. REACH, JOHNNY..!
I GOT IT! IT'S HOLDING ME! BUT.. EVERYTHING ELSE... FLYING PAST... HOW.. DO WE... STOP IT..?
WE'VE UNLEASHED SOMETHING... MUCH MORE DANGEROUS... THAN THE SANDMAN..!
AND, ON THE OTHER SIDE OF THE ROOM... A DAZED, UNCOMPREHENDING FIGURE FEELS THE SEETHING SENSATION OF BLIND PANIC WELLING WITHIN HIM...
I NEVER BARGAINED FOR ANYTHING... LIKE THIS!
IT'S LIKE... THE END OF THE WORLD!
I MADE MY FEET... LIKE SANDY ANCHORS... BUT THEY CAN'T HOLD ME... MUCH LONGER..!
IT'S STARTING TO PULL ME... TOWARDS THE OPEN DOOR... INTO... WHAT?
THE FORCE IS GETTING STRONGER... PULLING TOO HARD... CAN'T FIGHT IT!
BUT IT WON'T GET ME...!
THERE'S STILL ONE WAY OUT...!
THEN, FORGETTING HIS CRUCIAL BATTLE WITH THE FF... FORGETTING HOW CLOSE HE HAD SEEMED TO ULTIMATE VICTORY... FORGETTING EVERYTHING SAVE THE MENACE THAT LOOMS AHEAD... SANDMAN LEAPS...
KLLASH!
THE WINDOW.. I MADE IT!

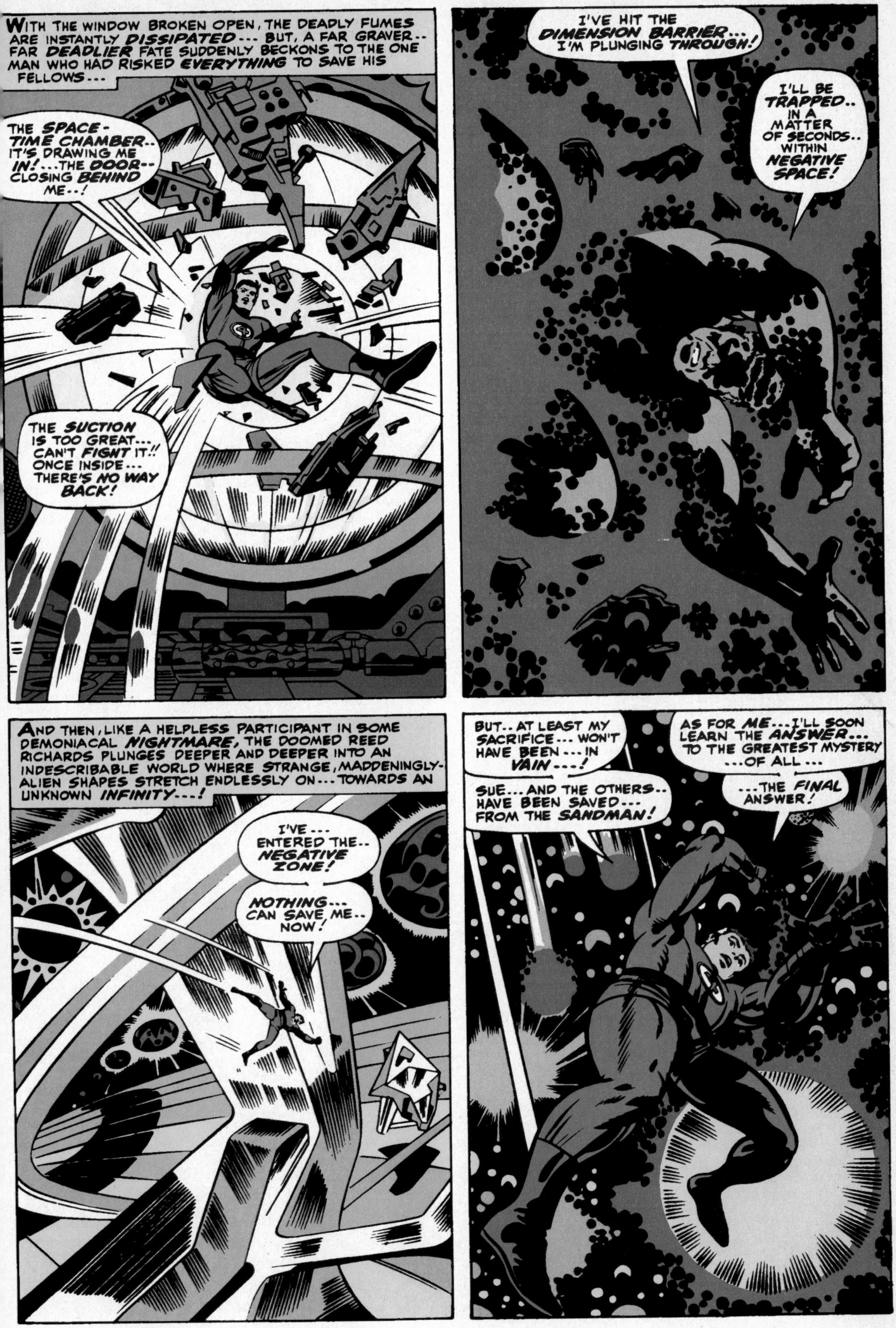
WITH THE WINDOW BROKEN OPEN, THE DEADLY FUMES ARE INSTANTLY DISSIPATED... BUT, A FAR GRAVER-- FAR DEADLIER FATE SUDDENLY BECKONS TO THE ONE MAN WHO HAD RISKED EVERYTHING TO SAVE HIS FELLOWS...
THE SPACE-TIME CHAMBER.. IT'S DRAWING ME IN!...THE DOOR-- CLOSING BEHIND ME--!
THE SUCTION IS TOO GREAT... CAN'T FIGHT IT!! ONCE INSIDE... THERE'S NO WAY BACK!
I'VE HIT THE DIMENSION BARRIER... I'M PLUNGING THROUGH!
I'LL BE TRAPPED.. IN A MATTER OF SECONDS.. WITHIN NEGATIVE SPACE!
AND THEN, LIKE A HELPLESS PARTICIPANT IN SOME DEMONIACAL NIGHTMARE, THE DOOMED REED RICHARDS PLUNGES DEEPER AND DEEPER INTO AN INDESCRIBABLE WORLD WHERE STRANGE, MADDENINGLY-ALIEN SHAPES STRETCH ENDLESSLY ON... TOWARDS AN UNKNOWN INFINITY...!
I'VE... ENTERED THE.. NEGATIVE ZONE!
NOTHING... CAN SAVE ME.. NOW!
BUT.. AT LEAST MY SACRIFICE... WON'T HAVE BEEN... IN VAIN...!
SUE... AND THE OTHERS.. HAVE BEEN SAVED... FROM THE SANDMAN!
AS FOR ME... I'LL SOON LEARN THE ANSWER... TO THE GREATEST MYSTERY... OF ALL...
...THE FINAL ANSWER!

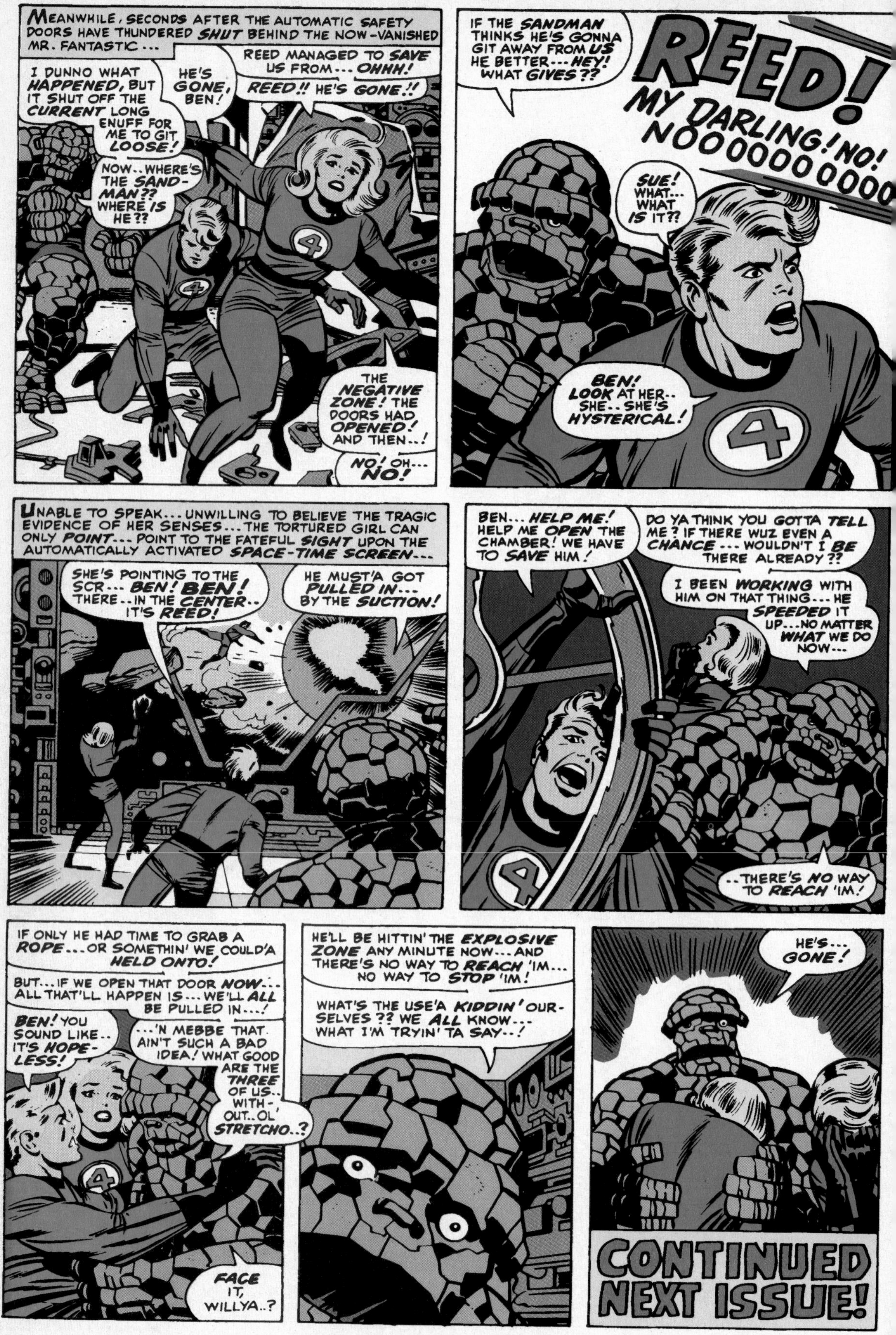
MEANWHILE, SECONDS AFTER THE AUTOMATIC SAFETY DOORS HAVE THUNDERED SHUT BEHIND THE NOW-VANISHED MR. FANTASTIC...
I DUNNO WHAT HAPPENED, BUT IT SHUT OFF THE CURRENT LONG ENUFF FOR ME TO GIT LOOSE!
HE'S GONE, BEN!
REED MANAGED TO SAVE US FROM... OHHH!
REED!! HE'S GONE!!
NOW.. WHERE'S THE SAND-MAN?? WHERE IS HE??
THE NEGATIVE ZONE! THE DOORS HAD OPENED! AND THEN..!
NO! OH... NO!
IF THE SANDMAN THINKS HE'S GONNA GIT AWAY FROM US HE BETTER--- HEY! WHAT GIVES??
REED! MY DARLING! NO! NOOOOOOOOOOO
SUE! WHAT... WHAT IS IT??
BEN! LOOK AT HER.. SHE.. SHE'S HYSTERICAL!
UNABLE TO SPEAK... UNWILLING TO BELIEVE THE TRAGIC EVIDENCE OF HER SENSES... THE TORTURED GIRL CAN ONLY POINT... POINT TO THE FATEFUL SIGHT UPON THE AUTOMATICALLY ACTIVATED SPACE-TIME SCREEN...
SHE'S POINTING TO THE SCR... BEN! BEN! THERE.. IN THE CENTER.. IT'S REED!
HE MUST'A GOT PULLED IN... BY THE SUCTION!
BEN... HELP ME! HELP ME OPEN THE CHAMBER! WE HAVE TO SAVE HIM!
DO YA THINK YOU GOTTA TELL ME? IF THERE WUZ EVEN A CHANCE... WOULDN'T I BE THERE ALREADY??
I BEEN WORKING WITH HIM ON THAT THING... HE SPEEDED IT UP... NO MATTER WHAT WE DO NOW...
..THERE'S NO WAY TO REACH 'IM!
IF ONLY HE HAD TIME TO GRAB A ROPE... OR SOMETHIN' WE COULD'A HELD ONTO!
BUT... IF WE OPEN THAT DOOR NOW... ALL THAT'LL HAPPEN IS... WE'LL ALL BE PULLED IN...!
BEN! YOU SOUND LIKE.. IT'S HOPE-LESS!
...'N MEBBE THAT AIN'T SUCH A BAD IDEA! WHAT GOOD ARE THE THREE OF US.. WITH-OUT.. OL' STRETCHO..?
FACE IT, WILLYA..?
HE'LL BE HITTIN' THE EXPLOSIVE ZONE ANY MINUTE NOW... AND THERE'S NO WAY TO REACH 'IM... NO WAY TO STOP 'IM!
WHAT'S THE USE'A KIDDIN' OUR-SELVES?? WE ALL KNOW... WHAT I'M TRYIN' TA SAY..!
HE'S... GONE!
CONTINUED NEXT ISSUE!

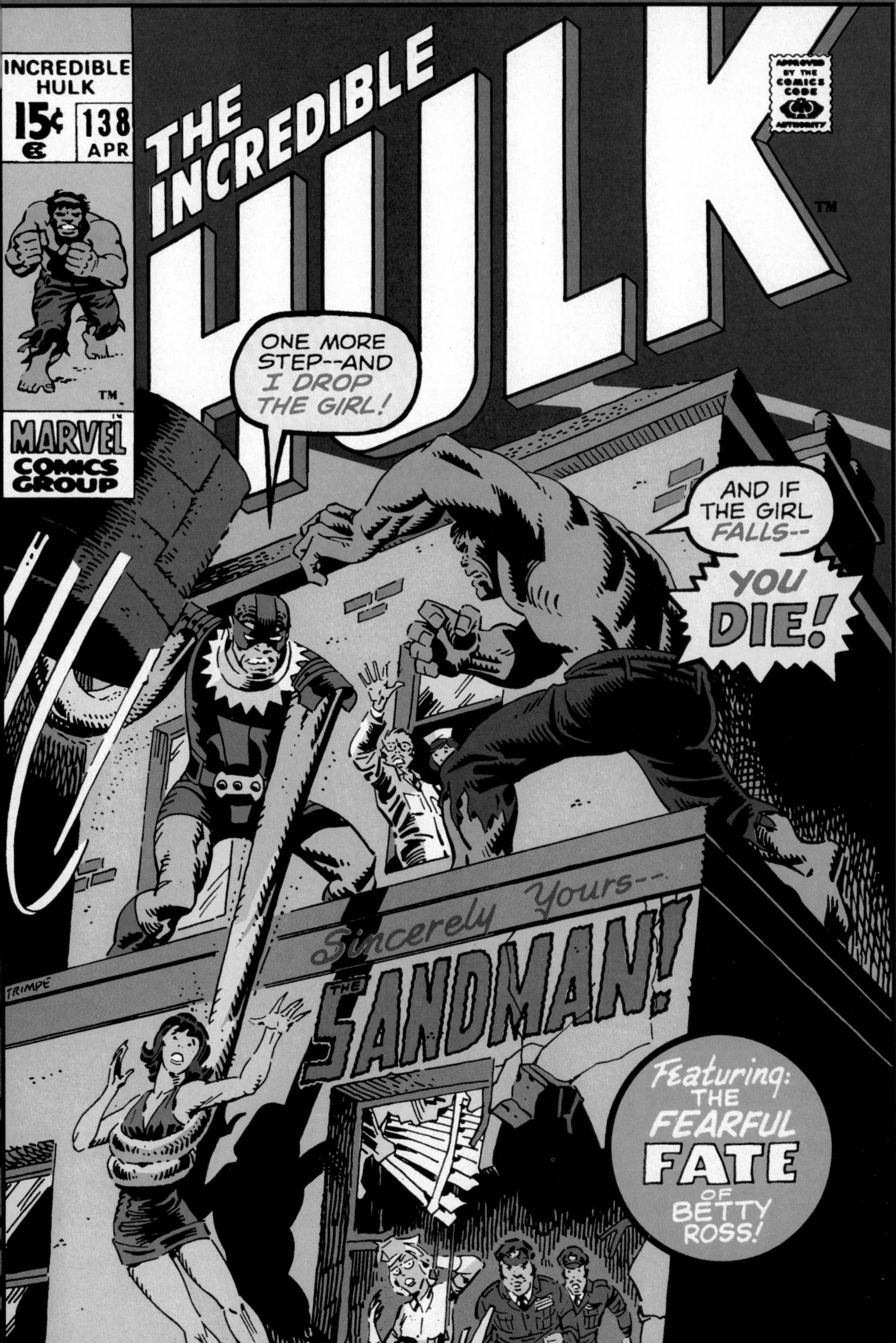
INCREDIBLE HULK
15¢
138 APR
THE INCREDIBLE HULK
TM
MARVEL COMICS GROUP
ONE MORE STEP--AND I DROP THE GIRL!
AND IF THE GIRL FALLS--
YOU DIE!
Sincerely Yours--
THE SANDMAN!
TRIMPE
Featuring: THE FEARFUL FATE OF BETTY ROSS!

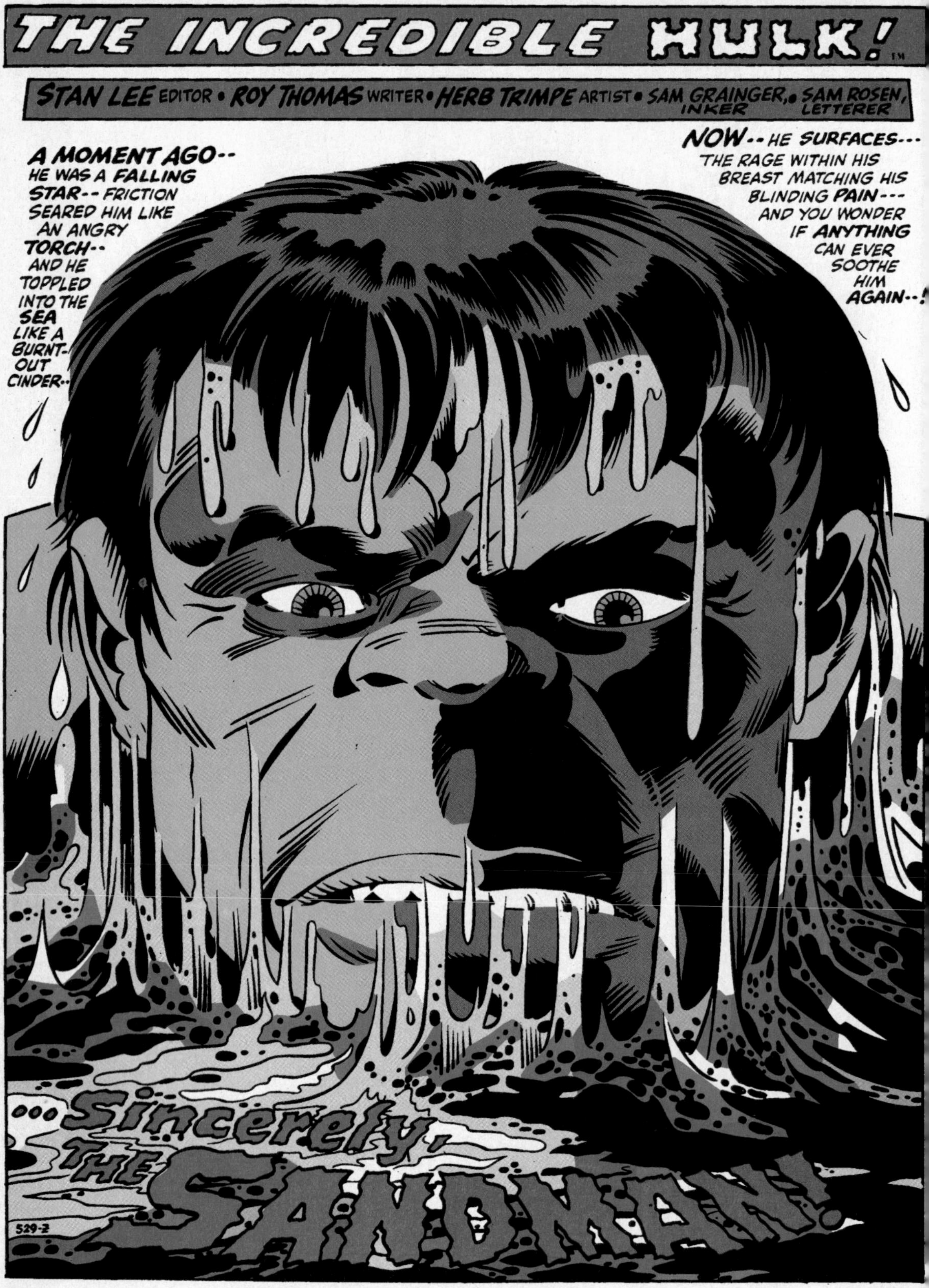
THE INCREDIBLE HULK!
STAN LEE EDITOR • ROY THOMAS WRITER • HERB TRIMPE ARTIST • SAM GRAINGER, INKER • SAM ROSEN, LETTERER
A MOMENT AGO-- HE WAS A FALLING STAR-- FRICTION SEARED HIM LIKE AN ANGRY TORCH-- AND HE TOPPLED INTO THE SEA LIKE A BURNT-OUT CINDER--
NOW-- HE SURFACES--- THE RAGE WITHIN HIS BREAST MATCHING HIS BLINDING PAIN--- AND YOU WONDER IF ANYTHING CAN EVER SOOTHE HIM AGAIN--!
...Sincerely, THE SANDMAN!
529-2

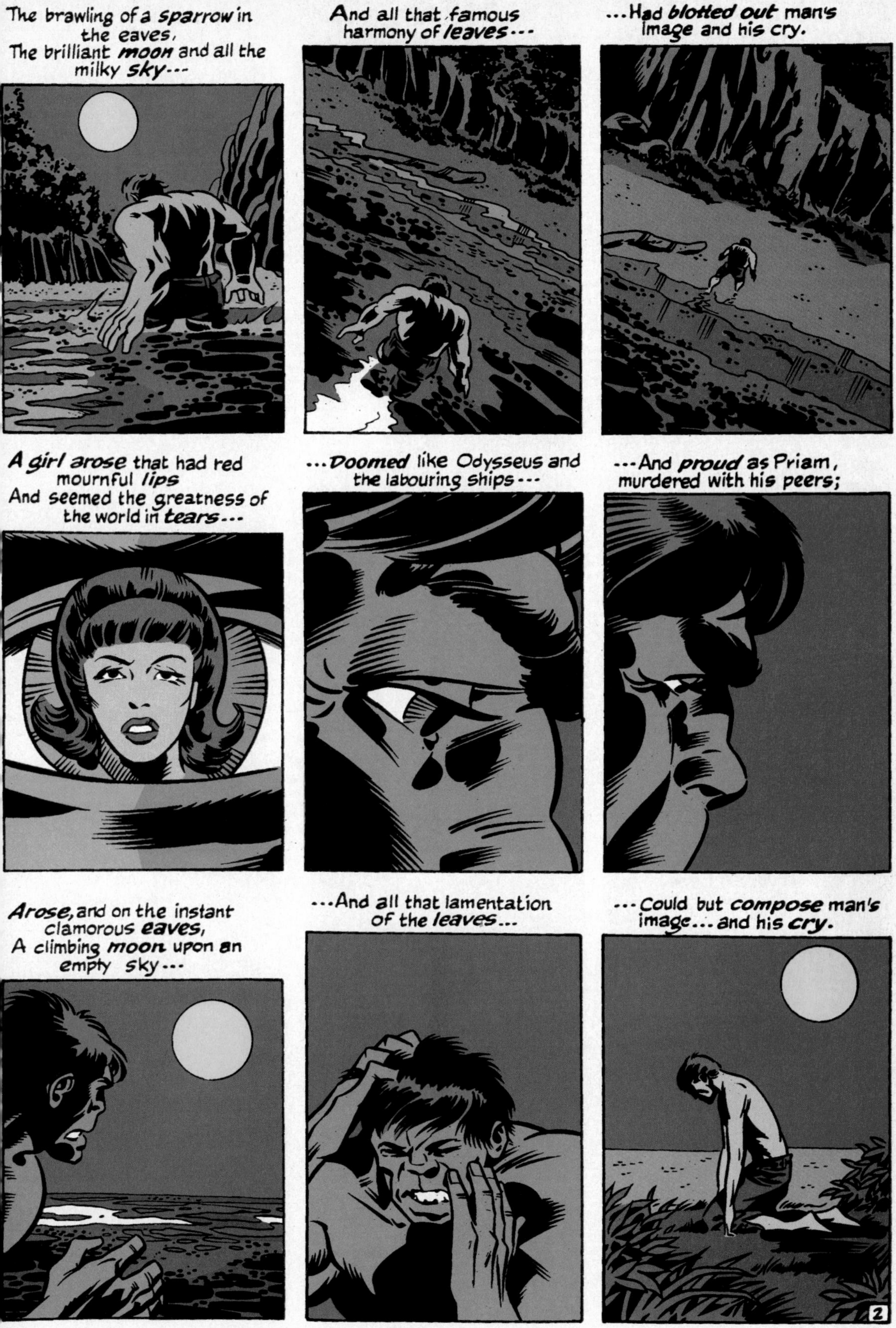

The brawling of a sparrow in the eaves,
The brilliant moon and all the milky sky---
And all that famous harmony of leaves---
...Had blotted out man's image and his cry.
A girl arose that had red mournful lips
And seemed the greatness of the world in tears---
...Doomed like Odysseus and the labouring ships---
---And proud as Priam, murdered with his peers;
Arose, and on the instant clamorous eaves,
A climbing moon upon an empty sky---
---And all that lamentation of the leaves...
---Could but compose man's image... and his cry.
2

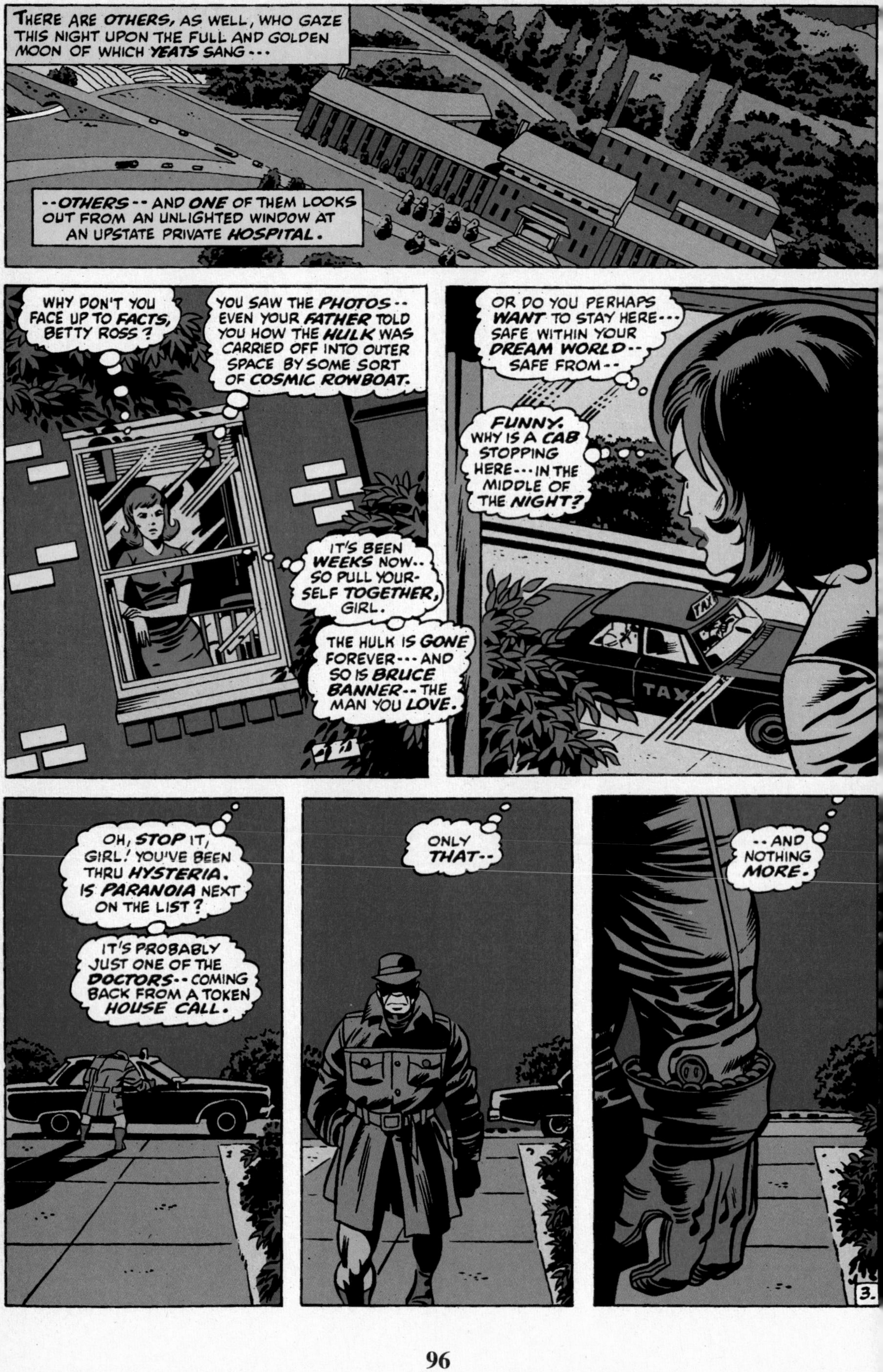
THERE ARE OTHERS, AS WELL, WHO GAZE THIS NIGHT UPON THE FULL AND GOLDEN MOON OF WHICH YEATS SANG...
--OTHERS-- AND ONE OF THEM LOOKS OUT FROM AN UNLIGHTED WINDOW AT AN UPSTATE PRIVATE HOSPITAL.
WHY DON'T YOU FACE UP TO FACTS, BETTY ROSS?
YOU SAW THE PHOTOS-- EVEN YOUR FATHER TOLD YOU HOW THE HULK WAS CARRIED OFF INTO OUTER SPACE BY SOME SORT OF COSMIC ROWBOAT.
IT'S BEEN WEEKS NOW.. SO PULL YOURSELF TOGETHER, GIRL.
THE HULK IS GONE FOREVER--- AND SO IS BRUCE BANNER-- THE MAN YOU LOVE.
OR DO YOU PERHAPS WANT TO STAY HERE--- SAFE WITHIN YOUR DREAM WORLD-- SAFE FROM--
FUNNY. WHY IS A CAB STOPPING HERE--- IN THE MIDDLE OF THE NIGHT?
TAXI
OH, STOP IT, GIRL! YOU'VE BEEN THRU HYSTERIA. IS PARANOIA NEXT ON THE LIST?
IT'S PROBABLY JUST ONE OF THE DOCTORS-- COMING BACK FROM A TOKEN HOUSE CALL.
ONLY THAT--
--AND NOTHING MORE.
3.

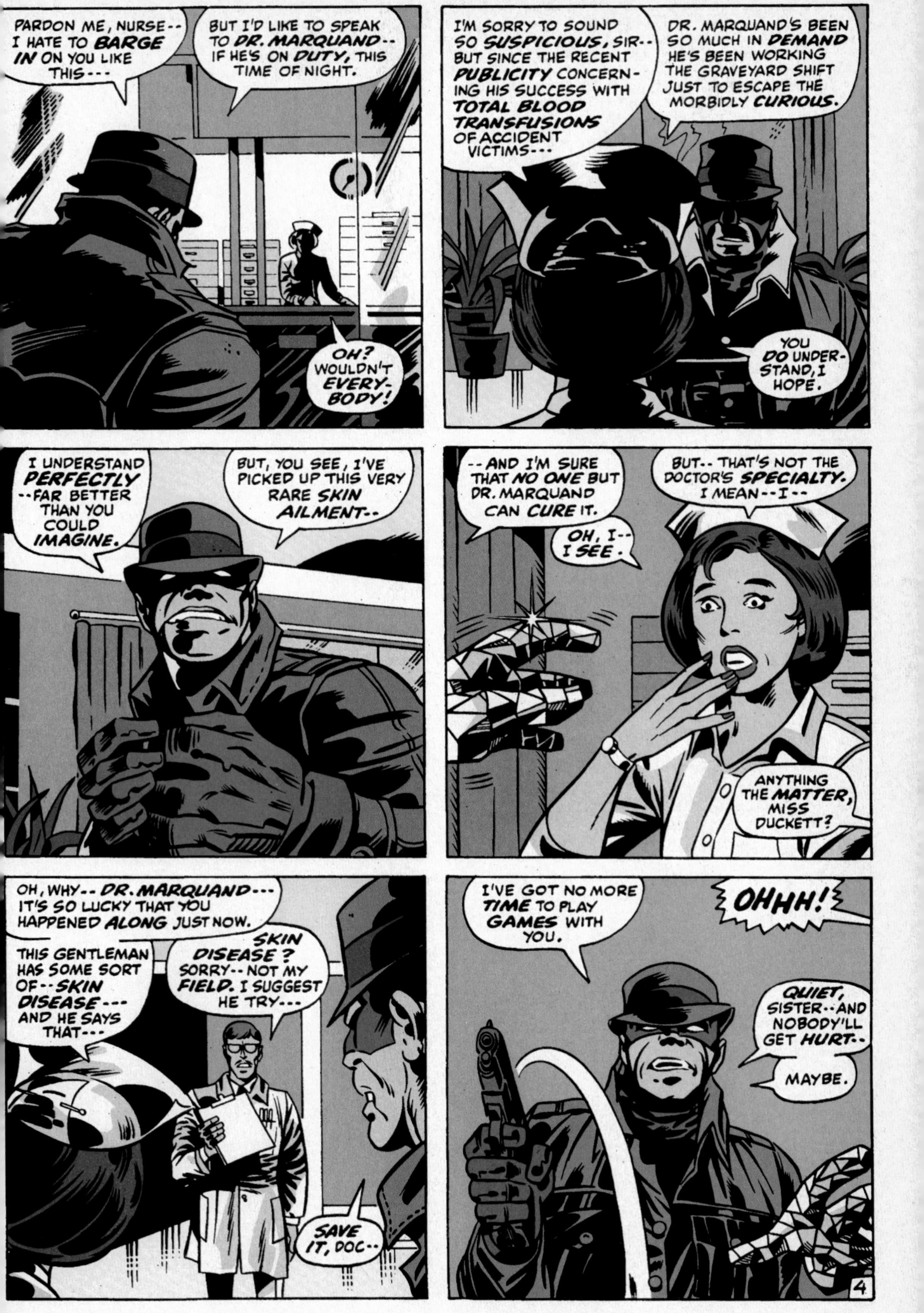
PARDON ME, NURSE-- I HATE TO BARGE IN ON YOU LIKE THIS---
BUT I'D LIKE TO SPEAK TO DR. MARQUAND-- IF HE'S ON DUTY, THIS TIME OF NIGHT.
OH? WOULDN'T EVERY-BODY!
I'M SORRY TO SOUND SO SUSPICIOUS, SIR-- BUT SINCE THE RECENT PUBLICITY CONCERNING HIS SUCCESS WITH TOTAL BLOOD TRANSFUSIONS OF ACCIDENT VICTIMS---
DR. MARQUAND'S BEEN SO MUCH IN DEMAND HE'S BEEN WORKING THE GRAVEYARD SHIFT JUST TO ESCAPE THE MORBIDLY CURIOUS.
YOU DO UNDERSTAND, I HOPE.
I UNDERSTAND PERFECTLY --FAR BETTER THAN YOU COULD IMAGINE.
BUT, YOU SEE, I'VE PICKED UP THIS VERY RARE SKIN AILMENT--
--AND I'M SURE THAT NO ONE BUT DR. MARQUAND CAN CURE IT.
OH, I-- I SEE.
BUT-- THAT'S NOT THE DOCTOR'S SPECIALTY. I MEAN--I--
ANYTHING THE MATTER, MISS DUCKETT?
OH, WHY-- DR. MARQUAND--- IT'S SO LUCKY THAT YOU HAPPENED ALONG JUST NOW.
THIS GENTLEMAN HAS SOME SORT OF--SKIN DISEASE--- AND HE SAYS THAT---
SKIN DISEASE? SORRY-- NOT MY FIELD. I SUGGEST HE TRY---
SAVE IT, DOC--
I'VE GOT NO MORE TIME TO PLAY GAMES WITH YOU.
OHHH!
QUIET, SISTER--AND NOBODY'LL GET HURT--
MAYBE.
4

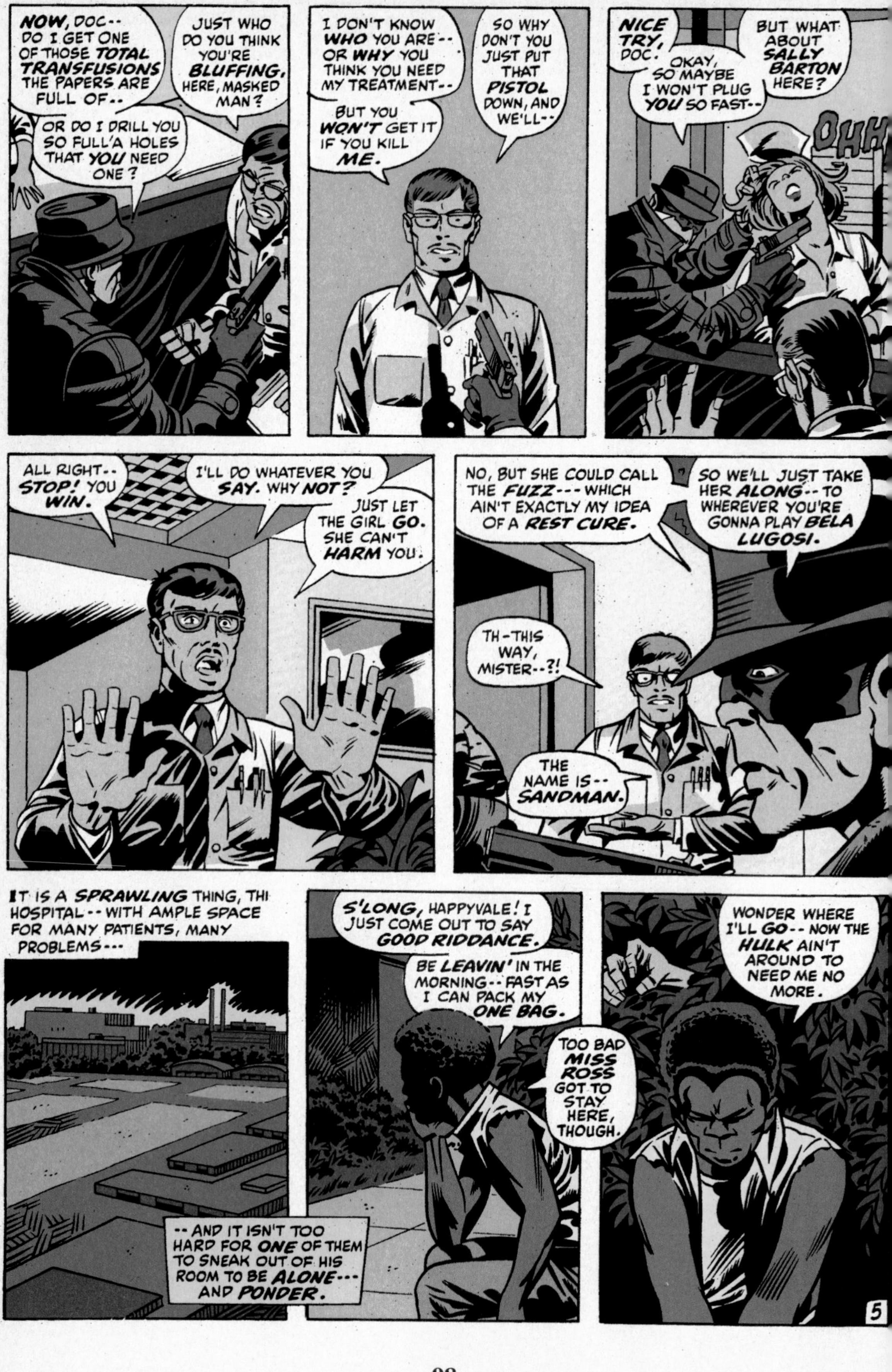
NOW, DOC-- DO I GET ONE OF THOSE TOTAL TRANSFUSIONS THE PAPERS ARE FULL OF--
OR DO I DRILL YOU SO FULL'A HOLES THAT YOU NEED ONE?
JUST WHO DO YOU THINK YOU'RE BLUFFING, HERE, MASKED MAN?
I DON'T KNOW WHO YOU ARE-- OR WHY YOU THINK YOU NEED MY TREATMENT--
BUT YOU WON'T GET IT IF YOU KILL ME.
SO WHY DON'T YOU JUST PUT THAT PISTOL DOWN, AND WE'LL--
NICE TRY, DOC.
OKAY, SO MAYBE I WON'T PLUG YOU SO FAST--
BUT WHAT ABOUT SALLY BARTON HERE?
OHH
ALL RIGHT-- STOP! YOU WIN.
I'LL DO WHATEVER YOU SAY. WHY NOT?
JUST LET THE GIRL GO. SHE CAN'T HARM YOU.
NO, BUT SHE COULD CALL THE FUZZ--- WHICH AIN'T EXACTLY MY IDEA OF A REST CURE.
SO WE'LL JUST TAKE HER ALONG-- TO WHEREVER YOU'RE GONNA PLAY BELA LUGOSI.
TH-THIS WAY, MISTER--?!
THE NAME IS-- SANDMAN.
IT IS A SPRAWLING THING, THIS HOSPITAL-- WITH AMPLE SPACE FOR MANY PATIENTS, MANY PROBLEMS---
--AND IT ISN'T TOO HARD FOR ONE OF THEM TO SNEAK OUT OF HIS ROOM TO BE ALONE--- AND PONDER.
S'LONG, HAPPYVALE! I JUST COME OUT TO SAY GOOD RIDDANCE.
BE LEAVIN' IN THE MORNING-- FAST AS I CAN PACK MY ONE BAG.
TOO BAD MISS ROSS GOT TO STAY HERE, THOUGH.
WONDER WHERE I'LL GO-- NOW THE HULK AIN'T AROUND TO NEED ME NO MORE.
5

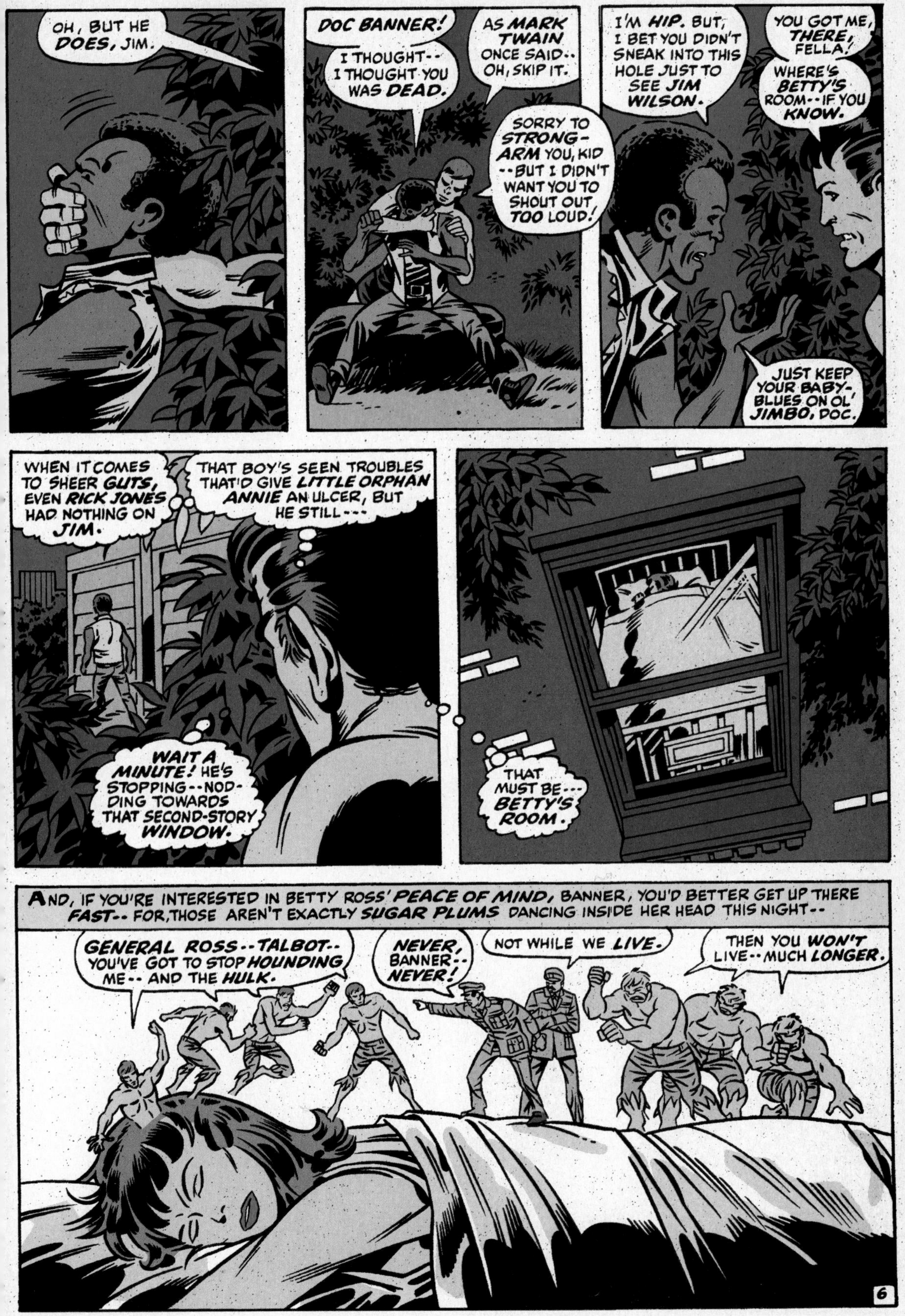

OH, BUT HE DOES, JIM.
DOC BANNER!
I THOUGHT-- I THOUGHT YOU WAS DEAD.
AS MARK TWAIN ONCE SAID.. OH, SKIP IT.
SORRY TO STRONG-ARM YOU, KID --BUT I DIDN'T WANT YOU TO SHOUT OUT TOO LOUD!
I'M HIP. BUT, I BET YOU DIDN'T SNEAK INTO THIS HOLE JUST TO SEE JIM WILSON.
YOU GOT ME, THERE, FELLA!
WHERE'S BETTY'S ROOM--IF YOU KNOW.
JUST KEEP YOUR BABY-BLUES ON OL' JIMBO, DOC.
WHEN IT COMES TO SHEER GUTS, EVEN RICK JONES HAD NOTHING ON JIM.
THAT BOY'S SEEN TROUBLES THAT'D GIVE LITTLE ORPHAN ANNIE AN ULCER, BUT HE STILL---
WAIT A MINUTE! HE'S STOPPING--NODDING TOWARDS THAT SECOND-STORY WINDOW.
THAT MUST BE--- BETTY'S ROOM.
AND, IF YOU'RE INTERESTED IN BETTY ROSS' PEACE OF MIND, BANNER, YOU'D BETTER GET UP THERE FAST-- FOR, THOSE AREN'T EXACTLY SUGAR PLUMS DANCING INSIDE HER HEAD THIS NIGHT--
GENERAL ROSS--TALBOT-- YOU'VE GOT TO STOP HOUNDING ME-- AND THE HULK.
NEVER, BANNER-- NEVER!
NOT WHILE WE LIVE.
THEN YOU WON'T LIVE--MUCH LONGER.
6

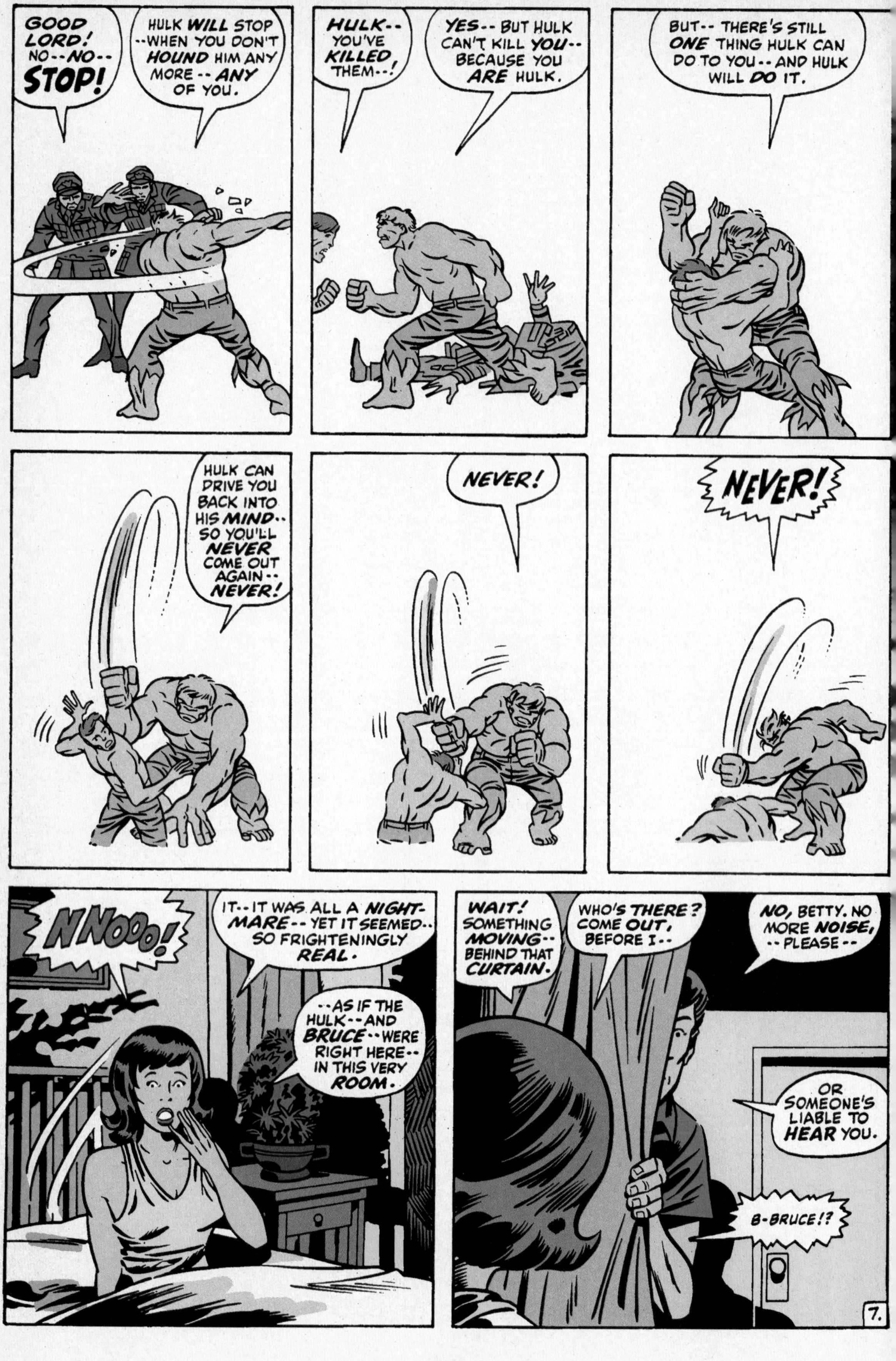
GOOD LORD! NO--NO--STOP!
HULK WILL STOP --WHEN YOU DON'T HOUND HIM ANY MORE--ANY OF YOU.
HULK-- YOU'VE KILLED THEM--!
YES-- BUT HULK CAN'T KILL YOU-- BECAUSE YOU ARE HULK.
BUT-- THERE'S STILL ONE THING HULK CAN DO TO YOU--AND HULK WILL DO IT.
HULK CAN DRIVE YOU BACK INTO HIS MIND-- SO YOU'LL NEVER COME OUT AGAIN-- NEVER!
NEVER!
NEVER!
NNOOOO!
IT--IT WAS ALL A NIGHTMARE-- YET IT SEEMED-- SO FRIGHTENINGLY REAL.
--AS IF THE HULK--AND BRUCE--WERE RIGHT HERE-- IN THIS VERY ROOM.
WAIT! SOMETHING MOVING-- BEHIND THAT CURTAIN.
WHO'S THERE? COME OUT, BEFORE I--
NO, BETTY. NO MORE NOISE, --PLEASE--
OR SOMEONE'S LIABLE TO HEAR YOU.
B-BRUCE!?
7.

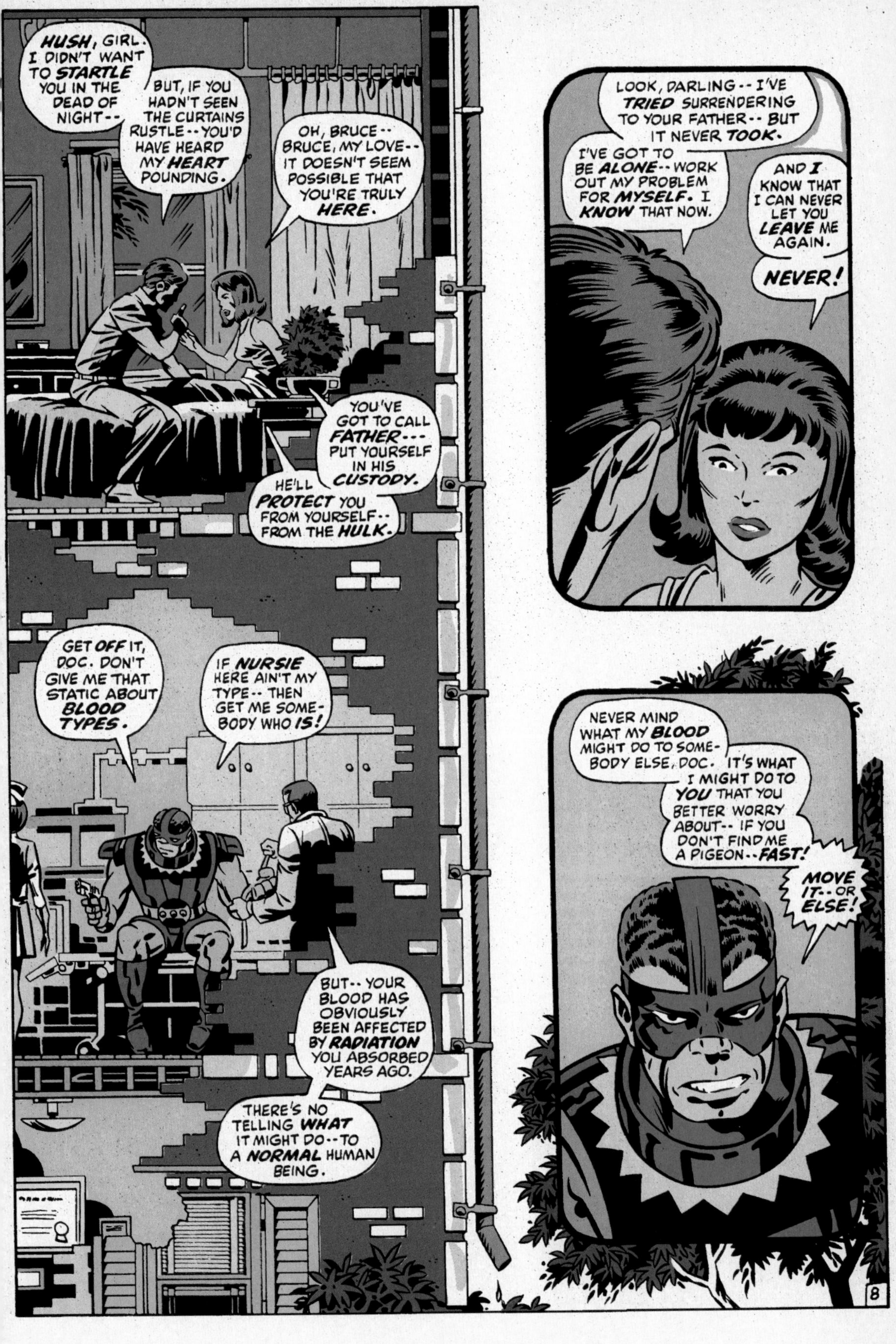
HUSH, GIRL. I DIDN'T WANT TO STARTLE YOU IN THE DEAD OF NIGHT--
BUT, IF YOU HADN'T SEEN THE CURTAINS RUSTLE--YOU'D HAVE HEARD MY HEART POUNDING.
OH, BRUCE--BRUCE, MY LOVE--IT DOESN'T SEEM POSSIBLE THAT YOU'RE TRULY HERE.
YOU'VE GOT TO CALL FATHER---PUT YOURSELF IN HIS CUSTODY.
HE'LL PROTECT YOU FROM YOURSELF--FROM THE HULK.
LOOK, DARLING--I'VE TRIED SURRENDERING TO YOUR FATHER--BUT IT NEVER TOOK.
I'VE GOT TO BE ALONE--WORK OUT MY PROBLEM FOR MYSELF. I KNOW THAT NOW.
AND I KNOW THAT I CAN NEVER LET YOU LEAVE ME AGAIN.
NEVER!
GET OFF IT, DOC. DON'T GIVE ME THAT STATIC ABOUT BLOOD TYPES.
IF NURSIE HERE AIN'T MY TYPE--THEN GET ME SOMEBODY WHO IS!
BUT--YOUR BLOOD HAS OBVIOUSLY BEEN AFFECTED BY RADIATION YOU ABSORBED YEARS AGO.
THERE'S NO TELLING WHAT IT MIGHT DO--TO A NORMAL HUMAN BEING.
NEVER MIND WHAT MY BLOOD MIGHT DO TO SOMEBODY ELSE, DOC. IT'S WHAT I MIGHT DO TO YOU THAT YOU BETTER WORRY ABOUT--IF YOU DON'T FIND ME A PIGEON--FAST!
MOVE IT--OR ELSE!
8

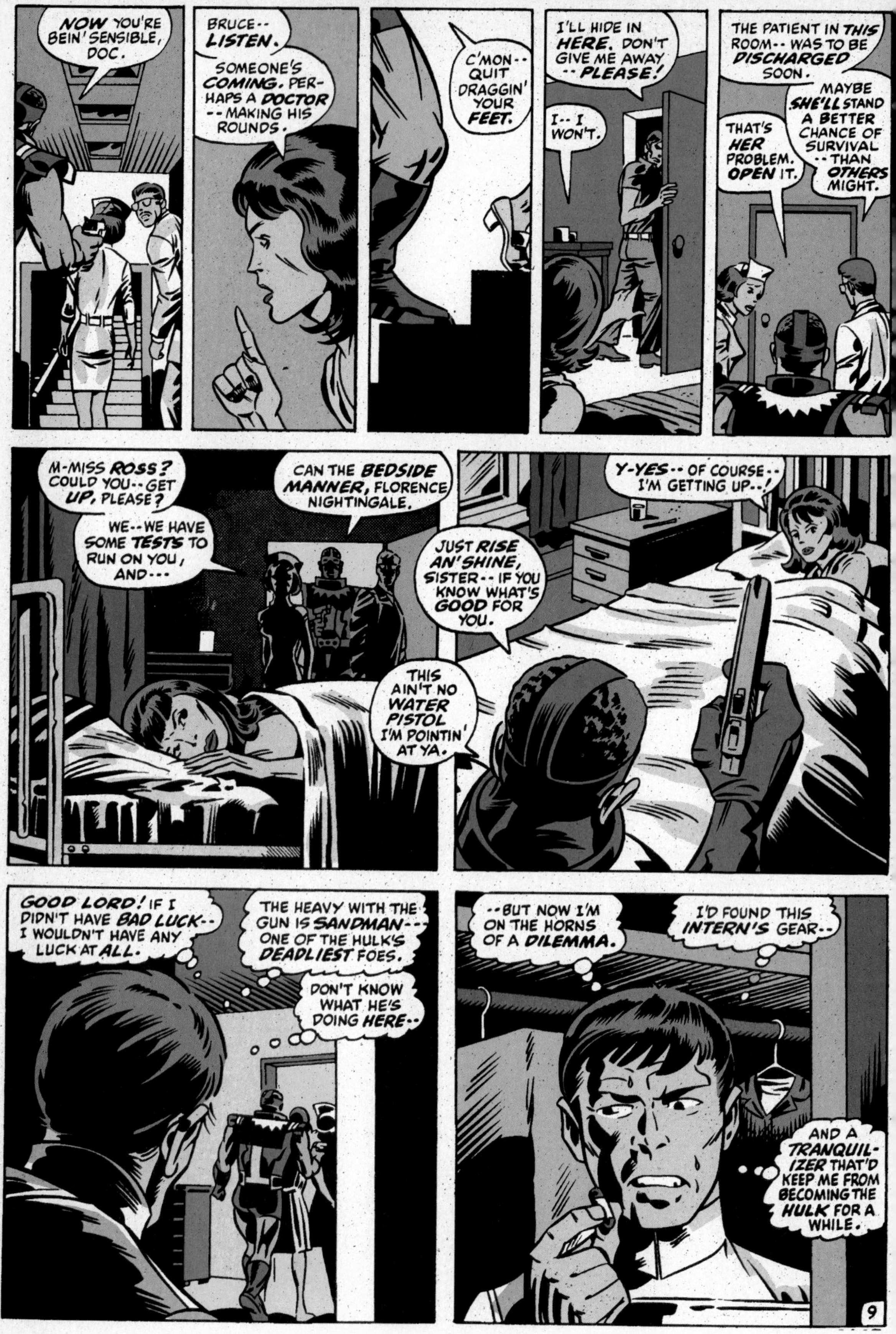
NOW YOU'RE BEIN' SENSIBLE, DOC.
BRUCE-- LISTEN.
SOMEONE'S COMING. PERHAPS A DOCTOR -- MAKING HIS ROUNDS.
C'MON -- QUIT DRAGGIN' YOUR FEET.
I'LL HIDE IN HERE. DON'T GIVE ME AWAY -- PLEASE!
I-- I WON'T.
THE PATIENT IN THIS ROOM-- WAS TO BE DISCHARGED SOON.
MAYBE SHE'LL STAND A BETTER CHANCE OF SURVIVAL -- THAN OTHERS MIGHT.
THAT'S HER PROBLEM. OPEN IT.
M-MISS ROSS? COULD YOU-- GET UP, PLEASE?
WE--WE HAVE SOME TESTS TO RUN ON YOU, AND---
CAN THE BEDSIDE MANNER, FLORENCE NIGHTINGALE.
Y-YES-- OF COURSE-- I'M GETTING UP--!
JUST RISE AN' SHINE, SISTER-- IF YOU KNOW WHAT'S GOOD FOR YOU.
THIS AIN'T NO WATER PISTOL I'M POINTIN' AT YA.
GOOD LORD! IF I DIDN'T HAVE BAD LUCK-- I WOULDN'T HAVE ANY LUCK AT ALL.
THE HEAVY WITH THE GUN IS SANDMAN--- ONE OF THE HULK'S DEADLIEST FOES.
DON'T KNOW WHAT HE'S DOING HERE--
--BUT NOW I'M ON THE HORNS OF A DILEMMA.
I'D FOUND THIS INTERN'S GEAR--
AND A TRANQUILIZER THAT'D KEEP ME FROM BECOMING THE HULK FOR A WHILE.
9

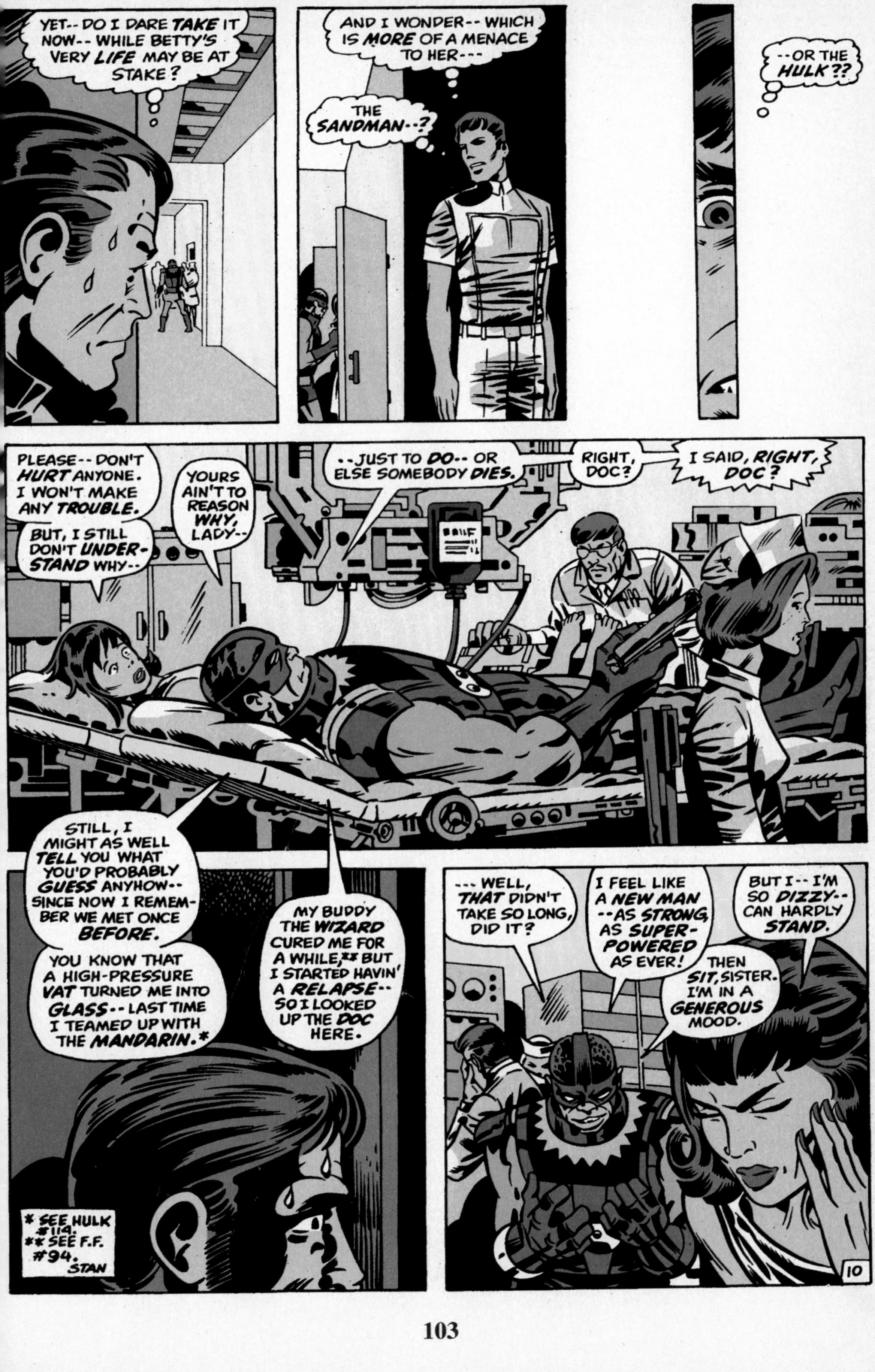
YET-- DO I DARE TAKE IT NOW-- WHILE BETTY'S VERY LIFE MAY BE AT STAKE?
AND I WONDER-- WHICH IS MORE OF A MENACE TO HER---
THE SANDMAN--?
--OR THE HULK??
PLEASE-- DON'T HURT ANYONE. I WON'T MAKE ANY TROUBLE.
BUT, I STILL DON'T UNDERSTAND WHY--
YOURS AIN'T TO REASON WHY, LADY--
--JUST TO DO-- OR ELSE SOMEBODY DIES.
RIGHT, DOC?
I SAID, RIGHT, DOC?
STILL, I MIGHT AS WELL TELL YOU WHAT YOU'D PROBABLY GUESS ANYHOW-- SINCE NOW I REMEMBER WE MET ONCE BEFORE.
YOU KNOW THAT A HIGH-PRESSURE VAT TURNED ME INTO GLASS-- LAST TIME I TEAMED UP WITH THE MANDARIN.*
MY BUDDY THE WIZARD CURED ME FOR A WHILE,** BUT I STARTED HAVIN' A RELAPSE-- SO I LOOKED UP THE DOC HERE.
* SEE HULK #114. ** SEE F.F. #94. STAN
--- WELL, THAT DIDN'T TAKE SO LONG, DID IT?
I FEEL LIKE A NEW MAN --AS STRONG, AS SUPER-POWERED AS EVER!
BUT I-- I'M SO DIZZY-- CAN HARDLY STAND.
THEN SIT, SISTER. I'M IN A GENEROUS MOOD.
10

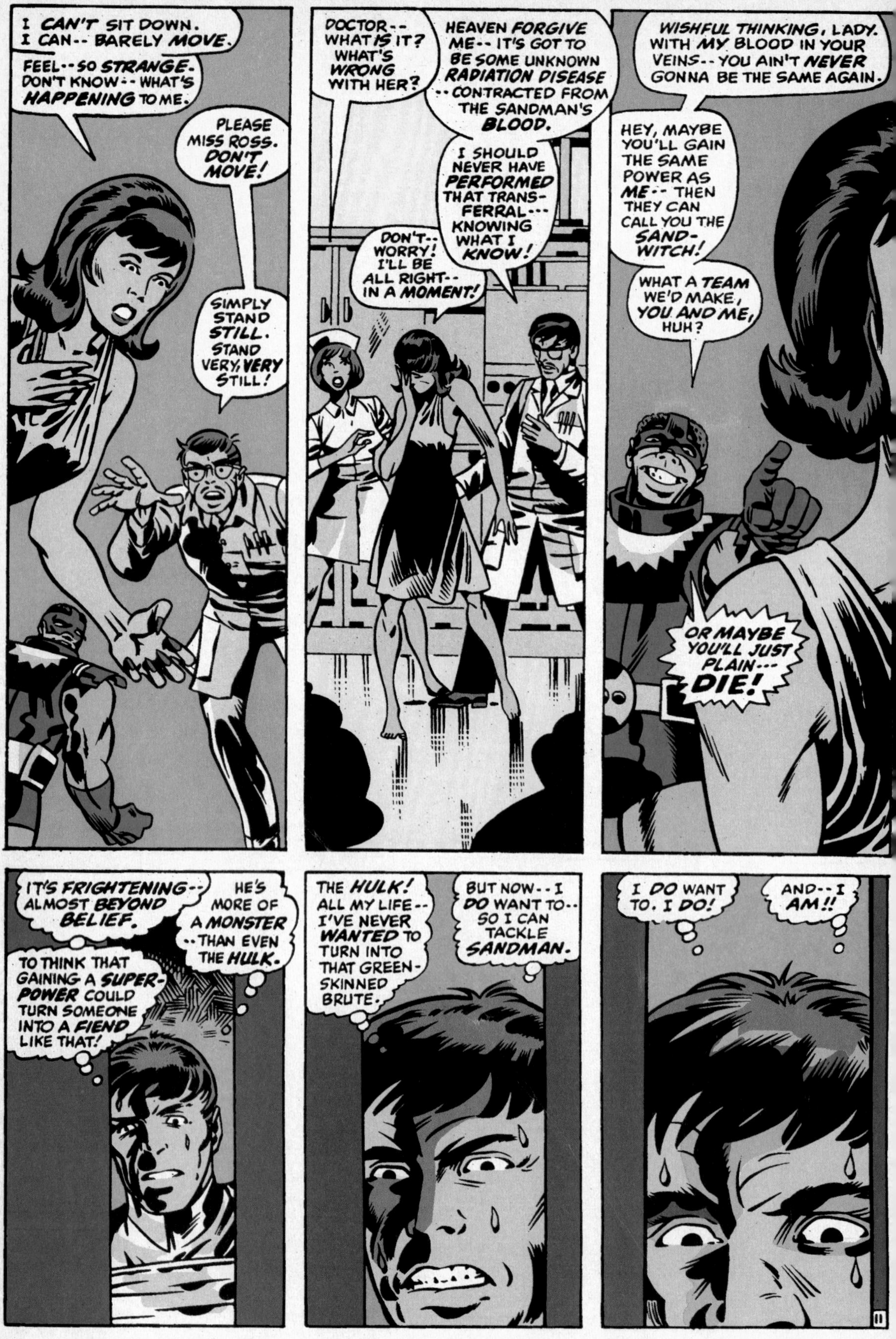

I CAN'T SIT DOWN. I CAN-- BARELY MOVE.
FEEL--SO STRANGE. DON'T KNOW--WHAT'S HAPPENING TO ME.
PLEASE MISS ROSS. DON'T MOVE!
SIMPLY STAND STILL. STAND VERY, VERY STILL!
DOCTOR-- WHAT IS IT? WHAT'S WRONG WITH HER?
HEAVEN FORGIVE ME-- IT'S GOT TO BE SOME UNKNOWN RADIATION DISEASE --CONTRACTED FROM THE SANDMAN'S BLOOD.
I SHOULD NEVER HAVE PERFORMED THAT TRANS-FERRAL--- KNOWING WHAT I KNOW!
DON'T-- WORRY! I'LL BE ALL RIGHT-- IN A MOMENT!
WISHFUL THINKING, LADY. WITH MY BLOOD IN YOUR VEINS-- YOU AIN'T NEVER GONNA BE THE SAME AGAIN.
HEY, MAYBE YOU'LL GAIN THE SAME POWER AS ME-- THEN THEY CAN CALL YOU THE SAND-WITCH!
WHAT A TEAM WE'D MAKE, YOU AND ME, HUH?
OR MAYBE YOU'LL JUST PLAIN--- DIE!
IT'S FRIGHTENING-- ALMOST BEYOND BELIEF.
HE'S MORE OF A MONSTER --THAN EVEN THE HULK.
TO THINK THAT GAINING A SUPER-POWER COULD TURN SOMEONE INTO A FIEND LIKE THAT!
THE HULK! ALL MY LIFE-- I'VE NEVER WANTED TO TURN INTO THAT GREEN-SKINNED BRUTE.
BUT NOW-- I DO WANT TO-- SO I CAN TACKLE SANDMAN.
I DO WANT TO. I DO!
AND-- I AM!!
11

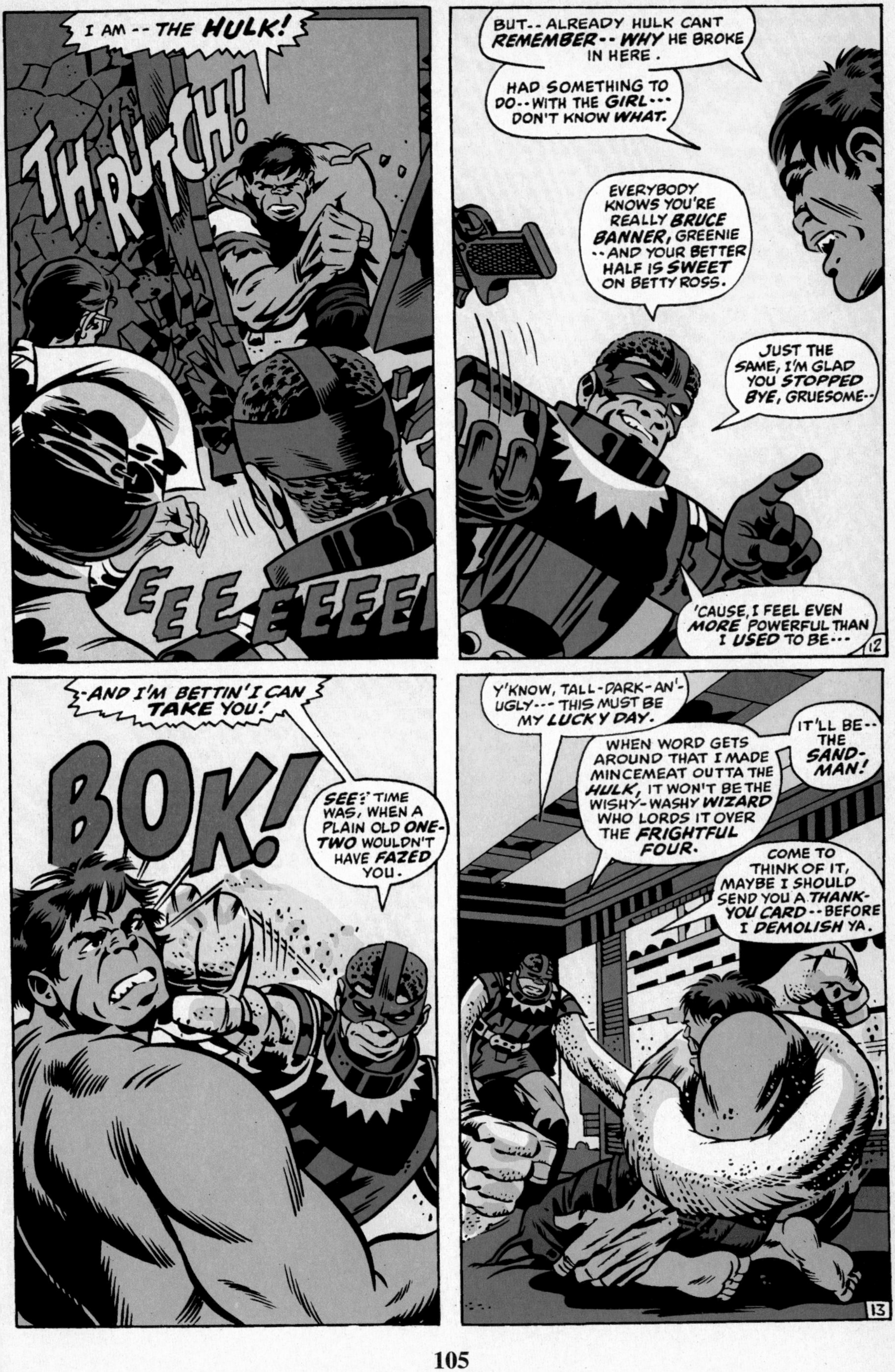
I AM -- THE HULK!
THRUTCH!
EEEEEEEE
BUT-- ALREADY HULK CANT REMEMBER-- WHY HE BROKE IN HERE.
HAD SOMETHING TO DO--WITH THE GIRL--- DON'T KNOW WHAT.
EVERYBODY KNOWS YOU'RE REALLY BRUCE BANNER, GREENIE --AND YOUR BETTER HALF IS SWEET ON BETTY ROSS.
JUST THE SAME, I'M GLAD YOU STOPPED BYE, GRUESOME--
'CAUSE, I FEEL EVEN MORE POWERFUL THAN I USED TO BE---
12
-AND I'M BETTIN' I CAN TAKE YOU!
BOK!
SEE? TIME WAS, WHEN A PLAIN OLD ONE-TWO WOULDN'T HAVE FAZED YOU.
Y'KNOW, TALL-DARK-AN'-UGLY--- THIS MUST BE MY LUCKY DAY.
WHEN WORD GETS AROUND THAT I MADE MINCEMEAT OUTTA THE HULK, IT WON'T BE THE WISHY-WASHY WIZARD WHO LORDS IT OVER THE FRIGHTFUL FOUR.
IT'LL BE-- THE SANDMAN!
COME TO THINK OF IT, MAYBE I SHOULD SEND YOU A THANK-YOU CARD--BEFORE I DEMOLISH YA.
13

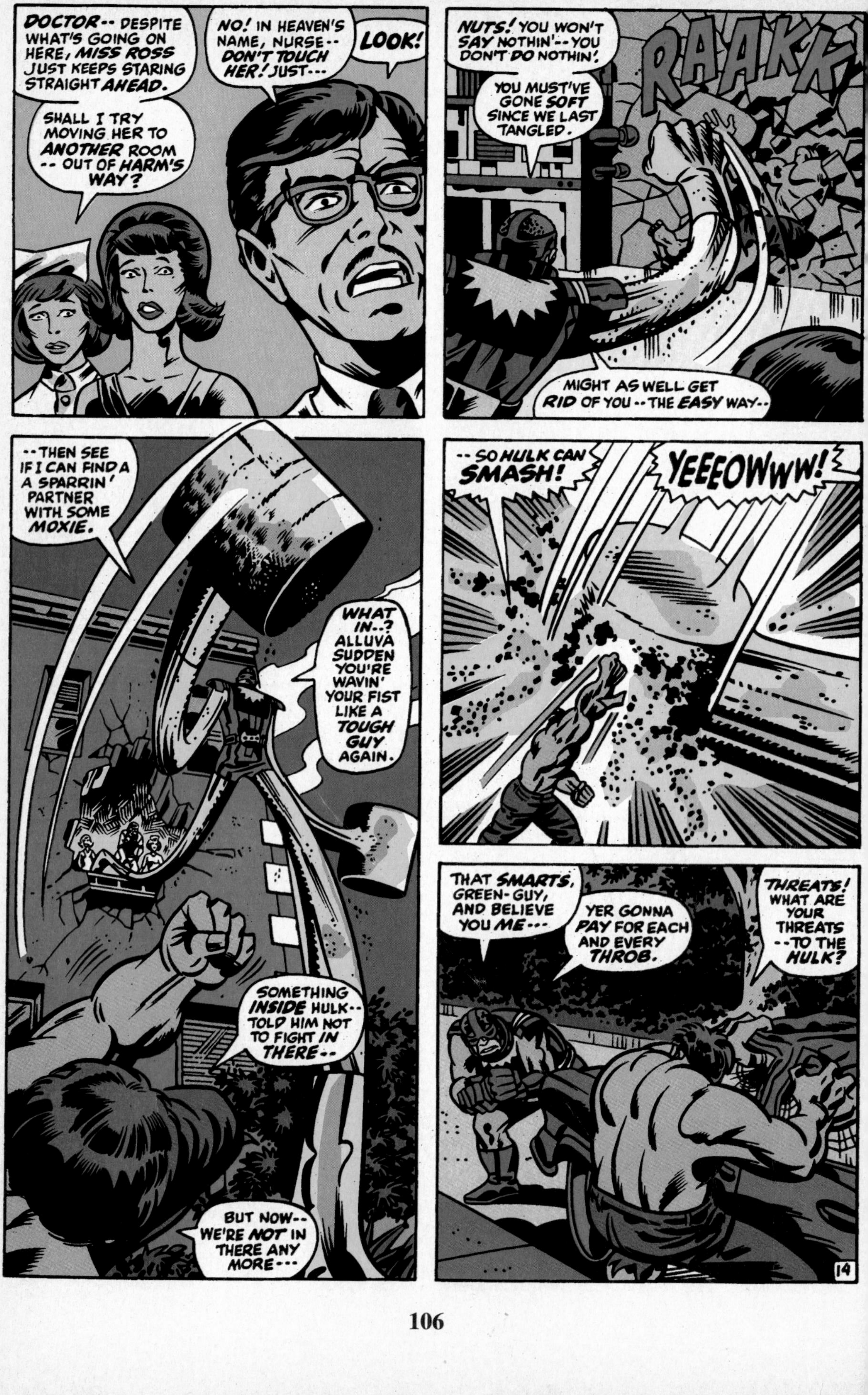
DOCTOR-- DESPITE WHAT'S GOING ON HERE, MISS ROSS JUST KEEPS STARING STRAIGHT AHEAD.
SHALL I TRY MOVING HER TO ANOTHER ROOM -- OUT OF HARM'S WAY?
NO! IN HEAVEN'S NAME, NURSE-- DON'T TOUCH HER! JUST---
LOOK!
NUTS! YOU WON'T SAY NOTHIN'-- YOU DON'T DO NOTHIN'!
YOU MUST'VE GONE SOFT SINCE WE LAST TANGLED.
RAAKK
MIGHT AS WELL GET RID OF YOU -- THE EASY WAY--
--THEN SEE IF I CAN FIND A A SPARRIN' PARTNER WITH SOME MOXIE.
WHAT IN..? ALLUVA SUDDEN YOU'RE WAVIN' YOUR FIST LIKE A TOUGH GUY AGAIN.
SOMETHING INSIDE HULK-- TOLD HIM NOT TO FIGHT IN THERE--
BUT NOW-- WE'RE NOT IN THERE ANY MORE---
-- SO HULK CAN SMASH!
YEEEOWWW!
THAT SMARTS, GREEN-GUY, AND BELIEVE YOU ME---
YER GONNA PAY FOR EACH AND EVERY THROB.
THREATS! WHAT ARE YOUR THREATS --TO THE HULK?
14

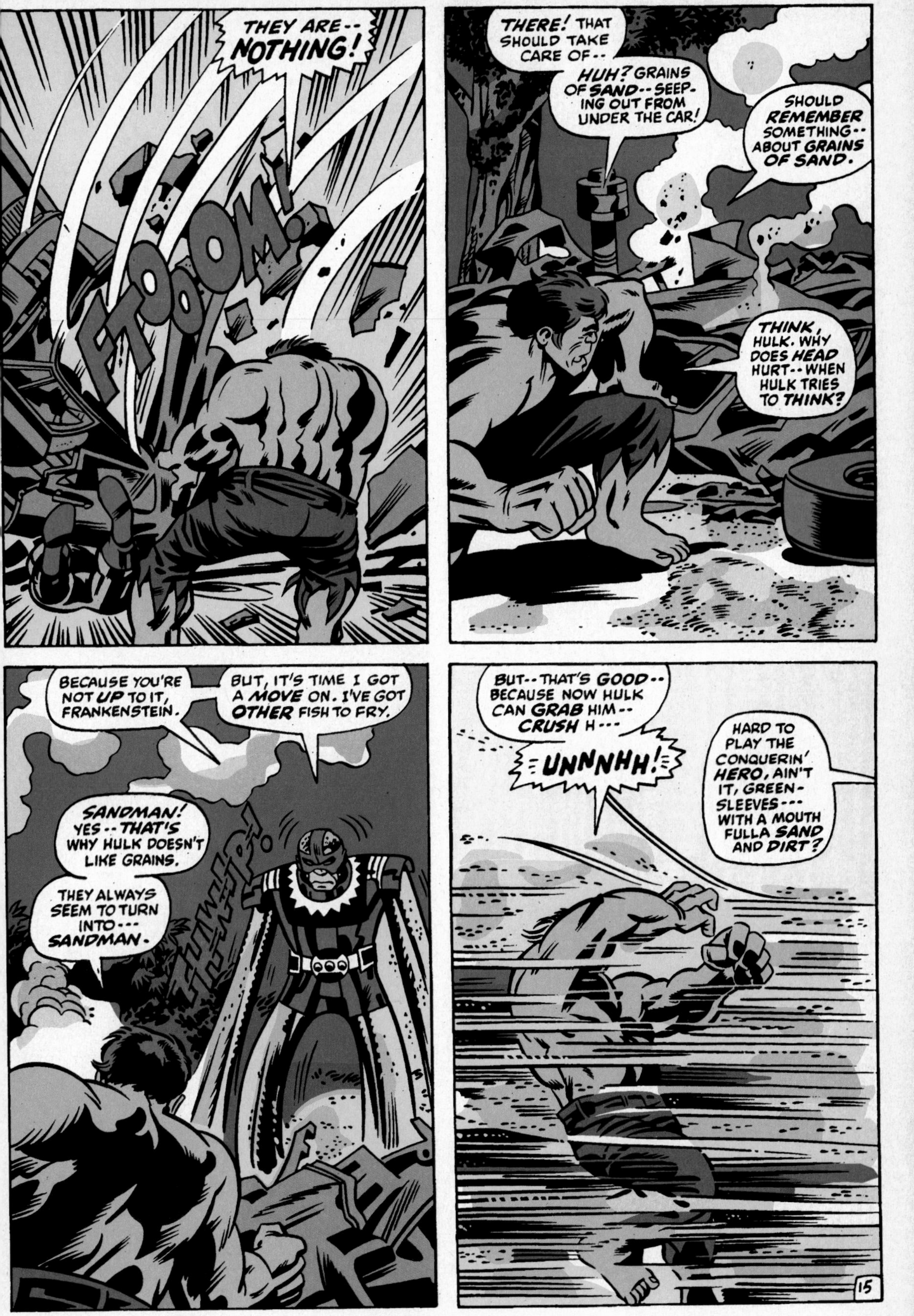

THEY ARE -- NOTHING!
FTOOOM!
THERE! THAT SHOULD TAKE CARE OF --
HUH? GRAINS OF SAND -- SEEPING OUT FROM UNDER THE CAR!
SHOULD REMEMBER SOMETHING -- ABOUT GRAINS OF SAND.
THINK, HULK. WHY DOES HEAD HURT -- WHEN HULK TRIES TO THINK?
BECAUSE YOU'RE NOT UP TO IT, FRANKENSTEIN.
BUT, IT'S TIME I GOT A MOVE ON. I'VE GOT OTHER FISH TO FRY.
SANDMAN! YES -- THAT'S WHY HULK DOESN'T LIKE GRAINS.
THEY ALWAYS SEEM TO TURN INTO --- SANDMAN.
BUT -- THAT'S GOOD -- BECAUSE NOW HULK CAN GRAB HIM -- CRUSH H ---
UNNNHH!
HARD TO PLAY THE CONQUERIN' HERO, AIN'T IT, GREEN-SLEEVES --- WITH A MOUTH FULLA SAND AND DIRT?
15

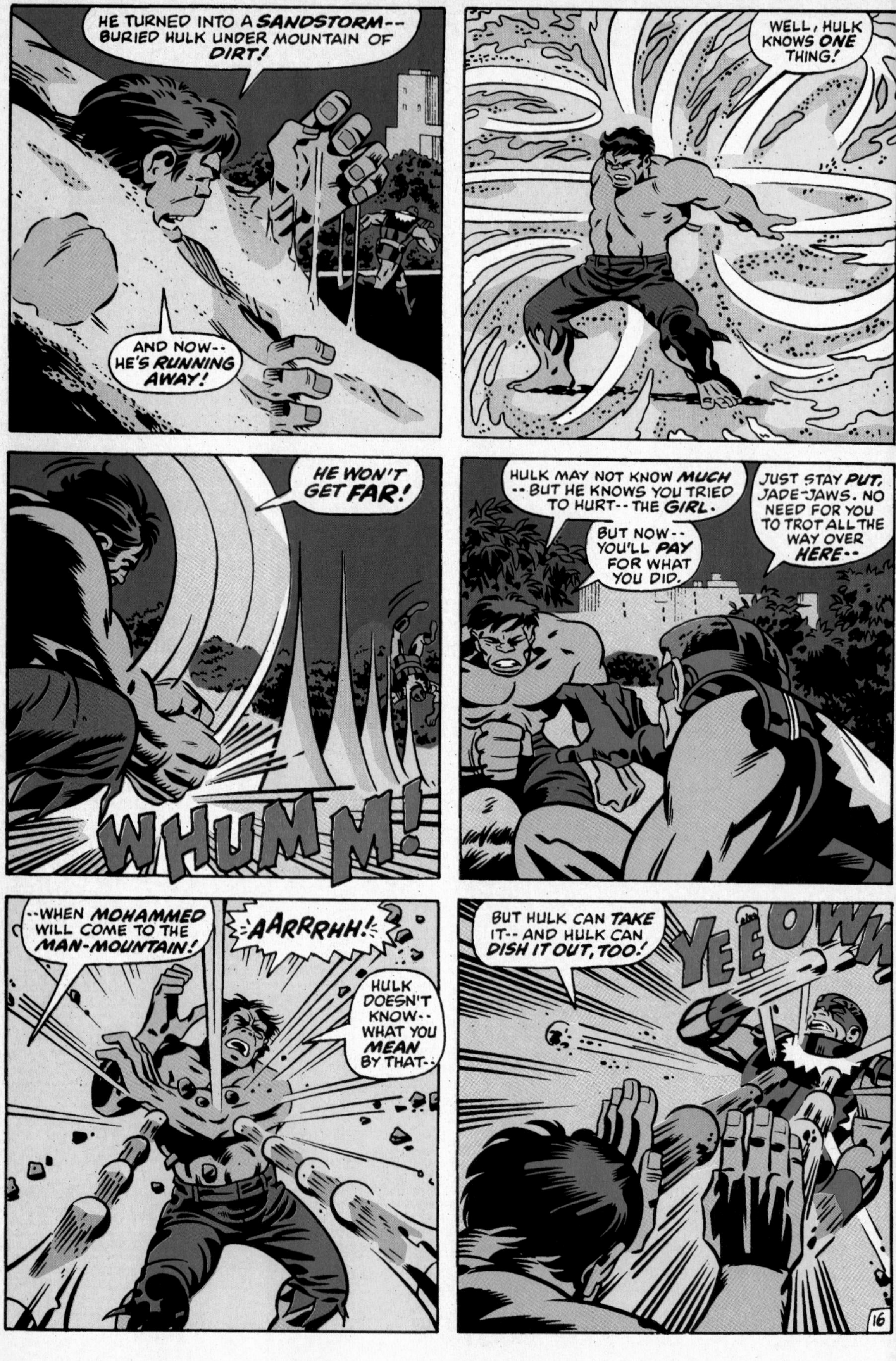
HE TURNED INTO A SANDSTORM-- BURIED HULK UNDER MOUNTAIN OF DIRT!
AND NOW-- HE'S RUNNING AWAY!
WELL, HULK KNOWS ONE THING!
HE WON'T GET FAR!
WHUMM!
HULK MAY NOT KNOW MUCH -- BUT HE KNOWS YOU TRIED TO HURT-- THE GIRL.
BUT NOW-- YOU'LL PAY FOR WHAT YOU DID.
JUST STAY PUT, JADE-JAWS. NO NEED FOR YOU TO TROT ALL THE WAY OVER HERE--
--WHEN MOHAMMED WILL COME TO THE MAN-MOUNTAIN!
AARRRHH!
HULK DOESN'T KNOW-- WHAT YOU MEAN BY THAT--
BUT HULK CAN TAKE IT-- AND HULK CAN DISH IT OUT, TOO!
YEEOWW
16

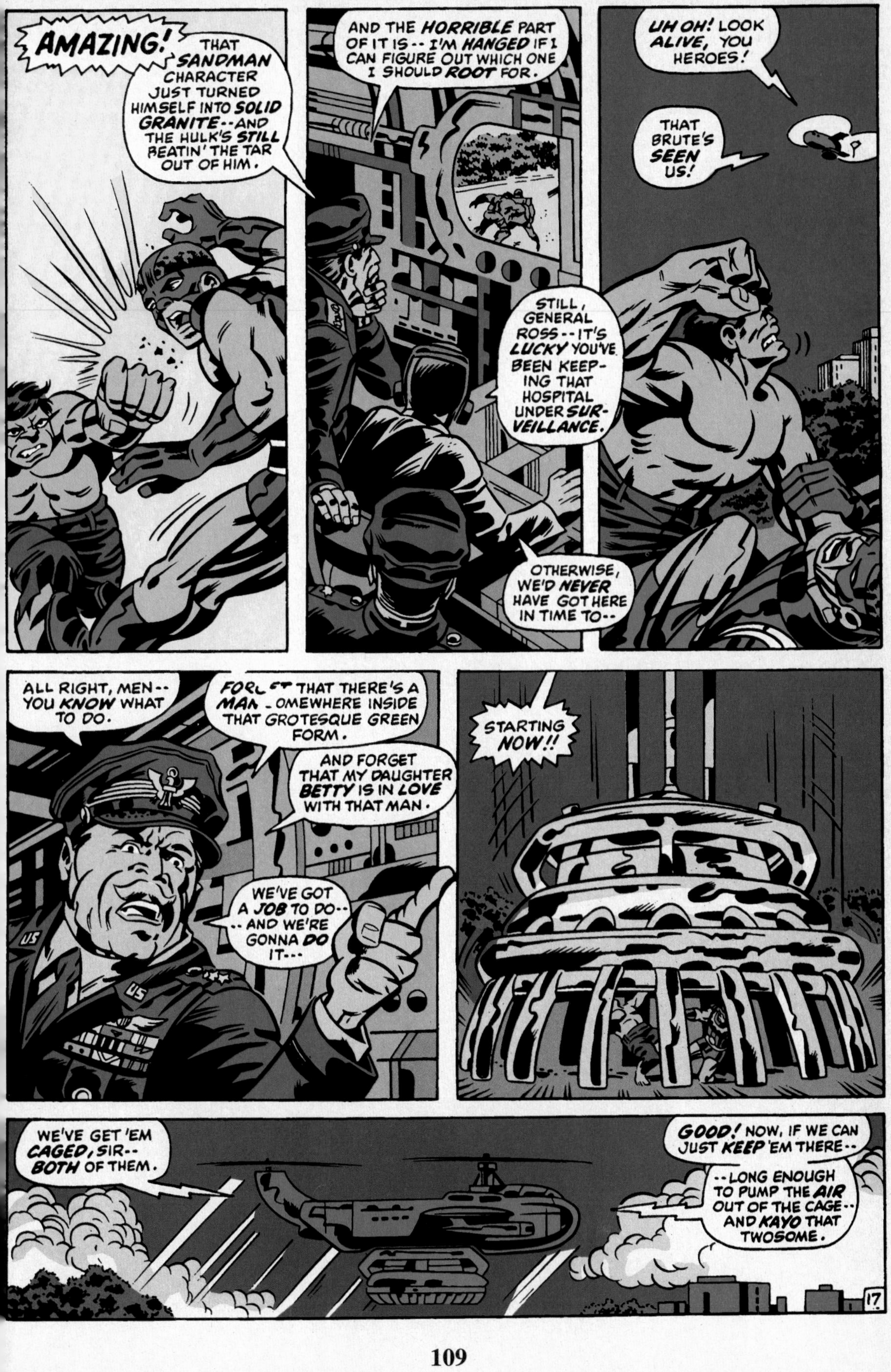
AMAZING! THAT SANDMAN CHARACTER JUST TURNED HIMSELF INTO SOLID GRANITE--AND THE HULK'S STILL BEATIN' THE TAR OUT OF HIM.
AND THE HORRIBLE PART OF IT IS--I'M HANGED IF I CAN FIGURE OUT WHICH ONE I SHOULD ROOT FOR.
STILL, GENERAL ROSS--IT'S LUCKY YOU'VE BEEN KEEPING THAT HOSPITAL UNDER SURVEILLANCE.
OTHERWISE, WE'D NEVER HAVE GOT HERE IN TIME TO--
UH OH! LOOK ALIVE, YOU HEROES!
THAT BRUTE'S SEEN US!
ALL RIGHT, MEN--YOU KNOW WHAT TO DO.
FOR T THAT THERE'S A MA OMEWHERE INSIDE THAT GROTESQUE GREEN FORM.
AND FORGET THAT MY DAUGHTER BETTY IS IN LOVE WITH THAT MAN.
WE'VE GOT A JOB TO DO----AND WE'RE GONNA DO IT---
STARTING NOW!!
WE'VE GET 'EM CAGED, SIR--BOTH OF THEM.
GOOD! NOW, IF WE CAN JUST KEEP 'EM THERE--
--LONG ENOUGH TO PUMP THE AIR OUT OF THE CAGE--AND KAYO THAT TWOSOME.
17

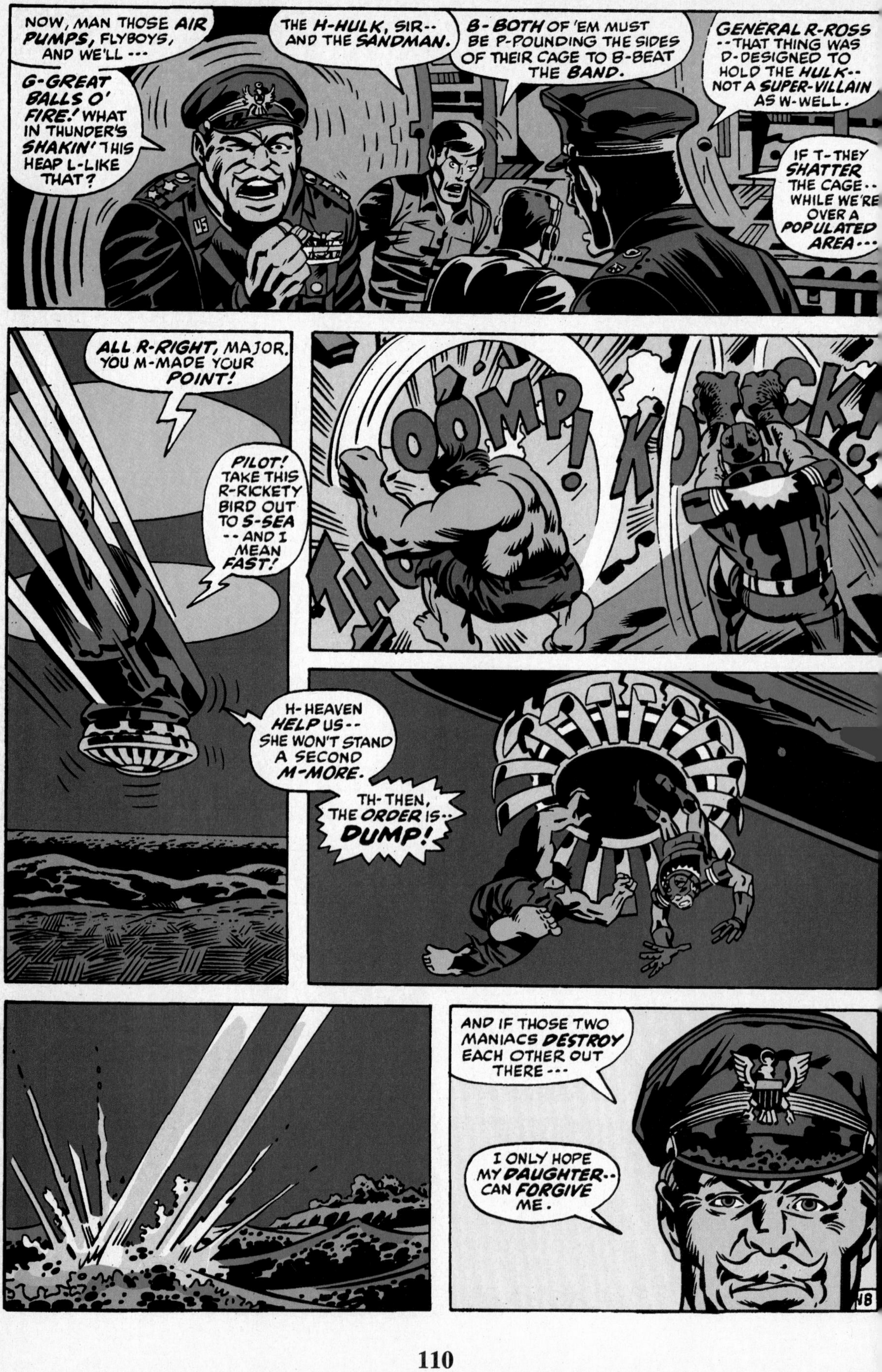
NOW, MAN THOSE AIR PUMPS, FLYBOYS, AND WE'LL ---
G-GREAT BALLS O' FIRE! WHAT IN THUNDER'S SHAKIN' THIS HEAP L-LIKE THAT?
THE H-HULK, SIR-- AND THE SANDMAN.
B-BOTH OF 'EM MUST BE P-POUNDING THE SIDES OF THEIR CAGE TO B-BEAT THE BAND.
GENERAL R-ROSS --THAT THING WAS D-DESIGNED TO HOLD THE HULK-- NOT A SUPER-VILLAIN AS W-WELL.
IF T-THEY SHATTER THE CAGE-- WHILE WE'RE OVER A POPULATED AREA---
ALL R-RIGHT, MAJOR. YOU M-MADE YOUR POINT!
PILOT! TAKE THIS R-RICKETY BIRD OUT TO S-SEA --AND I MEAN FAST!
THOOMP! KKOCK!
H-HEAVEN HELP US-- SHE WON'T STAND A SECOND M-MORE.
TH-THEN, THE ORDER IS-- DUMP!
AND IF THOSE TWO MANIACS DESTROY EACH OTHER OUT THERE ---
I ONLY HOPE MY DAUGHTER-- CAN FORGIVE ME.

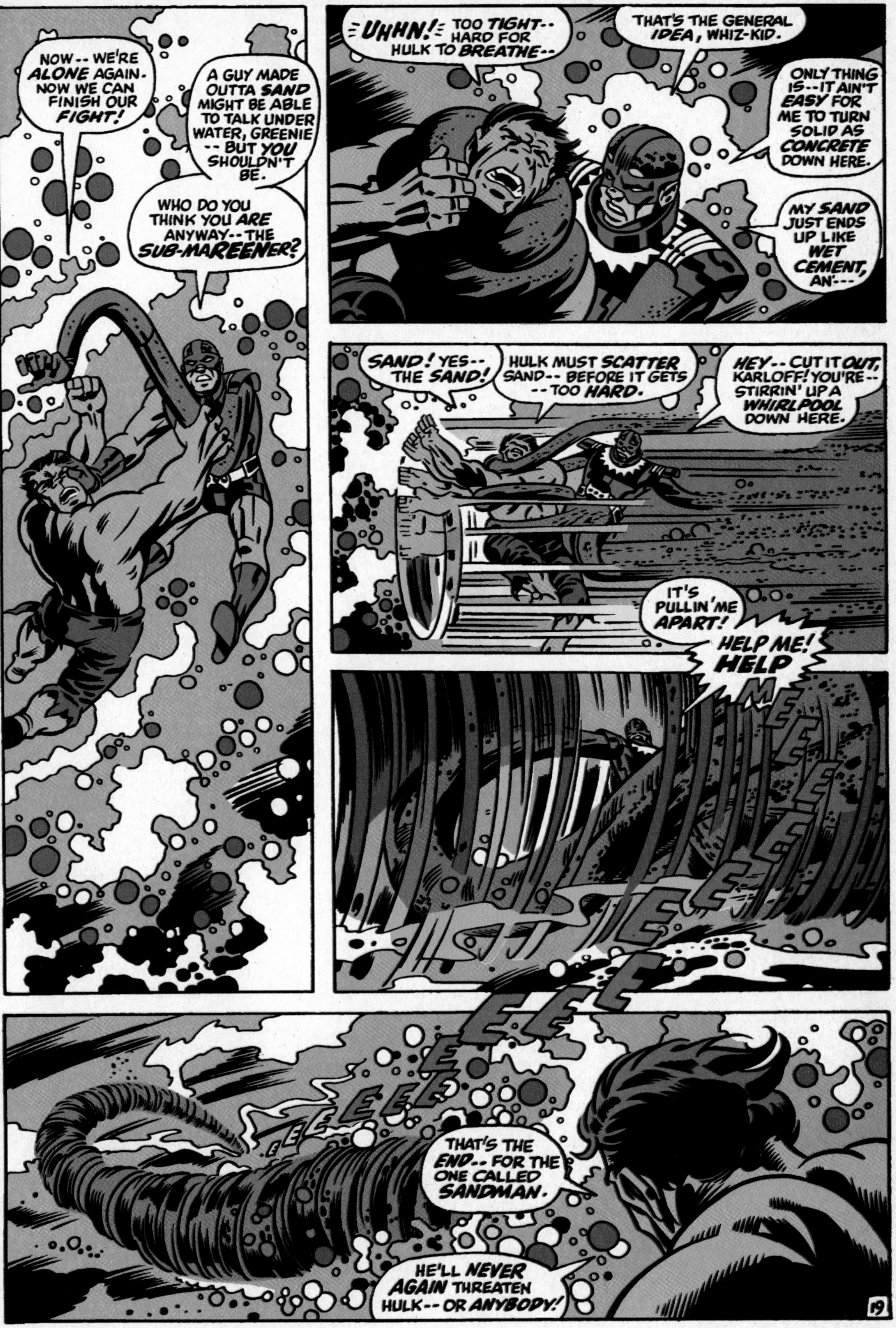
NOW -- WE'RE ALONE AGAIN. NOW WE CAN FINISH OUR FIGHT!
A GUY MADE OUTTA SAND MIGHT BE ABLE TO TALK UNDER WATER, GREENIE -- BUT YOU SHOULDN'T BE.
WHO DO YOU THINK YOU ARE ANYWAY-- THE SUB-MAREENER?
UHHN! TOO TIGHT-- HARD FOR HULK TO BREATHE--
THAT'S THE GENERAL IDEA, WHIZ-KID.
ONLY THING IS--IT AIN'T EASY FOR ME TO TURN SOLID AS CONCRETE DOWN HERE.
MY SAND JUST ENDS UP LIKE WET CEMENT, AN'---
SAND! YES-- THE SAND!
HULK MUST SCATTER SAND-- BEFORE IT GETS --TOO HARD.
HEY-- CUT IT OUT, KARLOFF! YOU'RE-- STIRRIN' UP A WHIRLPOOL DOWN HERE.
IT'S PULLIN' ME APART!
HELP ME! HELP MEEEEEEEEEEEEEEEE
THAT'S THE END.. FOR THE ONE CALLED SANDMAN.
HE'LL NEVER AGAIN THREATEN HULK-- OR ANYBODY!
19

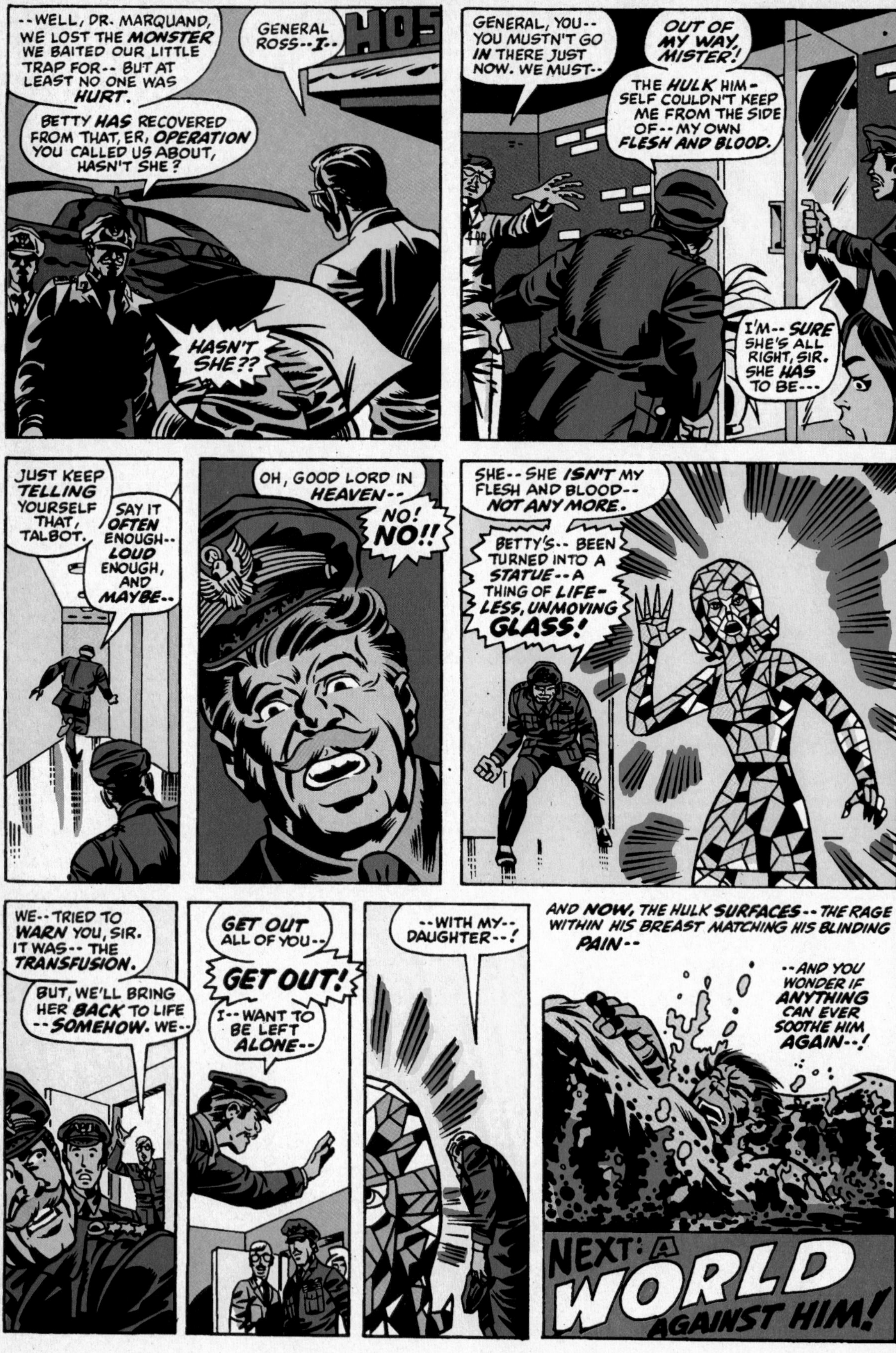
--WELL, DR. MARQUAND, WE LOST THE MONSTER WE BAITED OUR LITTLE TRAP FOR-- BUT AT LEAST NO ONE WAS HURT.
BETTY HAS RECOVERED FROM THAT, ER, OPERATION YOU CALLED US ABOUT, HASN'T SHE?
GENERAL ROSS--I--
HASN'T SHE??
HOS
GENERAL, YOU-- YOU MUSTN'T GO IN THERE JUST NOW. WE MUST--
OUT OF MY WAY, MISTER!
THE HULK HIMSELF COULDN'T KEEP ME FROM THE SIDE OF-- MY OWN FLESH AND BLOOD.
I'M-- SURE SHE'S ALL RIGHT, SIR. SHE HAS TO BE---
JUST KEEP TELLING YOURSELF THAT, TALBOT.
SAY IT OFTEN ENOUGH-- LOUD ENOUGH, AND MAYBE--
OH, GOOD LORD IN HEAVEN--
NO! NO!!
SHE-- SHE ISN'T MY FLESH AND BLOOD-- NOT ANY MORE.
BETTY'S-- BEEN TURNED INTO A STATUE-- A THING OF LIFELESS, UNMOVING GLASS!
WE-- TRIED TO WARN YOU, SIR. IT WAS-- THE TRANSFUSION.
BUT, WE'LL BRING HER BACK TO LIFE --SOMEHOW. WE--
GET OUT ALL OF YOU--
GET OUT!
I-- WANT TO BE LEFT ALONE--
--WITH MY-- DAUGHTER--!
AND NOW, THE HULK SURFACES-- THE RAGE WITHIN HIS BREAST MATCHING HIS BLINDING PAIN--
--AND YOU WONDER IF ANYTHING CAN EVER SOOTHE HIM AGAIN--!
NEXT: A WORLD AGAINST HIM!

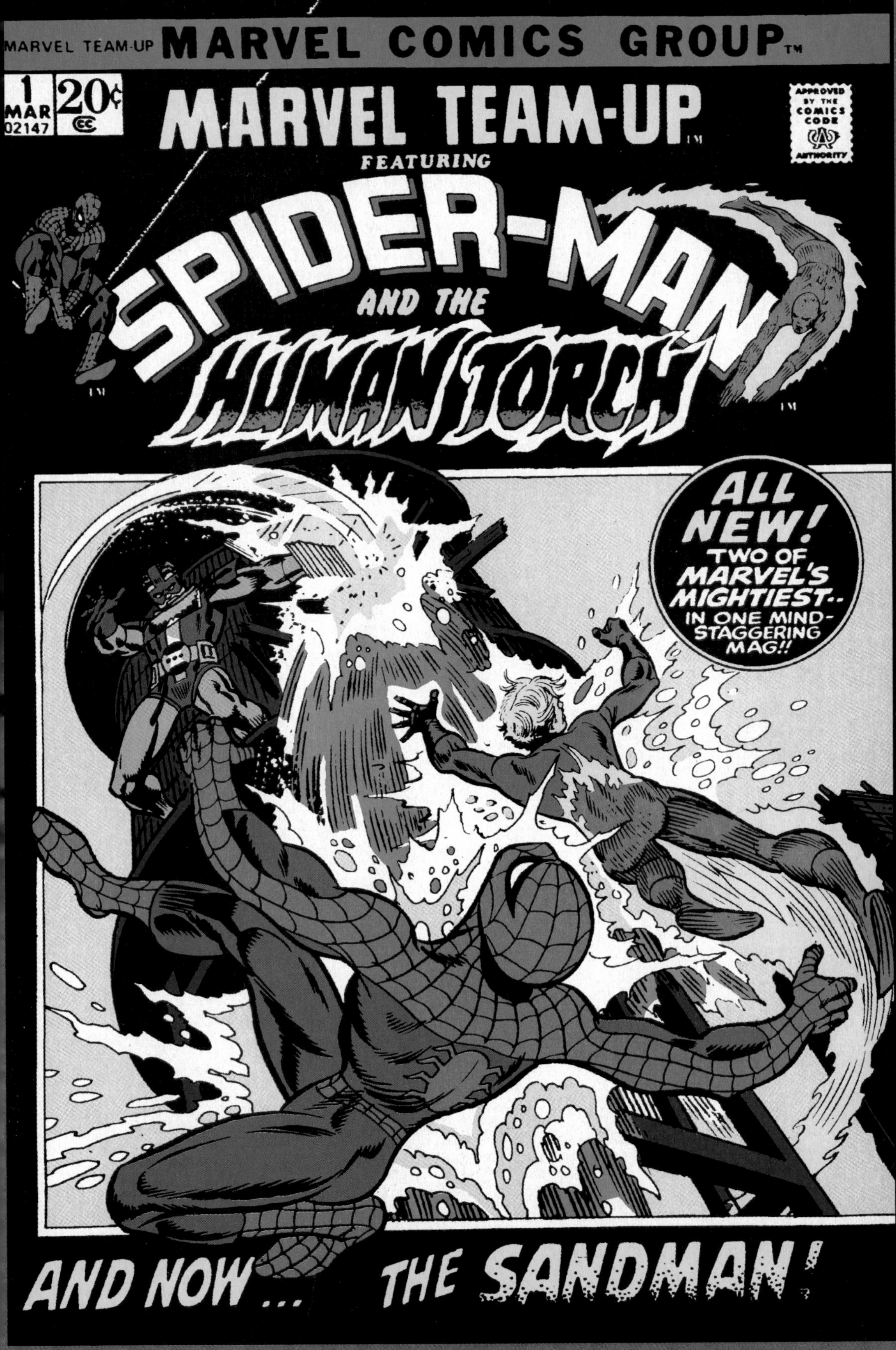

MARVEL TEAM-UP MARVEL COMICS GROUP™
1 MAR 02147
20¢
APPROVED BY THE COMICS CODE AUTHORITY
MARVEL TEAM-UP™
FEATURING
SPIDER-MAN™
AND THE
HUMAN TORCH™
ALL NEW! TWO OF MARVEL'S MIGHTIEST.. IN ONE MIND-STAGGERING MAG!!
AND NOW... THE SANDMAN!

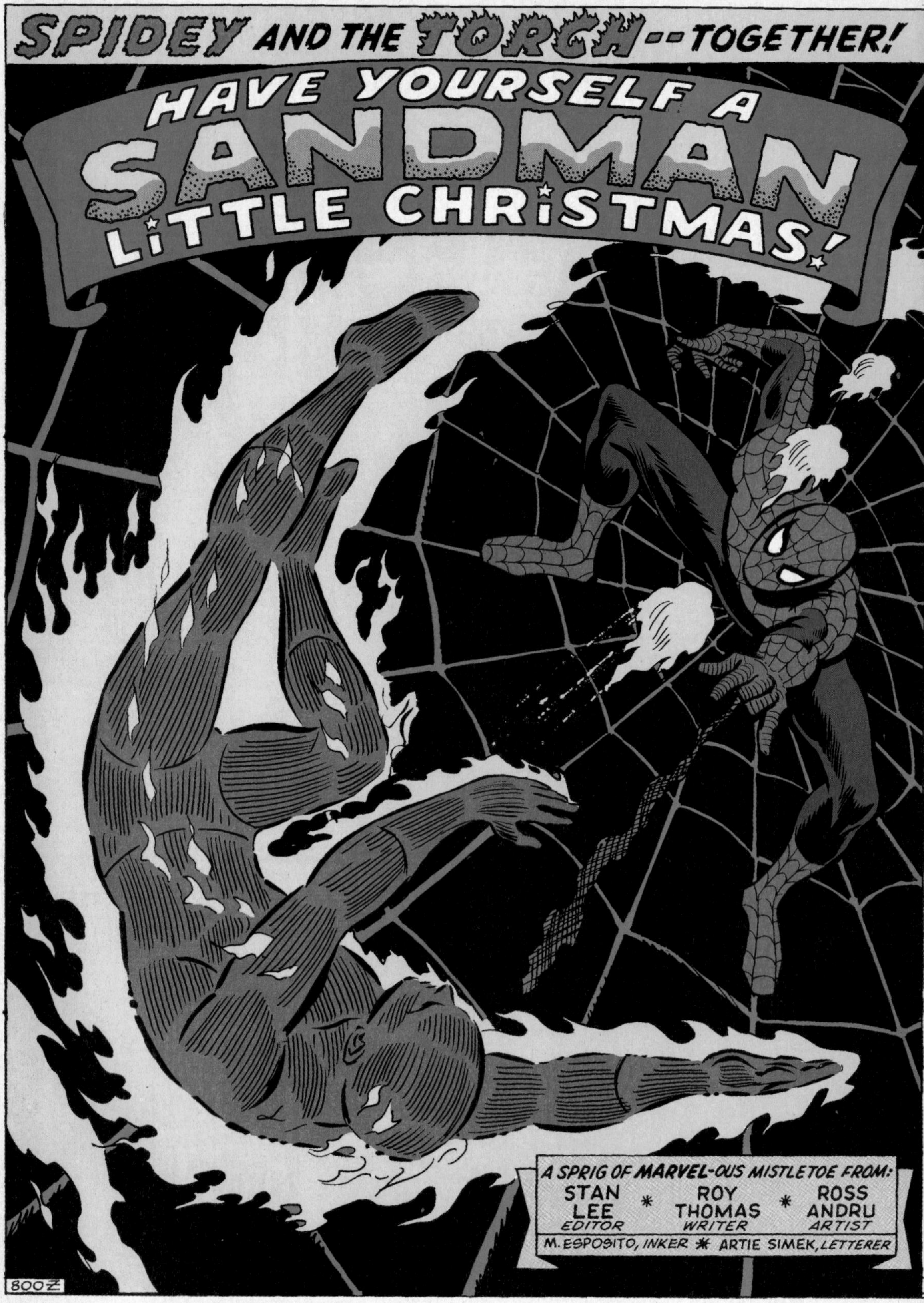

SPIDEY AND THE TORCH--TOGETHER!
HAVE YOURSELF A SANDMAN LITTLE CHRISTMAS!
A SPRIG OF MARVEL-OUS MISTLETOE FROM:
STAN LEE EDITOR * ROY THOMAS WRITER * ROSS ANDRU ARTIST
M. ESPOSITO, INKER * ARTIE SIMEK, LETTERER
800Z

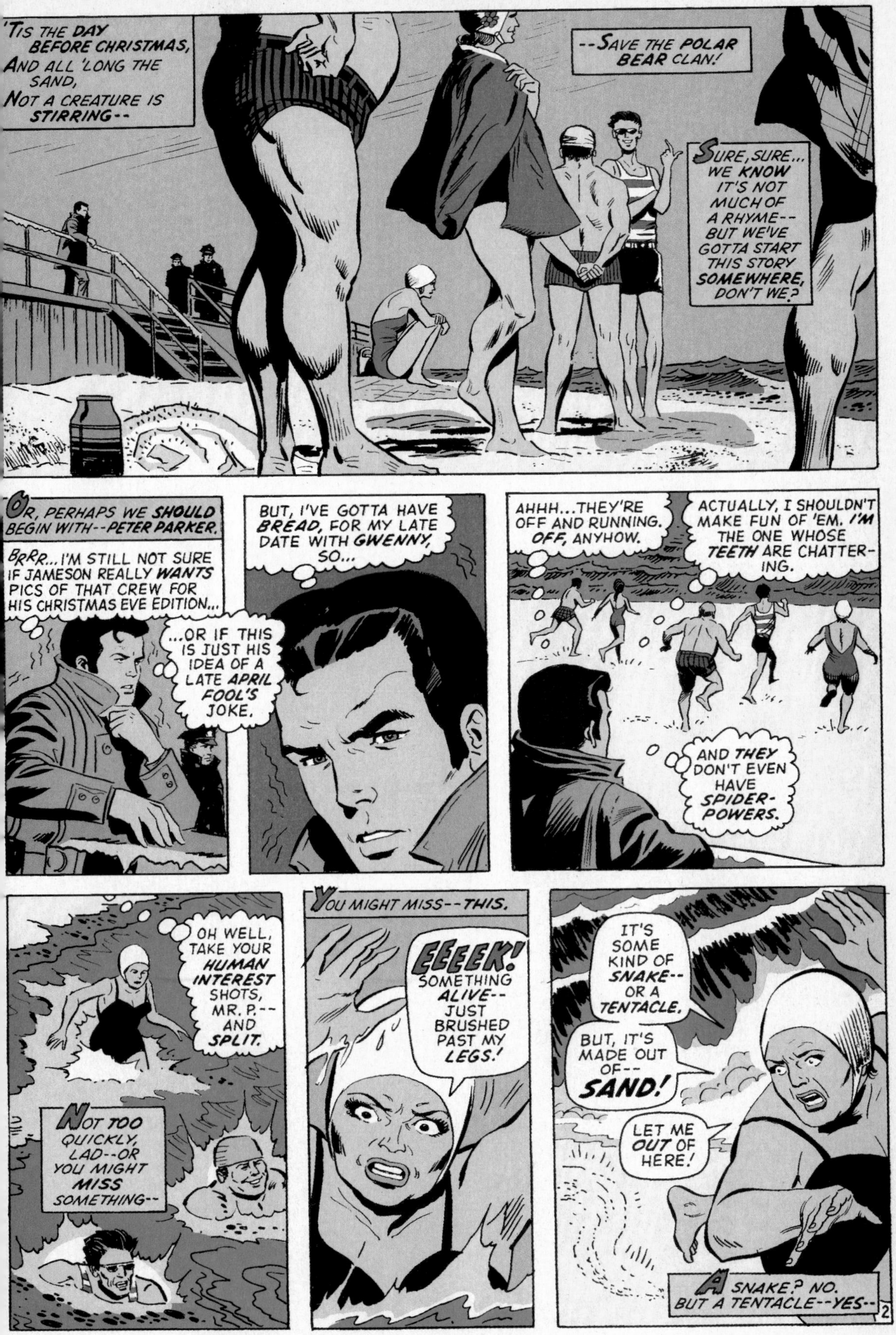
'TIS THE DAY BEFORE CHRISTMAS, AND ALL 'LONG THE SAND, NOT A CREATURE IS STIRRING--
--SAVE THE POLAR BEAR CLAN!
SURE, SURE... WE KNOW IT'S NOT MUCH OF A RHYME-- BUT WE'VE GOTTA START THIS STORY SOMEWHERE, DON'T WE?
OR, PERHAPS WE SHOULD BEGIN WITH--PETER PARKER.
BRRR... I'M STILL NOT SURE IF JAMESON REALLY WANTS PICS OF THAT CREW FOR HIS CHRISTMAS EVE EDITION...
...OR IF THIS IS JUST HIS IDEA OF A LATE APRIL FOOL'S JOKE.
BUT, I'VE GOTTA HAVE BREAD, FOR MY LATE DATE WITH GWENNY, SO...
AHHH...THEY'RE OFF AND RUNNING. OFF, ANYHOW.
ACTUALLY, I SHOULDN'T MAKE FUN OF 'EM. I'M THE ONE WHOSE TEETH ARE CHATTERING.
AND THEY DON'T EVEN HAVE SPIDER-POWERS.
OH WELL, TAKE YOUR HUMAN INTEREST SHOTS, MR. P.-- AND SPLIT.
NOT TOO QUICKLY, LAD--OR YOU MIGHT MISS SOMETHING--
YOU MIGHT MISS--THIS.
EEEEK! SOMETHING ALIVE-- JUST BRUSHED PAST MY LEGS!
IT'S SOME KIND OF SNAKE-- OR A TENTACLE.
BUT, IT'S MADE OUT OF-- SAND!
LET ME OUT OF HERE!
A SNAKE? NO. BUT A TENTACLE--YES--
2

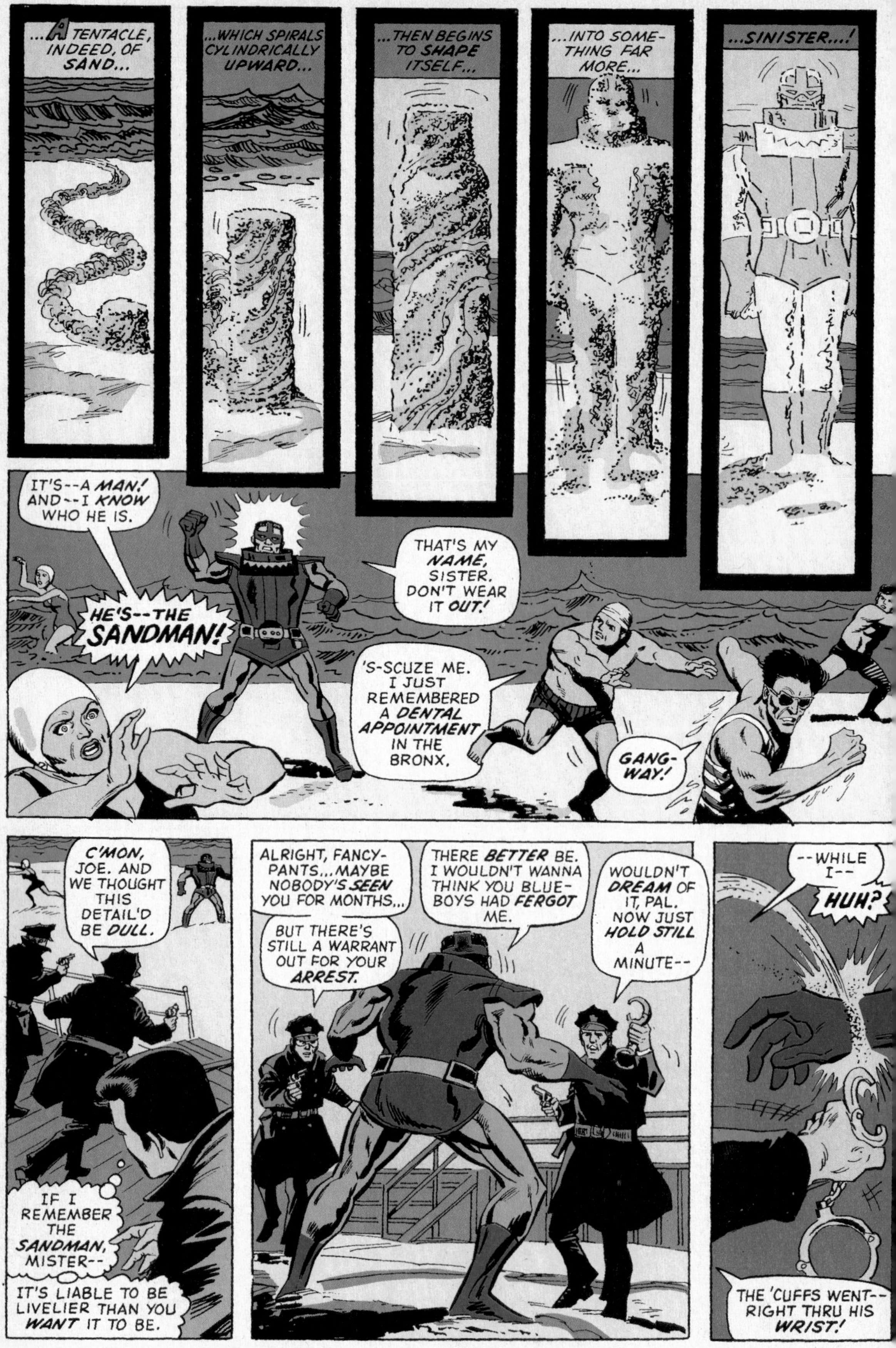
...A TENTACLE, INDEED, OF SAND...
...WHICH SPIRALS CYLINDRICALLY UPWARD...
...THEN BEGINS TO SHAPE ITSELF...
...INTO SOMETHING FAR MORE...
...SINISTER...!
IT'S--A MAN! AND--I KNOW WHO HE IS.
HE'S--THE SANDMAN!
THAT'S MY NAME, SISTER. DON'T WEAR IT OUT!
'S-SCUZE ME. I JUST REMEMBERED A DENTAL APPOINTMENT IN THE BRONX.
GANG-WAY!
C'MON, JOE. AND WE THOUGHT THIS DETAIL'D BE DULL.
IF I REMEMBER THE SANDMAN, MISTER--
IT'S LIABLE TO BE LIVELIER THAN YOU WANT IT TO BE.
ALRIGHT, FANCY-PANTS...MAYBE NOBODY'S SEEN YOU FOR MONTHS...
BUT THERE'S STILL A WARRANT OUT FOR YOUR ARREST.
THERE BETTER BE. I WOULDN'T WANNA THINK YOU BLUE-BOYS HAD FERGOT ME.
WOULDN'T DREAM OF IT, PAL. NOW JUST HOLD STILL A MINUTE--
--WHILE I--
HUH?
THE 'CUFFS WENT--RIGHT THRU HIS WRIST!

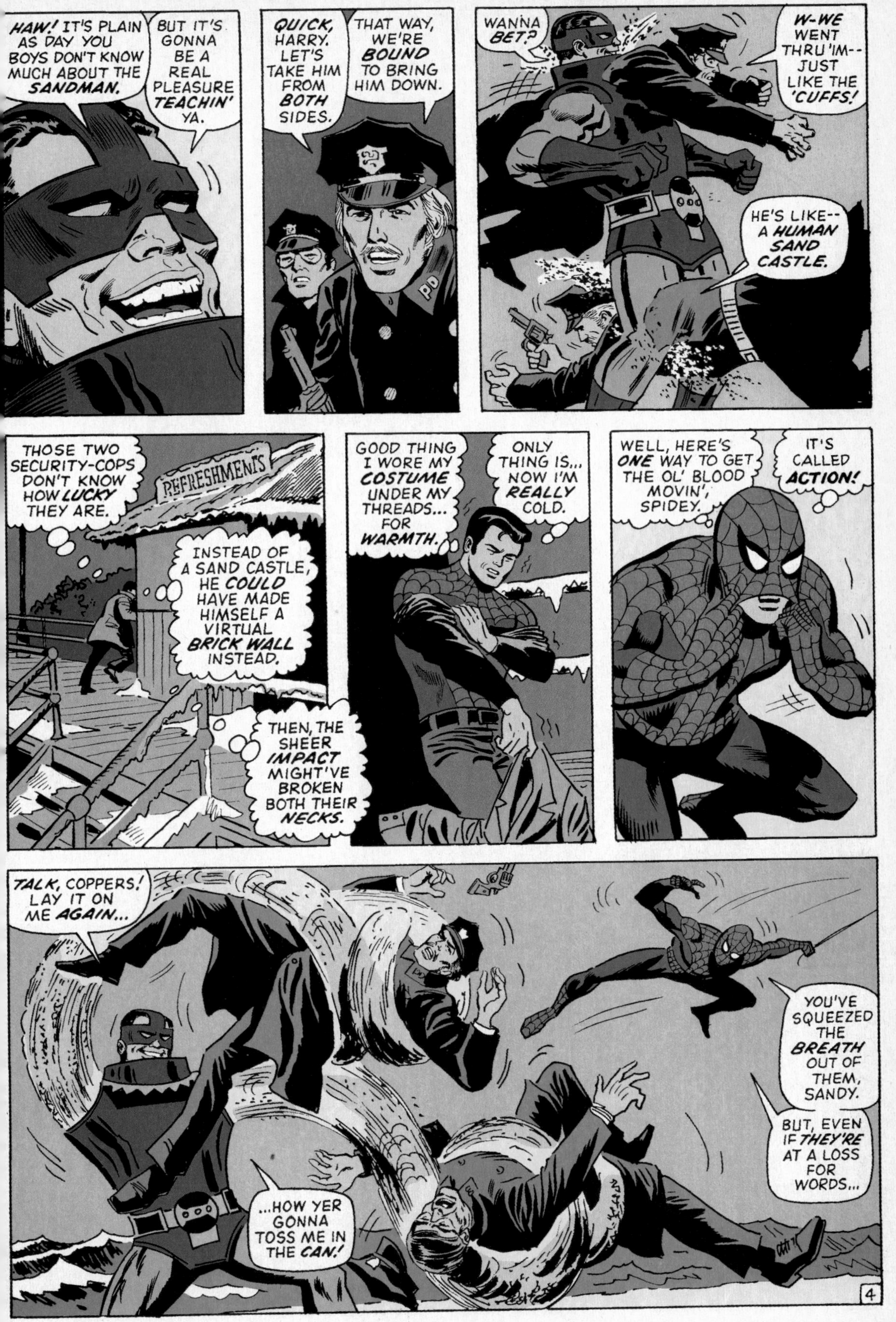
HAW! IT'S PLAIN AS DAY YOU BOYS DON'T KNOW MUCH ABOUT THE SANDMAN.
BUT IT'S GONNA BE A REAL PLEASURE TEACHIN' YA.
QUICK, HARRY. LET'S TAKE HIM FROM BOTH SIDES.
THAT WAY, WE'RE BOUND TO BRING HIM DOWN.
WANNA BET?
W-WE WENT THRU 'IM--JUST LIKE THE 'CUFFS!
HE'S LIKE--A HUMAN SAND CASTLE.
THOSE TWO SECURITY-COPS DON'T KNOW HOW LUCKY THEY ARE.
REFRESHMENTS
INSTEAD OF A SAND CASTLE, HE COULD HAVE MADE HIMSELF A VIRTUAL BRICK WALL INSTEAD.
THEN, THE SHEER IMPACT MIGHT'VE BROKEN BOTH THEIR NECKS.
GOOD THING I WORE MY COSTUME UNDER MY THREADS... FOR WARMTH.
ONLY THING IS... NOW I'M REALLY COLD.
WELL, HERE'S ONE WAY TO GET THE OL' BLOOD MOVIN', SPIDEY.
IT'S CALLED ACTION!
TALK, COPPERS! LAY IT ON ME AGAIN...
...HOW YER GONNA TOSS ME IN THE CAN!
YOU'VE SQUEEZED THE BREATH OUT OF THEM, SANDY.
BUT, EVEN IF THEY'RE AT A LOSS FOR WORDS...
4

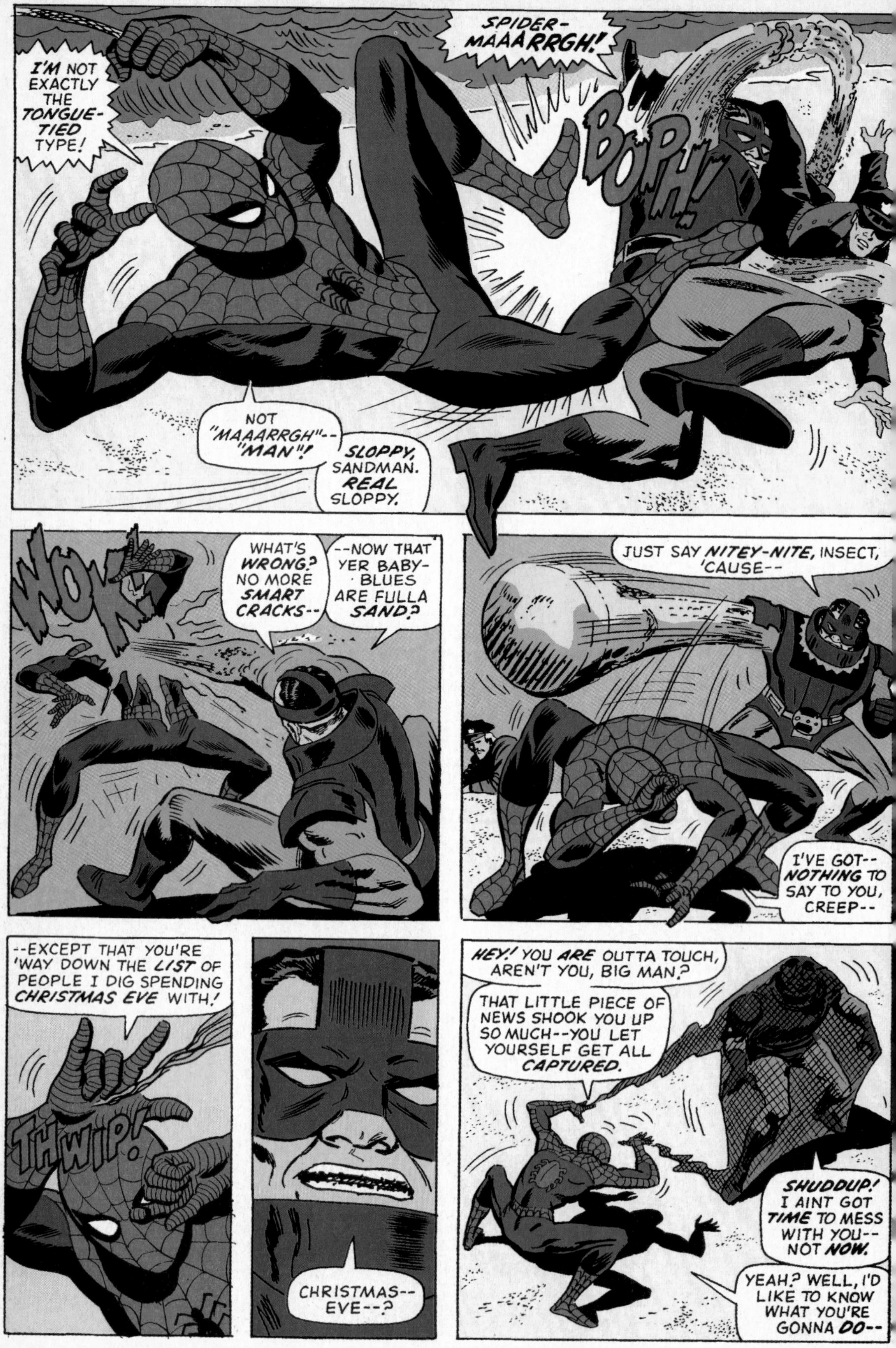
I'M NOT EXACTLY THE TONGUE-TIED TYPE!
SPIDER-MAAARRGH!
BOPH!
NOT "MAAARRGH"-- "MAN"!
SLOPPY, SANDMAN. REAL SLOPPY.
WOK
WHAT'S WRONG? NO MORE SMART CRACKS--
--NOW THAT YER BABY-BLUES ARE FULLA SAND?
JUST SAY NITEY-NITE, INSECT, 'CAUSE--
I'VE GOT-- NOTHING TO SAY TO YOU, CREEP--
--EXCEPT THAT YOU'RE 'WAY DOWN THE LIST OF PEOPLE I DIG SPENDING CHRISTMAS EVE WITH!
THWIP!
CHRISTMAS-- EVE--?
HEY! YOU ARE OUTTA TOUCH, AREN'T YOU, BIG MAN?
THAT LITTLE PIECE OF NEWS SHOOK YOU UP SO MUCH--YOU LET YOURSELF GET ALL CAPTURED.
SHUDDUP! I AINT GOT TIME TO MESS WITH YOU-- NOT NOW.
YEAH? WELL, I'D LIKE TO KNOW WHAT YOU'RE GONNA DO--

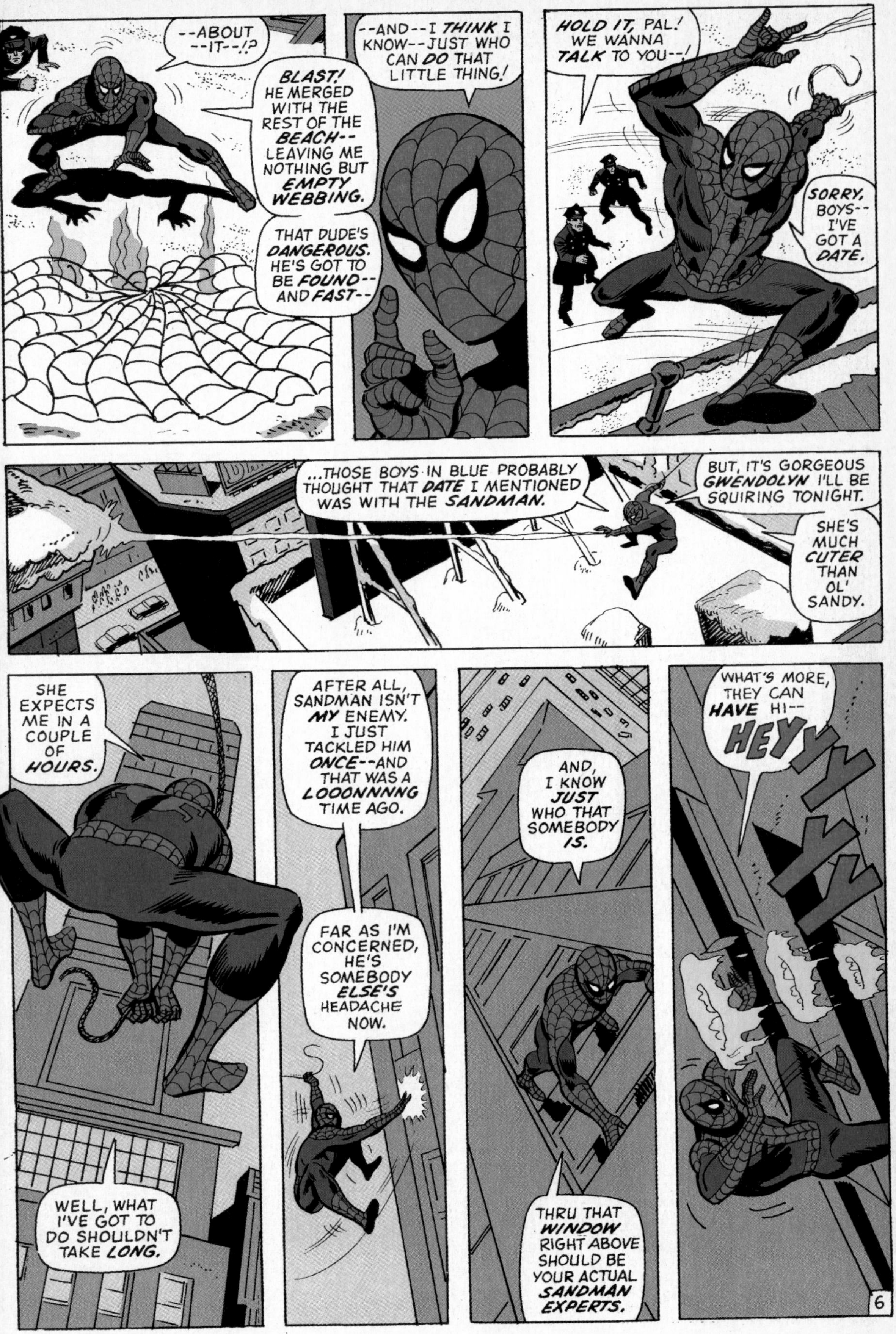
--ABOUT --IT--!?
BLAST! HE MERGED WITH THE REST OF THE BEACH-- LEAVING ME NOTHING BUT EMPTY WEBBING.
THAT DUDE'S DANGEROUS. HE'S GOT TO BE FOUND-- AND FAST--
--AND--I THINK I KNOW--JUST WHO CAN DO THAT LITTLE THING!
HOLD IT, PAL! WE WANNA TALK TO YOU--!
SORRY, BOYS-- I'VE GOT A DATE.
...THOSE BOYS IN BLUE PROBABLY THOUGHT THAT DATE I MENTIONED WAS WITH THE SANDMAN.
BUT, IT'S GORGEOUS GWENDOLYN I'LL BE SQUIRING TONIGHT.
SHE'S MUCH CUTER THAN OL' SANDY.
SHE EXPECTS ME IN A COUPLE OF HOURS.
WELL, WHAT I'VE GOT TO DO SHOULDN'T TAKE LONG.
AFTER ALL, SANDMAN ISN'T MY ENEMY. I JUST TACKLED HIM ONCE--AND THAT WAS A LOOONNNNG TIME AGO.
FAR AS I'M CONCERNED, HE'S SOMEBODY ELSE'S HEADACHE NOW.
AND, I KNOW JUST WHO THAT SOMEBODY IS.
THRU THAT WINDOW RIGHT ABOVE SHOULD BE YOUR ACTUAL SANDMAN EXPERTS.
WHAT'S MORE, THEY CAN HAVE HI--
HEYYYYY
6

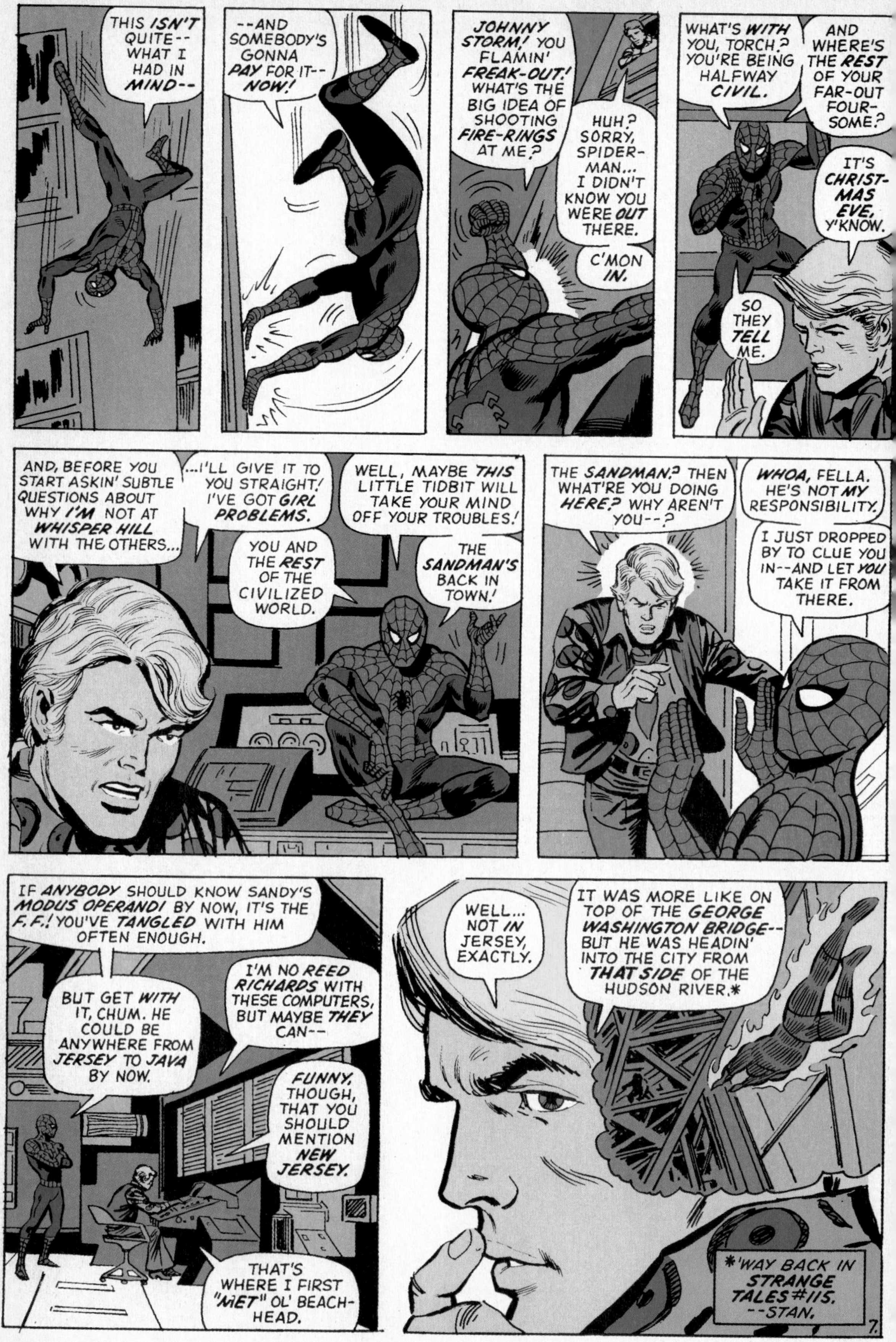

THIS ISN'T QUITE-- WHAT I HAD IN MIND--
--AND SOMEBODY'S GONNA PAY FOR IT-- NOW!
JOHNNY STORM! YOU FLAMIN' FREAK-OUT! WHAT'S THE BIG IDEA OF SHOOTING FIRE-RINGS AT ME?
HUH? SORRY, SPIDER-MAN... I DIDN'T KNOW YOU WERE OUT THERE.
C'MON IN.
WHAT'S WITH YOU, TORCH? YOU'RE BEING HALFWAY CIVIL.
AND WHERE'S THE REST OF YOUR FAR-OUT FOUR-SOME?
IT'S CHRIST-MAS EVE, Y'KNOW.
SO THEY TELL ME.
AND, BEFORE YOU START ASKIN' SUBTLE QUESTIONS ABOUT WHY I'M NOT AT WHISPER HILL WITH THE OTHERS...
...I'LL GIVE IT TO YOU STRAIGHT! I'VE GOT GIRL PROBLEMS.
YOU AND THE REST OF THE CIVILIZED WORLD.
WELL, MAYBE THIS LITTLE TIDBIT WILL TAKE YOUR MIND OFF YOUR TROUBLES!
THE SANDMAN'S BACK IN TOWN!
THE SANDMAN? THEN WHAT'RE YOU DOING HERE? WHY AREN'T YOU--?
WHOA, FELLA. HE'S NOT MY RESPONSIBILITY.
I JUST DROPPED BY TO CLUE YOU IN--AND LET YOU TAKE IT FROM THERE.
IF ANYBODY SHOULD KNOW SANDY'S MODUS OPERANDI BY NOW, IT'S THE F.F.! YOU'VE TANGLED WITH HIM OFTEN ENOUGH.
BUT GET WITH IT, CHUM. HE COULD BE ANYWHERE FROM JERSEY TO JAVA BY NOW.
I'M NO REED RICHARDS WITH THESE COMPUTERS, BUT MAYBE THEY CAN--
FUNNY, THOUGH, THAT YOU SHOULD MENTION NEW JERSEY.
THAT'S WHERE I FIRST "MET" OL' BEACH-HEAD.
WELL... NOT IN JERSEY, EXACTLY.
IT WAS MORE LIKE ON TOP OF THE GEORGE WASHINGTON BRIDGE--BUT HE WAS HEADIN' INTO THE CITY FROM THAT SIDE OF THE HUDSON RIVER.*
*'WAY BACK IN STRANGE TALES #115. --STAN.
7.

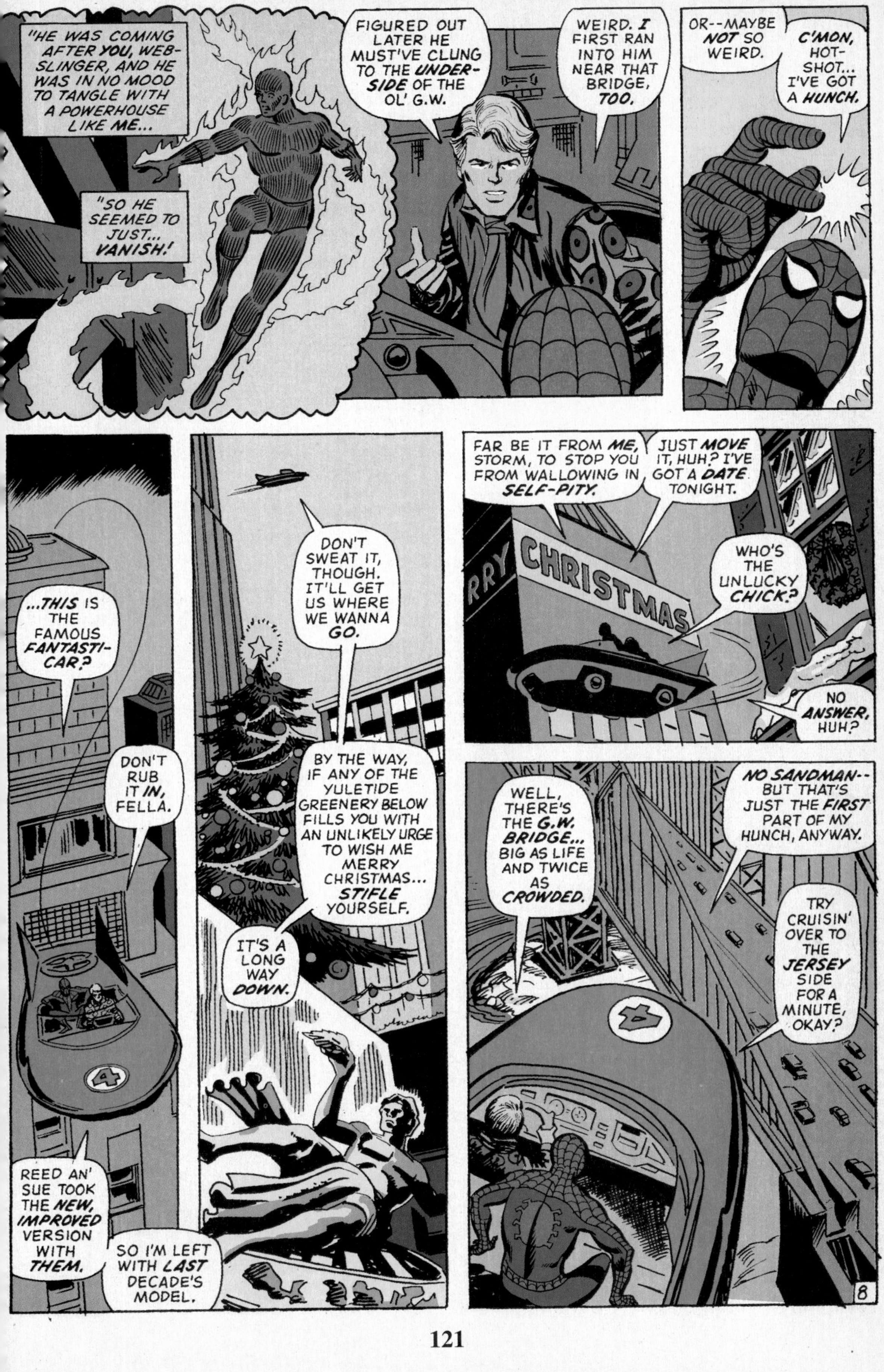
"HE WAS COMING AFTER YOU, WEB-SLINGER, AND HE WAS IN NO MOOD TO TANGLE WITH A POWERHOUSE LIKE ME...
"SO HE SEEMED TO JUST... VANISH!'
FIGURED OUT LATER HE MUST'VE CLUNG TO THE UNDER-SIDE OF THE OL' G.W.
WEIRD. I FIRST RAN INTO HIM NEAR THAT BRIDGE, TOO.
OR--MAYBE NOT SO WEIRD.
C'MON, HOT-SHOT... I'VE GOT A HUNCH.
...THIS IS THE FAMOUS FANTASTI-CAR?
DON'T RUB IT IN, FELLA.
REED AN' SUE TOOK THE NEW, IMPROVED VERSION WITH THEM.
SO I'M LEFT WITH LAST DECADE'S MODEL.
DON'T SWEAT IT, THOUGH. IT'LL GET US WHERE WE WANNA GO.
BY THE WAY, IF ANY OF THE YULETIDE GREENERY BELOW FILLS YOU WITH AN UNLIKELY URGE TO WISH ME MERRY CHRISTMAS... STIFLE YOURSELF.
IT'S A LONG WAY DOWN.
FAR BE IT FROM ME, STORM, TO STOP YOU FROM WALLOWING IN SELF-PITY.
JUST MOVE IT, HUH? I'VE GOT A DATE TONIGHT.
RRY CHRISTMAS
WHO'S THE UNLUCKY CHICK?
NO ANSWER, HUH?
WELL, THERE'S THE G.W. BRIDGE... BIG AS LIFE AND TWICE AS CROWDED.
NO SANDMAN-- BUT THAT'S JUST THE FIRST PART OF MY HUNCH, ANYWAY.
TRY CRUISIN' OVER TO THE JERSEY SIDE FOR A MINUTE, OKAY?
8

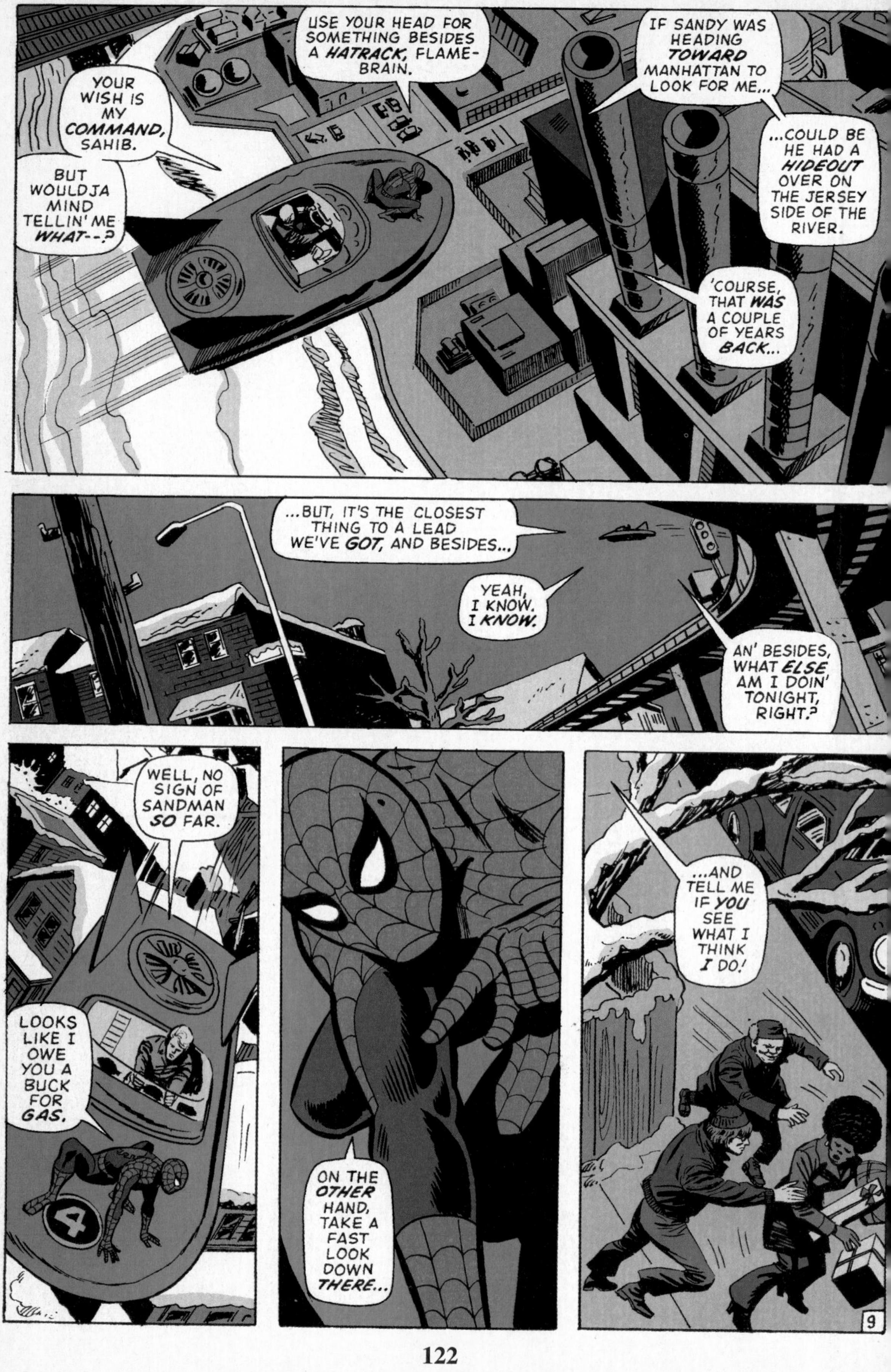
YOUR WISH IS MY COMMAND, SAHIB.
BUT WOULDJA MIND TELLIN' ME WHAT--?
USE YOUR HEAD FOR SOMETHING BESIDES A HATRACK, FLAME-BRAIN.
IF SANDY WAS HEADING TOWARD MANHATTAN TO LOOK FOR ME...
...COULD BE HE HAD A HIDEOUT OVER ON THE JERSEY SIDE OF THE RIVER.
'COURSE, THAT WAS A COUPLE OF YEARS BACK...
...BUT, IT'S THE CLOSEST THING TO A LEAD WE'VE GOT, AND BESIDES...
YEAH, I KNOW. I KNOW.
AN' BESIDES, WHAT ELSE AM I DOIN' TONIGHT, RIGHT?
WELL, NO SIGN OF SANDMAN SO FAR.
LOOKS LIKE I OWE YOU A BUCK FOR GAS.
4
ON THE OTHER HAND, TAKE A FAST LOOK DOWN THERE...
...AND TELL ME IF YOU SEE WHAT I THINK I DO!
9

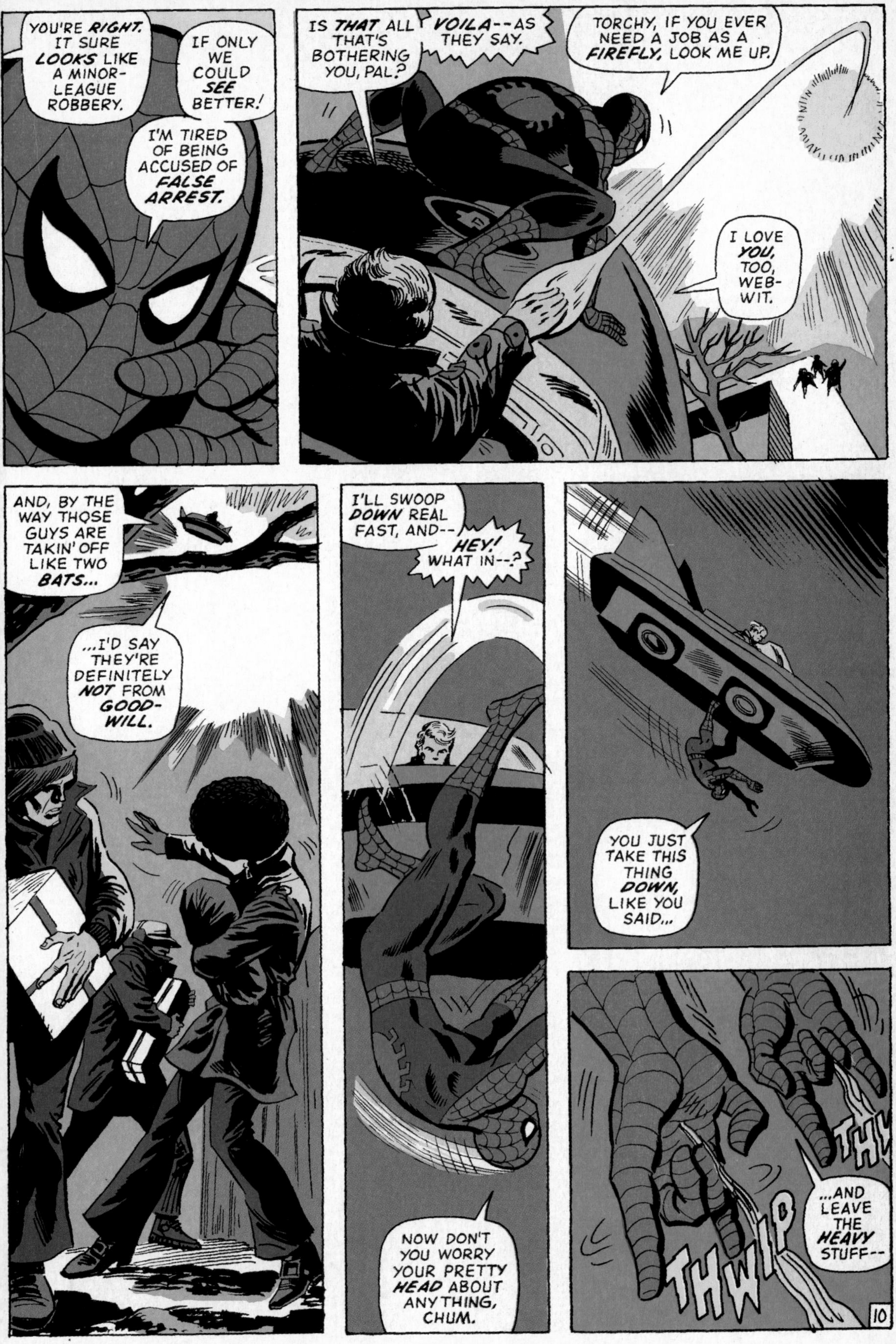
YOU'RE RIGHT. IT SURE LOOKS LIKE A MINOR-LEAGUE ROBBERY.
IF ONLY WE COULD SEE BETTER!
I'M TIRED OF BEING ACCUSED OF FALSE ARREST.
IS THAT ALL THAT'S BOTHERING YOU, PAL?
VOILA--AS THEY SAY.
TORCHY, IF YOU EVER NEED A JOB AS A FIREFLY, LOOK ME UP.
I LOVE YOU, TOO, WEB-WIT.
AND, BY THE WAY THOSE GUYS ARE TAKIN' OFF LIKE TWO BATS...
...I'D SAY THEY'RE DEFINITELY NOT FROM GOOD-WILL.
I'LL SWOOP DOWN REAL FAST, AND--
HEY! WHAT IN--?
NOW DON'T YOU WORRY YOUR PRETTY HEAD ABOUT ANYTHING, CHUM.
YOU JUST TAKE THIS THING DOWN, LIKE YOU SAID...
...AND LEAVE THE HEAVY STUFF--
THWIP
THW
10

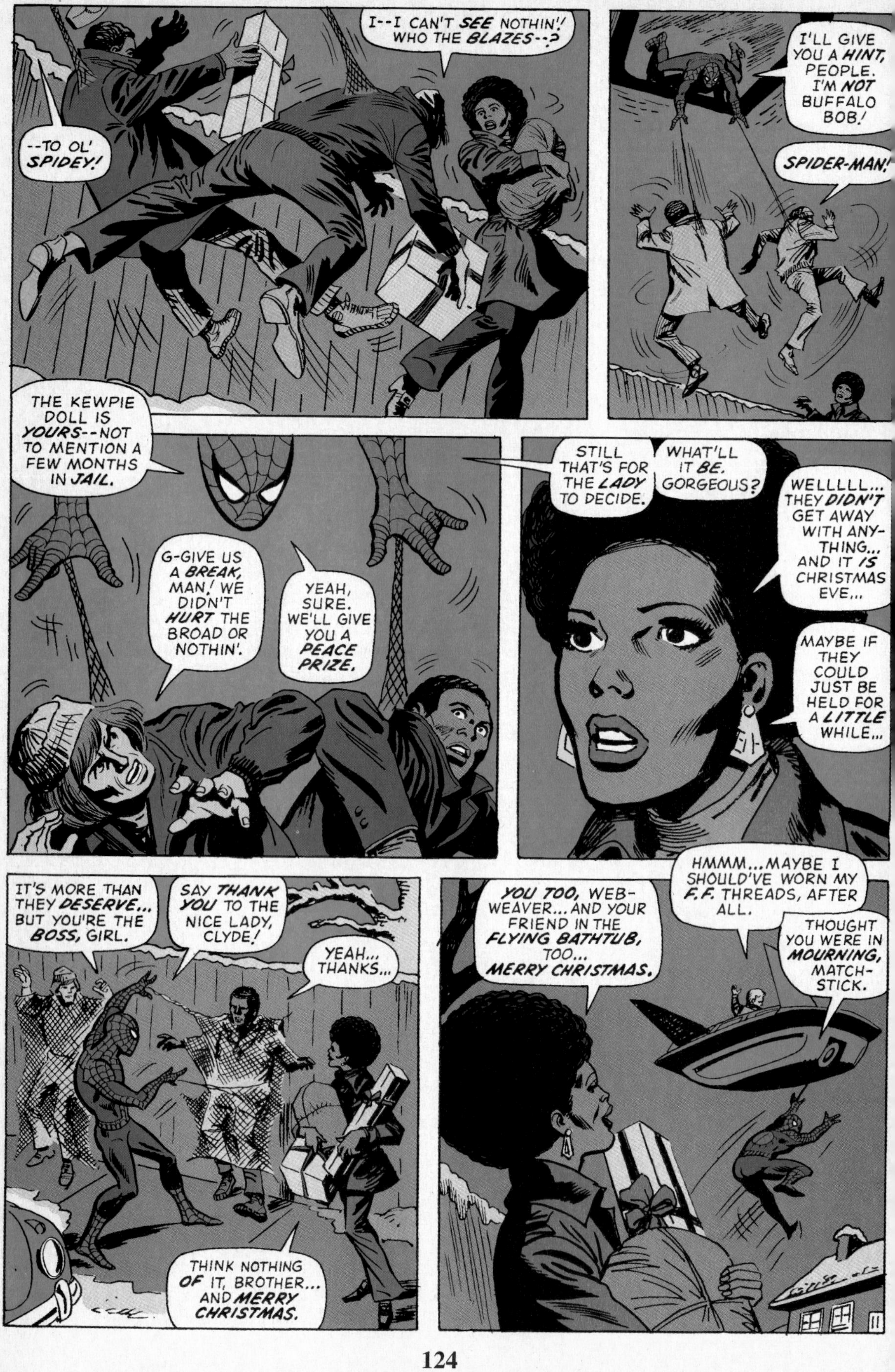
--TO OL' SPIDEY!
I--I CAN'T SEE NOTHIN'! WHO THE BLAZES--?
I'LL GIVE YOU A HINT, PEOPLE. I'M NOT BUFFALO BOB!
SPIDER-MAN!
THE KEWPIE DOLL IS YOURS--NOT TO MENTION A FEW MONTHS IN JAIL.
G-GIVE US A BREAK, MAN! WE DIDN'T HURT THE BROAD OR NOTHIN'.
YEAH, SURE. WE'LL GIVE YOU A PEACE PRIZE.
STILL THAT'S FOR THE LADY TO DECIDE.
WHAT'LL IT BE, GORGEOUS?
WELLLLL... THEY DIDN'T GET AWAY WITH ANYTHING... AND IT IS CHRISTMAS EVE...
MAYBE IF THEY COULD JUST BE HELD FOR A LITTLE WHILE...
IT'S MORE THAN THEY DESERVE... BUT YOU'RE THE BOSS, GIRL.
SAY THANK YOU TO THE NICE LADY, CLYDE!
YEAH... THANKS...
THINK NOTHING OF IT, BROTHER... AND MERRY CHRISTMAS.
YOU TOO, WEB-WEAVER... AND YOUR FRIEND IN THE FLYING BATHTUB, TOO... MERRY CHRISTMAS.
HMMM... MAYBE I SHOULD'VE WORN MY F.F. THREADS, AFTER ALL.
THOUGHT YOU WERE IN MOURNING, MATCH-STICK.
11

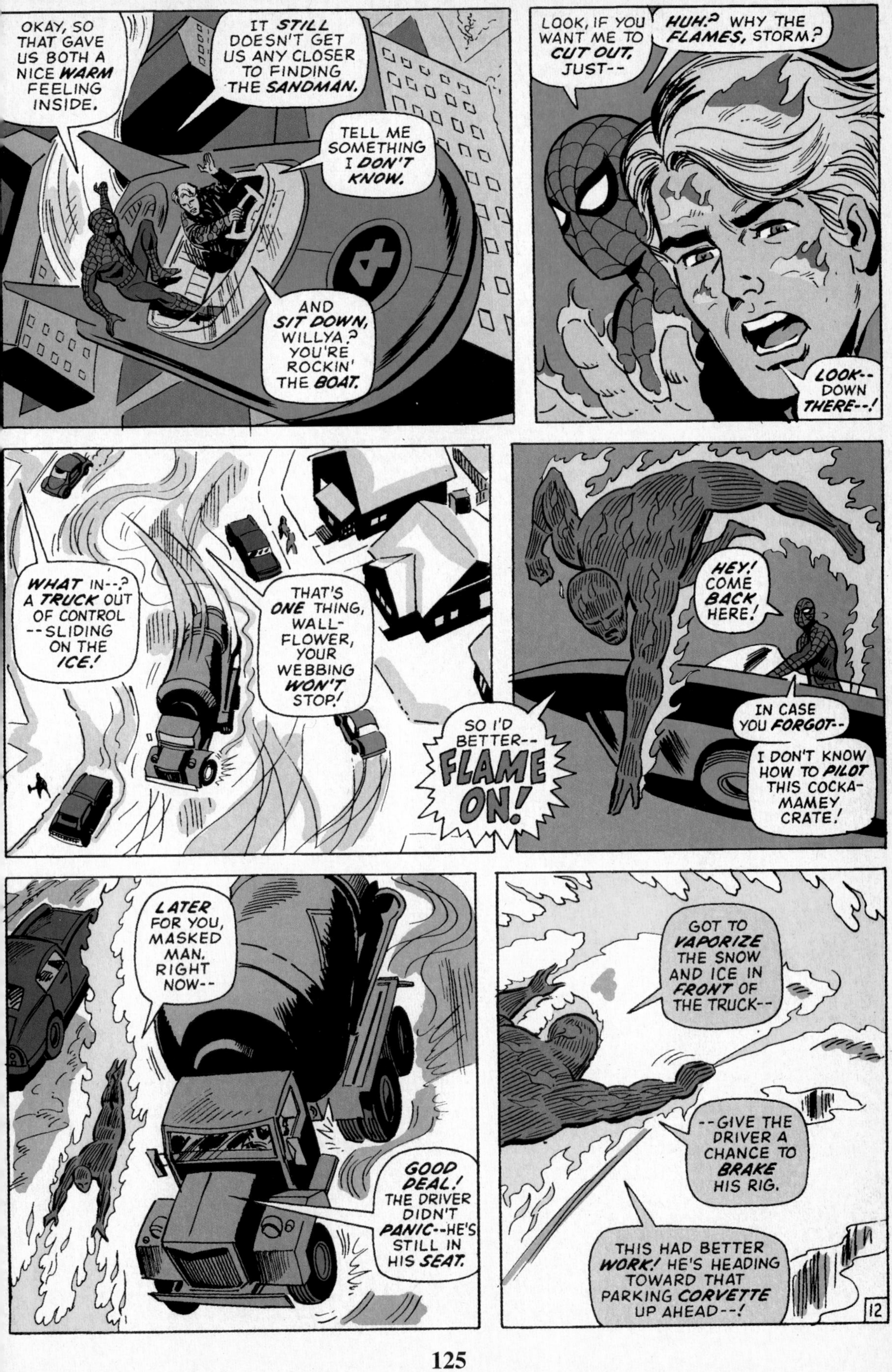

OKAY, SO THAT GAVE US BOTH A NICE WARM FEELING INSIDE.
IT STILL DOESN'T GET US ANY CLOSER TO FINDING THE SANDMAN.
TELL ME SOMETHING I DON'T KNOW.
AND SIT DOWN, WILLYA? YOU'RE ROCKIN' THE BOAT.
LOOK, IF YOU WANT ME TO CUT OUT, JUST--
HUH? WHY THE FLAMES, STORM?
LOOK-- DOWN THERE--!
WHAT IN--? A TRUCK OUT OF CONTROL --SLIDING ON THE ICE!
THAT'S ONE THING, WALL-FLOWER, YOUR WEBBING WON'T STOP!
SO I'D BETTER--
FLAME ON!
HEY! COME BACK HERE!
IN CASE YOU FORGOT--
I DON'T KNOW HOW TO PILOT THIS COCKA-MAMEY CRATE!
LATER FOR YOU, MASKED MAN. RIGHT NOW--
GOOD DEAL! THE DRIVER DIDN'T PANIC--HE'S STILL IN HIS SEAT.
GOT TO VAPORIZE THE SNOW AND ICE IN FRONT OF THE TRUCK--
--GIVE THE DRIVER A CHANCE TO BRAKE HIS RIG.
THIS HAD BETTER WORK! HE'S HEADING TOWARD THAT PARKING CORVETTE UP AHEAD--!
12

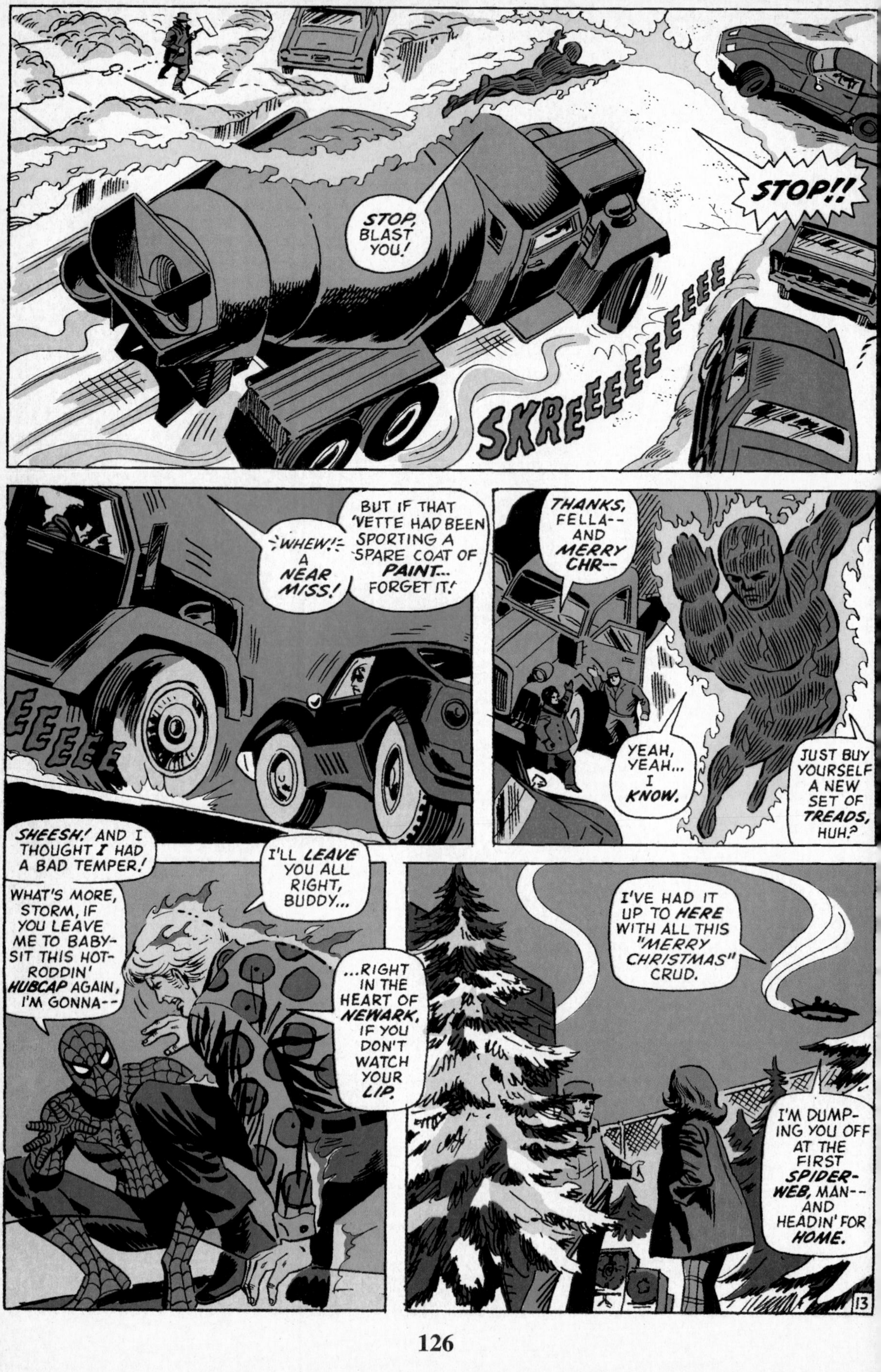
STOP, BLAST YOU!
STOP!!
SKREEEEEEEEEE
WHEW! A NEAR MISS!
BUT IF THAT 'VETTE HAD BEEN SPORTING A SPARE COAT OF PAINT... FORGET IT!
THANKS, FELLA-- AND MERRY CHR--
YEAH, YEAH... I KNOW.
JUST BUY YOURSELF A NEW SET OF TREADS, HUH?
SHEESH! AND I THOUGHT I HAD A BAD TEMPER!
WHAT'S MORE, STORM, IF YOU LEAVE ME TO BABY-SIT THIS HOT-RODDIN' HUBCAP AGAIN, I'M GONNA--
I'LL LEAVE YOU ALL RIGHT, BUDDY...
...RIGHT IN THE HEART OF NEWARK, IF YOU DON'T WATCH YOUR LIP.
I'VE HAD IT UP TO HERE WITH ALL THIS "MERRY CHRISTMAS" CRUD.
I'M DUMPING YOU OFF AT THE FIRST SPIDER-WEB, MAN-- AND HEADIN' FOR HOME.
13

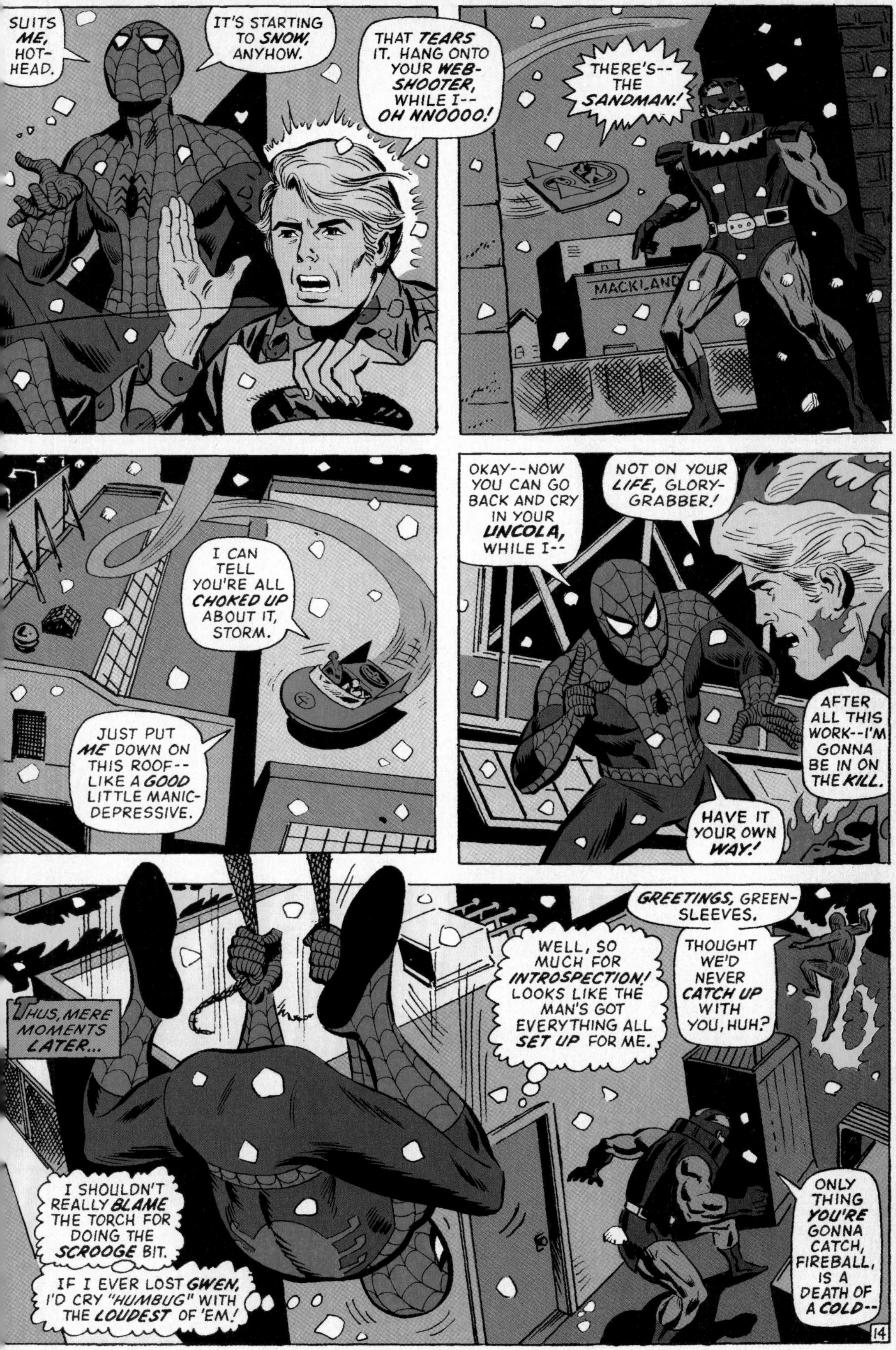

SUITS ME, HOT-HEAD.
IT'S STARTING TO SNOW, ANYHOW.
THAT TEARS IT. HANG ONTO YOUR WEB-SHOOTER, WHILE I-- OH NNOOOO!
THERE'S-- THE SANDMAN!
MACKLAND
I CAN TELL YOU'RE ALL CHOKED UP ABOUT IT, STORM.
JUST PUT ME DOWN ON THIS ROOF-- LIKE A GOOD LITTLE MANIC-DEPRESSIVE.
OKAY--NOW YOU CAN GO BACK AND CRY IN YOUR UNCOLA, WHILE I--
NOT ON YOUR LIFE, GLORY-GRABBER!
AFTER ALL THIS WORK--I'M GONNA BE IN ON THE KILL.
HAVE IT YOUR OWN WAY!
THUS, MERE MOMENTS LATER...
I SHOULDN'T REALLY BLAME THE TORCH FOR DOING THE SCROOGE BIT.
IF I EVER LOST GWEN, I'D CRY "HUMBUG" WITH THE LOUDEST OF 'EM!
WELL, SO MUCH FOR INTROSPECTION! LOOKS LIKE THE MAN'S GOT EVERYTHING ALL SET UP FOR ME.
GREETINGS, GREEN-SLEEVES.
THOUGHT WE'D NEVER CATCH UP WITH YOU, HUH?
ONLY THING YOU'RE GONNA CATCH, FIREBALL, IS A DEATH OF A COLD--
14

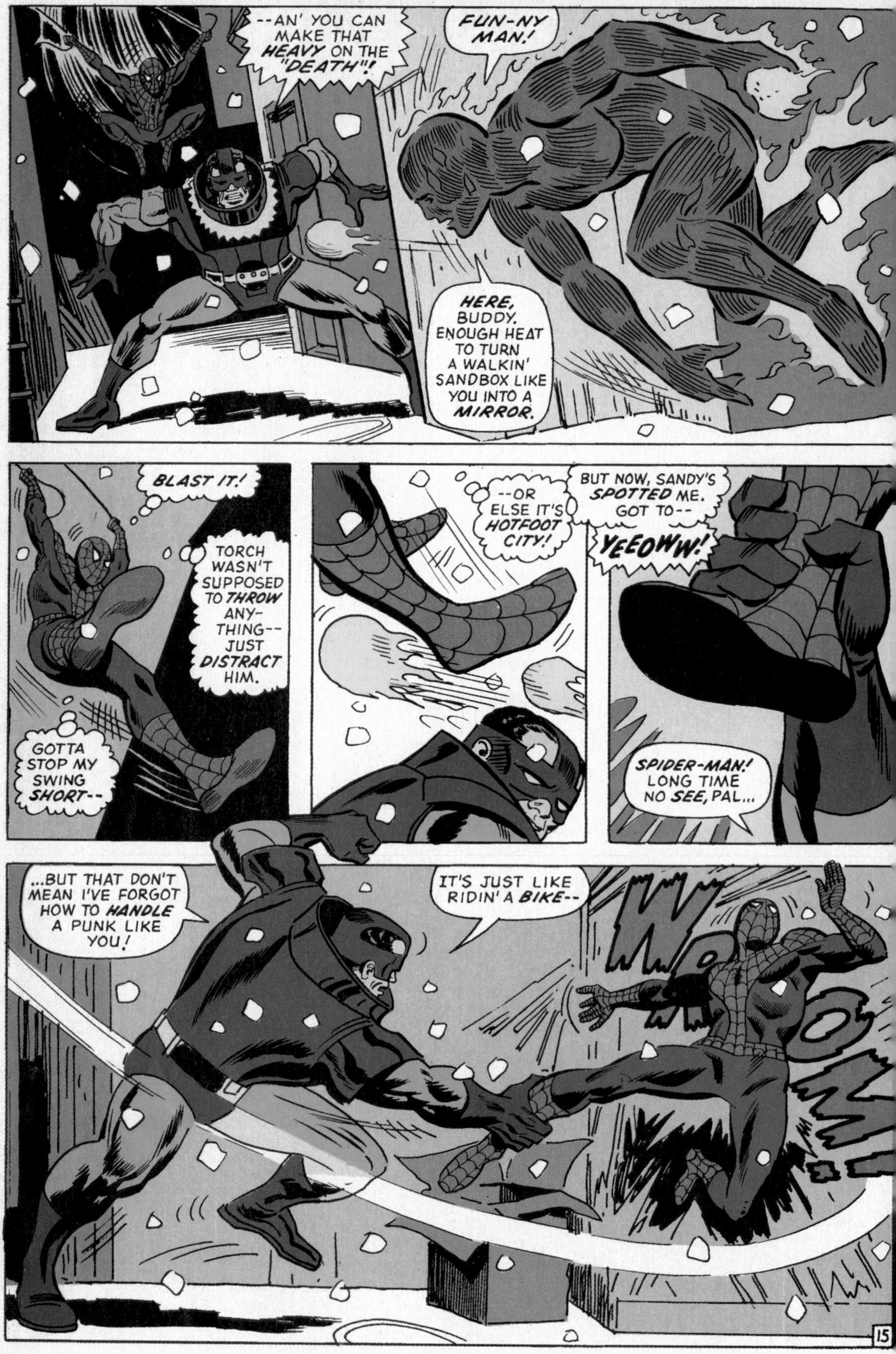
--AN' YOU CAN MAKE THAT HEAVY ON THE "DEATH"!
FUN-NY MAN!
HERE, BUDDY. ENOUGH HEAT TO TURN A WALKIN' SANDBOX LIKE YOU INTO A MIRROR.
BLAST IT!
TORCH WASN'T SUPPOSED TO THROW ANYTHING--JUST DISTRACT HIM.
GOTTA STOP MY SWING SHORT--
--OR ELSE IT'S HOTFOOT CITY!
BUT NOW, SANDY'S SPOTTED ME. GOT TO--
YEEOWW!
SPIDER-MAN! LONG TIME NO SEE, PAL...
...BUT THAT DON'T MEAN I'VE FORGOT HOW TO HANDLE A PUNK LIKE YOU!
IT'S JUST LIKE RIDIN' A BIKE--
15

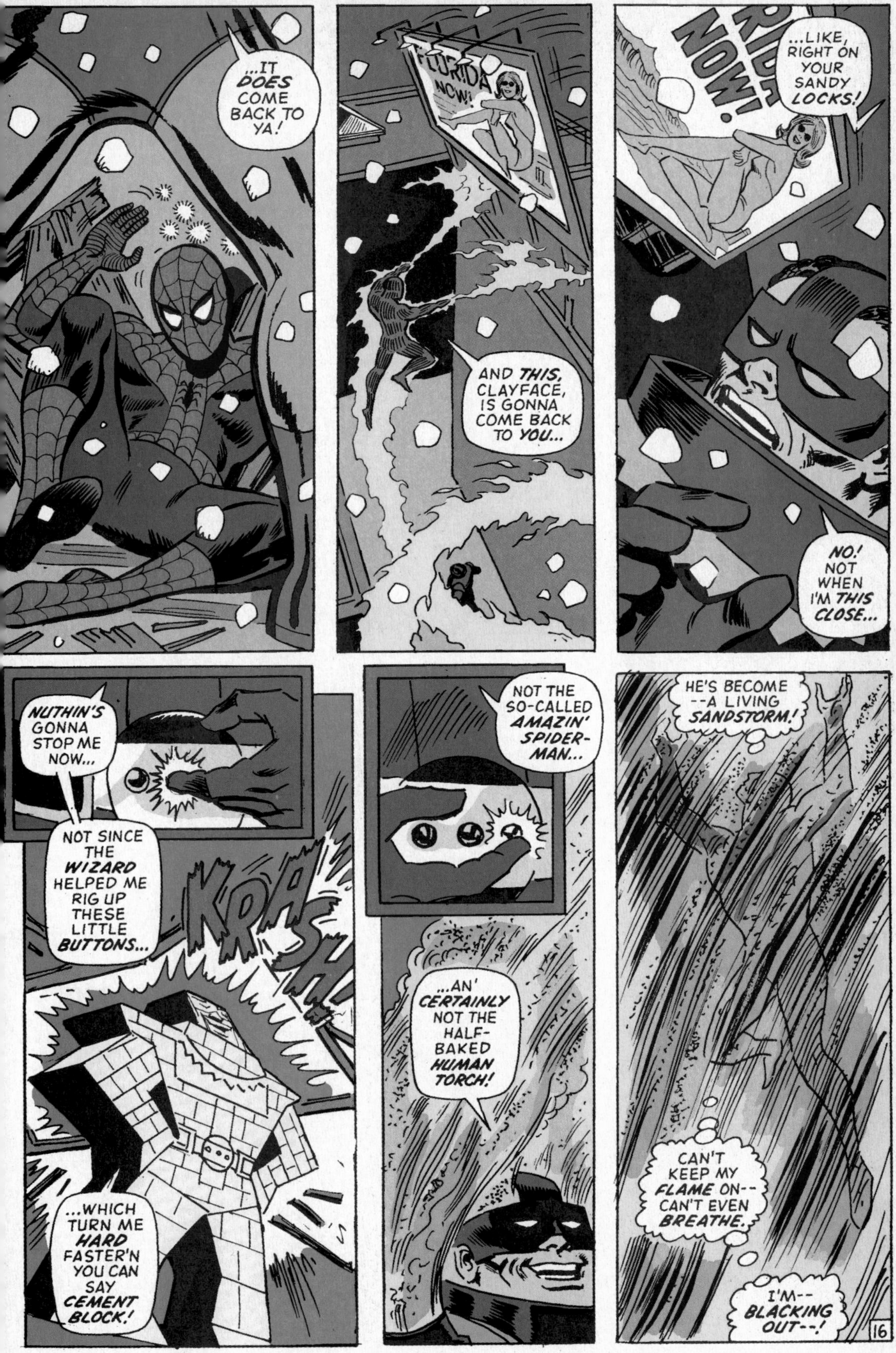
...IT DOES COME BACK TO YA!
FLORIDA NOW!
AND THIS, CLAYFACE, IS GONNA COME BACK TO YOU...
...LIKE, RIGHT ON YOUR SANDY LOCKS!
NO! NOT WHEN I'M THIS CLOSE...
NUTHIN'S GONNA STOP ME NOW...
NOT SINCE THE WIZARD HELPED ME RIG UP THESE LITTLE BUTTONS...
KRASH!
...WHICH TURN ME HARD FASTER'N YOU CAN SAY CEMENT BLOCK!
NOT THE SO-CALLED AMAZIN' SPIDER-MAN...
...AN' CERTAINLY NOT THE HALF-BAKED HUMAN TORCH!
HE'S BECOME --A LIVING SANDSTORM!
CAN'T KEEP MY FLAME ON--CAN'T EVEN BREATHE.
I'M--BLACKING OUT--!
16

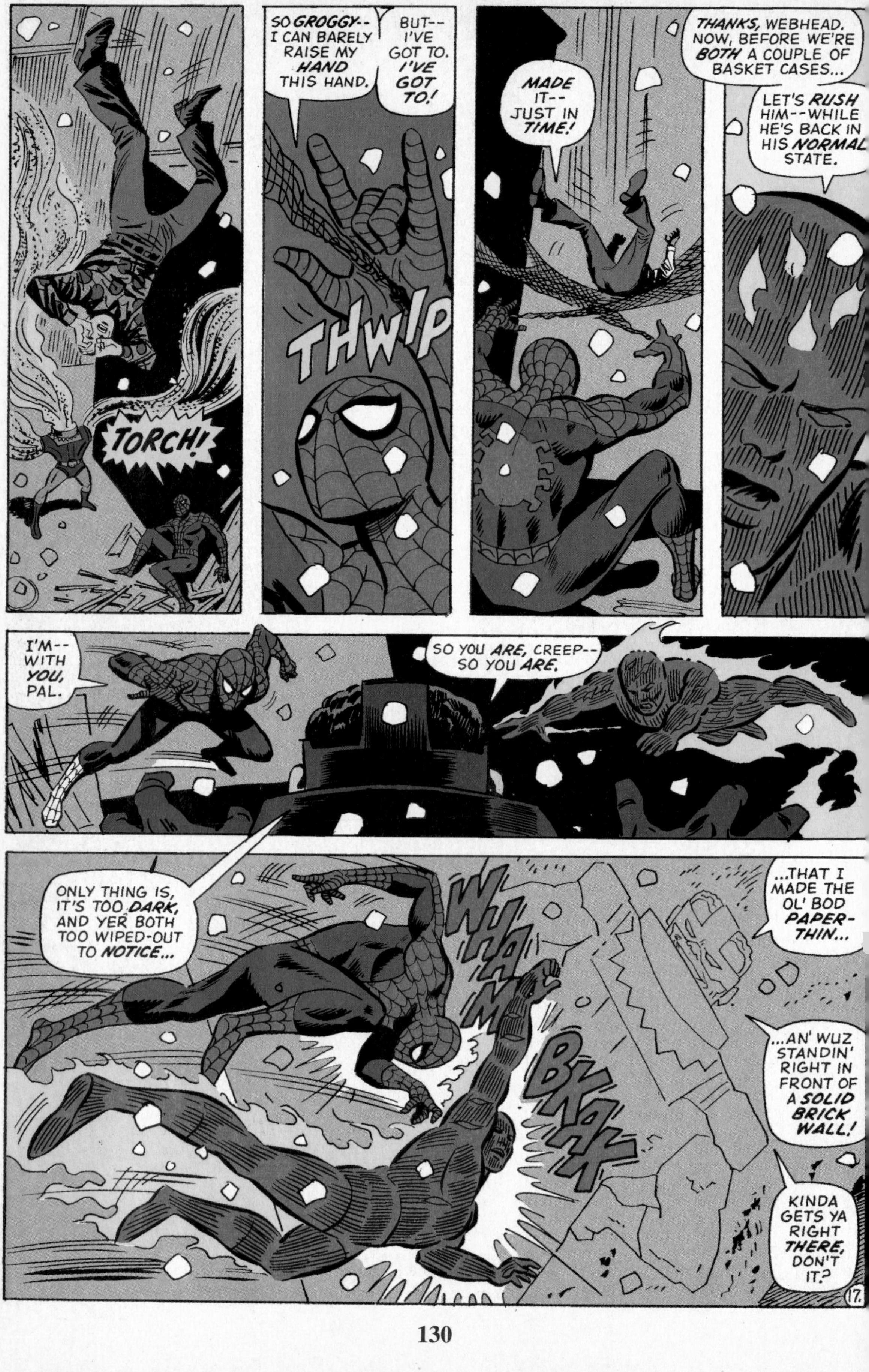
TORCH!
SO GROGGY-- I CAN BARELY RAISE MY HAND THIS HAND.
BUT-- I'VE GOT TO. I'VE GOT TO!
THWIP
MADE IT-- JUST IN TIME!
THANKS, WEBHEAD. NOW, BEFORE WE'RE BOTH A COUPLE OF BASKET CASES...
LET'S RUSH HIM--WHILE HE'S BACK IN HIS NORMAL STATE.
I'M-- WITH YOU, PAL.
SO YOU ARE, CREEP-- SO YOU ARE.
ONLY THING IS, IT'S TOO DARK, AND YER BOTH TOO WIPED-OUT TO NOTICE...
...THAT I MADE THE OL' BOD PAPER-THIN...
...AN' WUZ STANDIN' RIGHT IN FRONT OF A SOLID BRICK WALL!
KINDA GETS YA RIGHT THERE, DON'T IT?
WHAM
BKAK
17

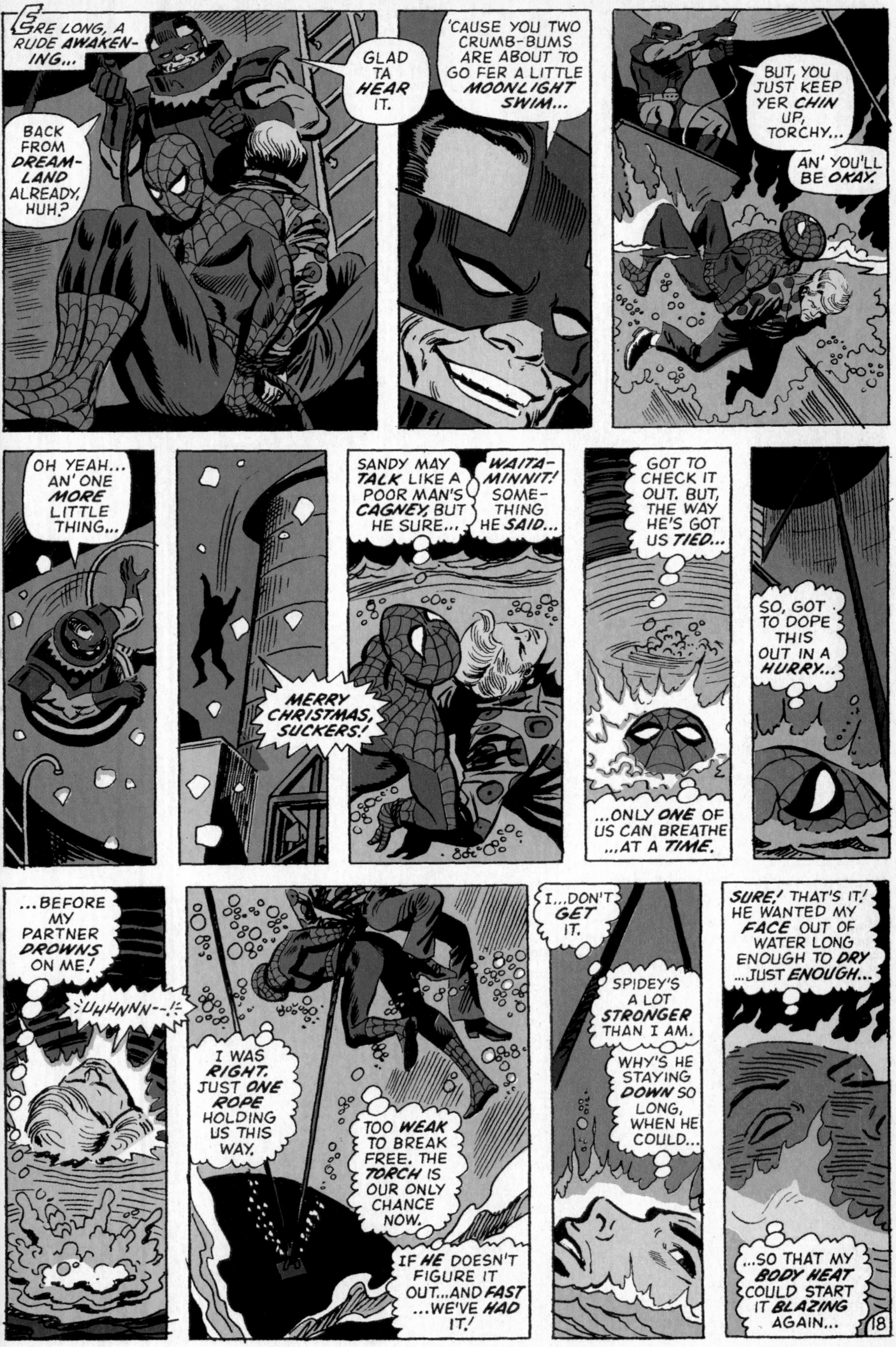

ERE LONG, A RUDE AWAKENING...
BACK FROM DREAM-LAND ALREADY, HUH?
GLAD TA HEAR IT.
'CAUSE YOU TWO CRUMB-BUMS ARE ABOUT TO GO FER A LITTLE MOONLIGHT SWIM...
BUT, YOU JUST KEEP YER CHIN UP, TORCHY...
AN' YOU'LL BE OKAY.
OH YEAH... AN' ONE MORE LITTLE THING...
MERRY CHRISTMAS, SUCKERS!
SANDY MAY TALK LIKE A POOR MAN'S CAGNEY, BUT HE SURE...
WAITA-MINNIT! SOME-THING HE SAID...
GOT TO CHECK IT OUT. BUT, THE WAY HE'S GOT US TIED...
...ONLY ONE OF US CAN BREATHE ...AT A TIME.
SO, GOT TO DOPE THIS OUT IN A HURRY...
...BEFORE MY PARTNER DROWNS ON ME!
UHHNNN--!
I WAS RIGHT. JUST ONE ROPE HOLDING US THIS WAY.
TOO WEAK TO BREAK FREE. THE TORCH IS OUR ONLY CHANCE NOW.
IF HE DOESN'T FIGURE IT OUT...AND FAST ...WE'VE HAD IT!
I...DON'T GET IT.
SPIDEY'S A LOT STRONGER THAN I AM.
WHY'S HE STAYING DOWN SO LONG, WHEN HE COULD...
SURE! THAT'S IT! HE WANTED MY FACE OUT OF WATER LONG ENOUGH TO DRY ...JUST ENOUGH...
...SO THAT MY BODY HEAT COULD START IT BLAZING AGAIN...
18

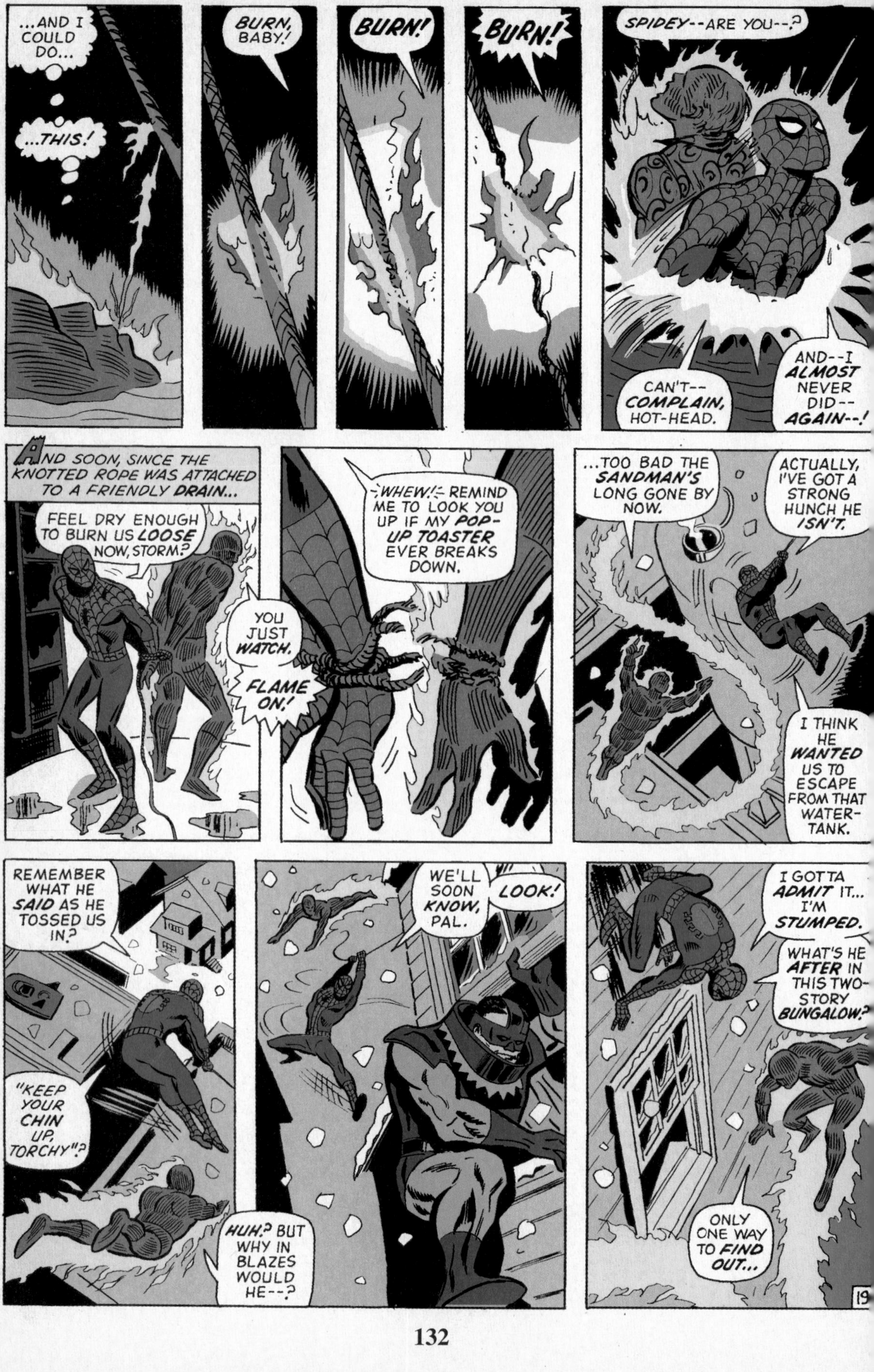
...AND I COULD DO...
...THIS!
BURN, BABY!
BURN!
BURN!
SPIDEY--ARE YOU--?
CAN'T-- COMPLAIN, HOT-HEAD.
AND--I ALMOST NEVER DID-- AGAIN--!
AND SOON, SINCE THE KNOTTED ROPE WAS ATTACHED TO A FRIENDLY DRAIN...
FEEL DRY ENOUGH TO BURN US LOOSE NOW, STORM?
YOU JUST WATCH.
FLAME ON!
WHEW!-- REMIND ME TO LOOK YOU UP IF MY POP-UP TOASTER EVER BREAKS DOWN.
...TOO BAD THE SANDMAN'S LONG GONE BY NOW.
ACTUALLY, I'VE GOT A STRONG HUNCH HE ISN'T.
I THINK HE WANTED US TO ESCAPE FROM THAT WATER-TANK.
REMEMBER WHAT HE SAID AS HE TOSSED US IN?
"KEEP YOUR CHIN UP, TORCHY"?
HUH? BUT WHY IN BLAZES WOULD HE--?
WE'LL SOON KNOW, PAL.
LOOK!
I GOTTA ADMIT IT... I'M STUMPED.
WHAT'S HE AFTER IN THIS TWO-STORY BUNGALOW?
ONLY ONE WAY TO FIND OUT...
19

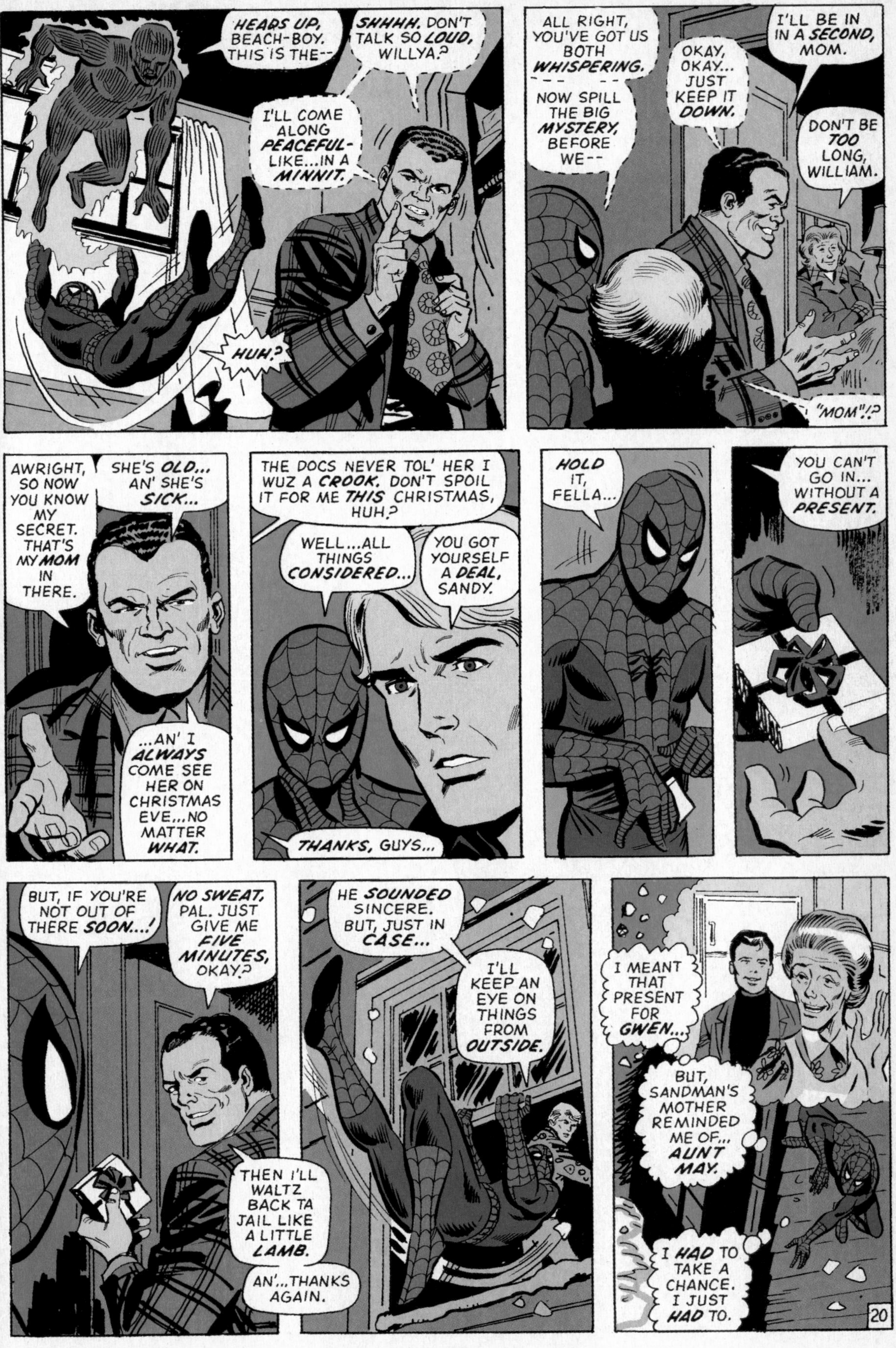
HEADS UP, BEACH-BOY. THIS IS THE--
SHHHH. DON'T TALK SO LOUD, WILLYA?
I'LL COME ALONG PEACEFUL-LIKE...IN A MINNIT.
HUH?
ALL RIGHT, YOU'VE GOT US BOTH WHISPERING.
NOW SPILL THE BIG MYSTERY, BEFORE WE--
OKAY, OKAY... JUST KEEP IT DOWN.
I'LL BE IN IN A SECOND, MOM.
DON'T BE TOO LONG, WILLIAM.
"MOM"!?
AWRIGHT, SO NOW YOU KNOW MY SECRET. THAT'S MY MOM IN THERE.
SHE'S OLD... AN' SHE'S SICK...
...AN' I ALWAYS COME SEE HER ON CHRISTMAS EVE...NO MATTER WHAT.
THE DOCS NEVER TOL' HER I WUZ A CROOK. DON'T SPOIL IT FOR ME THIS CHRISTMAS, HUH?
WELL...ALL THINGS CONSIDERED...
YOU GOT YOURSELF A DEAL, SANDY.
THANKS, GUYS...
HOLD IT, FELLA...
YOU CAN'T GO IN... WITHOUT A PRESENT.
BUT, IF YOU'RE NOT OUT OF THERE SOON...!
NO SWEAT, PAL. JUST GIVE ME FIVE MINUTES, OKAY?
THEN I'LL WALTZ BACK TA JAIL LIKE A LITTLE LAMB.
AN'...THANKS AGAIN.
HE SOUNDED SINCERE. BUT, JUST IN CASE...
I'LL KEEP AN EYE ON THINGS FROM OUTSIDE.
I MEANT THAT PRESENT FOR GWEN...
BUT, SANDMAN'S MOTHER REMINDED ME OF... AUNT MAY.
I HAD TO TAKE A CHANCE. I JUST HAD TO.
20

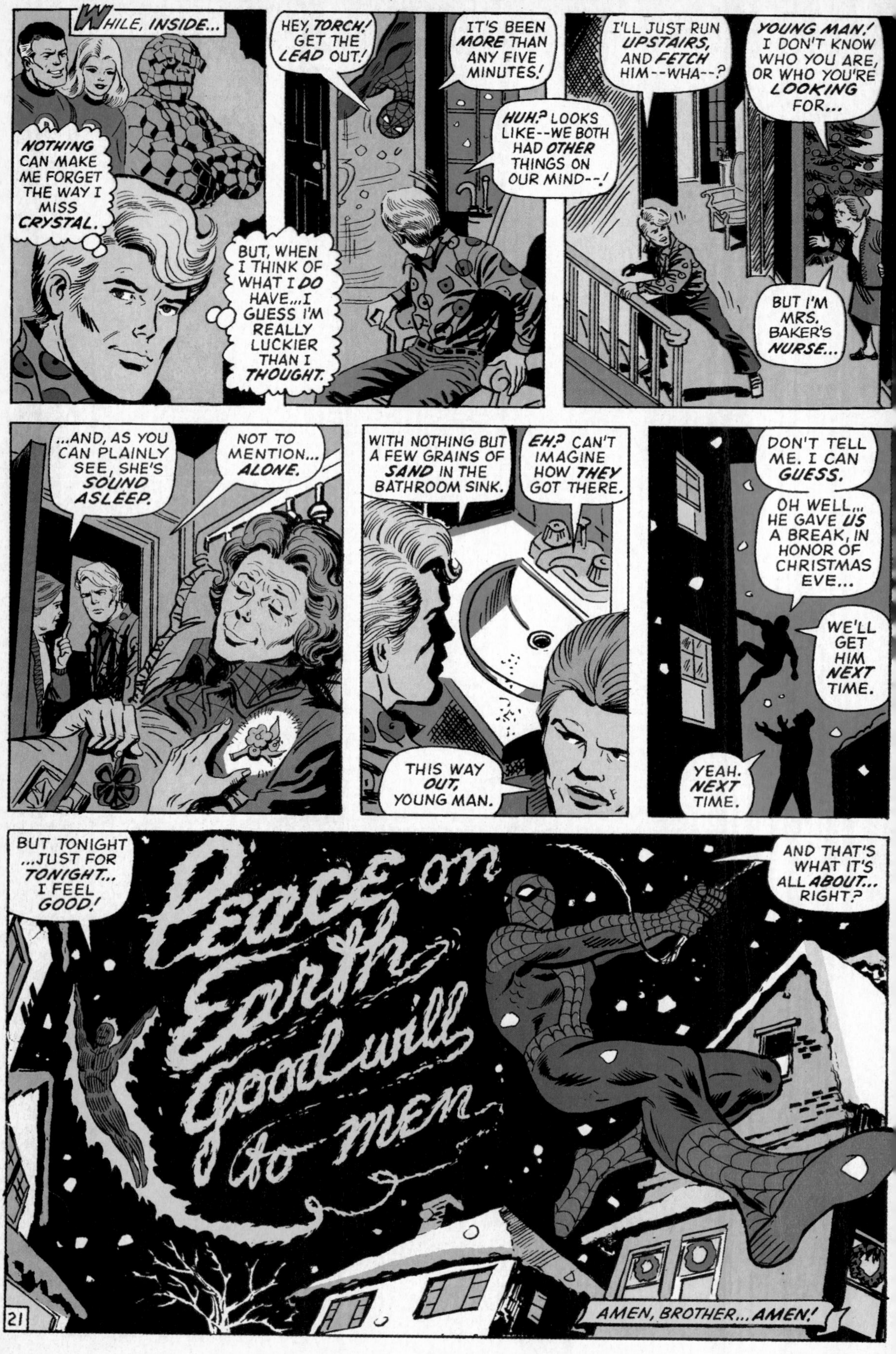

WHILE, INSIDE...
NOTHING CAN MAKE ME FORGET THE WAY I MISS CRYSTAL.
BUT, WHEN I THINK OF WHAT I DO HAVE...I GUESS I'M REALLY LUCKIER THAN I THOUGHT.
HEY, TORCH! GET THE LEAD OUT!
IT'S BEEN MORE THAN ANY FIVE MINUTES!
HUH? LOOKS LIKE--WE BOTH HAD OTHER THINGS ON OUR MIND--!
I'LL JUST RUN UPSTAIRS, AND FETCH HIM--WHA--?
YOUNG MAN! I DON'T KNOW WHO YOU ARE, OR WHO YOU'RE LOOKING FOR...
BUT I'M MRS. BAKER'S NURSE...
...AND, AS YOU CAN PLAINLY SEE, SHE'S SOUND ASLEEP.
NOT TO MENTION... ALONE.
WITH NOTHING BUT A FEW GRAINS OF SAND IN THE BATHROOM SINK.
EH? CAN'T IMAGINE HOW THEY GOT THERE.
THIS WAY OUT, YOUNG MAN.
DON'T TELL ME. I CAN GUESS.
OH WELL... HE GAVE US A BREAK, IN HONOR OF CHRISTMAS EVE...
WE'LL GET HIM NEXT TIME.
YEAH. NEXT TIME.
BUT TONIGHT ...JUST FOR TONIGHT... I FEEL GOOD!
Peace on Earth Good will to men
AND THAT'S WHAT IT'S ALL ABOUT... RIGHT?
21
AMEN, BROTHER... AMEN!

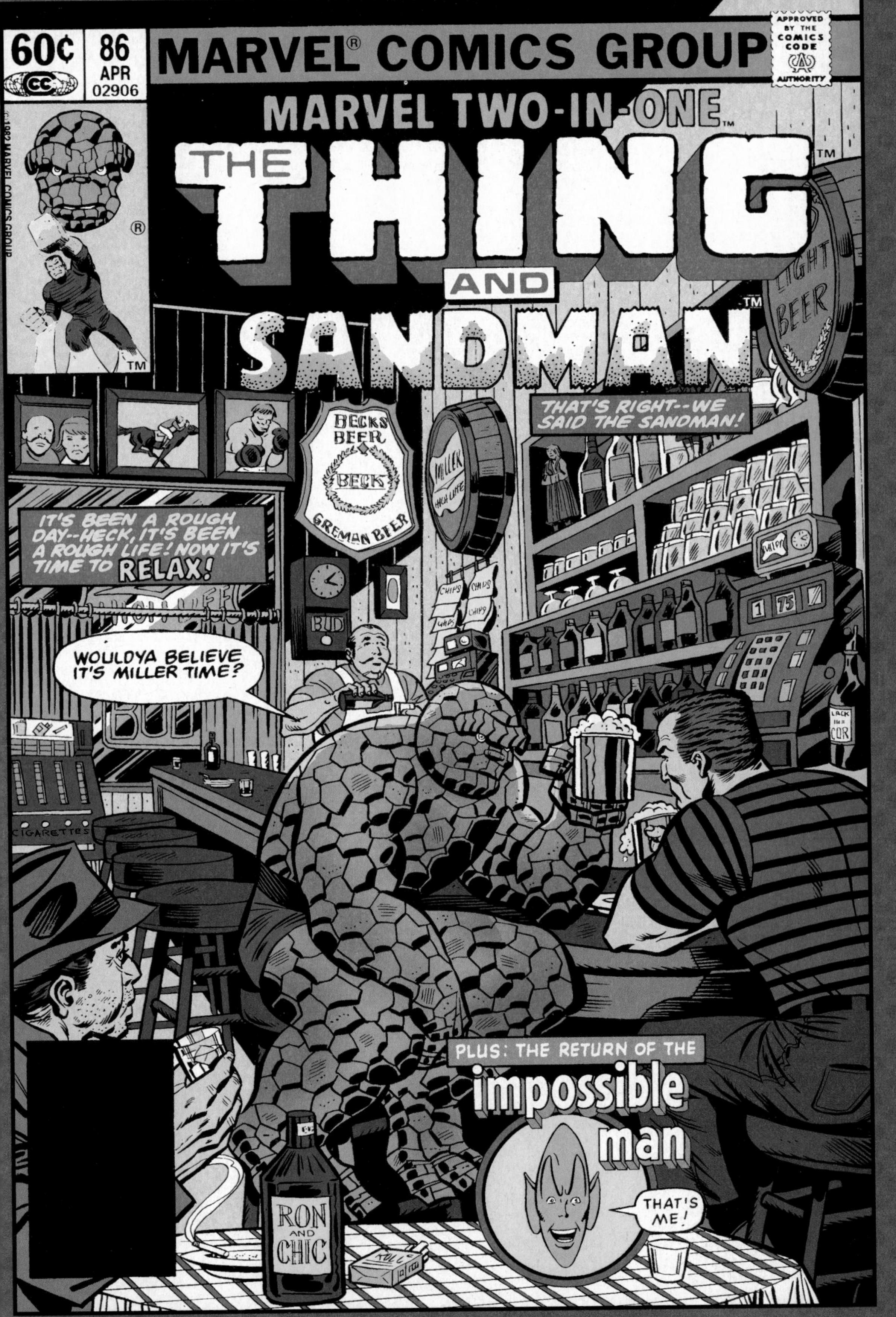
60¢
86
APR
02906
CC
MARVEL® COMICS GROUP
APPROVED BY THE COMICS CODE AUTHORITY
© 1982 MARVEL COMICS GROUP
MARVEL TWO-IN-ONE™
THE THING™
AND
SANDMAN™
THAT'S RIGHT--WE SAID THE SANDMAN!
IT'S BEEN A ROUGH DAY--HECK, IT'S BEEN A ROUGH LIFE! NOW IT'S TIME TO RELAX!
WOULDYA BELIEVE IT'S MILLER TIME?
BECKS BEER
BECK
GREMAN BEER
LIGHT BEER
BUD
CHIPS
CIGARETTES
PLUS: THE RETURN OF THE
impossible man
THAT'S ME!
RON AND CHIC

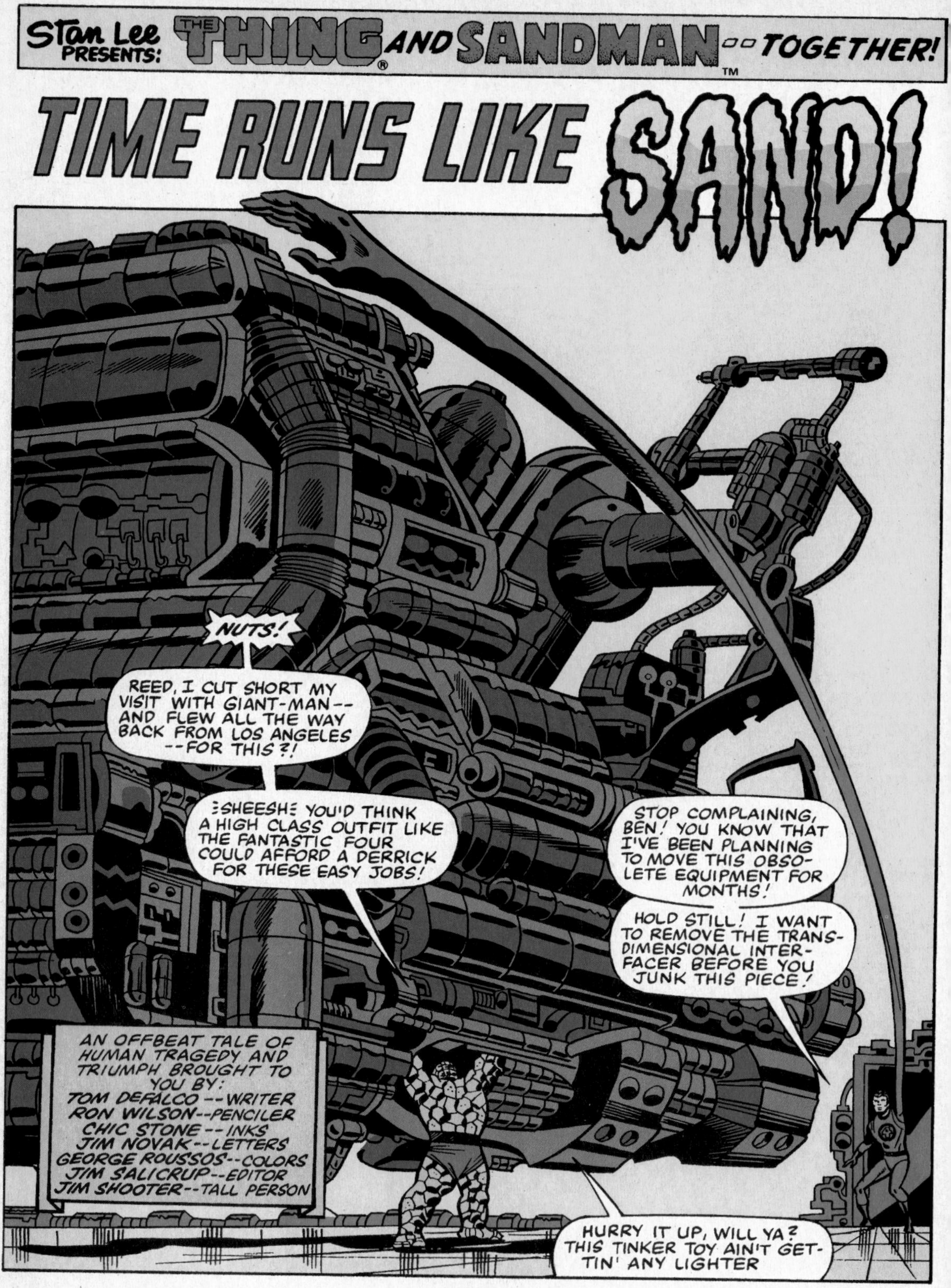
STAN LEE PRESENTS: THE THING® AND SANDMAN™ -- TOGETHER!
TIME RUNS LIKE SAND!
NUTS!
REED, I CUT SHORT MY VISIT WITH GIANT-MAN-- AND FLEW ALL THE WAY BACK FROM LOS ANGELES --FOR THIS?!
SHEESH! YOU'D THINK A HIGH CLASS OUTFIT LIKE THE FANTASTIC FOUR COULD AFFORD A DERRICK FOR THESE EASY JOBS!
STOP COMPLAINING, BEN! YOU KNOW THAT I'VE BEEN PLANNING TO MOVE THIS OBSOLETE EQUIPMENT FOR MONTHS!
HOLD STILL! I WANT TO REMOVE THE TRANS-DIMENSIONAL INTERFACER BEFORE YOU JUNK THIS PIECE!
AN OFFBEAT TALE OF HUMAN TRAGEDY AND TRIUMPH BROUGHT TO YOU BY: TOM DEFALCO--WRITER RON WILSON--PENCILER CHIC STONE--INKS JIM NOVAK--LETTERS GEORGE ROUSSOS--COLORS JIM SALICRUP--EDITOR JIM SHOOTER--TALL PERSON
HURRY IT UP, WILL YA? THIS TINKER TOY AIN'T GETTIN' ANY LIGHTER

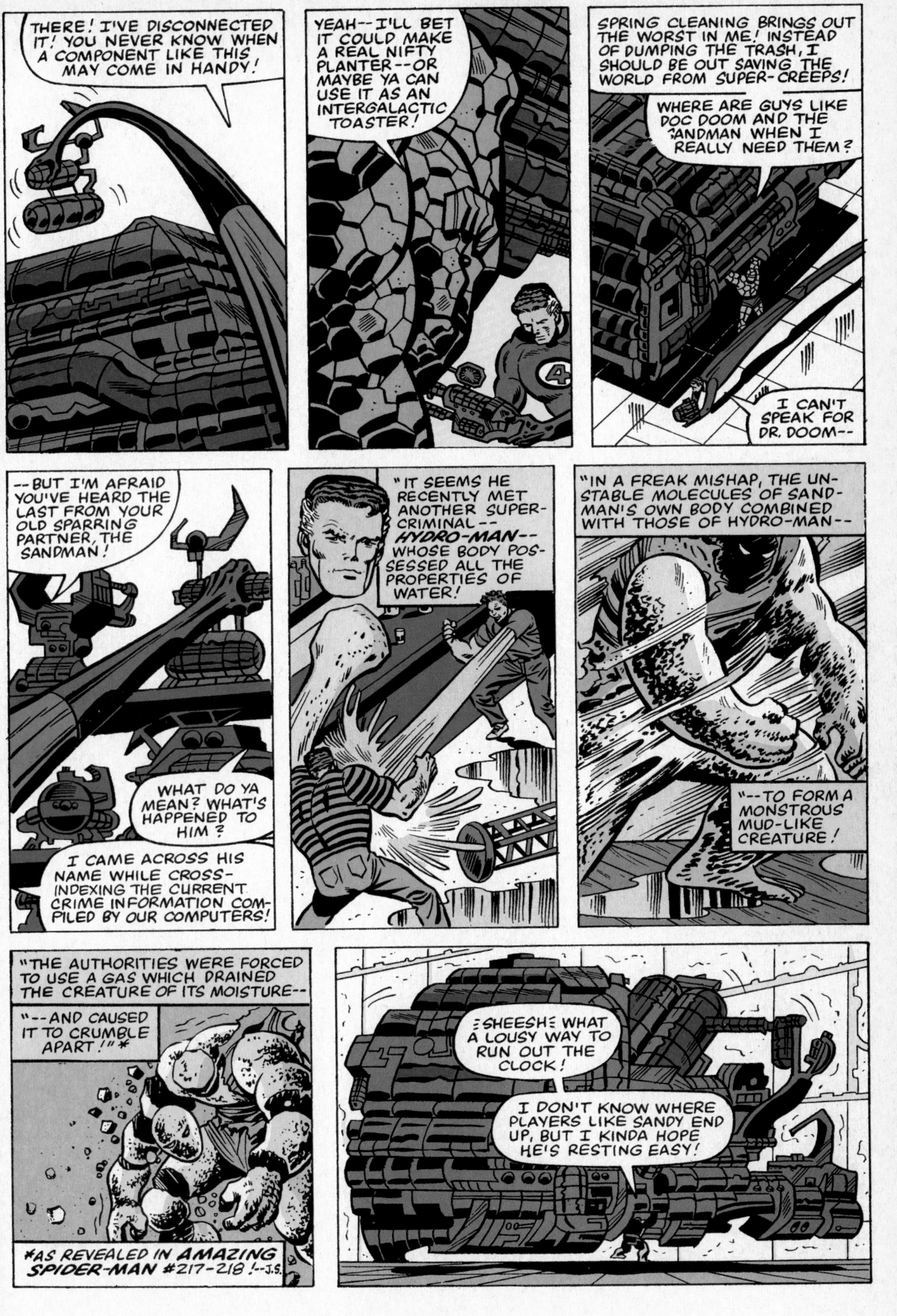
THERE! I'VE DISCONNECTED IT! YOU NEVER KNOW WHEN A COMPONENT LIKE THIS MAY COME IN HANDY!
YEAH--I'LL BET IT COULD MAKE A REAL NIFTY PLANTER--OR MAYBE YA CAN USE IT AS AN INTERGALACTIC TOASTER!
SPRING CLEANING BRINGS OUT THE WORST IN ME! INSTEAD OF DUMPING THE TRASH, I SHOULD BE OUT SAVING THE WORLD FROM SUPER-CREEPS!
WHERE ARE GUYS LIKE DOC DOOM AND THE SANDMAN WHEN I REALLY NEED THEM?
I CAN'T SPEAK FOR DR. DOOM--
--BUT I'M AFRAID YOU'VE HEARD THE LAST FROM YOUR OLD SPARRING PARTNER, THE SANDMAN!
WHAT DO YA MEAN? WHAT'S HAPPENED TO HIM?
I CAME ACROSS HIS NAME WHILE CROSS-INDEXING THE CURRENT CRIME INFORMATION COMPILED BY OUR COMPUTERS!
"IT SEEMS HE RECENTLY MET ANOTHER SUPER-CRIMINAL--HYDRO-MAN--WHOSE BODY POSSESSED ALL THE PROPERTIES OF WATER!
"IN A FREAK MISHAP, THE UNSTABLE MOLECULES OF SANDMAN'S OWN BODY COMBINED WITH THOSE OF HYDRO-MAN--
"--TO FORM A MONSTROUS MUD-LIKE CREATURE!
"THE AUTHORITIES WERE FORCED TO USE A GAS WHICH DRAINED THE CREATURE OF ITS MOISTURE--
"--AND CAUSED IT TO CRUMBLE APART!"*
*AS REVEALED IN AMAZING SPIDER-MAN #217-218!--J.S.
SHEESH! WHAT A LOUSY WAY TO RUN OUT THE CLOCK!
I DON'T KNOW WHERE PLAYERS LIKE SANDY END UP, BUT I KINDA HOPE HE'S RESTING EASY!

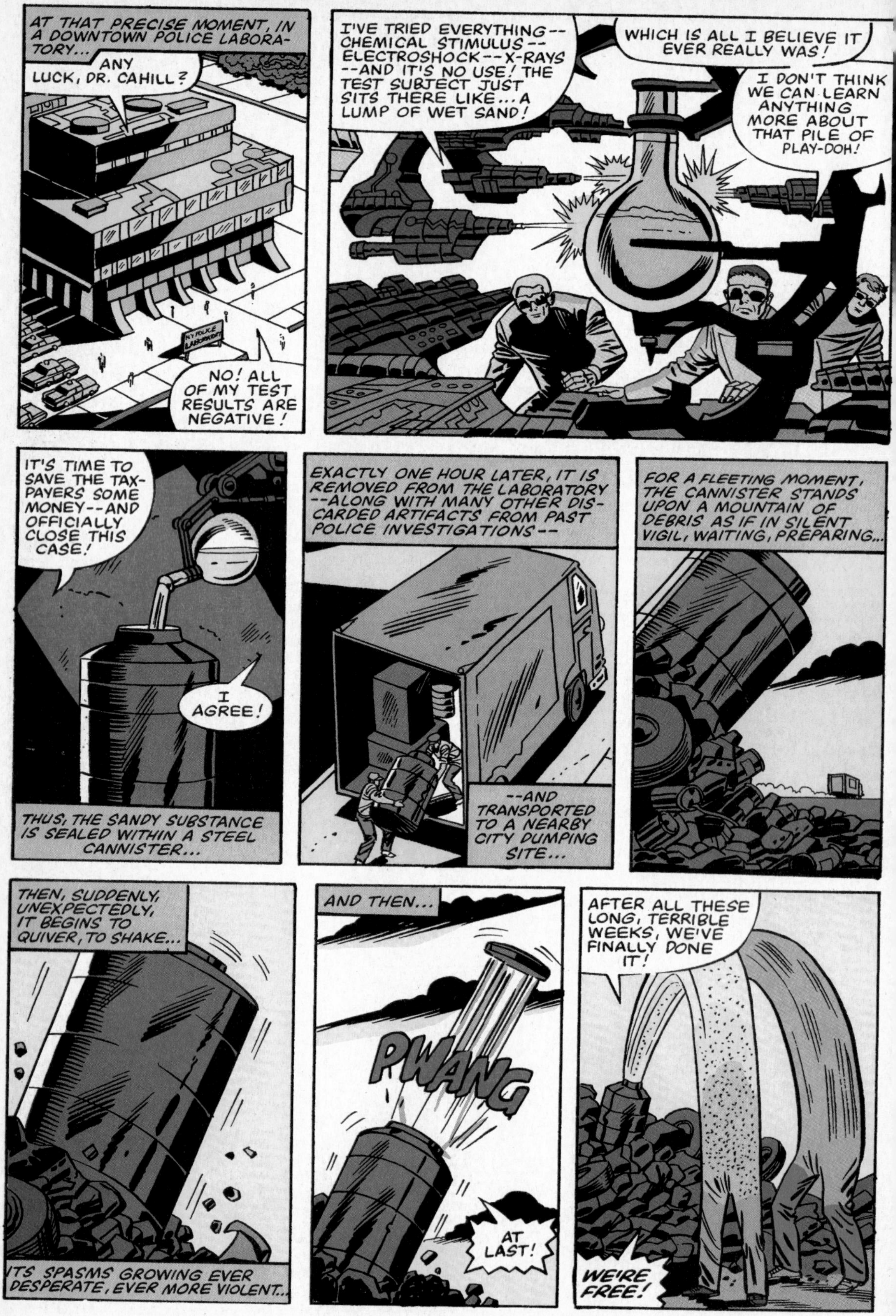
AT THAT PRECISE MOMENT, IN A DOWNTOWN POLICE LABORATORY...
ANY LUCK, DR. CAHILL?
NY POLICE LABORATORY
NO! ALL OF MY TEST RESULTS ARE NEGATIVE!
I'VE TRIED EVERYTHING-- CHEMICAL STIMULUS-- --ELECTROSHOCK--X-RAYS --AND IT'S NO USE! THE TEST SUBJECT JUST SITS THERE LIKE... A LUMP OF WET SAND!
WHICH IS ALL I BELIEVE IT EVER REALLY WAS!
I DON'T THINK WE CAN LEARN ANYTHING MORE ABOUT THAT PILE OF PLAY-DOH!
IT'S TIME TO SAVE THE TAXPAYERS SOME MONEY--AND OFFICIALLY CLOSE THIS CASE!
I AGREE!
THUS, THE SANDY SUBSTANCE IS SEALED WITHIN A STEEL CANNISTER...
EXACTLY ONE HOUR LATER, IT IS REMOVED FROM THE LABORATORY --ALONG WITH MANY OTHER DISCARDED ARTIFACTS FROM PAST POLICE INVESTIGATIONS--
--AND TRANSPORTED TO A NEARBY CITY DUMPING SITE...
FOR A FLEETING MOMENT, THE CANNISTER STANDS UPON A MOUNTAIN OF DEBRIS AS IF IN SILENT VIGIL, WAITING, PREPARING...
THEN, SUDDENLY, UNEXPECTEDLY, IT BEGINS TO QUIVER, TO SHAKE...
ITS SPASMS GROWING EVER DESPERATE, EVER MORE VIOLENT...
AND THEN...
PWANG
AT LAST!
AFTER ALL THESE LONG, TERRIBLE WEEKS, WE'VE FINALLY DONE IT!
WE'RE FREE!

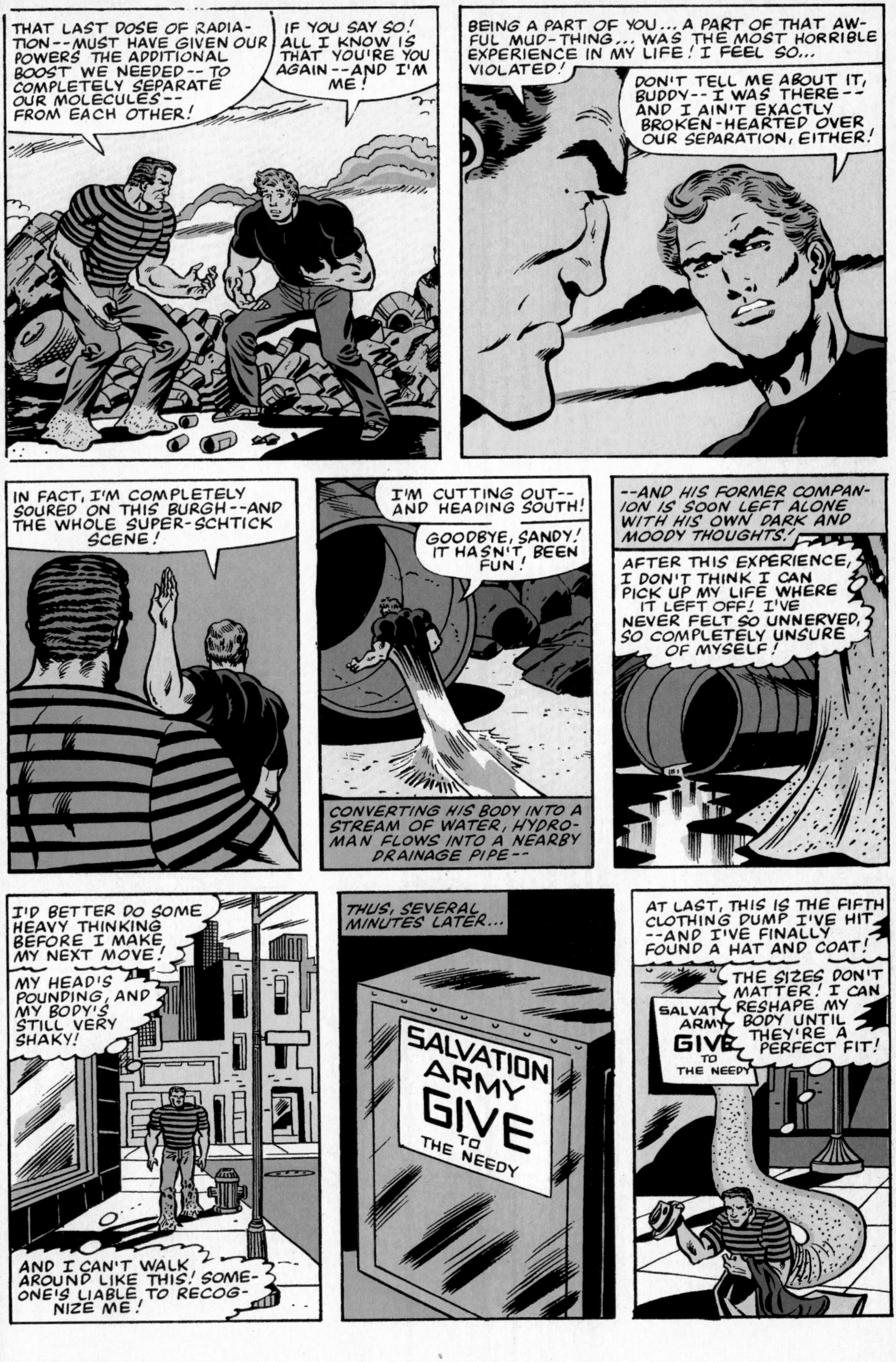
THAT LAST DOSE OF RADIATION--MUST HAVE GIVEN OUR POWERS THE ADDITIONAL BOOST WE NEEDED--TO COMPLETELY SEPARATE OUR MOLECULES--FROM EACH OTHER!
IF YOU SAY SO! ALL I KNOW IS THAT YOU'RE YOU AGAIN--AND I'M ME!
BEING A PART OF YOU... A PART OF THAT AWFUL MUD-THING... WAS THE MOST HORRIBLE EXPERIENCE IN MY LIFE! I FEEL SO... VIOLATED!
DON'T TELL ME ABOUT IT, BUDDY--I WAS THERE--AND I AIN'T EXACTLY BROKEN-HEARTED OVER OUR SEPARATION, EITHER!
IN FACT, I'M COMPLETELY SOURED ON THIS BURGH--AND THE WHOLE SUPER-SCHTICK SCENE!
I'M CUTTING OUT--AND HEADING SOUTH!
GOODBYE, SANDY! IT HASN'T BEEN FUN!
CONVERTING HIS BODY INTO A STREAM OF WATER, HYDRO-MAN FLOWS INTO A NEARBY DRAINAGE PIPE--
--AND HIS FORMER COMPANION IS SOON LEFT ALONE WITH HIS OWN DARK AND MOODY THOUGHTS!
AFTER THIS EXPERIENCE, I DON'T THINK I CAN PICK UP MY LIFE WHERE IT LEFT OFF! I'VE NEVER FELT SO UNNERVED, SO COMPLETELY UNSURE OF MYSELF!
I'D BETTER DO SOME HEAVY THINKING BEFORE I MAKE MY NEXT MOVE!
MY HEAD'S POUNDING, AND MY BODY'S STILL VERY SHAKY!
AND I CAN'T WALK AROUND LIKE THIS! SOMEONE'S LIABLE TO RECOGNIZE ME!
THUS, SEVERAL MINUTES LATER...
SALVATION ARMY GIVE TO THE NEEDY
AT LAST, THIS IS THE FIFTH CLOTHING DUMP I'VE HIT--AND I'VE FINALLY FOUND A HAT AND COAT!
THE SIZES DON'T MATTER! I CAN RESHAPE MY BODY UNTIL THEY'RE A PERFECT FIT!
SALVATION ARMY GIVE TO THE NEEDY

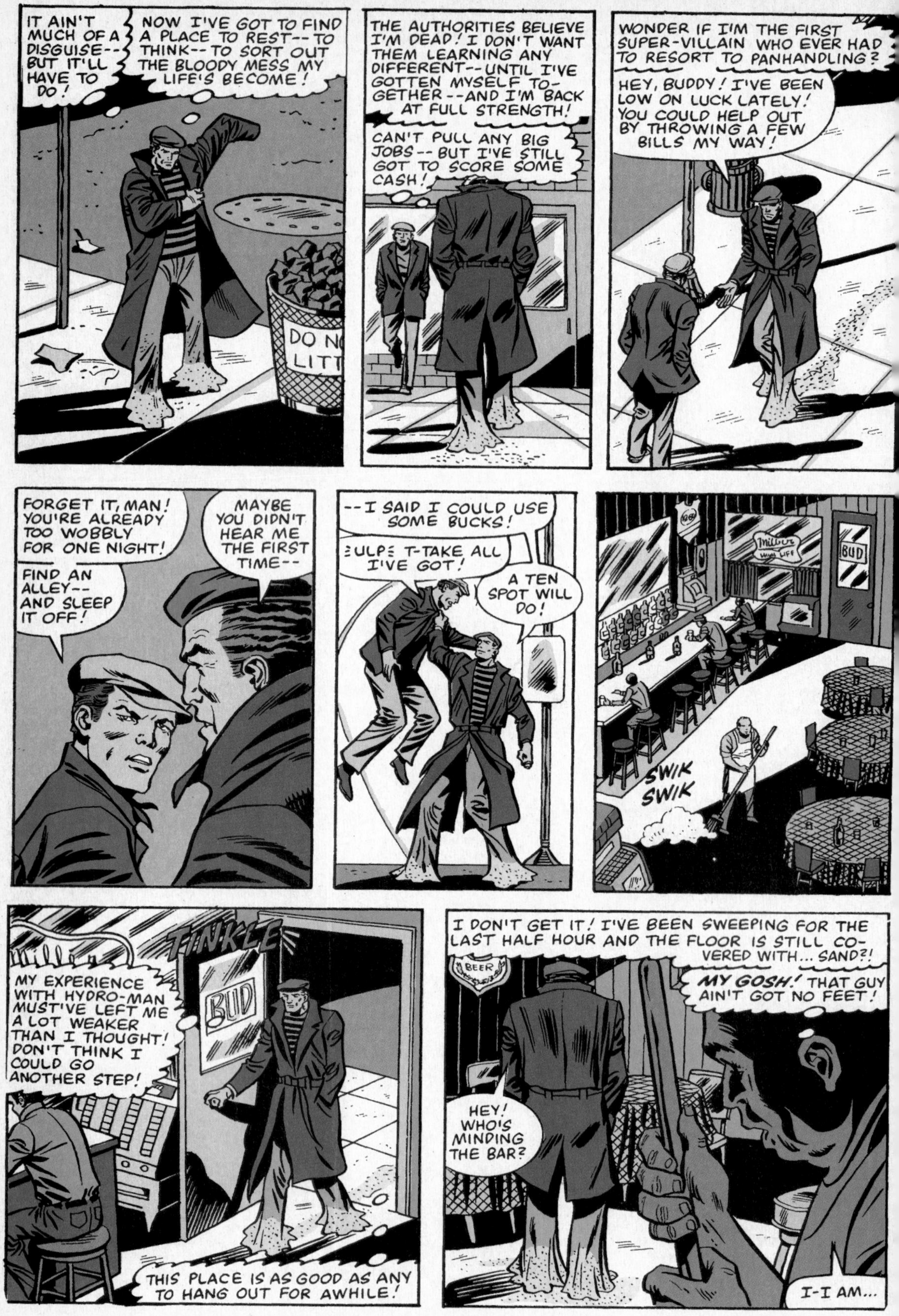
IT AIN'T MUCH OF A DISGUISE-- BUT IT'LL HAVE TO DO!
NOW I'VE GOT TO FIND A PLACE TO REST--TO THINK--TO SORT OUT THE BLOODY MESS MY LIFE'S BECOME!
DO NO LITT
THE AUTHORITIES BELIEVE I'M DEAD! I DON'T WANT THEM LEARNING ANY DIFFERENT--UNTIL I'VE GOTTEN MYSELF TOGETHER--AND I'M BACK AT FULL STRENGTH!
CAN'T PULL ANY BIG JOBS--BUT I'VE STILL GOT TO SCORE SOME CASH!
WONDER IF I'M THE FIRST SUPER-VILLAIN WHO EVER HAD TO RESORT TO PANHANDLING?
HEY, BUDDY! I'VE BEEN LOW ON LUCK LATELY! YOU COULD HELP OUT BY THROWING A FEW BILLS MY WAY!
FORGET IT, MAN! YOU'RE ALREADY TOO WOBBLY FOR ONE NIGHT!
FIND AN ALLEY-- AND SLEEP IT OFF!
MAYBE YOU DIDN'T HEAR ME THE FIRST TIME--
--I SAID I COULD USE SOME BUCKS!
GULP! T-TAKE ALL I'VE GOT!
A TEN SPOT WILL DO!
BUD
SWIK SWIK
TINKLE
BUD
MY EXPERIENCE WITH HYDRO-MAN MUST'VE LEFT ME A LOT WEAKER THAN I THOUGHT! DON'T THINK I COULD GO ANOTHER STEP!
THIS PLACE IS AS GOOD AS ANY TO HANG OUT FOR AWHILE!
I DON'T GET IT! I'VE BEEN SWEEPING FOR THE LAST HALF HOUR AND THE FLOOR IS STILL COVERED WITH... SAND?!
MY GOSH! THAT GUY AIN'T GOT NO FEET!
BEER
HEY! WHO'S MINDING THE BAR?
I-I AM...

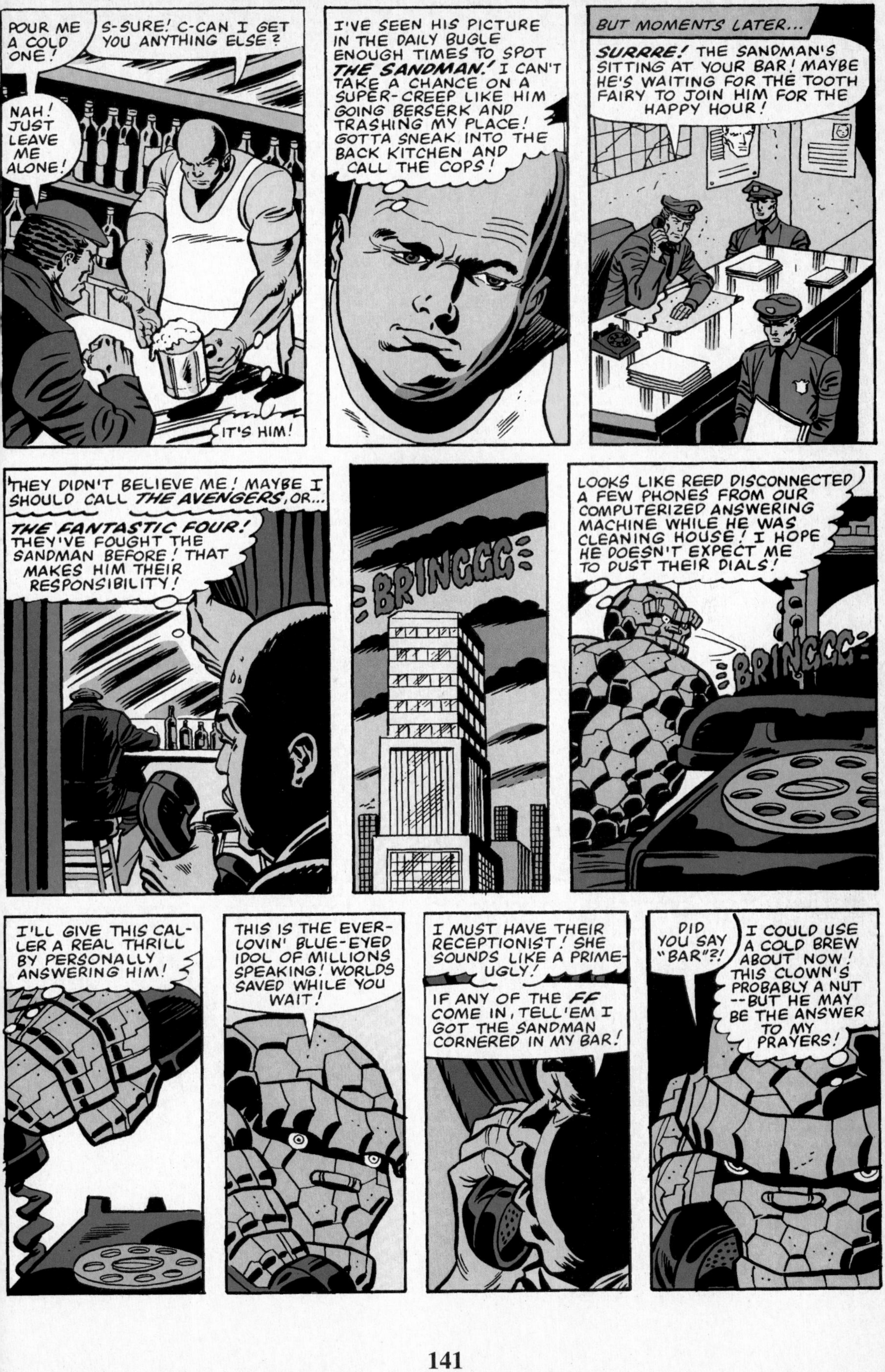
POUR ME A COLD ONE!
S-SURE! C-CAN I GET YOU ANYTHING ELSE?
NAH! JUST LEAVE ME ALONE!
IT'S HIM!
I'VE SEEN HIS PICTURE IN THE DAILY BUGLE ENOUGH TIMES TO SPOT THE SANDMAN! I CAN'T TAKE A CHANCE ON A SUPER-CREEP LIKE HIM GOING BERSERK AND TRASHING MY PLACE! GOTTA SNEAK INTO THE BACK KITCHEN AND CALL THE COPS!
BUT MOMENTS LATER...
SURRRE! THE SANDMAN'S SITTING AT YOUR BAR! MAYBE HE'S WAITING FOR THE TOOTH FAIRY TO JOIN HIM FOR THE HAPPY HOUR!
THEY DIDN'T BELIEVE ME! MAYBE I SHOULD CALL THE AVENGERS, OR...
THE FANTASTIC FOUR! THEY'VE FOUGHT THE SANDMAN BEFORE! THAT MAKES HIM THEIR RESPONSIBILITY!
BRINGGG
LOOKS LIKE REED DISCONNECTED A FEW PHONES FROM OUR COMPUTERIZED ANSWERING MACHINE WHILE HE WAS CLEANING HOUSE! I HOPE HE DOESN'T EXPECT ME TO DUST THEIR DIALS!
BRINGGG
I'LL GIVE THIS CALLER A REAL THRILL BY PERSONALLY ANSWERING HIM!
THIS IS THE EVER-LOVIN' BLUE-EYED IDOL OF MILLIONS SPEAKING! WORLDS SAVED WHILE YOU WAIT!
I MUST HAVE THEIR RECEPTIONIST! SHE SOUNDS LIKE A PRIME-UGLY!
IF ANY OF THE FF COME IN, TELL'EM I GOT THE SANDMAN CORNERED IN MY BAR!
DID YOU SAY "BAR"?!
I COULD USE A COLD BREW ABOUT NOW! THIS CLOWN'S PROBABLY A NUT --BUT HE MAY BE THE ANSWER TO MY PRAYERS!

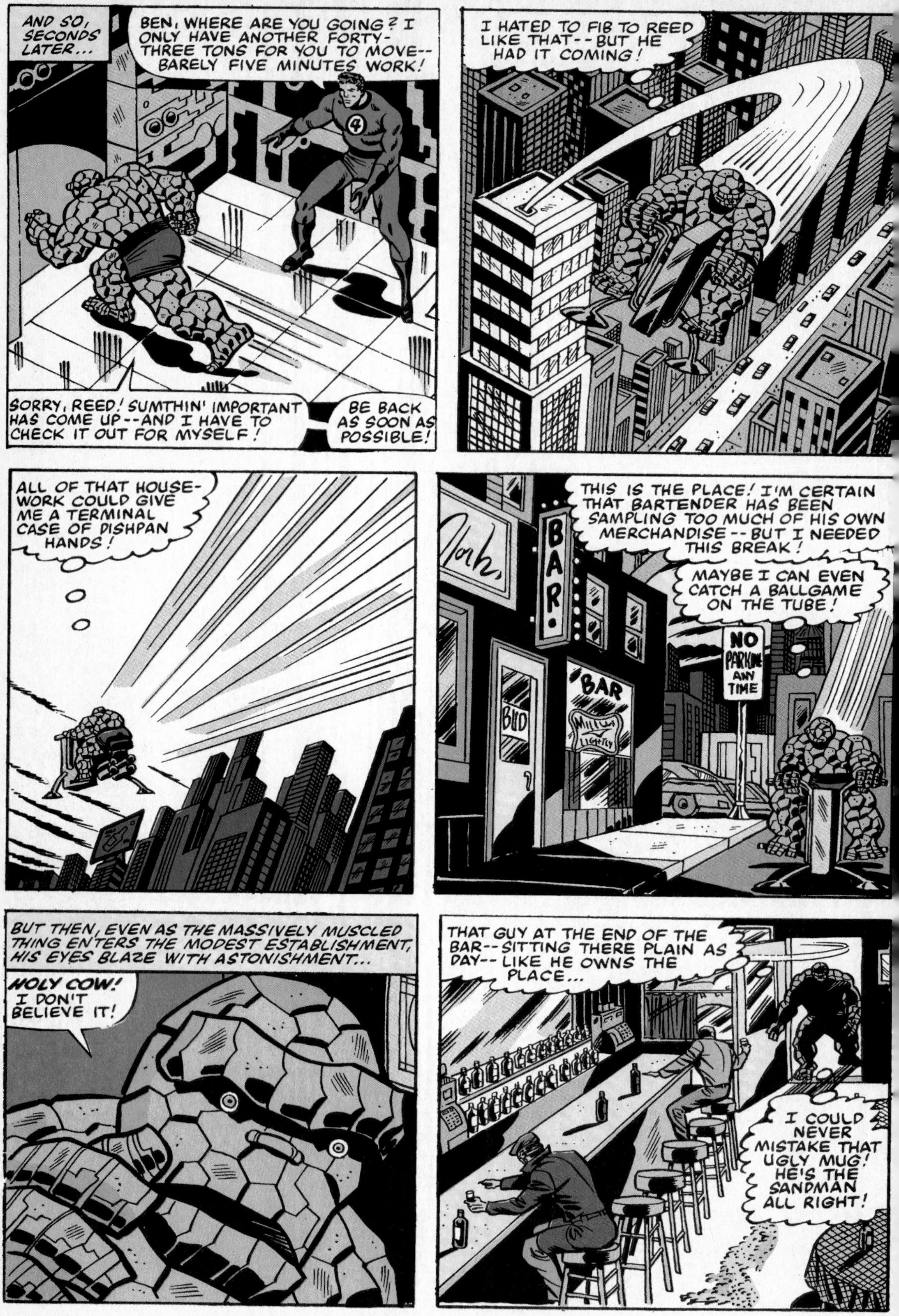
AND SO, SECONDS LATER...
BEN, WHERE ARE YOU GOING? I ONLY HAVE ANOTHER FORTY-THREE TONS FOR YOU TO MOVE-- BARELY FIVE MINUTES WORK!
SORRY, REED! SUMTHIN' IMPORTANT HAS COME UP--AND I HAVE TO CHECK IT OUT FOR MYSELF!
BE BACK AS SOON AS POSSIBLE!
I HATED TO FIB TO REED LIKE THAT--BUT HE HAD IT COMING!
ALL OF THAT HOUSE-WORK COULD GIVE ME A TERMINAL CASE OF DISHPAN HANDS!
THIS IS THE PLACE! I'M CERTAIN THAT BARTENDER HAS BEEN SAMPLING TOO MUCH OF HIS OWN MERCHANDISE--BUT I NEEDED THIS BREAK!
MAYBE I CAN EVEN CATCH A BALLGAME ON THE TUBE!
BAR
BAR
NO PARKING ANY TIME
BUT THEN, EVEN AS THE MASSIVELY MUSCLED THING ENTERS THE MODEST ESTABLISHMENT, HIS EYES BLAZE WITH ASTONISHMENT...
HOLY COW! I DON'T BELIEVE IT!
THAT GUY AT THE END OF THE BAR--SITTING THERE PLAIN AS DAY--LIKE HE OWNS THE PLACE...
I COULD NEVER MISTAKE THAT UGLY MUG! HE'S THE SANDMAN ALL RIGHT!

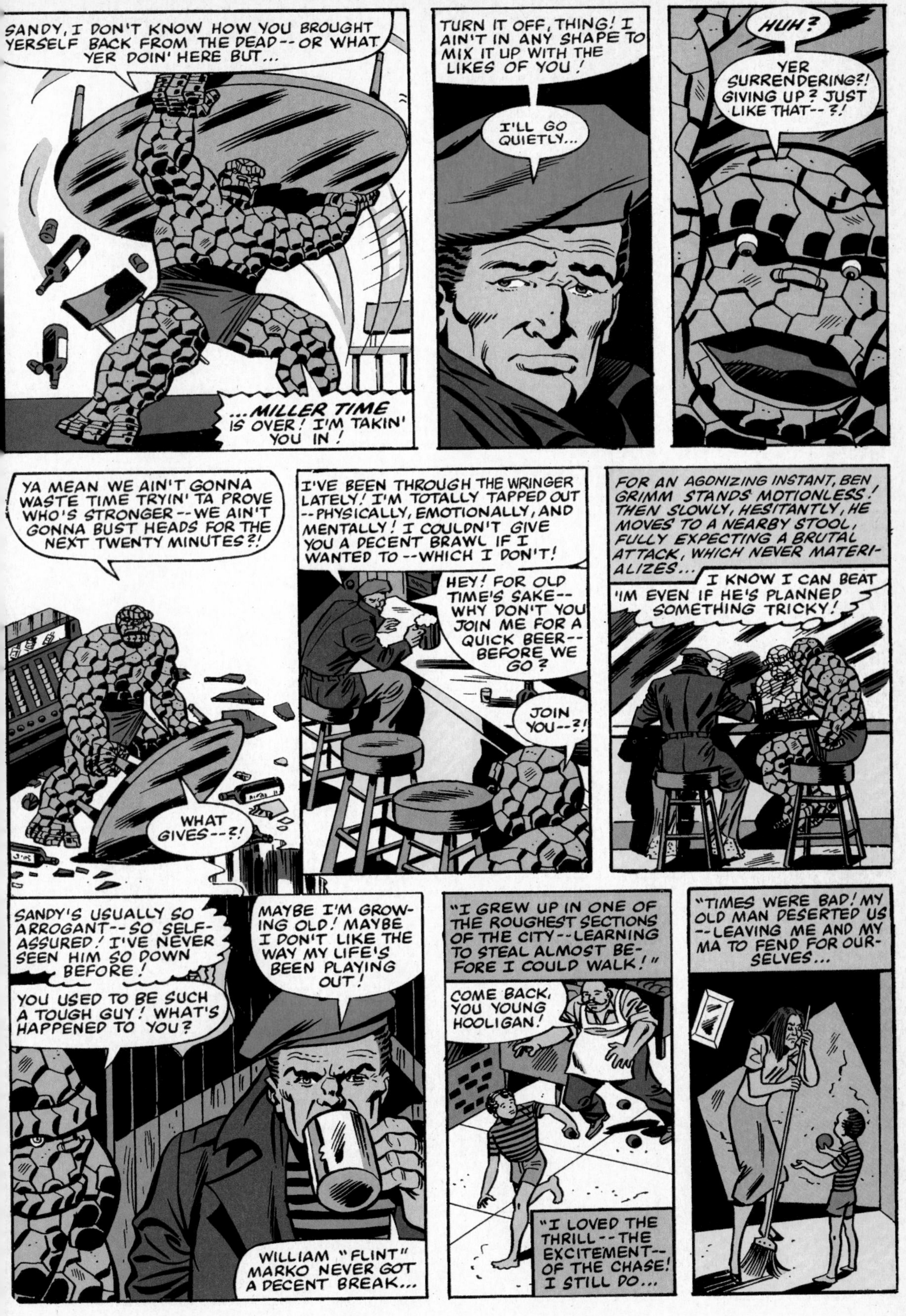
SANDY, I DON'T KNOW HOW YOU BROUGHT YERSELF BACK FROM THE DEAD--OR WHAT YER DOIN' HERE BUT...
...MILLER TIME IS OVER! I'M TAKIN' YOU IN!
TURN IT OFF, THING! I AIN'T IN ANY SHAPE TO MIX IT UP WITH THE LIKES OF YOU!
I'LL GO QUIETLY...
HUH?
YER SURRENDERING?! GIVING UP? JUST LIKE THAT--?!
YA MEAN WE AIN'T GONNA WASTE TIME TRYIN' TA PROVE WHO'S STRONGER--WE AIN'T GONNA BUST HEADS FOR THE NEXT TWENTY MINUTES?!
WHAT GIVES--?!
I'VE BEEN THROUGH THE WRINGER LATELY! I'M TOTALLY TAPPED OUT --PHYSICALLY, EMOTIONALLY, AND MENTALLY! I COULDN'T GIVE YOU A DECENT BRAWL IF I WANTED TO--WHICH I DON'T!
HEY! FOR OLD TIME'S SAKE--WHY DON'T YOU JOIN ME FOR A QUICK BEER--BEFORE WE GO?
JOIN YOU--?!
FOR AN AGONIZING INSTANT, BEN GRIMM STANDS MOTIONLESS! THEN SLOWLY, HESITANTLY, HE MOVES TO A NEARBY STOOL, FULLY EXPECTING A BRUTAL ATTACK, WHICH NEVER MATERIALIZES...
I KNOW I CAN BEAT 'IM EVEN IF HE'S PLANNED SOMETHING TRICKY!
SANDY'S USUALLY SO ARROGANT--SO SELF-ASSURED! I'VE NEVER SEEN HIM SO DOWN BEFORE!
YOU USED TO BE SUCH A TOUGH GUY! WHAT'S HAPPENED TO YOU?
MAYBE I'M GROWING OLD! MAYBE I DON'T LIKE THE WAY MY LIFE'S BEEN PLAYING OUT!
WILLIAM "FLINT" MARKO NEVER GOT A DECENT BREAK...
"I GREW UP IN ONE OF THE ROUGHEST SECTIONS OF THE CITY--LEARNING TO STEAL ALMOST BEFORE I COULD WALK!"
COME BACK, YOU YOUNG HOOLIGAN!
"I LOVED THE THRILL--THE EXCITEMENT--OF THE CHASE! I STILL DO...
"TIMES WERE BAD! MY OLD MAN DESERTED US--LEAVING ME AND MY MA TO FEND FOR OURSELVES...

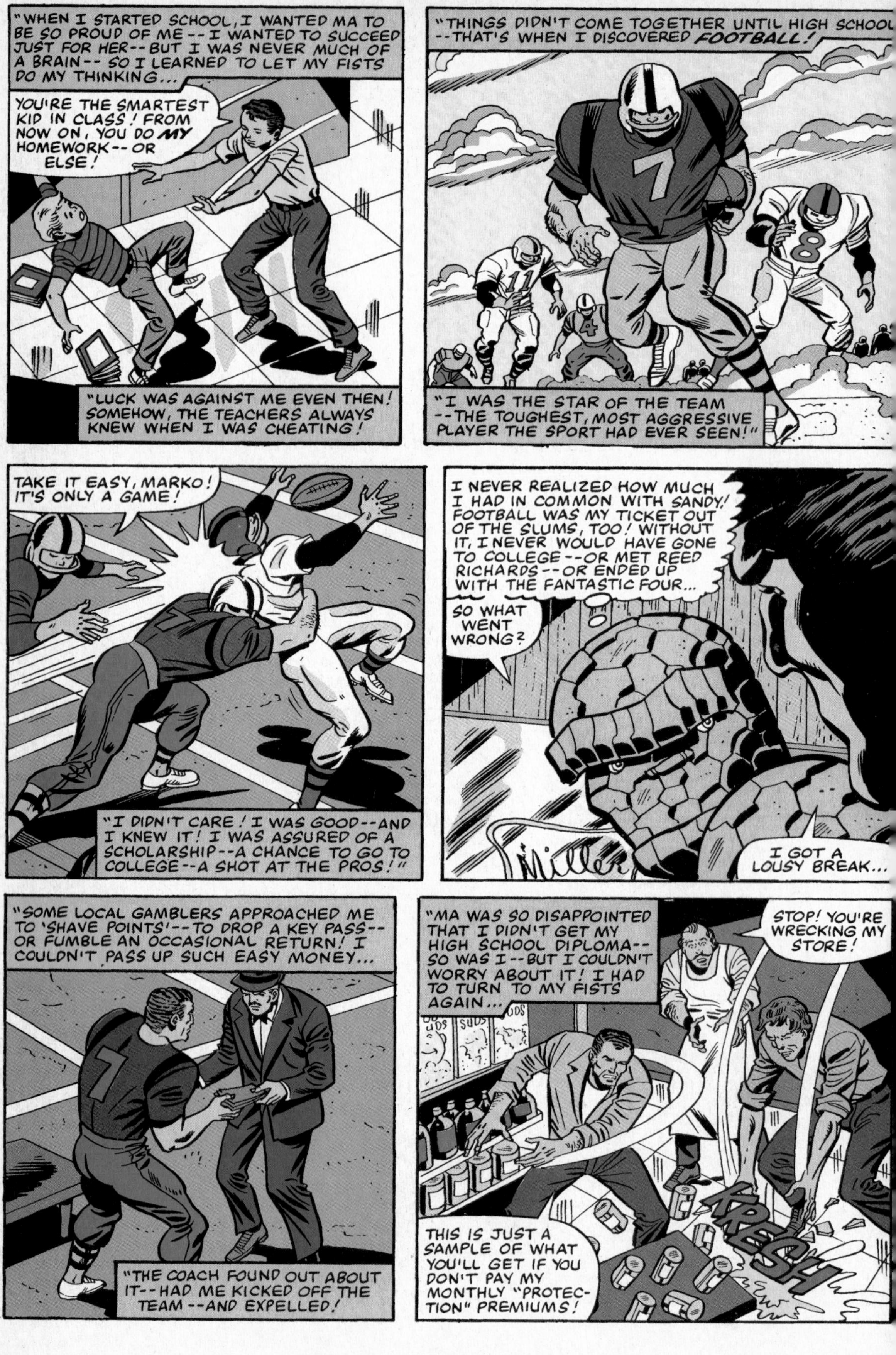
"WHEN I STARTED SCHOOL, I WANTED MA TO BE SO PROUD OF ME -- I WANTED TO SUCCEED JUST FOR HER -- BUT I WAS NEVER MUCH OF A BRAIN -- SO I LEARNED TO LET MY FISTS DO MY THINKING...
YOU'RE THE SMARTEST KID IN CLASS! FROM NOW ON, YOU DO MY HOMEWORK -- OR ELSE!
"LUCK WAS AGAINST ME EVEN THEN! SOMEHOW, THE TEACHERS ALWAYS KNEW WHEN I WAS CHEATING!
"THINGS DIDN'T COME TOGETHER UNTIL HIGH SCHOOL -- THAT'S WHEN I DISCOVERED FOOTBALL!
"I WAS THE STAR OF THE TEAM -- THE TOUGHEST, MOST AGGRESSIVE PLAYER THE SPORT HAD EVER SEEN!"
TAKE IT EASY, MARKO! IT'S ONLY A GAME!
"I DIDN'T CARE! I WAS GOOD -- AND I KNEW IT! I WAS ASSURED OF A SCHOLARSHIP -- A CHANCE TO GO TO COLLEGE -- A SHOT AT THE PROS!"
I NEVER REALIZED HOW MUCH I HAD IN COMMON WITH SANDY! FOOTBALL WAS MY TICKET OUT OF THE SLUMS, TOO! WITHOUT IT, I NEVER WOULD HAVE GONE TO COLLEGE -- OR MET REED RICHARDS -- OR ENDED UP WITH THE FANTASTIC FOUR...
SO WHAT WENT WRONG?
I GOT A LOUSY BREAK...
Miller
"SOME LOCAL GAMBLERS APPROACHED ME TO 'SHAVE POINTS' -- TO DROP A KEY PASS -- OR FUMBLE AN OCCASIONAL RETURN! I COULDN'T PASS UP SUCH EASY MONEY...
"THE COACH FOUND OUT ABOUT IT -- HAD ME KICKED OFF THE TEAM -- AND EXPELLED!
"MA WAS SO DISAPPOINTED THAT I DIDN'T GET MY HIGH SCHOOL DIPLOMA -- SO WAS I -- BUT I COULDN'T WORRY ABOUT IT! I HAD TO TURN TO MY FISTS AGAIN...
STOP! YOU'RE WRECKING MY STORE!
THIS IS JUST A SAMPLE OF WHAT YOU'LL GET IF YOU DON'T PAY MY MONTHLY "PROTECTION" PREMIUMS!
KRESH

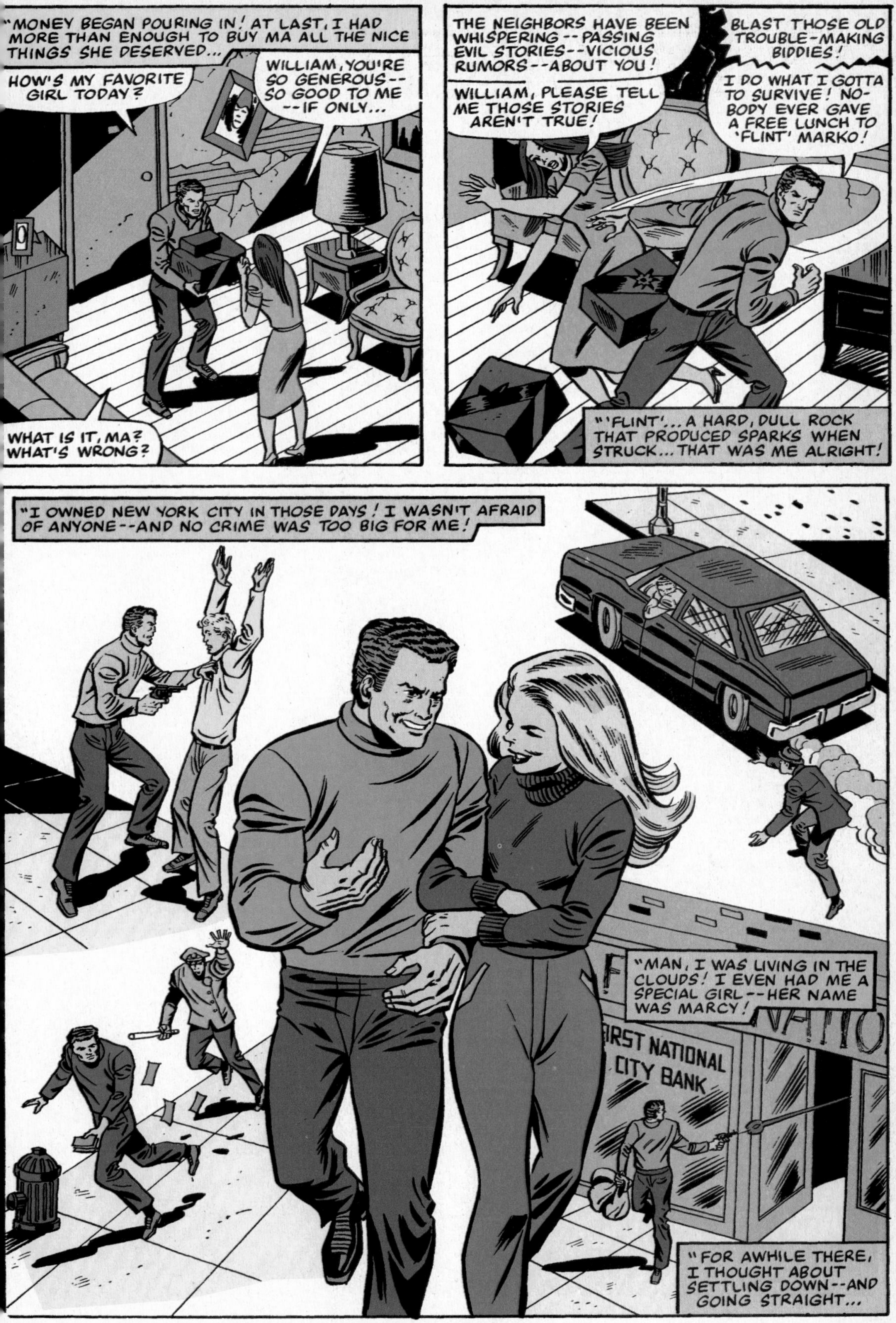

"MONEY BEGAN POURING IN! AT LAST, I HAD MORE THAN ENOUGH TO BUY MA ALL THE NICE THINGS SHE DESERVED...
HOW'S MY FAVORITE GIRL TODAY?
WILLIAM, YOU'RE SO GENEROUS-- SO GOOD TO ME --IF ONLY...
WHAT IS IT, MA? WHAT'S WRONG?
THE NEIGHBORS HAVE BEEN WHISPERING--PASSING EVIL STORIES--VICIOUS RUMORS--ABOUT YOU!
WILLIAM, PLEASE TELL ME THOSE STORIES AREN'T TRUE!
BLAST THOSE OLD TROUBLE-MAKING BIDDIES!
I DO WHAT I GOTTA TO SURVIVE! NOBODY EVER GAVE A FREE LUNCH TO 'FLINT' MARKO!
"'FLINT'... A HARD, DULL ROCK THAT PRODUCED SPARKS WHEN STRUCK... THAT WAS ME ALRIGHT!
"I OWNED NEW YORK CITY IN THOSE DAYS! I WASN'T AFRAID OF ANYONE--AND NO CRIME WAS TOO BIG FOR ME!
"MAN, I WAS LIVING IN THE CLOUDS! I EVEN HAD ME A SPECIAL GIRL--HER NAME WAS MARCY!
IRST NATIONAL CITY BANK
"FOR AWHILE THERE, I THOUGHT ABOUT SETTLING DOWN--AND GOING STRAIGHT...

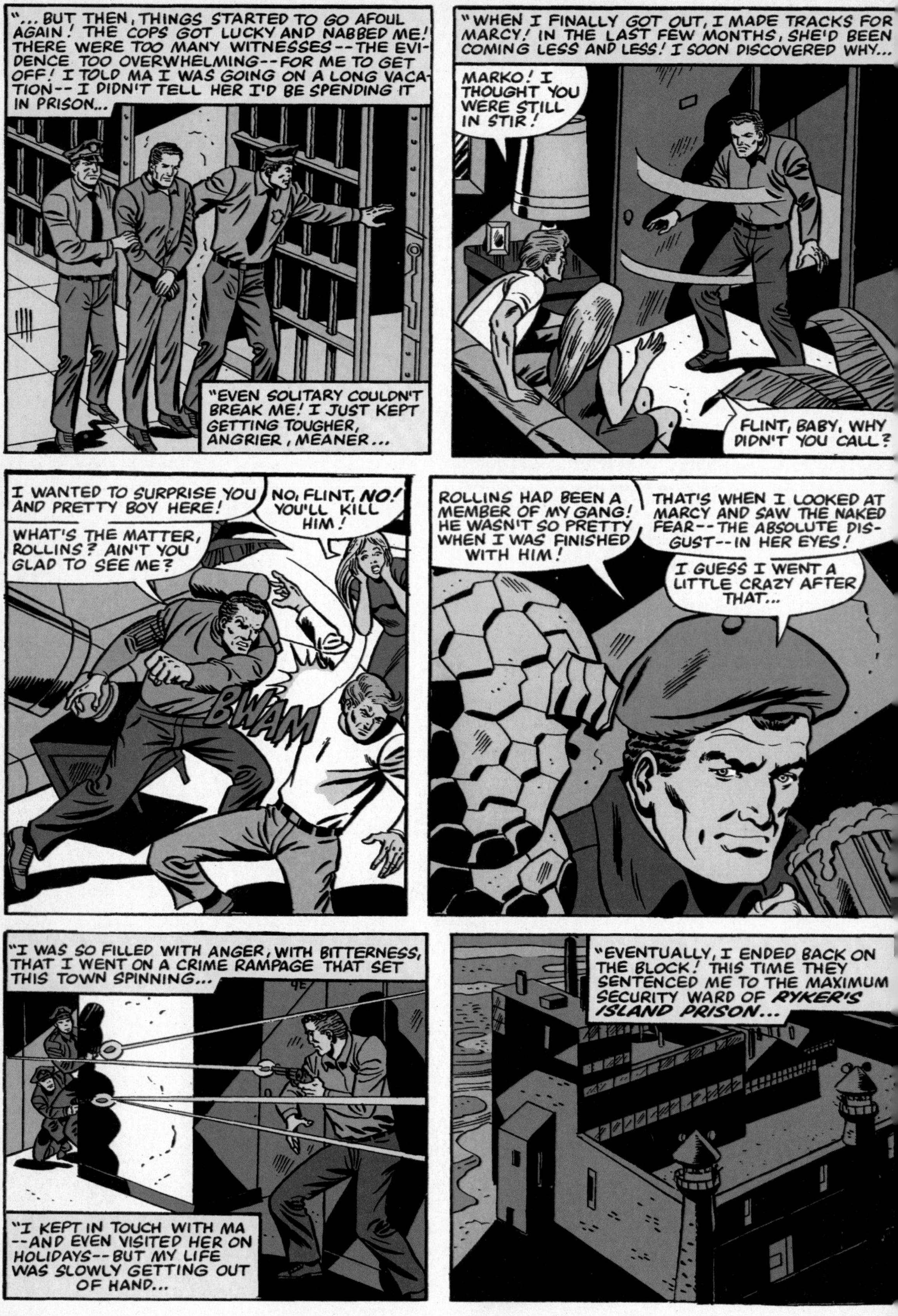
"...BUT THEN, THINGS STARTED TO GO AFOUL AGAIN! THE COPS GOT LUCKY AND NABBED ME! THERE WERE TOO MANY WITNESSES--THE EVIDENCE TOO OVERWHELMING--FOR ME TO GET OFF! I TOLD MA I WAS GOING ON A LONG VACATION--I DIDN'T TELL HER I'D BE SPENDING IT IN PRISON...
"EVEN SOLITARY COULDN'T BREAK ME! I JUST KEPT GETTING TOUGHER, ANGRIER, MEANER...
"WHEN I FINALLY GOT OUT, I MADE TRACKS FOR MARCY! IN THE LAST FEW MONTHS, SHE'D BEEN COMING LESS AND LESS! I SOON DISCOVERED WHY...
MARKO! I THOUGHT YOU WERE STILL IN STIR!
FLINT, BABY, WHY DIDN'T YOU CALL?
I WANTED TO SURPRISE YOU AND PRETTY BOY HERE!
WHAT'S THE MATTER, ROLLINS? AIN'T YOU GLAD TO SEE ME?
NO, FLINT, NO! YOU'LL KILL HIM!
BWAM
ROLLINS HAD BEEN A MEMBER OF MY GANG! HE WASN'T SO PRETTY WHEN I WAS FINISHED WITH HIM!
THAT'S WHEN I LOOKED AT MARCY AND SAW THE NAKED FEAR--THE ABSOLUTE DISGUST--IN HER EYES!
I GUESS I WENT A LITTLE CRAZY AFTER THAT...
"I WAS SO FILLED WITH ANGER, WITH BITTERNESS, THAT I WENT ON A CRIME RAMPAGE THAT SET THIS TOWN SPINNING...
"I KEPT IN TOUCH WITH MA--AND EVEN VISITED HER ON HOLIDAYS--BUT MY LIFE WAS SLOWLY GETTING OUT OF HAND...
"EVENTUALLY, I ENDED BACK ON THE BLOCK! THIS TIME THEY SENTENCED ME TO THE MAXIMUM SECURITY WARD OF RYKER'S ISLAND PRISON...

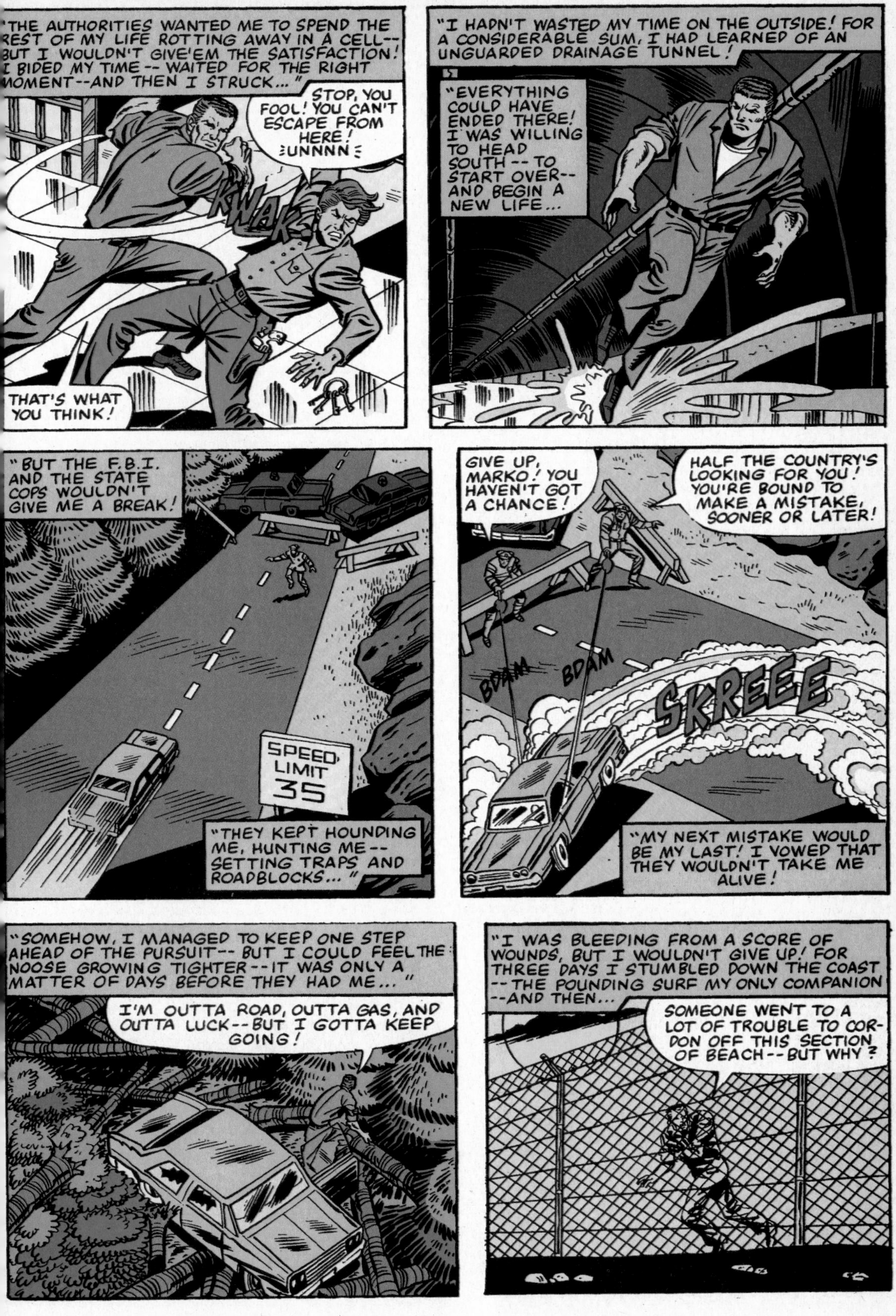
"THE AUTHORITIES WANTED ME TO SPEND THE REST OF MY LIFE ROTTING AWAY IN A CELL-- BUT I WOULDN'T GIVE 'EM THE SATISFACTION! I BIDED MY TIME -- WAITED FOR THE RIGHT MOMENT--AND THEN I STRUCK..."
STOP, YOU FOOL! YOU CAN'T ESCAPE FROM HERE! UNNNN
KWAK
THAT'S WHAT YOU THINK!
"I HADN'T WASTED MY TIME ON THE OUTSIDE! FOR A CONSIDERABLE SUM, I HAD LEARNED OF AN UNGUARDED DRAINAGE TUNNEL!
"EVERYTHING COULD HAVE ENDED THERE! I WAS WILLING TO HEAD SOUTH -- TO START OVER-- AND BEGIN A NEW LIFE...
"BUT THE F.B.I. AND THE STATE COPS WOULDN'T GIVE ME A BREAK!
SPEED LIMIT 35
"THEY KEPT HOUNDING ME, HUNTING ME-- SETTING TRAPS AND ROADBLOCKS..."
GIVE UP, MARKO! YOU HAVEN'T GOT A CHANCE!
HALF THE COUNTRY'S LOOKING FOR YOU! YOU'RE BOUND TO MAKE A MISTAKE, SOONER OR LATER!
BDAM
BDAM
SKREEE
"MY NEXT MISTAKE WOULD BE MY LAST! I VOWED THAT THEY WOULDN'T TAKE ME ALIVE!
"SOMEHOW, I MANAGED TO KEEP ONE STEP AHEAD OF THE PURSUIT-- BUT I COULD FEEL THE NOOSE GROWING TIGHTER--IT WAS ONLY A MATTER OF DAYS BEFORE THEY HAD ME..."
I'M OUTTA ROAD, OUTTA GAS, AND OUTTA LUCK--BUT I GOTTA KEEP GOING!
"I WAS BLEEDING FROM A SCORE OF WOUNDS, BUT I WOULDN'T GIVE UP! FOR THREE DAYS I STUMBLED DOWN THE COAST --THE POUNDING SURF MY ONLY COMPANION --AND THEN...
SOMEONE WENT TO A LOT OF TROUBLE TO CORDON OFF THIS SECTION OF BEACH--BUT WHY?

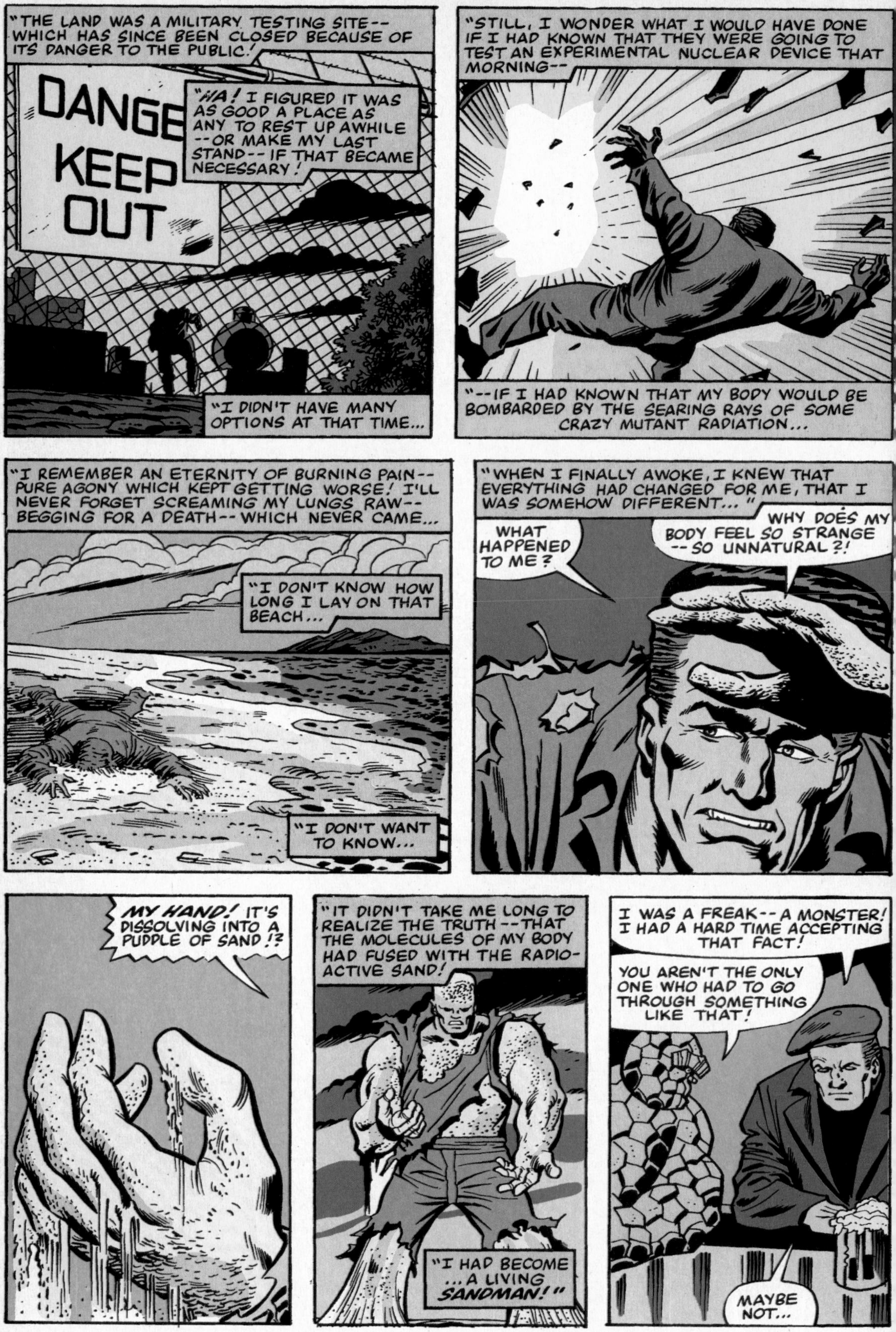
"THE LAND WAS A MILITARY TESTING SITE--WHICH HAS SINCE BEEN CLOSED BECAUSE OF ITS DANGER TO THE PUBLIC!
DANGE KEEP OUT
"HA! I FIGURED IT WAS AS GOOD A PLACE AS ANY TO REST UP AWHILE --OR MAKE MY LAST STAND--IF THAT BECAME NECESSARY!
"I DIDN'T HAVE MANY OPTIONS AT THAT TIME...
"STILL, I WONDER WHAT I WOULD HAVE DONE IF I HAD KNOWN THAT THEY WERE GOING TO TEST AN EXPERIMENTAL NUCLEAR DEVICE THAT MORNING--
"--IF I HAD KNOWN THAT MY BODY WOULD BE BOMBARDED BY THE SEARING RAYS OF SOME CRAZY MUTANT RADIATION...
"I REMEMBER AN ETERNITY OF BURNING PAIN--PURE AGONY WHICH KEPT GETTING WORSE! I'LL NEVER FORGET SCREAMING MY LUNGS RAW--BEGGING FOR A DEATH--WHICH NEVER CAME...
"I DON'T KNOW HOW LONG I LAY ON THAT BEACH...
"I DON'T WANT TO KNOW...
"WHEN I FINALLY AWOKE, I KNEW THAT EVERYTHING HAD CHANGED FOR ME, THAT I WAS SOMEHOW DIFFERENT..."
WHAT HAPPENED TO ME?
WHY DOES MY BODY FEEL SO STRANGE --SO UNNATURAL?!
MY HAND! IT'S DISSOLVING INTO A PUDDLE OF SAND!?
"IT DIDN'T TAKE ME LONG TO REALIZE THE TRUTH--THAT THE MOLECULES OF MY BODY HAD FUSED WITH THE RADIO-ACTIVE SAND!
"I HAD BECOME ...A LIVING SANDMAN!"
I WAS A FREAK--A MONSTER! I HAD A HARD TIME ACCEPTING THAT FACT!
YOU AREN'T THE ONLY ONE WHO HAD TO GO THROUGH SOMETHING LIKE THAT!
MAYBE NOT...

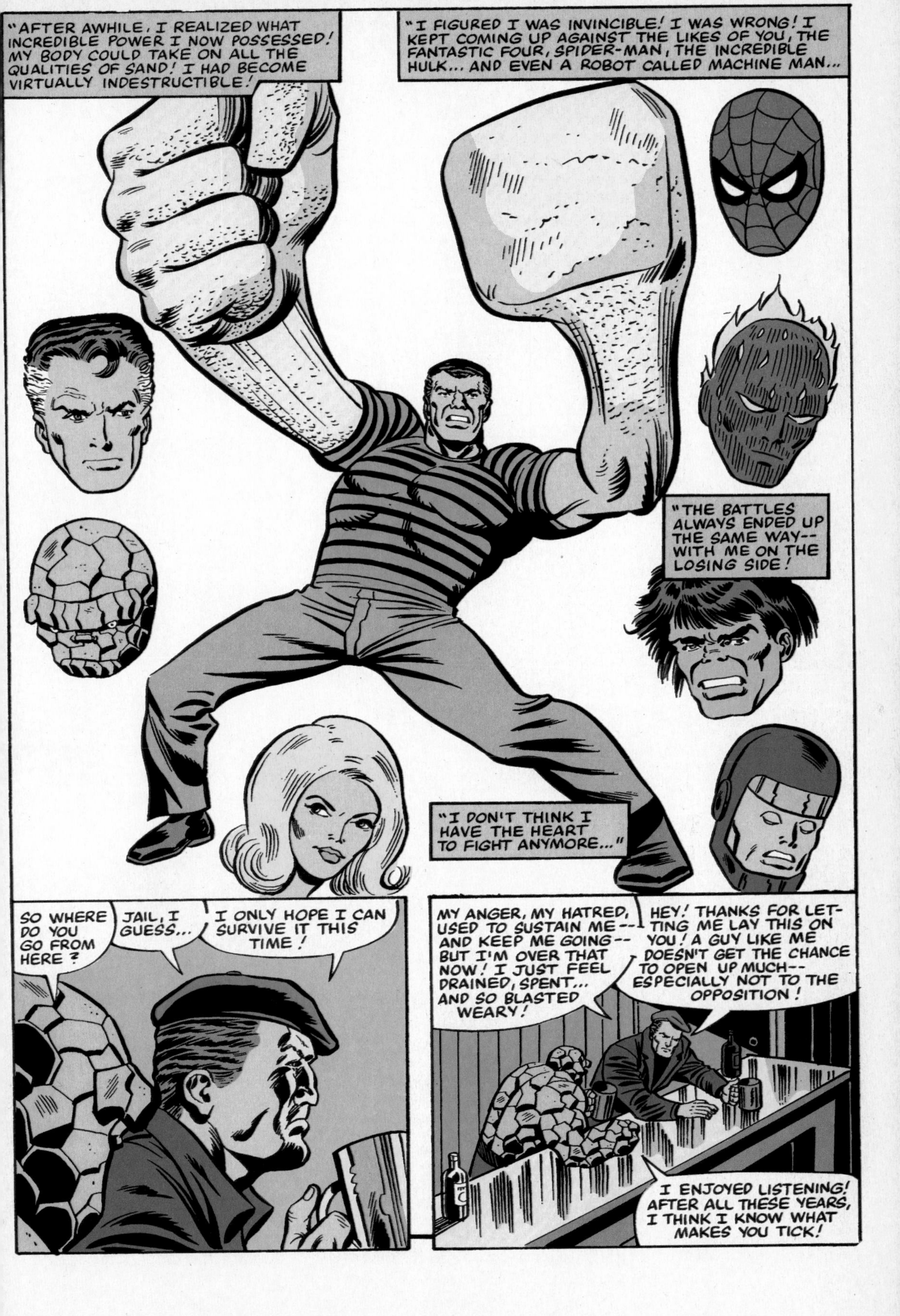
"AFTER AWHILE, I REALIZED WHAT INCREDIBLE POWER I NOW POSSESSED! MY BODY COULD TAKE ON ALL THE QUALITIES OF SAND! I HAD BECOME VIRTUALLY INDESTRUCTIBLE!
"I FIGURED I WAS INVINCIBLE! I WAS WRONG! I KEPT COMING UP AGAINST THE LIKES OF YOU, THE FANTASTIC FOUR, SPIDER-MAN, THE INCREDIBLE HULK... AND EVEN A ROBOT CALLED MACHINE MAN...
"THE BATTLES ALWAYS ENDED UP THE SAME WAY-- WITH ME ON THE LOSING SIDE!
"I DON'T THINK I HAVE THE HEART TO FIGHT ANYMORE..."
SO WHERE DO YOU GO FROM HERE?
JAIL, I GUESS...
I ONLY HOPE I CAN SURVIVE IT THIS TIME!
MY ANGER, MY HATRED, USED TO SUSTAIN ME-- AND KEEP ME GOING-- BUT I'M OVER THAT NOW! I JUST FEEL DRAINED, SPENT... AND SO BLASTED WEARY!
HEY! THANKS FOR LETTING ME LAY THIS ON YOU! A GUY LIKE ME DOESN'T GET THE CHANCE TO OPEN UP MUCH-- ESPECIALLY NOT TO THE OPPOSITION!
I ENJOYED LISTENING! AFTER ALL THESE YEARS, I THINK I KNOW WHAT MAKES YOU TICK!

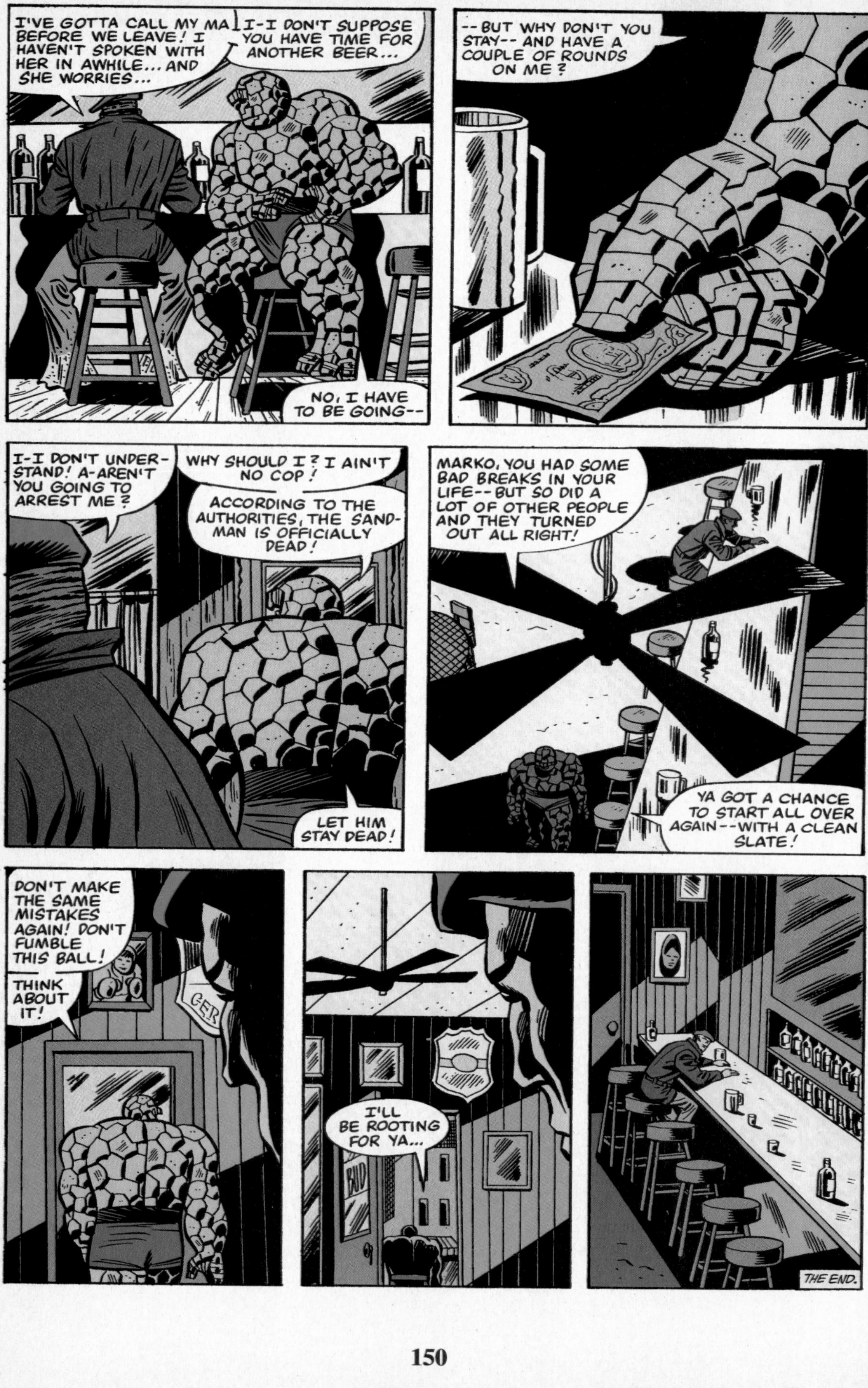
I'VE GOTTA CALL MY MA BEFORE WE LEAVE! I HAVEN'T SPOKEN WITH HER IN AWHILE... AND SHE WORRIES...
I-I DON'T SUPPOSE YOU HAVE TIME FOR ANOTHER BEER...
NO, I HAVE TO BE GOING--
--BUT WHY DON'T YOU STAY-- AND HAVE A COUPLE OF ROUNDS ON ME?
I-I DON'T UNDER-STAND! A-AREN'T YOU GOING TO ARREST ME?
WHY SHOULD I? I AIN'T NO COP!
ACCORDING TO THE AUTHORITIES, THE SAND-MAN IS OFFICIALLY DEAD!
LET HIM STAY DEAD!
MARKO, YOU HAD SOME BAD BREAKS IN YOUR LIFE--BUT SO DID A LOT OF OTHER PEOPLE AND THEY TURNED OUT ALL RIGHT!
YA GOT A CHANCE TO START ALL OVER AGAIN--WITH A CLEAN SLATE!
DON'T MAKE THE SAME MISTAKES AGAIN! DON'T FUMBLE THIS BALL!
THINK ABOUT IT!
I'LL BE ROOTING FOR YA...
THE END.

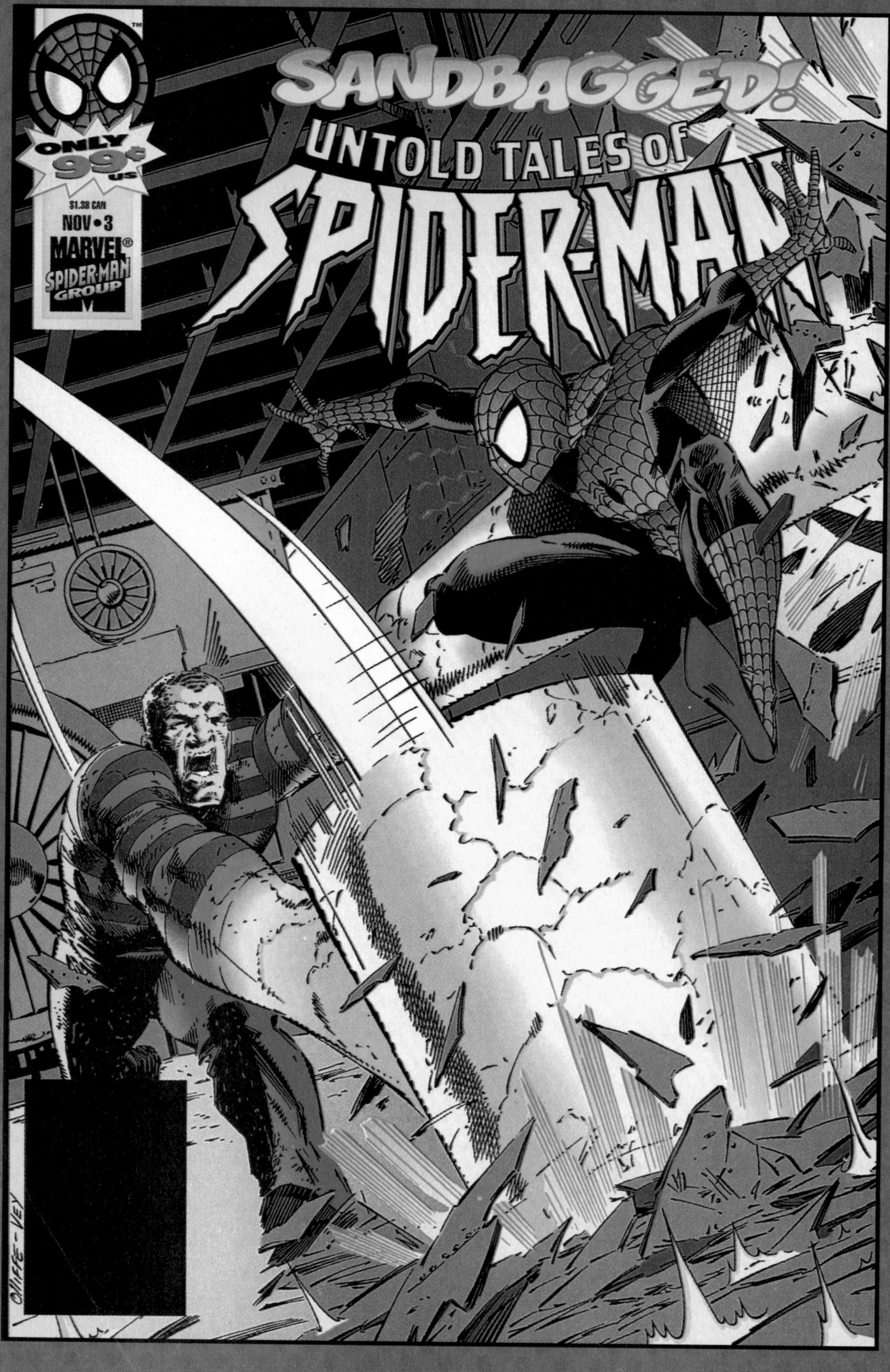
ONLY
99¢
US
$1.38 CAN
NOV • 3
MARVEL®
SPIDER-MAN GROUP
SANDBAGGED!
UNTOLD TALES OF
SPIDER-MAN

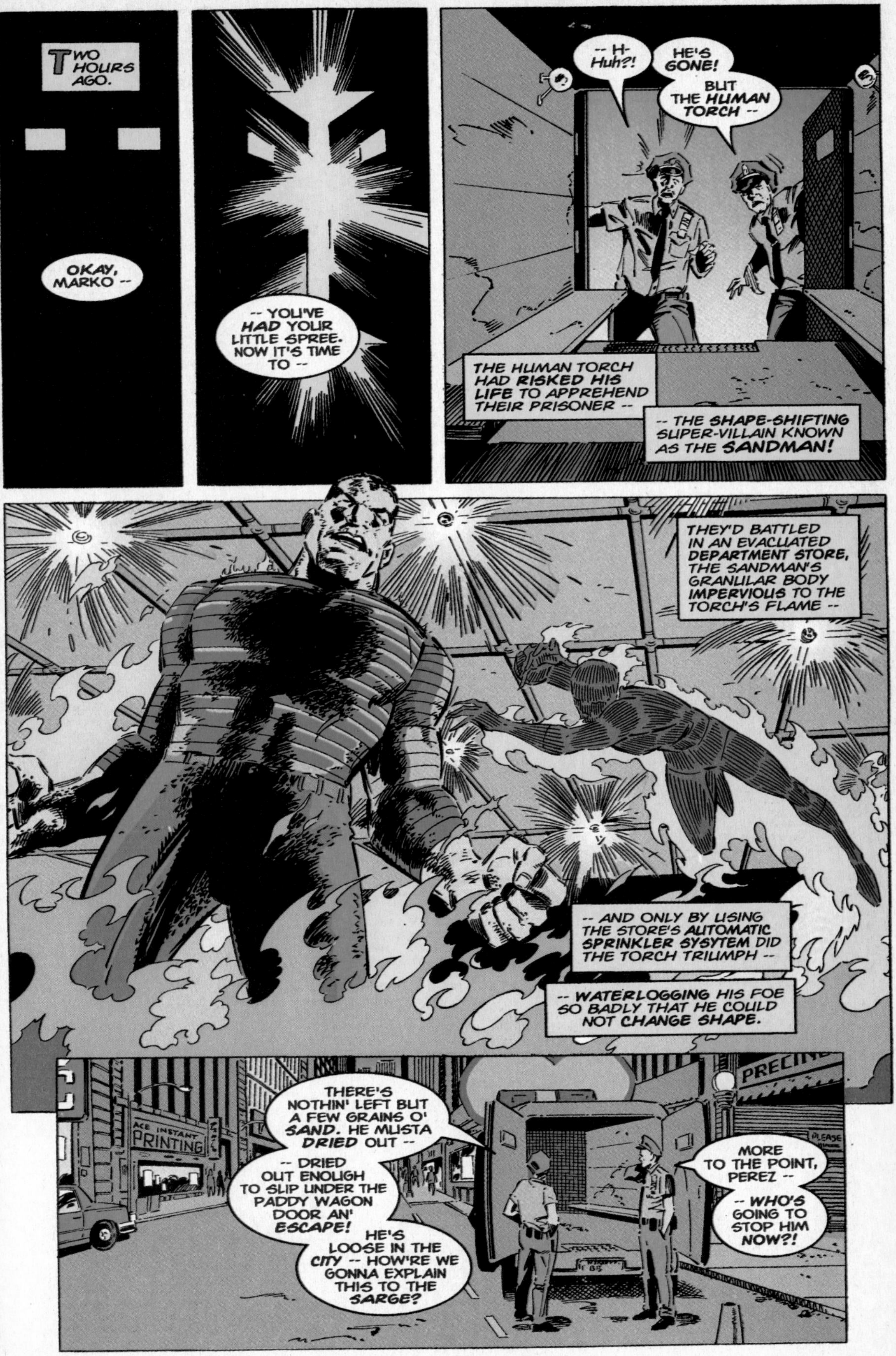
TWO HOURS AGO.
OKAY, MARKO --
-- YOU'VE HAD YOUR LITTLE SPREE. NOW IT'S TIME TO --
-- H-Huh?!
HE'S GONE!
BUT THE HUMAN TORCH --
THE HUMAN TORCH HAD RISKED HIS LIFE TO APPREHEND THEIR PRISONER --
-- THE SHAPE-SHIFTING SUPER-VILLAIN KNOWN AS THE SANDMAN!
THEY'D BATTLED IN AN EVACUATED DEPARTMENT STORE, THE SANDMAN'S GRANULAR BODY IMPERVIOUS TO THE TORCH'S FLAME --
-- AND ONLY BY USING THE STORE'S AUTOMATIC SPRINKLER SYSYTEM DID THE TORCH TRIUMPH --
-- WATERLOGGING HIS FOE SO BADLY THAT HE COULD NOT CHANGE SHAPE.
ACE INSTANT PRINTING
PRECIN
THERE'S NOTHIN' LEFT BUT A FEW GRAINS O' SAND. HE MUSTA DRIED OUT --
-- DRIED OUT ENOUGH TO SLIP UNDER THE PADDY WAGON DOOR AN' ESCAPE!
HE'S LOOSE IN THE CITY -- HOW'RE WE GONNA EXPLAIN THIS TO THE SARGE?
MORE TO THE POINT, PEREZ --
-- WHO'S GOING TO STOP HIM NOW?!

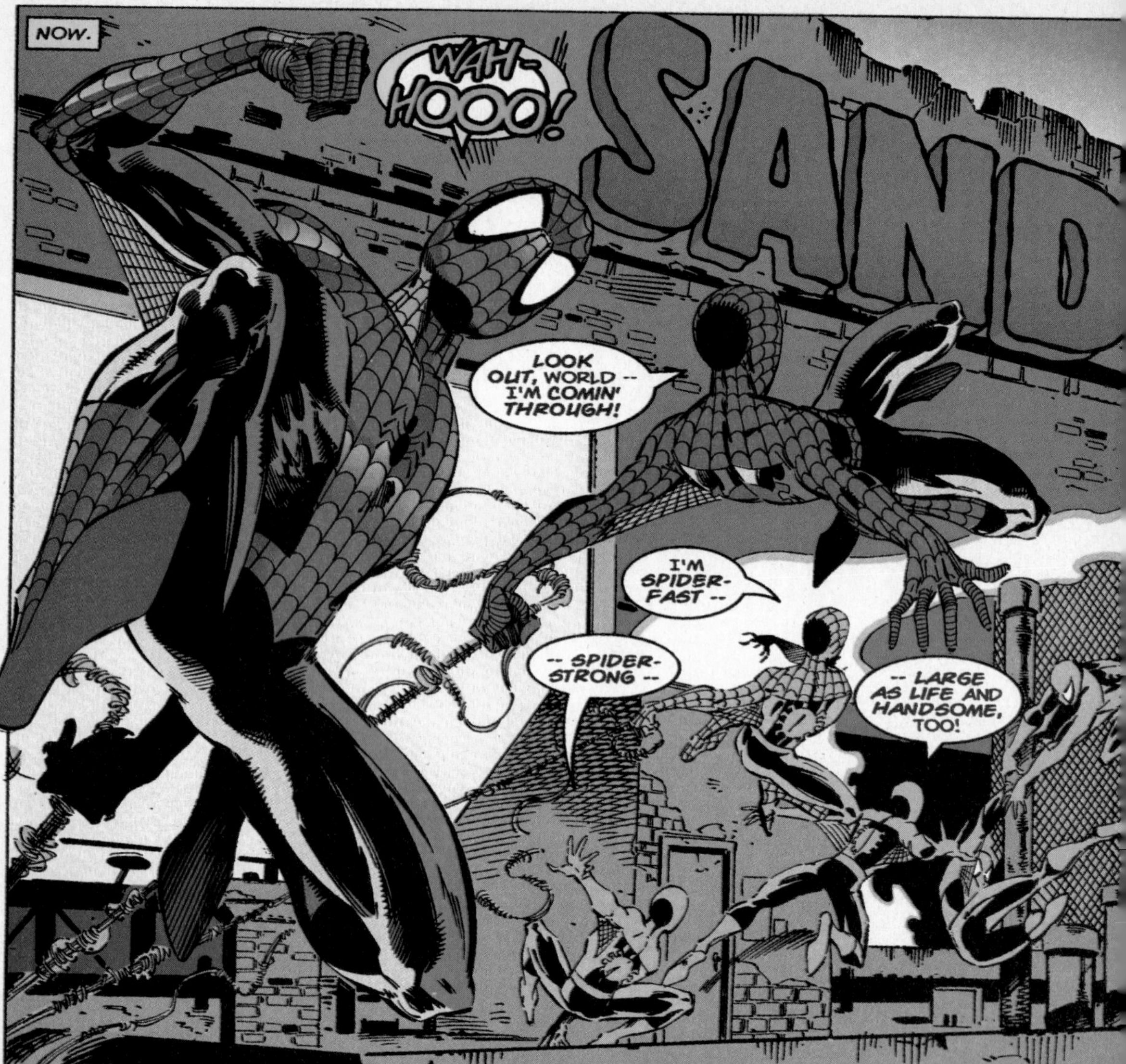
NOW.
WAH-HOOO!
SAND
LOOK OUT, WORLD -- I'M COMIN' THROUGH!
I'M SPIDER-FAST --
-- SPIDER-STRONG --
-- LARGE AS LIFE AND HANDSOME, TOO!

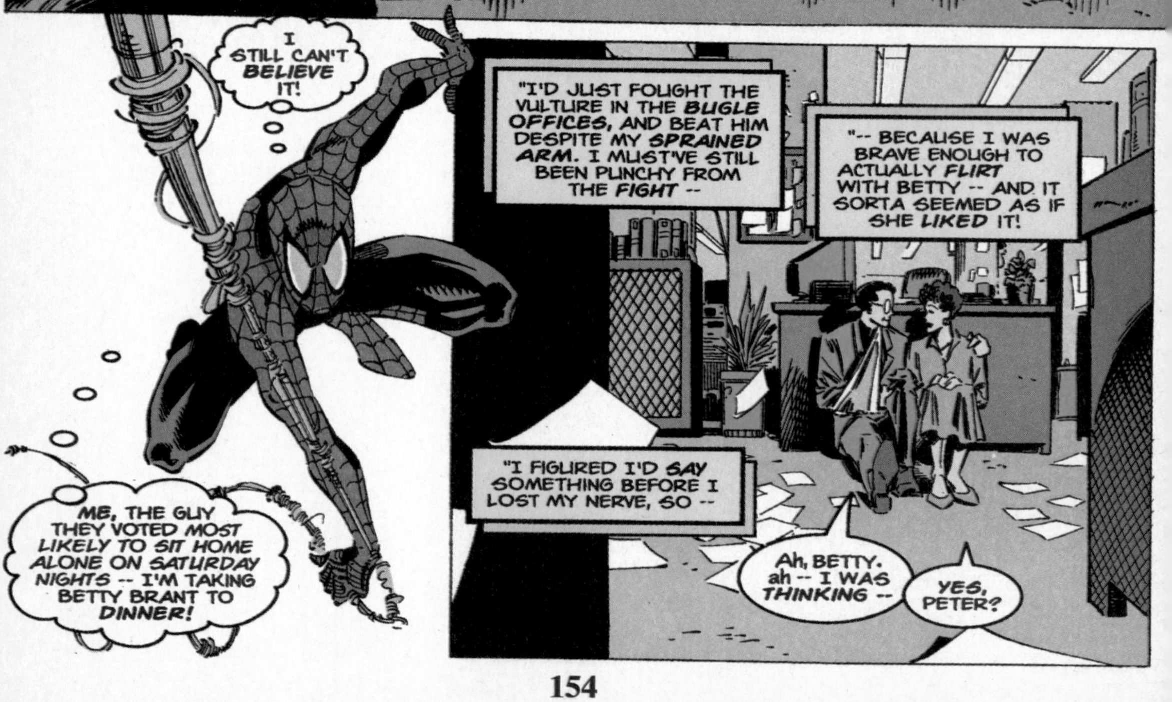
I STILL CAN'T BELIEVE IT!
"I'D JUST FOUGHT THE VULTURE IN THE BUGLE OFFICES, AND BEAT HIM DESPITE MY SPRAINED ARM. I MUST'VE STILL BEEN PUNCHY FROM THE FIGHT --
"-- BECAUSE I WAS BRAVE ENOUGH TO ACTUALLY FLIRT WITH BETTY -- AND IT SORTA SEEMED AS IF SHE LIKED IT!
"I FIGURED I'D SAY SOMETHING BEFORE I LOST MY NERVE, SO --
Ah, BETTY. ah -- I WAS THINKING --
YES, PETER?
ME, THE GUY THEY VOTED MOST LIKELY TO SIT HOME ALONE ON SATURDAY NIGHTS -- I'M TAKING BETTY BRANT TO DINNER!

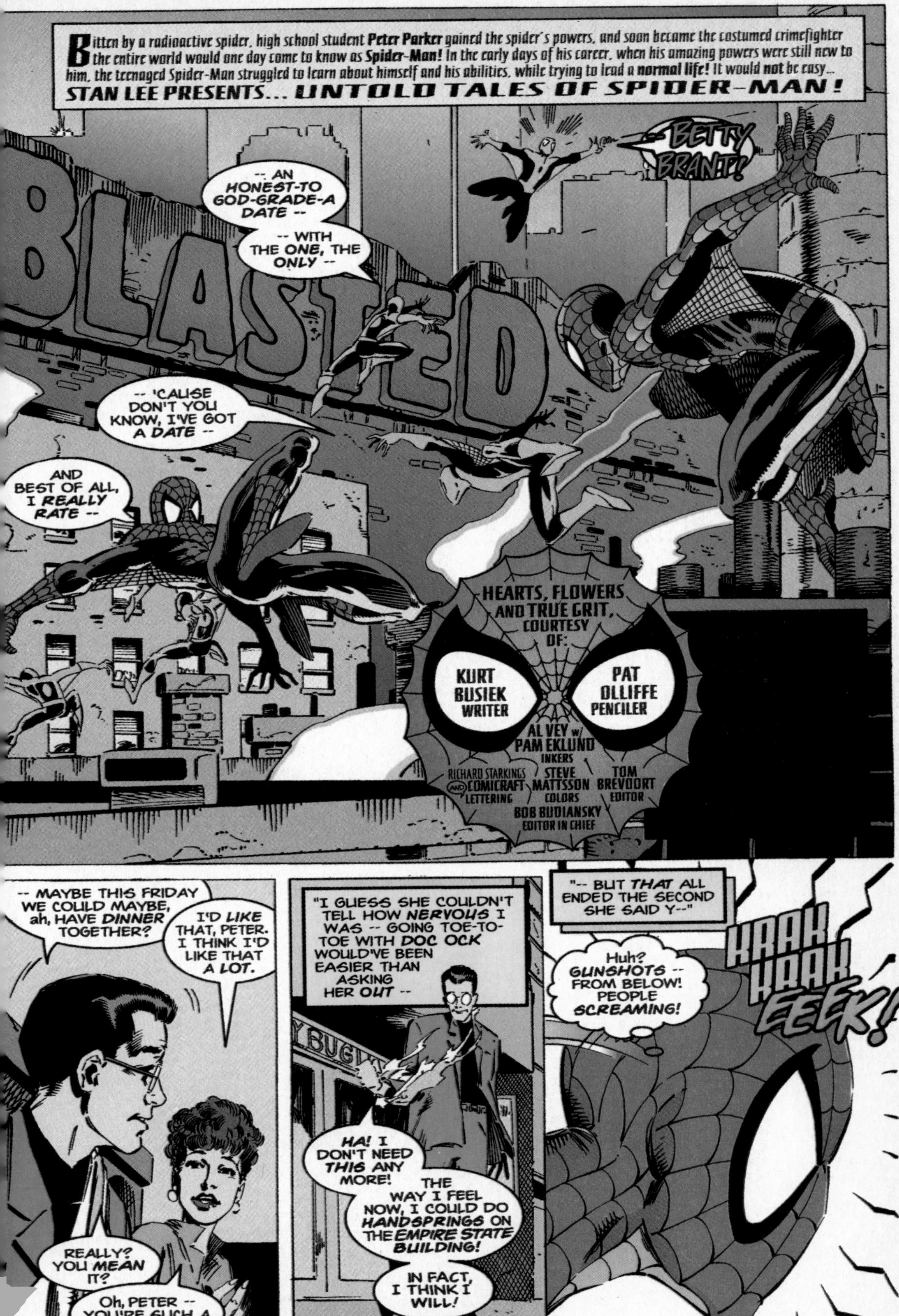

Bitten by a radioactive spider, high school student Peter Parker gained the spider's powers, and soon became the costumed crimefighter the entire world would one day come to know as Spider-Man! In the early days of his career, when his amazing powers were still new to him, the teenaged Spider-Man struggled to learn about himself and his abilities, while trying to lead a normal life! It would not be easy...
STAN LEE PRESENTS... UNTOLD TALES OF SPIDER-MAN!
BLASTED
-- AN HONEST-TO GOD-GRADE-A DATE --
-- WITH THE ONE, THE ONLY --
-- BETTY BRANT!
-- 'CAUSE DON'T YOU KNOW, I'VE GOT A DATE --
AND BEST OF ALL, I REALLY RATE --
HEARTS, FLOWERS AND TRUE GRIT, COURTESY OF:
KURT BUSIEK WRITER
PAT OLLIFFE PENCILER
AL VEY w/ PAM EKLUND INKERS
RICHARD STARKINGS AND COMICRAFT LETTERING
STEVE MATTSSON COLORS
TOM BREVOORT EDITOR
BOB BUDIANSKY EDITOR IN CHIEF
-- MAYBE THIS FRIDAY WE COULD MAYBE, ah, HAVE DINNER TOGETHER?
I'D LIKE THAT, PETER. I THINK I'D LIKE THAT A LOT.
REALLY? YOU MEAN IT?
Oh, PETER -- YOU'RE SUCH A KIDDER!
"I GUESS SHE COULDN'T TELL HOW NERVOUS I WAS -- GOING TOE-TO-TOE WITH DOC OCK WOULD'VE BEEN EASIER THAN ASKING HER OUT --
HA! I DON'T NEED THIS ANY MORE!
THE WAY I FEEL NOW, I COULD DO HANDSPRINGS ON THE EMPIRE STATE BUILDING!
IN FACT, I THINK I WILL!
"-- BUT THAT ALL ENDED THE SECOND SHE SAID Y--"
KRAK KRAK EEEK!
Huh? GUNSHOTS -- FROM BELOW! PEOPLE SCREAMING!

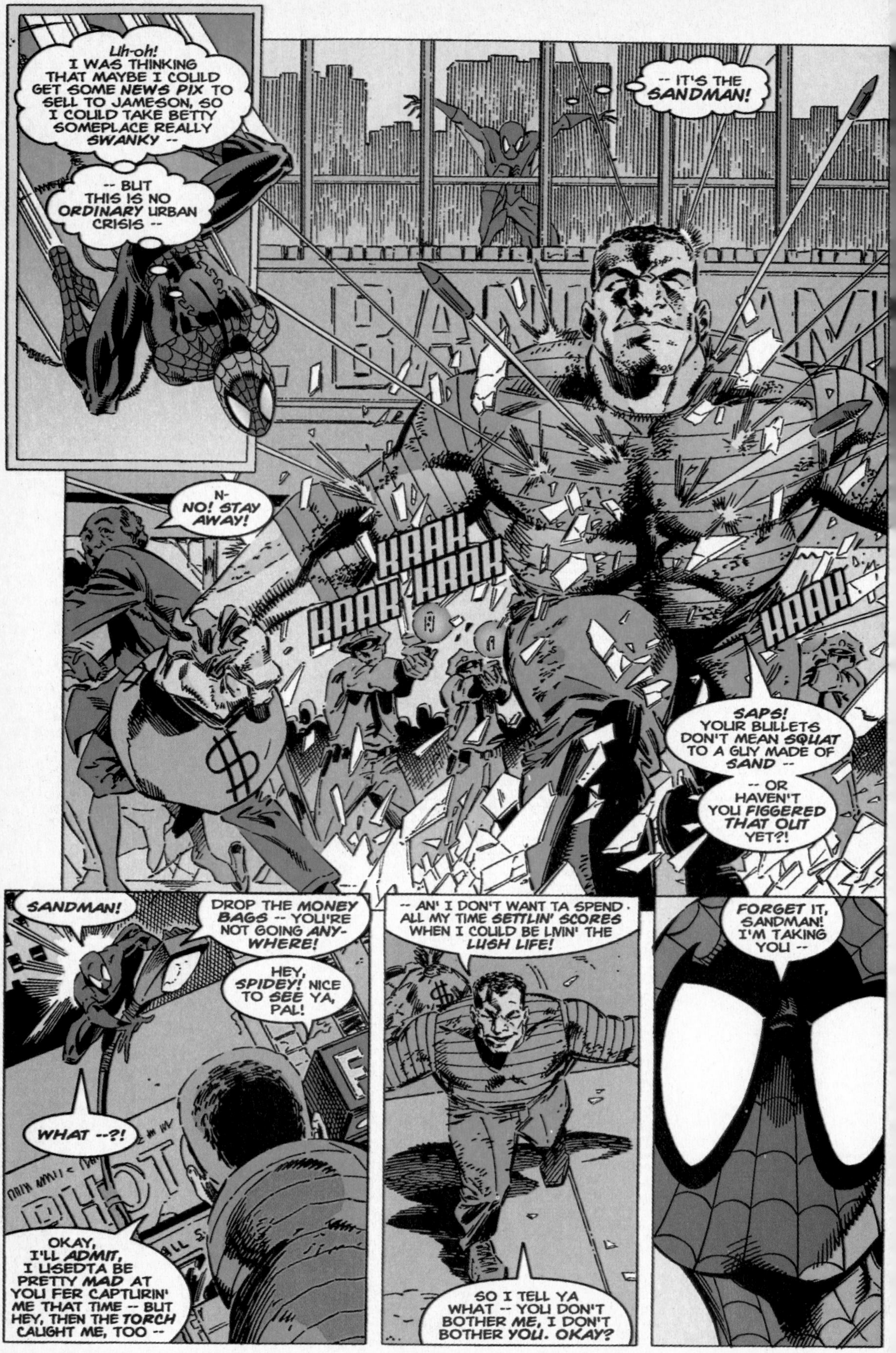
Uh-oh! I WAS THINKING THAT MAYBE I COULD GET SOME NEWS PIX TO SELL TO JAMESON, SO I COULD TAKE BETTY SOMEPLACE REALLY SWANKY --
-- BUT THIS IS NO ORDINARY URBAN CRISIS --
-- IT'S THE SANDMAN!
N-NO! STAY AWAY!
KRAK
KRAK KRAK
KRAK
KRAK
SAPS! YOUR BULLETS DON'T MEAN SQUAT TO A GUY MADE OF SAND --
-- OR HAVEN'T YOU FIGGERED THAT OUT YET?!
SANDMAN!
DROP THE MONEY BAGS -- YOU'RE NOT GOING ANYWHERE!
HEY, SPIDEY! NICE TO SEE YA, PAL!
WHAT --?!
OKAY, I'LL ADMIT, I USEDTA BE PRETTY MAD AT YOU FER CAPTURIN' ME THAT TIME -- BUT HEY, THEN THE TORCH CAUGHT ME, TOO --
-- AN' I DON'T WANT TA SPEND ALL MY TIME SETTLIN' SCORES WHEN I COULD BE LIVIN' THE LUSH LIFE!
SO I TELL YA WHAT -- YOU DON'T BOTHER ME, I DON'T BOTHER YOU. OKAY?
FORGET IT, SANDMAN! I'M TAKING YOU --

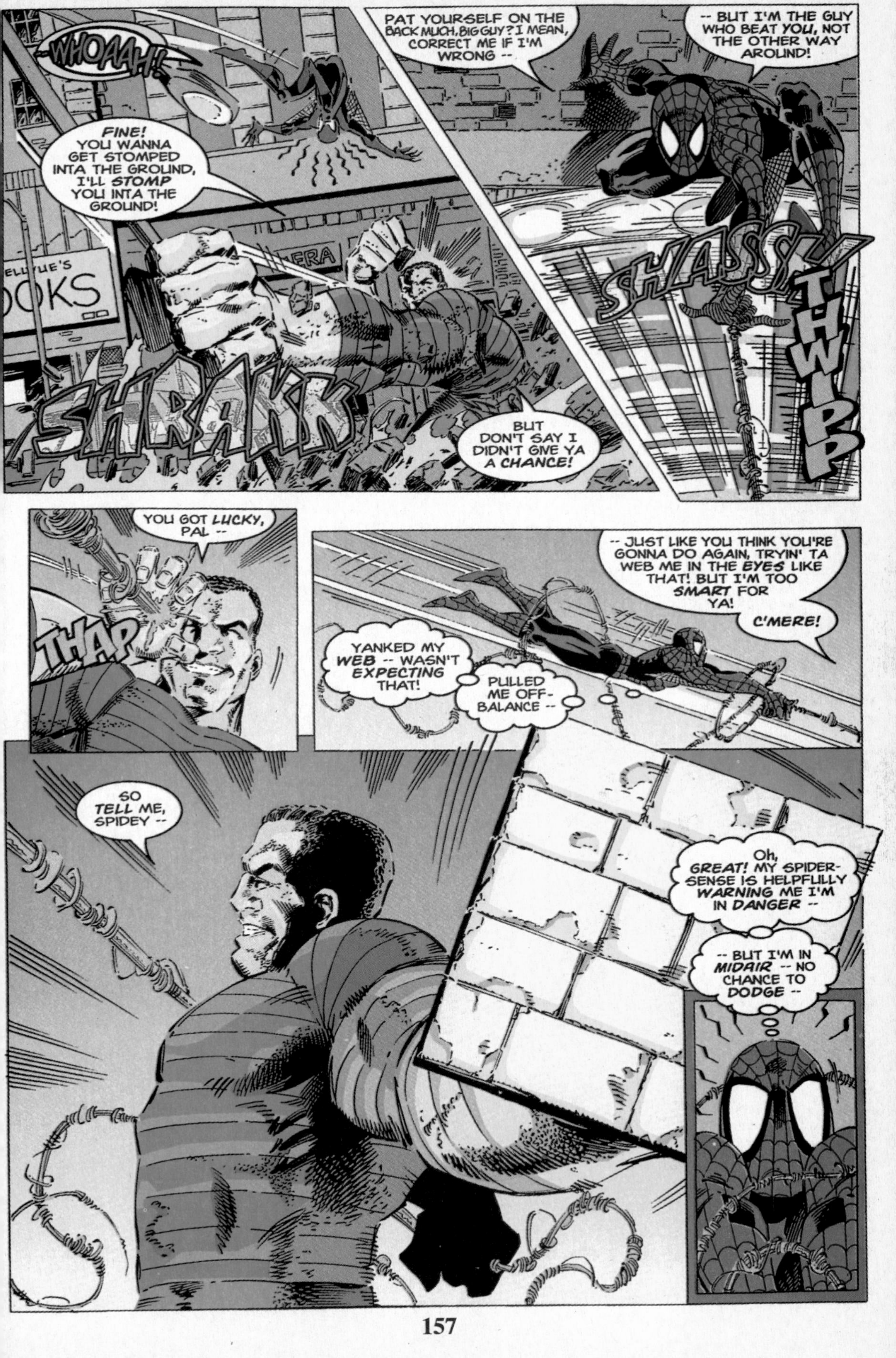
WHOAAH!
FINE! YOU WANNA GET STOMPED INTA THE GROUND, I'LL STOMP YOU INTA THE GROUND!
PAT YOURSELF ON THE BACK MUCH, BIG GUY? I MEAN, CORRECT ME IF I'M WRONG --
-- BUT I'M THE GUY WHO BEAT YOU, NOT THE OTHER WAY AROUND!
SHRAKK
SHASSSH
THWIPP
BUT DON'T SAY I DIDN'T GIVE YA A CHANCE!
YOU GOT LUCKY, PAL --
THAP
-- JUST LIKE YOU THINK YOU'RE GONNA DO AGAIN, TRYIN' TA WEB ME IN THE EYES LIKE THAT! BUT I'M TOO SMART FOR YA!
C'MERE!
YANKED MY WEB -- WASN'T EXPECTING THAT!
PULLED ME OFF-BALANCE --
SO TELL ME, SPIDEY --
Oh, GREAT! MY SPIDER-SENSE IS HELPFULLY WARNING ME I'M IN DANGER --
-- BUT I'M IN MIDAIR -- NO CHANCE TO DODGE --

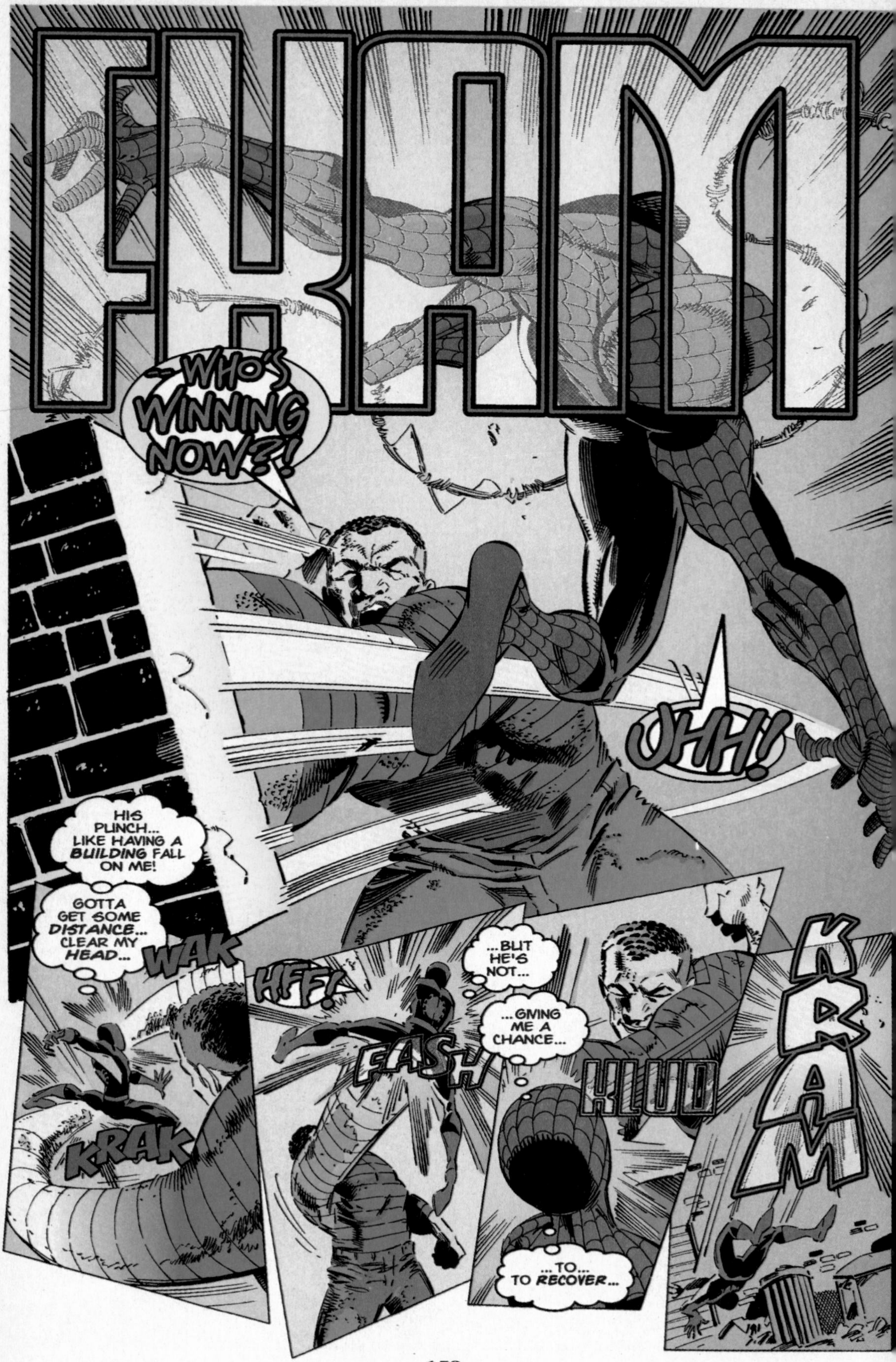
FRAM
-- WHO'S WINNING NOW?!
UHH!
HIS PUNCH... LIKE HAVING A BUILDING FALL ON ME!
GOTTA GET SOME DISTANCE... CLEAR MY HEAD...
WAK
KRAK
HFF!
FASH
...BUT HE'S NOT...
...GIVING ME A CHANCE...
KLUD
...TO... TO RECOVER...
KRAM

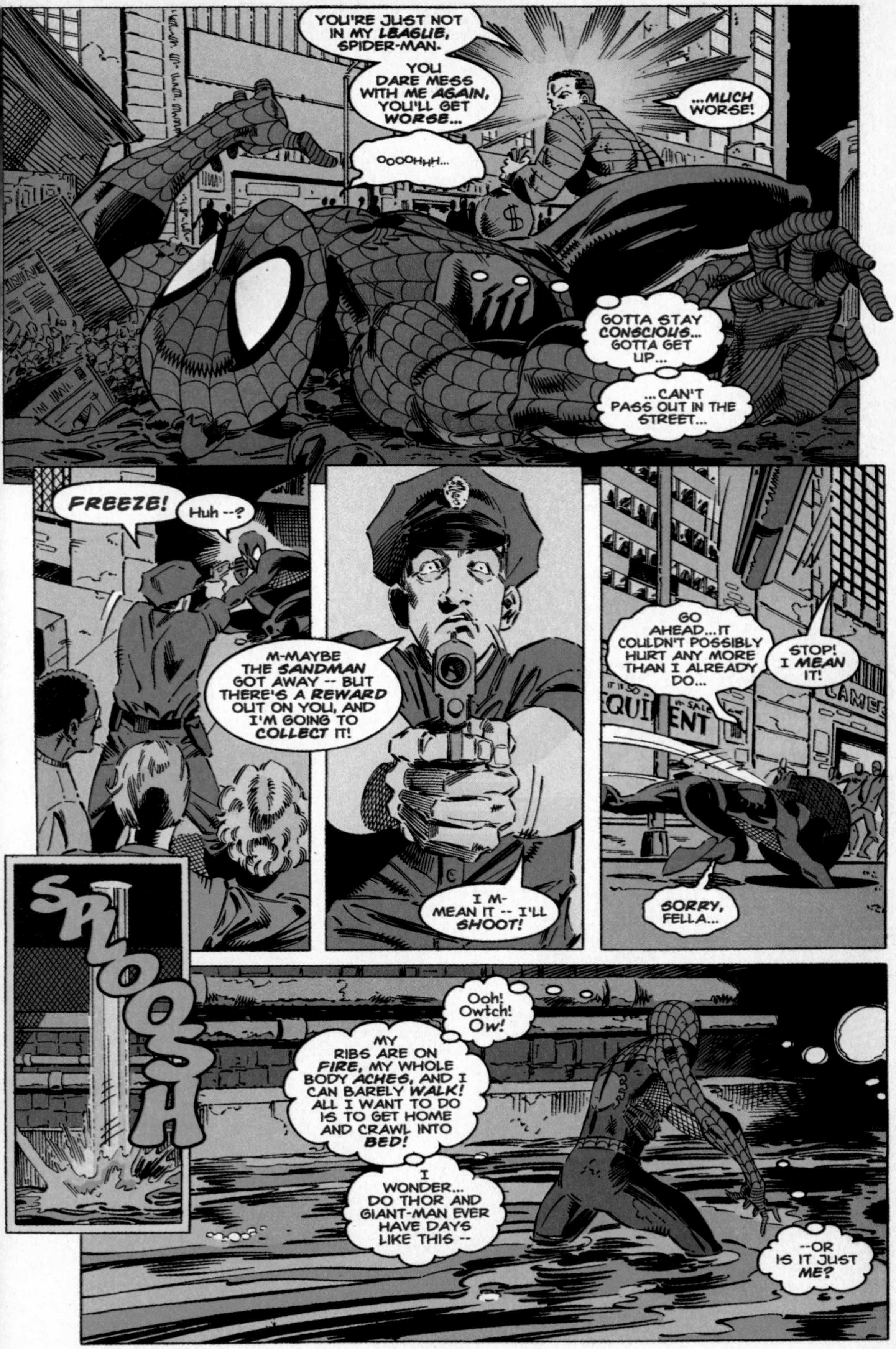
YOU'RE JUST NOT IN MY LEAGUE, SPIDER-MAN.
YOU DARE MESS WITH ME AGAIN, YOU'LL GET WORSE...
...MUCH WORSE!
OOOOHHH...
GOTTA STAY CONSCIOUS... GOTTA GET UP...
...CAN'T PASS OUT IN THE STREET...
FREEZE!
Huh --?
M-MAYBE THE SANDMAN GOT AWAY -- BUT THERE'S A REWARD OUT ON YOU, AND I'M GOING TO COLLECT IT!
I M-MEAN IT -- I'LL SHOOT!
GO AHEAD...IT COULDN'T POSSIBLY HURT ANY MORE THAN I ALREADY DO...
STOP! I MEAN IT!
SORRY, FELLA...
SPLOOSH
Ooh! Owtch! Ow!
MY RIBS ARE ON FIRE, MY WHOLE BODY ACHES, AND I CAN BARELY WALK! ALL I WANT TO DO IS TO GET HOME AND CRAWL INTO BED!
I WONDER... DO THOR AND GIANT-MAN EVER HAVE DAYS LIKE THIS --
--OR IS IT JUST ME?

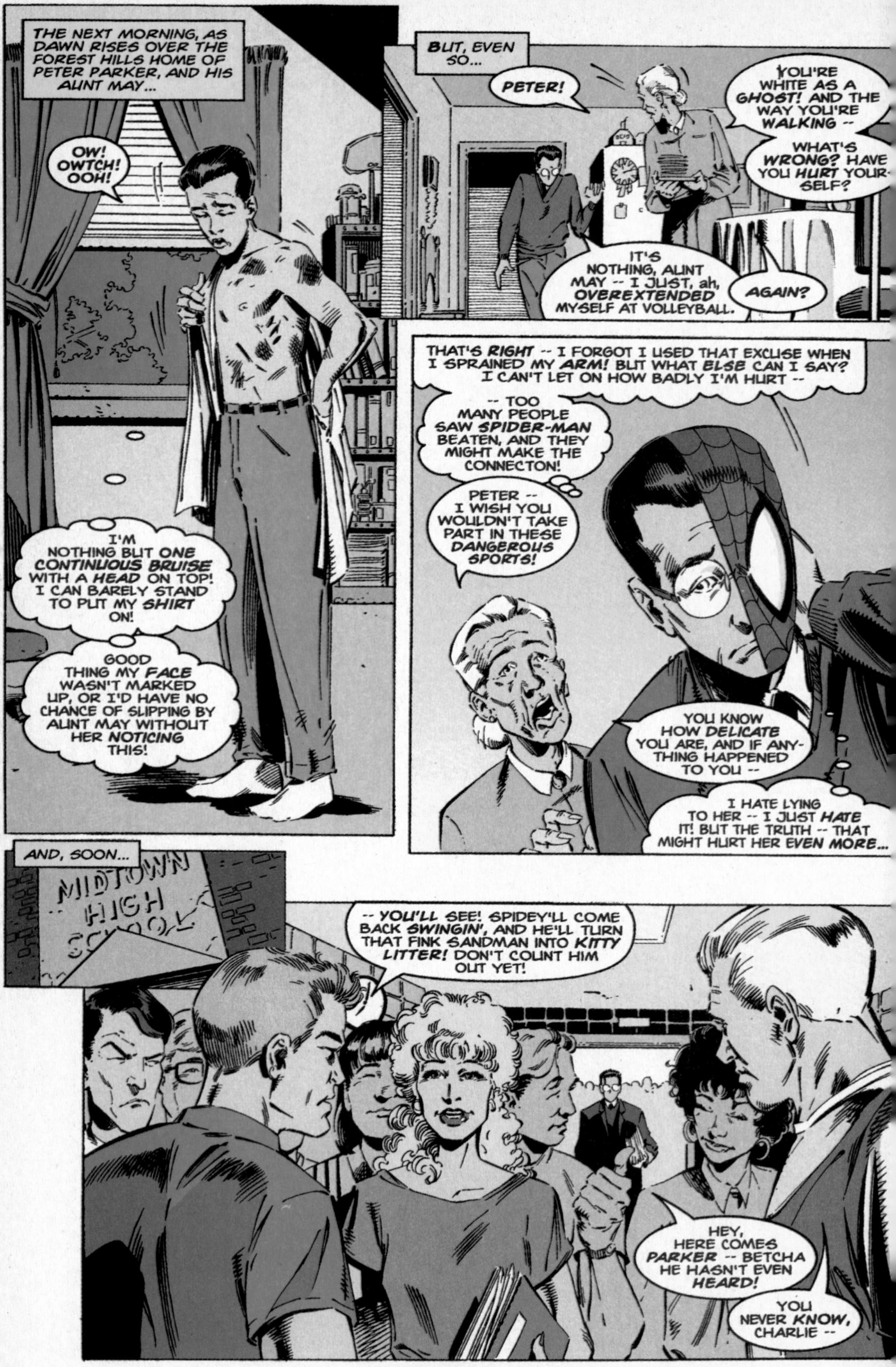
THE NEXT MORNING, AS DAWN RISES OVER THE FOREST HILLS HOME OF PETER PARKER, AND HIS AUNT MAY...
OW! OWTCH! OOH!
I'M NOTHING BUT ONE CONTINUOUS BRUISE WITH A HEAD ON TOP! I CAN BARELY STAND TO PUT MY SHIRT ON!
GOOD THING MY FACE WASN'T MARKED UP, OR I'D HAVE NO CHANCE OF SLIPPING BY AUNT MAY WITHOUT HER NOTICING THIS!
BUT, EVEN SO...
PETER!
YOU'RE WHITE AS A GHOST! AND THE WAY YOU'RE WALKING --
WHAT'S WRONG? HAVE YOU HURT YOURSELF?
IT'S NOTHING, AUNT MAY -- I JUST, ah, OVEREXTENDED MYSELF AT VOLLEYBALL.
AGAIN?
THAT'S RIGHT -- I FORGOT I USED THAT EXCUSE WHEN I SPRAINED MY ARM! BUT WHAT ELSE CAN I SAY? I CAN'T LET ON HOW BADLY I'M HURT --
-- TOO MANY PEOPLE SAW SPIDER-MAN BEATEN, AND THEY MIGHT MAKE THE CONNECTON!
PETER -- I WISH YOU WOULDN'T TAKE PART IN THESE DANGEROUS SPORTS!
YOU KNOW HOW DELICATE YOU ARE, AND IF ANYTHING HAPPENED TO YOU --
I HATE LYING TO HER -- I JUST HATE IT! BUT THE TRUTH -- THAT MIGHT HURT HER EVEN MORE...
AND, SOON...
MIDTOWN HIGH SCHOOL
-- YOU'LL SEE! SPIDEY'LL COME BACK SWINGIN', AND HE'LL TURN THAT FINK SANDMAN INTO KITTY LITTER! DON'T COUNT HIM OUT YET!
HEY, HERE COMES PARKER -- BETCHA HE HASN'T EVEN HEARD!
YOU NEVER KNOW, CHARLIE --

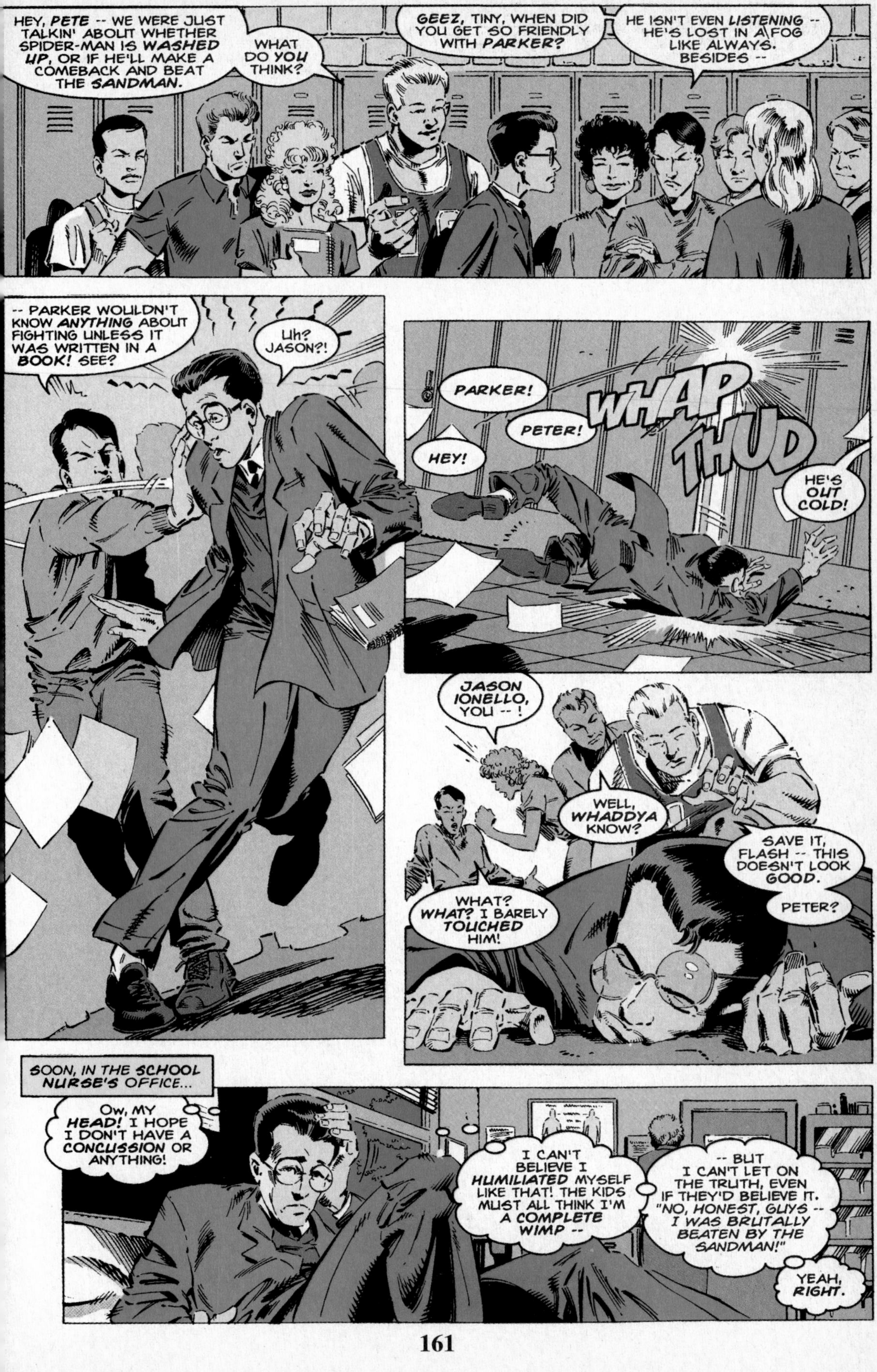
HEY, PETE -- WE WERE JUST TALKIN' ABOUT WHETHER SPIDER-MAN IS WASHED UP, OR IF HE'LL MAKE A COMEBACK AND BEAT THE SANDMAN.
WHAT DO YOU THINK?
GEEZ, TINY, WHEN DID YOU GET SO FRIENDLY WITH PARKER?
HE ISN'T EVEN LISTENING -- HE'S LOST IN A FOG LIKE ALWAYS. BESIDES --
-- PARKER WOULDN'T KNOW ANYTHING ABOUT FIGHTING UNLESS IT WAS WRITTEN IN A BOOK! SEE?
UH? JASON?!
PARKER!
PETER!
HEY!
WHAP
THUD
HE'S OUT COLD!
JASON IONELLO, YOU -- !
WELL, WHADDYA KNOW?
WHAT? WHAT? I BARELY TOUCHED HIM!
SAVE IT, FLASH -- THIS DOESN'T LOOK GOOD.
PETER?
SOON, IN THE SCHOOL NURSE'S OFFICE...
OW, MY HEAD! I HOPE I DON'T HAVE A CONCUSSION OR ANYTHING!
I CAN'T BELIEVE I HUMILIATED MYSELF LIKE THAT! THE KIDS MUST ALL THINK I'M A COMPLETE WIMP --
-- BUT I CAN'T LET ON THE TRUTH, EVEN IF THEY'D BELIEVE IT. "NO, HONEST, GUYS -- I WAS BRUTALLY BEATEN BY THE SANDMAN!"
YEAH, RIGHT.

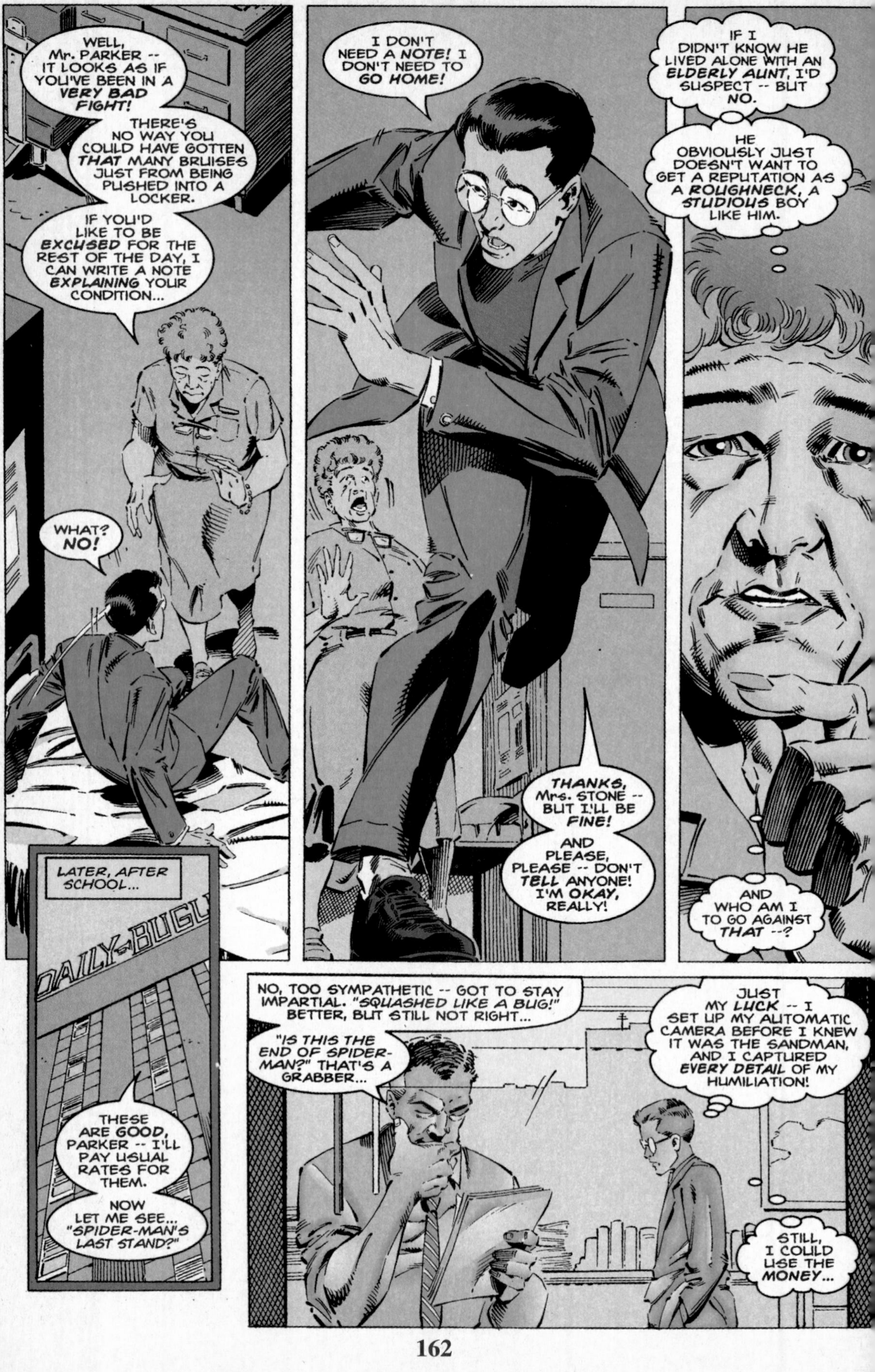
WELL, Mr. PARKER -- IT LOOKS AS IF YOU'VE BEEN IN A VERY BAD FIGHT!
THERE'S NO WAY YOU COULD HAVE GOTTEN THAT MANY BRUISES JUST FROM BEING PUSHED INTO A LOCKER.
IF YOU'D LIKE TO BE EXCUSED FOR THE REST OF THE DAY, I CAN WRITE A NOTE EXPLAINING YOUR CONDITION...
WHAT? NO!
I DON'T NEED A NOTE! I DON'T NEED TO GO HOME!
THANKS, Mrs. STONE -- BUT I'LL BE FINE!
AND PLEASE, PLEASE -- DON'T TELL ANYONE! I'M OKAY, REALLY!
IF I DIDN'T KNOW HE LIVED ALONE WITH AN ELDERLY AUNT, I'D SUSPECT -- BUT NO.
HE OBVIOUSLY JUST DOESN'T WANT TO GET A REPUTATION AS A ROUGHNECK, A STUDIOUS BOY LIKE HIM.
AND WHO AM I TO GO AGAINST THAT --?
LATER, AFTER SCHOOL...
DAILY BUGL
THESE ARE GOOD, PARKER -- I'LL PAY USUAL RATES FOR THEM.
NOW LET ME SEE... "SPIDER-MAN'S LAST STAND?"
NO, TOO SYMPATHETIC -- GOT TO STAY IMPARTIAL. "SQUASHED LIKE A BUG!" BETTER, BUT STILL NOT RIGHT...
"IS THIS THE END OF SPIDER-MAN?" THAT'S A GRABBER...
JUST MY LUCK -- I SET UP MY AUTOMATIC CAMERA BEFORE I KNEW IT WAS THE SANDMAN, AND I CAPTURED EVERY DETAIL OF MY HUMILIATION!
STILL, I COULD USE THE MONEY...

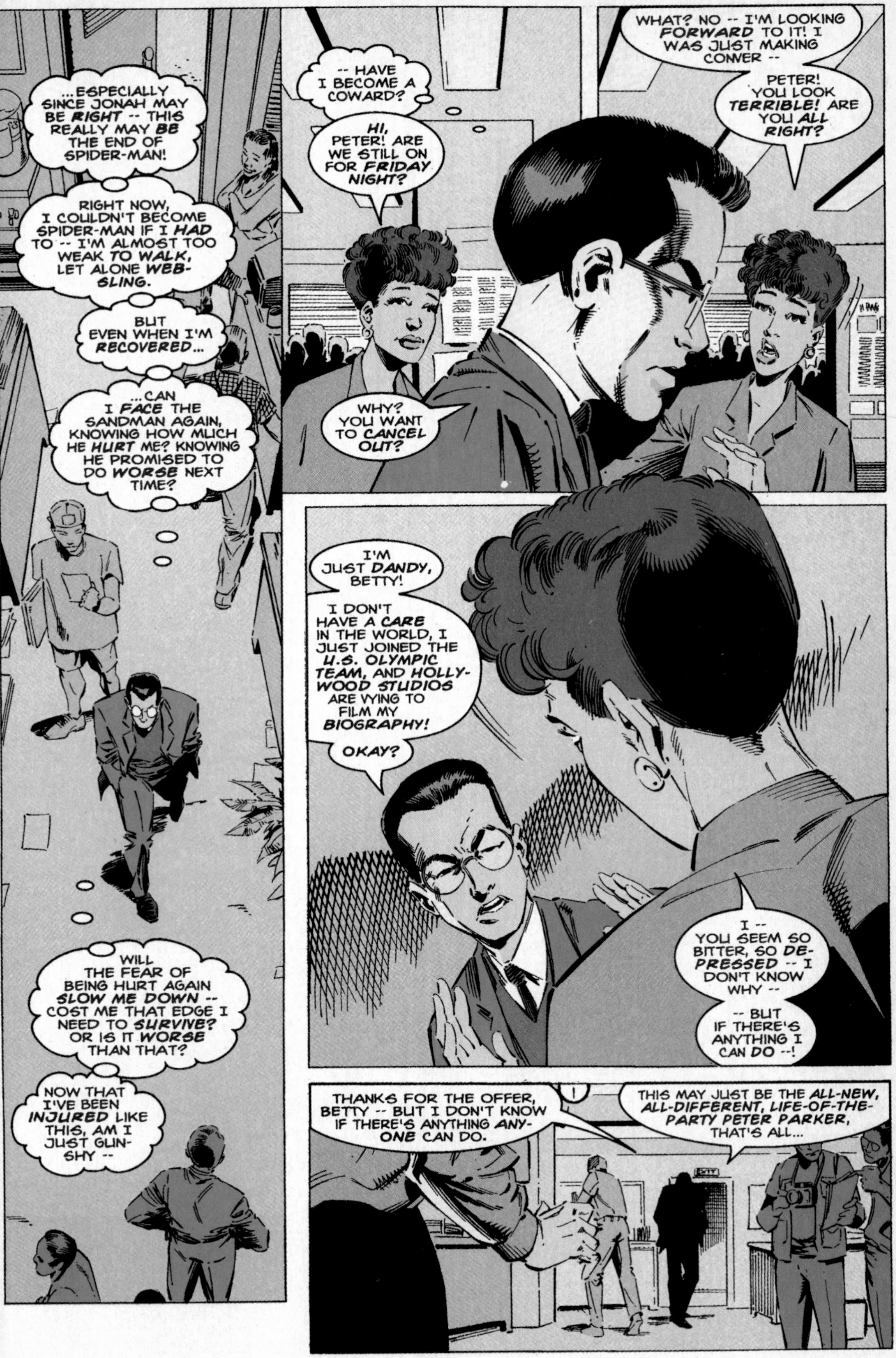
...ESPECIALLY SINCE JONAH MAY BE RIGHT -- THIS REALLY MAY BE THE END OF SPIDER-MAN!
RIGHT NOW, I COULDN'T BECOME SPIDER-MAN IF I HAD TO -- I'M ALMOST TOO WEAK TO WALK, LET ALONE WEB-SLING.
BUT EVEN WHEN I'M RECOVERED...
...CAN I FACE THE SANDMAN AGAIN, KNOWING HOW MUCH HE HURT ME? KNOWING HE PROMISED TO DO WORSE NEXT TIME?
WILL THE FEAR OF BEING HURT AGAIN SLOW ME DOWN -- COST ME THAT EDGE I NEED TO SURVIVE? OR IS IT WORSE THAN THAT?
NOW THAT I'VE BEEN INJURED LIKE THIS, AM I JUST GUN-SHY --
-- HAVE I BECOME A COWARD?
HI, PETER! ARE WE STILL ON FOR FRIDAY NIGHT?
WHY? YOU WANT TO CANCEL OUT?
WHAT? NO -- I'M LOOKING FORWARD TO IT! I WAS JUST MAKING CONVER --
PETER! YOU LOOK TERRIBLE! ARE YOU ALL RIGHT?
I'M JUST DANDY, BETTY!
I DON'T HAVE A CARE IN THE WORLD, I JUST JOINED THE U.S. OLYMPIC TEAM, AND HOLLY-WOOD STUDIOS ARE VYING TO FILM MY BIOGRAPHY!
OKAY?
I -- YOU SEEM SO BITTER, SO DE-PRESSED -- I DON'T KNOW WHY --
-- BUT IF THERE'S ANYTHING I CAN DO --!
THANKS FOR THE OFFER, BETTY -- BUT I DON'T KNOW IF THERE'S ANYTHING ANY-ONE CAN DO.
THIS MAY JUST BE THE ALL-NEW, ALL-DIFFERENT, LIFE-OF-THE-PARTY PETER PARKER, THAT'S ALL...

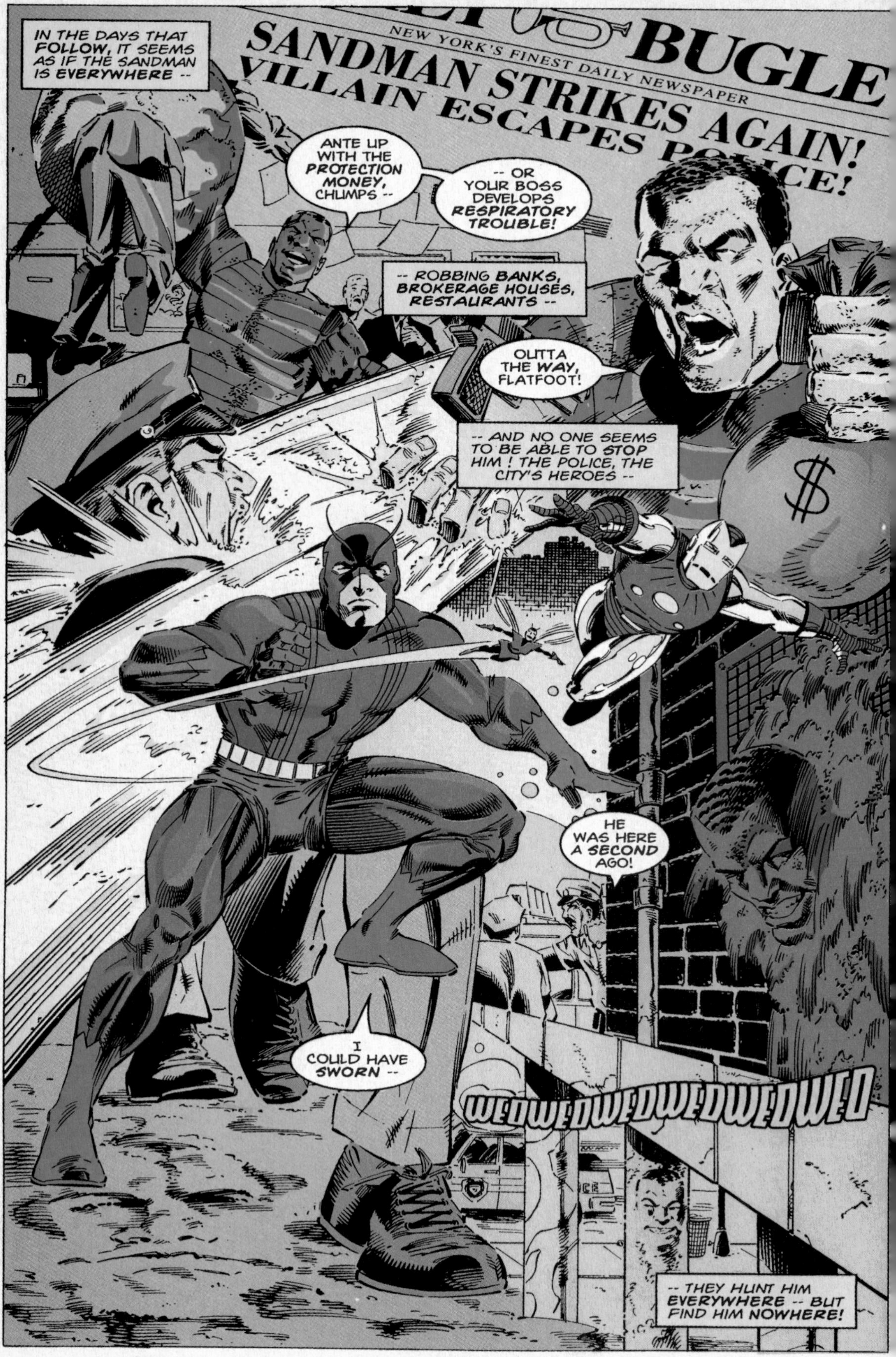
IN THE DAYS THAT FOLLOW, IT SEEMS AS IF THE SANDMAN IS EVERYWHERE --
NEW YORK'S FINEST DAILY NEWSPAPER
BUGLE
SANDMAN STRIKES AGAIN!
VILLAIN ESCAPES POLICE!
ANTE UP WITH THE PROTECTION MONEY, CHUMPS --
-- OR YOUR BOSS DEVELOPS RESPIRATORY TROUBLE!
-- ROBBING BANKS, BROKERAGE HOUSES, RESTAURANTS --
OUTTA THE WAY, FLATFOOT!
-- AND NO ONE SEEMS TO BE ABLE TO STOP HIM ! THE POLICE, THE CITY'S HEROES --
$
HE WAS HERE A SECOND AGO!
I COULD HAVE SWORN --
WEDWEDWEDWEDWEDWED
-- THEY HUNT HIM EVERYWHERE -- BUT FIND HIM NOWHERE!

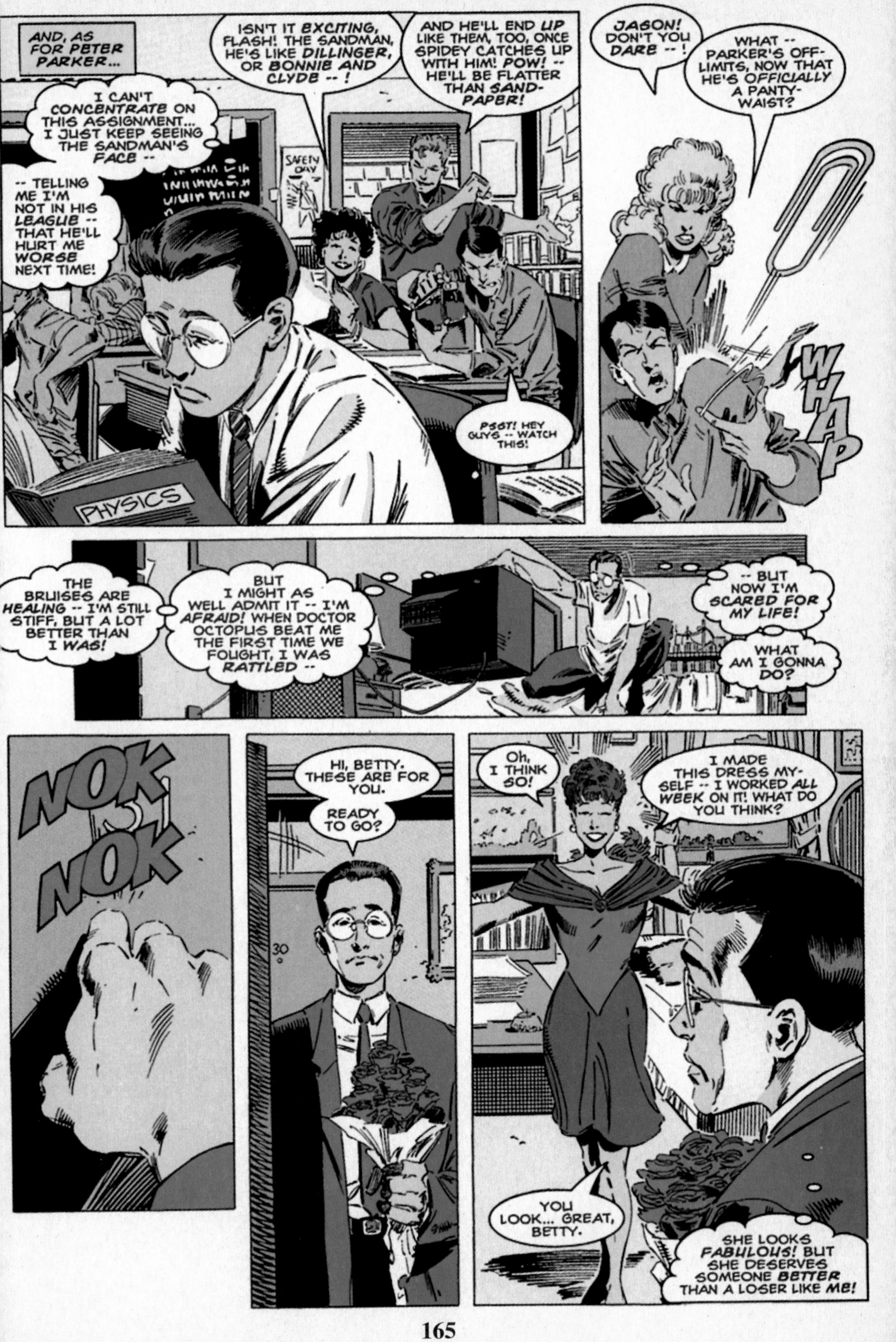
AND, AS FOR PETER PARKER...
I CAN'T CONCENTRATE ON THIS ASSIGNMENT... I JUST KEEP SEEING THE SANDMAN'S FACE --
-- TELLING ME I'M NOT IN HIS LEAGUE -- THAT HE'LL HURT ME WORSE NEXT TIME!
ISN'T IT EXCITING, FLASH! THE SANDMAN, HE'S LIKE DILLINGER, OR BONNIE AND CLYDE -- !
AND HE'LL END UP LIKE THEM, TOO, ONCE SPIDEY CATCHES UP WITH HIM! POW! -- HE'LL BE FLATTER THAN SAND-PAPER!
SAFETY DAY
PHYSICS
PSST! HEY GUYS -- WATCH THIS!
JASON! DON'T YOU DARE -- !
WHAT -- PARKER'S OFF-LIMITS, NOW THAT HE'S OFFICIALLY A PANTY-WAIST?
WHAP
THE BRUISES ARE HEALING -- I'M STILL STIFF, BUT A LOT BETTER THAN I WAS!
BUT I MIGHT AS WELL ADMIT IT -- I'M AFRAID! WHEN DOCTOR OCTOPUS BEAT ME THE FIRST TIME WE FOUGHT, I WAS RATTLED --
-- BUT NOW I'M SCARED FOR MY LIFE!
WHAT AM I GONNA DO?
NOK NOK
HI, BETTY. THESE ARE FOR YOU.
READY TO GO?
Oh, I THINK SO!
I MADE THIS DRESS MY-SELF -- I WORKED ALL WEEK ON IT! WHAT DO YOU THINK?
YOU LOOK... GREAT, BETTY.
SHE LOOKS FABULOUS! BUT SHE DESERVES SOMEONE BETTER THAN A LOSER LIKE ME!

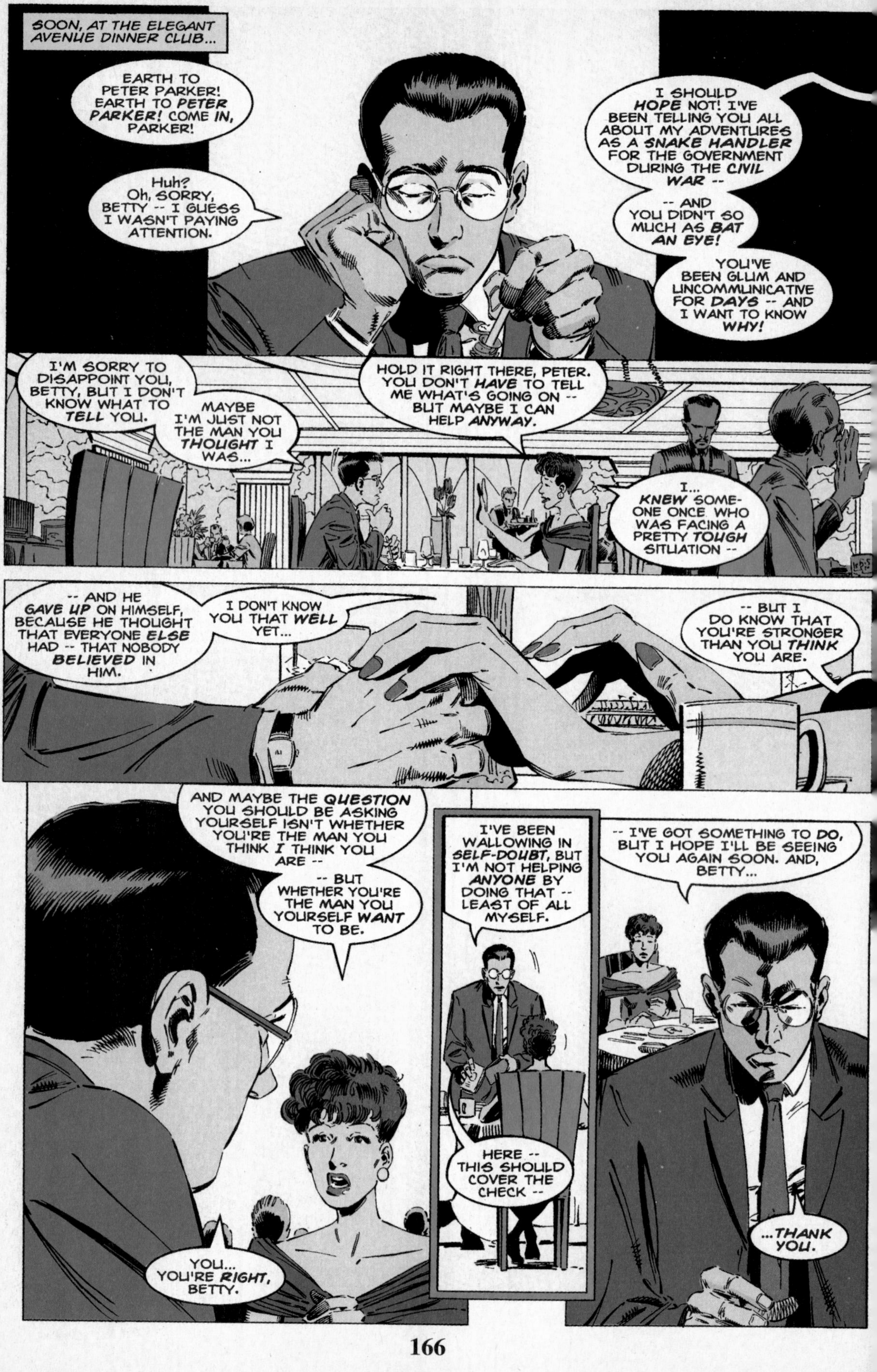
SOON, AT THE ELEGANT AVENUE DINNER CLUB...
EARTH TO PETER PARKER! EARTH TO PETER PARKER! COME IN, PARKER!
Huh? Oh, SORRY, BETTY -- I GUESS I WASN'T PAYING ATTENTION.
I SHOULD HOPE NOT! I'VE BEEN TELLING YOU ALL ABOUT MY ADVENTURES AS A SNAKE HANDLER FOR THE GOVERNMENT DURING THE CIVIL WAR --
-- AND YOU DIDN'T SO MUCH AS BAT AN EYE!
YOU'VE BEEN GLUM AND UNCOMMUNICATIVE FOR DAYS -- AND I WANT TO KNOW WHY!
I'M SORRY TO DISAPPOINT YOU, BETTY, BUT I DON'T KNOW WHAT TO TELL YOU.
MAYBE I'M JUST NOT THE MAN YOU THOUGHT I WAS...
HOLD IT RIGHT THERE, PETER. YOU DON'T HAVE TO TELL ME WHAT'S GOING ON -- BUT MAYBE I CAN HELP ANYWAY.
I... KNEW SOME-ONE ONCE WHO WAS FACING A PRETTY TOUGH SITUATION --
-- AND HE GAVE UP ON HIMSELF, BECAUSE HE THOUGHT THAT EVERYONE ELSE HAD -- THAT NOBODY BELIEVED IN HIM.
I DON'T KNOW YOU THAT WELL YET...
-- BUT I DO KNOW THAT YOU'RE STRONGER THAN YOU THINK YOU ARE.
AND MAYBE THE QUESTION YOU SHOULD BE ASKING YOURSELF ISN'T WHETHER YOU'RE THE MAN YOU THINK I THINK YOU ARE --
-- BUT WHETHER YOU'RE THE MAN YOU YOURSELF WANT TO BE.
YOU... YOU'RE RIGHT, BETTY.
I'VE BEEN WALLOWING IN SELF-DOUBT, BUT I'M NOT HELPING ANYONE BY DOING THAT -- LEAST OF ALL MYSELF.
HERE -- THIS SHOULD COVER THE CHECK --
-- I'VE GOT SOMETHING TO DO, BUT I HOPE I'LL BE SEEING YOU AGAIN SOON. AND, BETTY...
...THANK YOU.

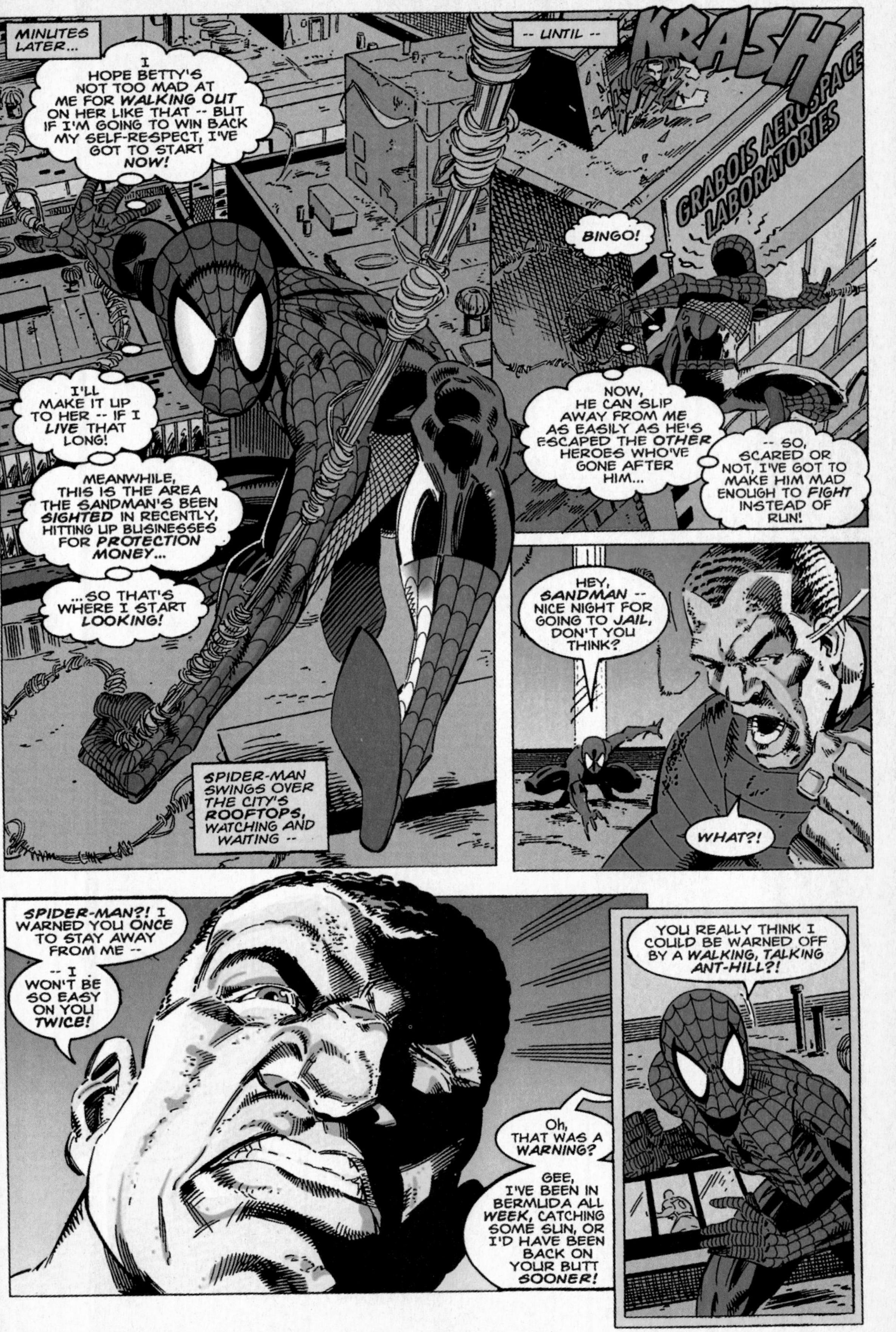
MINUTES LATER...
I HOPE BETTY'S NOT TOO MAD AT ME FOR WALKING OUT ON HER LIKE THAT -- BUT IF I'M GOING TO WIN BACK MY SELF-RESPECT, I'VE GOT TO START NOW!
I'LL MAKE IT UP TO HER -- IF I LIVE THAT LONG!
MEANWHILE, THIS IS THE AREA THE SANDMAN'S BEEN SIGHTED IN RECENTLY, HITTING UP BUSINESSES FOR PROTECTION MONEY...
...SO THAT'S WHERE I START LOOKING!
SPIDER-MAN SWINGS OVER THE CITY'S ROOFTOPS, WATCHING AND WAITING --
-- UNTIL --
KRASH
GRABOIS AEROSPACE LABORATORIES
BINGO!
NOW, HE CAN SLIP AWAY FROM ME AS EASILY AS HE'S ESCAPED THE OTHER HEROES WHO'VE GONE AFTER HIM...
-- SO, SCARED OR NOT, I'VE GOT TO MAKE HIM MAD ENOUGH TO FIGHT INSTEAD OF RUN!
HEY, SANDMAN -- NICE NIGHT FOR GOING TO JAIL, DON'T YOU THINK?
WHAT?!
SPIDER-MAN?! I WARNED YOU ONCE TO STAY AWAY FROM ME --
-- I WON'T BE SO EASY ON YOU TWICE!
YOU REALLY THINK I COULD BE WARNED OFF BY A WALKING, TALKING ANT-HILL?!
Oh, THAT WAS A WARNING?
GEE, I'VE BEEN IN BERMUDA ALL WEEK, CATCHING SOME SUN, OR I'D HAVE BEEN BACK ON YOUR BUTT SOONER!

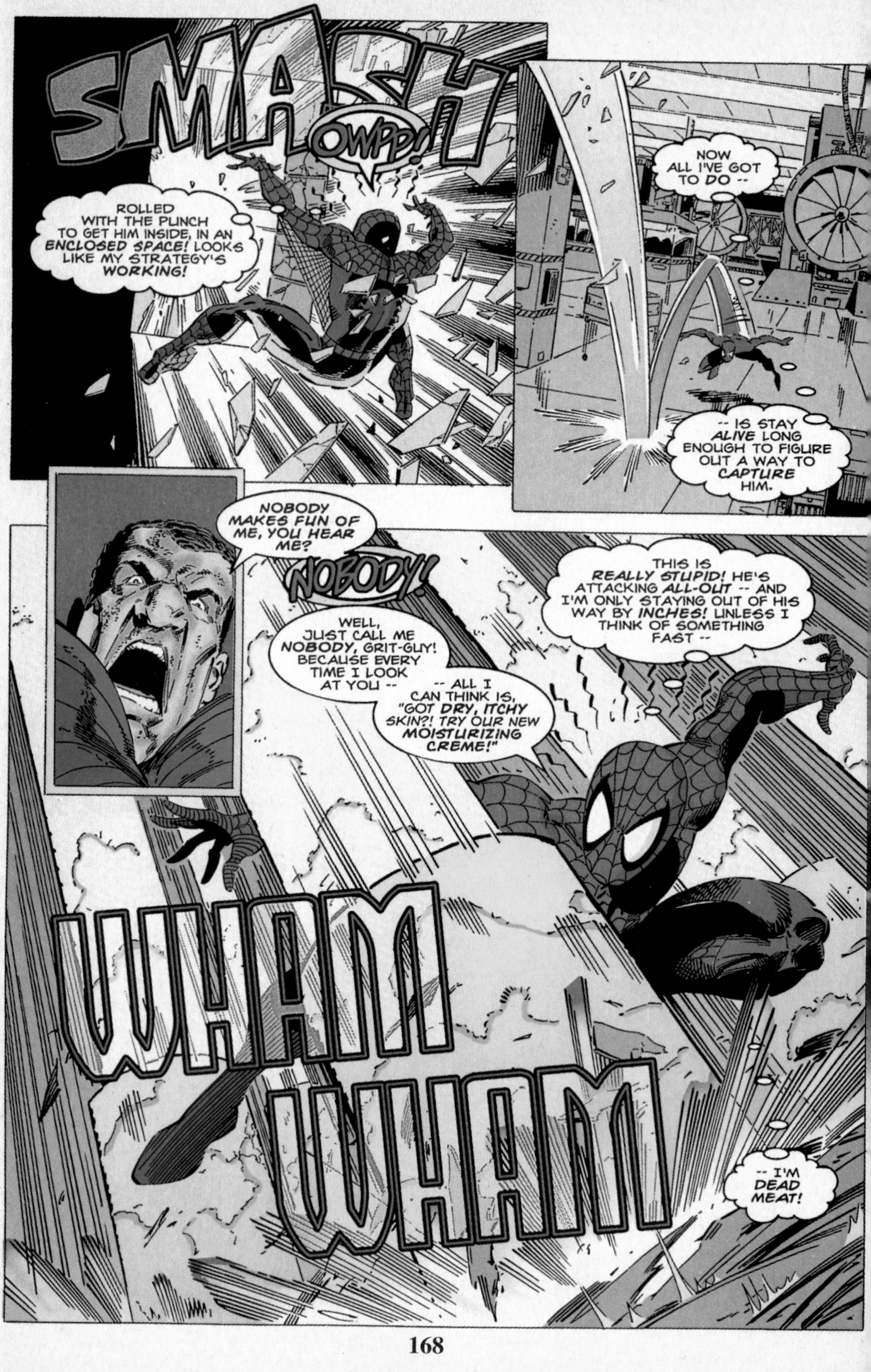
SMASH
OWPP!!
ROLLED WITH THE PUNCH TO GET HIM INSIDE, IN AN ENCLOSED SPACE! LOOKS LIKE MY STRATEGY'S WORKING!
NOW ALL I'VE GOT TO DO --
-- IS STAY ALIVE LONG ENOUGH TO FIGURE OUT A WAY TO CAPTURE HIM.
NOBODY MAKES FUN OF ME, YOU HEAR ME?
NOBODY!
WELL, JUST CALL ME NOBODY, GRIT-GUY! BECAUSE EVERY TIME I LOOK AT YOU --
-- ALL I CAN THINK IS, "GOT DRY, ITCHY SKIN?! TRY OUR NEW MOISTURIZING CREME!"
THIS IS REALLY STUPID! HE'S ATTACKING ALL-OUT -- AND I'M ONLY STAYING OUT OF HIS WAY BY INCHES! UNLESS I THINK OF SOMETHING FAST --
-- I'M DEAD MEAT!
WHAM
WHAM

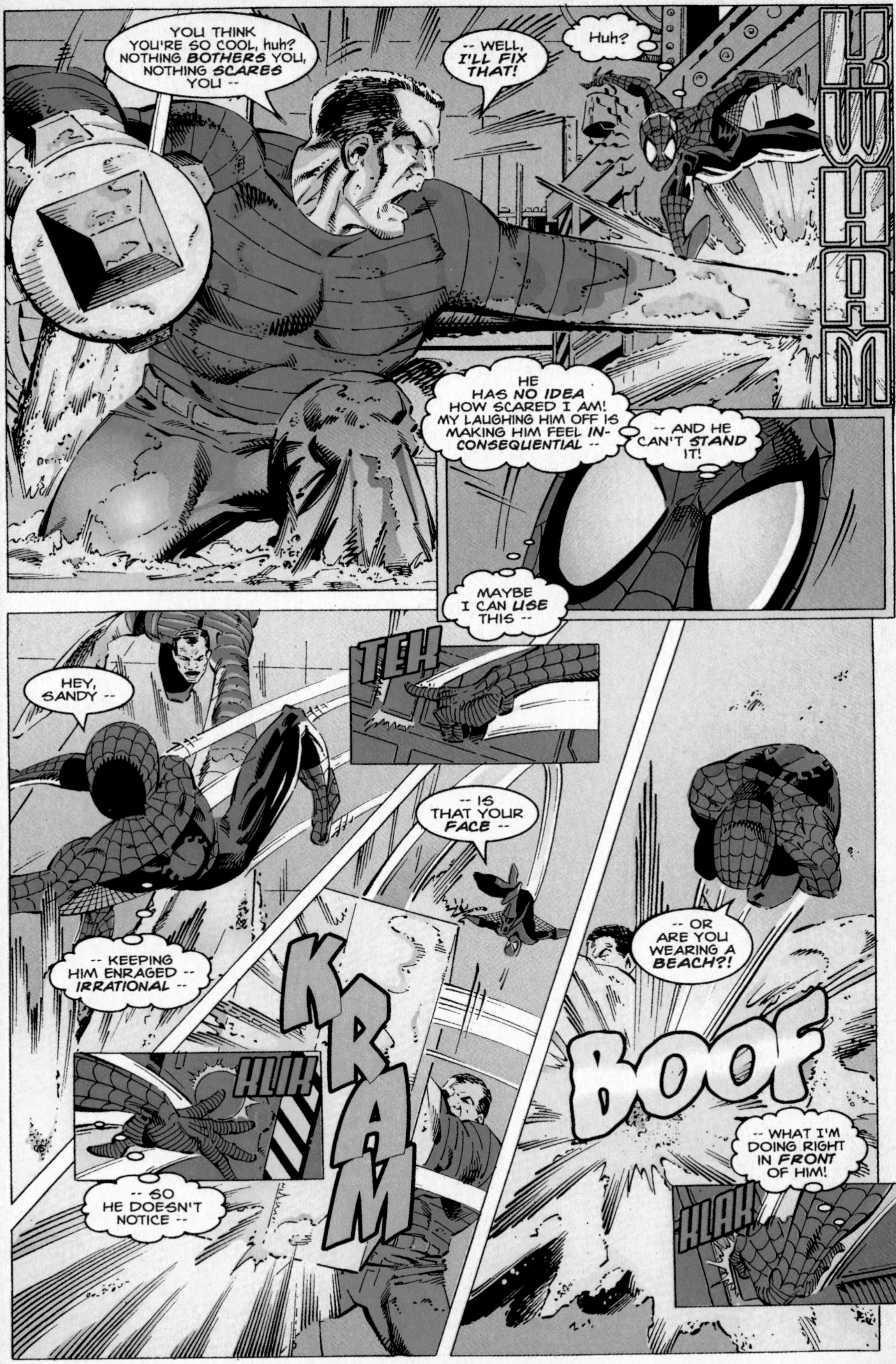
YOU THINK YOU'RE SO COOL, huh? NOTHING BOTHERS YOU, NOTHING SCARES YOU --
-- WELL, I'LL FIX THAT!
Huh?
KWHAM
HE HAS NO IDEA HOW SCARED I AM! MY LAUGHING HIM OFF IS MAKING HIM FEEL IN-CONSEQUENTIAL --
-- AND HE CAN'T STAND IT!
MAYBE I CAN USE THIS --
HEY, SANDY --
TEH
-- IS THAT YOUR FACE --
-- OR ARE YOU WEARING A BEACH?!
-- KEEPING HIM ENRAGED -- IRRATIONAL --
KRAM
BOOF
KLIK
-- SO HE DOESN'T NOTICE --
-- WHAT I'M DOING RIGHT IN FRONT OF HIM!
KLAK

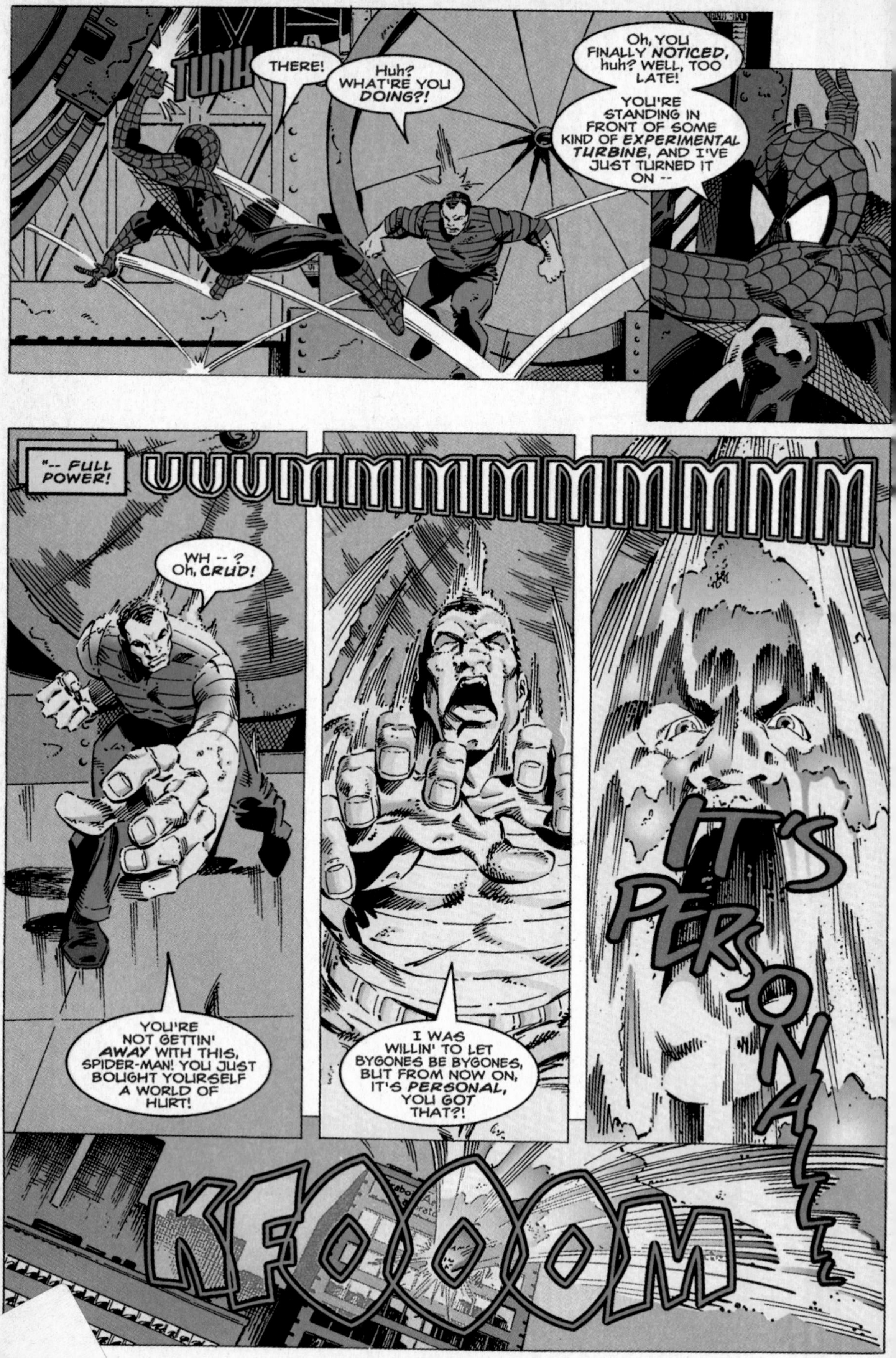
TUNK
THERE!
Huh? WHAT'RE YOU DOING?!
Oh, YOU FINALLY NOTICED, huh? WELL, TOO LATE!
YOU'RE STANDING IN FRONT OF SOME KIND OF EXPERIMENTAL TURBINE, AND I'VE JUST TURNED IT ON --
"-- FULL POWER!
UUUMMMMMMMMMMM
WH -- ? Oh, CRUD!
YOU'RE NOT GETTIN' AWAY WITH THIS, SPIDER-MAN! YOU JUST BOUGHT YOURSELF A WORLD OF HURT!
I WAS WILLIN' TO LET BYGONES BE BYGONES, BUT FROM NOW ON, IT'S PERSONAL, YOU GOT THAT?!
IT'S PERSONALLLL
KFOOOOM

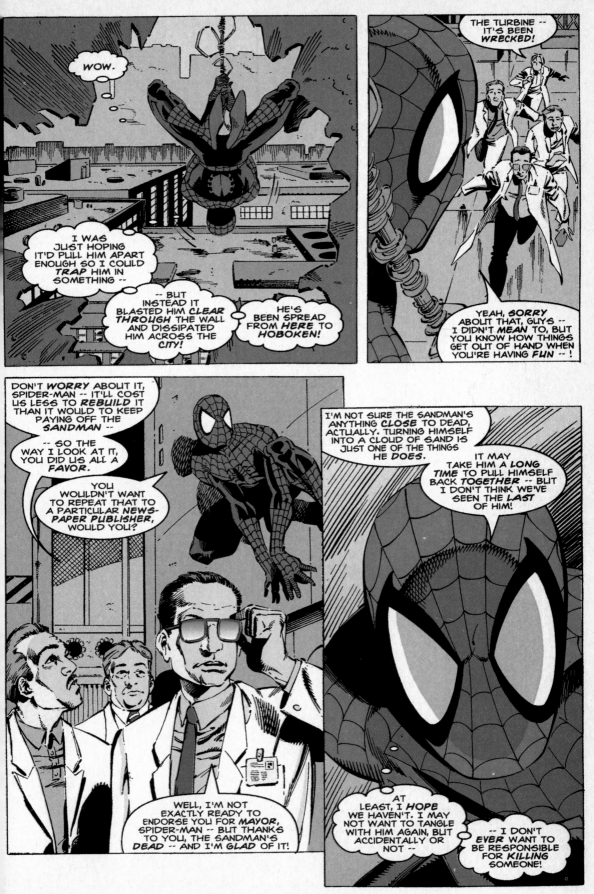

WOW.

I WAS JUST HOPING IT'D PULL HIM APART ENOUGH SO I COULD *TRAP* HIM IN SOMETHING --

-- BUT INSTEAD IT BLASTED HIM *CLEAR THROUGH* THE WALL AND DISSIPATED HIM ACROSS THE CITY!

HE'S BEEN SPREAD FROM *HERE* TO HOBOKEN!

THE TURBINE -- IT'S BEEN *WRECKED!*

YEAH, *SORRY* ABOUT THAT, GUYS -- I DIDN'T *MEAN* TO, BUT YOU KNOW HOW THINGS GET OUT OF HAND WHEN YOU'RE HAVING *FUN* --!

DON'T *WORRY* ABOUT IT, SPIDER-MAN -- IT'LL COST US LESS TO *REBUILD* IT THAN IT WOULD TO KEEP PAYING OFF THE *SANDMAN* --

-- SO THE WAY I LOOK AT IT, YOU DID US ALL A *FAVOR.*

YOU WOULDN'T WANT TO REPEAT THAT TO A PARTICULAR NEWS-PAPER PUBLISHER, WOULD YOU?

WELL, I'M NOT EXACTLY READY TO ENDORSE YOU FOR *MAYOR*, SPIDER-MAN -- BUT THANKS TO YOU, THE SANDMAN'S *DEAD* -- AND I'M GLAD OF IT!

I'M NOT SURE THE SANDMAN'S ANYTHING *CLOSE* TO DEAD, ACTUALLY. TURNING HIMSELF INTO A CLOUD OF SAND IS JUST ONE OF THE THINGS HE *DOES.*

IT MAY TAKE HIM A LONG *TIME* TO PULL HIMSELF BACK *TOGETHER* -- BUT I DON'T THINK WE'VE SEEN THE *LAST* OF HIM!

AT LEAST, I *HOPE* WE HAVEN'T. I MAY NOT WANT TO TANGLE WITH HIM AGAIN, BUT ACCIDENTALLY OR NOT --

-- I DON'T *EVER* WANT TO BE RESPONSIBLE FOR *KILLING* SOMEONE!

171

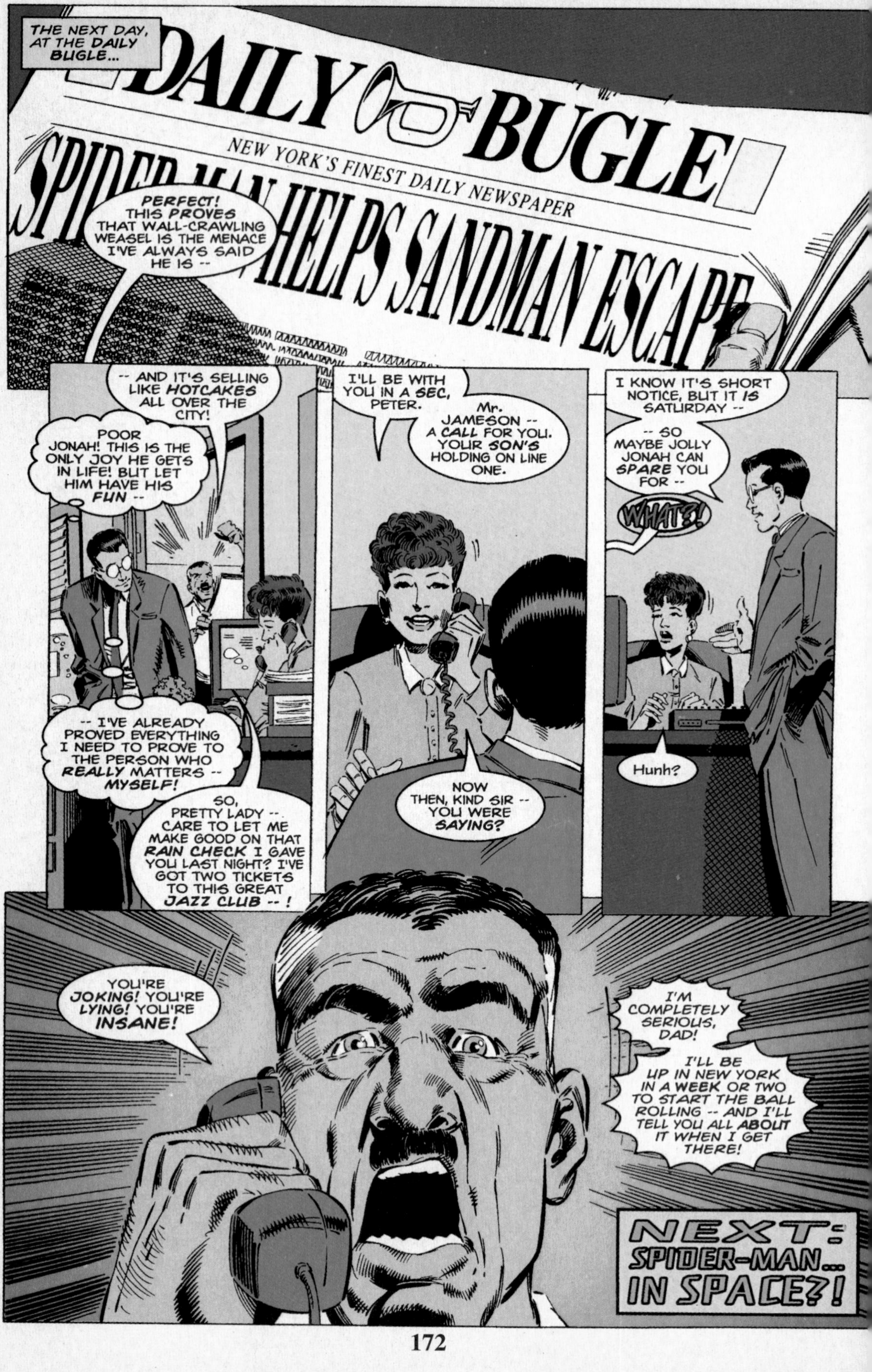
THE NEXT DAY, AT THE DAILY BUGLE...
DAILY BUGLE
NEW YORK'S FINEST DAILY NEWSPAPER
SPIDER-MAN HELPS SANDMAN ESCAPE
PERFECT! THIS PROVES THAT WALL-CRAWLING WEASEL IS THE MENACE I'VE ALWAYS SAID HE IS --
-- AND IT'S SELLING LIKE HOTCAKES ALL OVER THE CITY!
POOR JONAH! THIS IS THE ONLY JOY HE GETS IN LIFE! BUT LET HIM HAVE HIS FUN --
-- I'VE ALREADY PROVED EVERYTHING I NEED TO PROVE TO THE PERSON WHO REALLY MATTERS -- MYSELF!
SO, PRETTY LADY -- CARE TO LET ME MAKE GOOD ON THAT RAIN CHECK I GAVE YOU LAST NIGHT? I'VE GOT TWO TICKETS TO THIS GREAT JAZZ CLUB -- !
I'LL BE WITH YOU IN A SEC, PETER.
Mr. JAMESON -- A CALL FOR YOU. YOUR SON'S HOLDING ON LINE ONE.
NOW THEN, KIND SIR -- YOU WERE SAYING?
I KNOW IT'S SHORT NOTICE, BUT IT IS SATURDAY --
-- SO MAYBE JOLLY JONAH CAN SPARE YOU FOR --
WHAT?!
Hunh?
YOU'RE JOKING! YOU'RE LYING! YOU'RE INSANE!
I'M COMPLETELY SERIOUS, DAD!
I'LL BE UP IN NEW YORK IN A WEEK OR TWO TO START THE BALL ROLLING -- AND I'LL TELL YOU ALL ABOUT IT WHEN I GET THERE!
NEXT: SPIDER-MAN... IN SPACE?!

SANDMAN

Real name: William Baker
Occupation: Former professional criminal
Identity: Current identity secret
Legal status: Citizen of the United States with a criminal record
Current aliases: Sylvester Mann
Former aliases: Flint Marko
Place of birth: Queens, New York
Marital status: Divorced
Known relatives: Mrs. Baker (mother)
Group affiliation: Former member of the Frightful Four and Sinister Six, former ally of the Mandarin and Hydro-Man
Base of operations: Brooklyn, New York
First appearance: AMAZING SPIDER-MAN #4
Origin: MARVEL TWO-IN-ONE #86
History: William Baker was born and raised in a rough section of New York City. His father deserted him and his mother when he was three years old, leaving them impoverished. Baker learned to steal at an early age, and cheated and bluffed his way through public school. He excelled at football in high school, but ruined his chances for a legitimate career when he accepted money from a local gambling ring to intentionally lose an important game. Baker was found out and thrown off the team and expelled from school. He then found steady work as a henchman for a protection racket gang. At this point Baker adopted the name "Flint Marko." Marko became successful in the New York City underworld, but entertained thoughts of reforming to marry his girlfriend, Marcy Conroy. Arrested for a series of crimes, Marko was convicted and spent several years in solitary confinement growing increasingly hostile. Upon release, Marko discovered that Conroy had left him for a member of his gang named Vic Rollins. After exacting brutal revenge on Rollins, Marko embarked on a one-man crime wave throughout New York City. Eventually he was captured and imprisoned in the maximum security ward of Rykers Island Prison, New York. After a short time, he escaped through an unguarded drainpipe, the knowledge of which he had purchased while in confinement. He attempted to travel south to start a new life. However, Marko was pursued by the F.B.I. as well as state and local police departments. Narrowly evading the law numerous times, he made his way down the East Coast.

At one point, Marko found refuge in a military nuclear testing site near Savannah, Georgia. Marko was lying on a nearby beach when an experimental nuclear reactor's steam system exploded, bombarding him with a massive dose of radiation. After a short period of unconsciousness, Marko awoke to find that his body had weirdly taken on the properties of animated sand, and that he could transform himself into a sand-like form. Now able to elude the authorities with ease, the Sandman, as he now called himself, embarked on a career of criminal activity which brought him into conflict with Spider-Man, the Fantastic Four, the Hulk, and many other superhumanly powerful crimefighters (see individual entries).

The Sandman teamed with the Wizard, the Trapster, and Medusa, who together became known as the Frightful Four (see *Medusa, Trapster, Wizard, Appendix: Frightful Four*). The Sandman served as a member of the Frightful Four over many years, during which he sometimes acted independently of the team as well.

The Sandman's criminal career recently

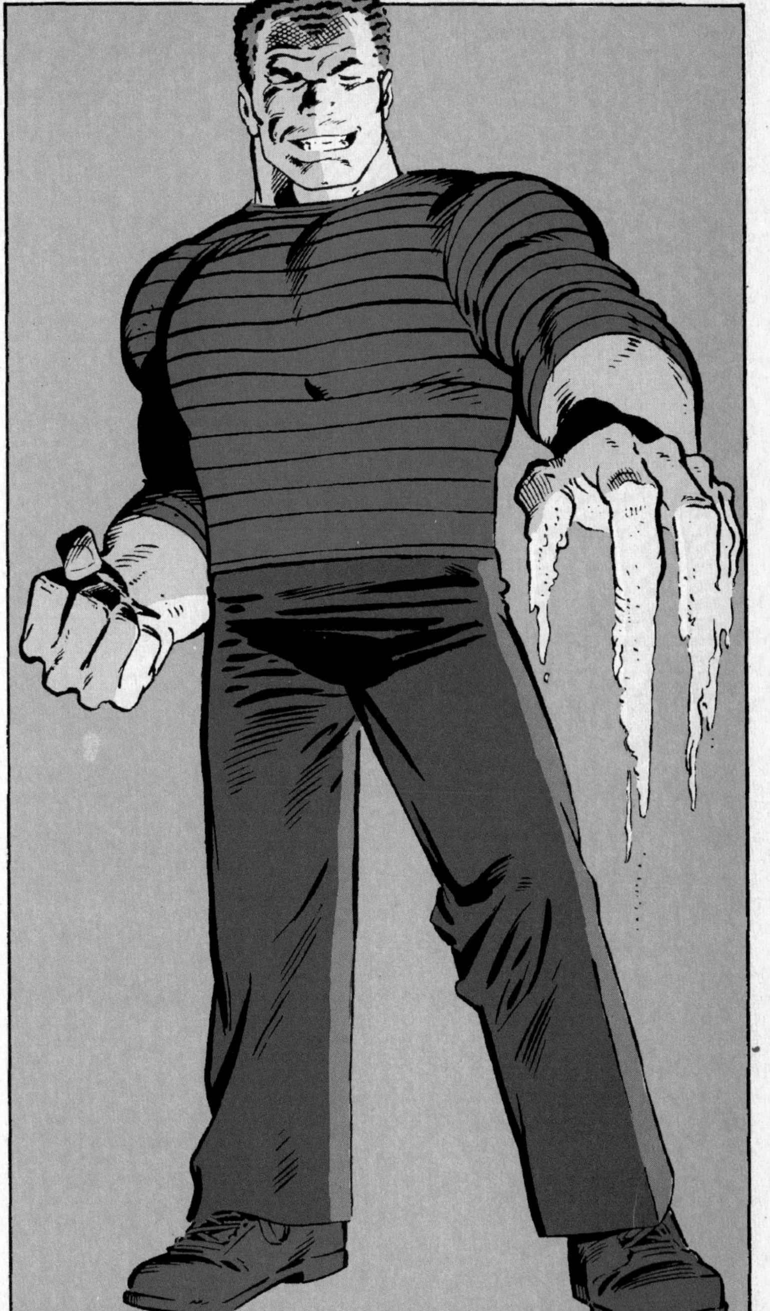

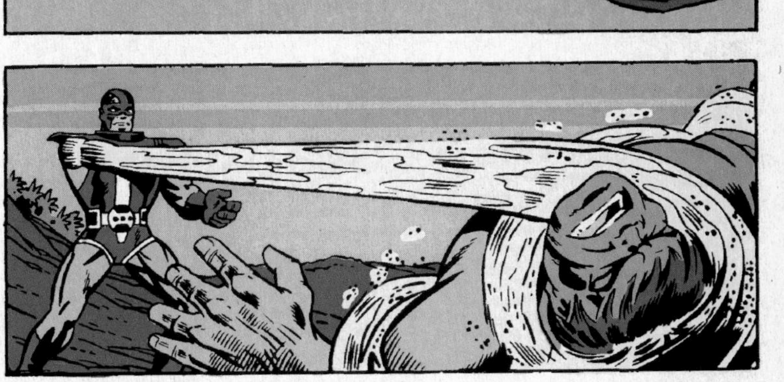

came to an apparent end. To battle Spider-Man, he had joined forces with a superhumanly powered criminal named Hydro-Man who could transform his body into animated water (see *Hydro-Man*). In a freak mishap, Sandman and Hydro-Man combined into a grotesque mud-like creature. The authorities subdued the mud creature with a special dessicating gas, which partially dehydrated the creature, rendering it harmless. The remaining amount of mud was sent to the police's forensic laboratory in Manhattan. There, police scientists sought to analyze the composition of the unusual mud, but determined with the instru-

ments at their disposal, that it was completely inanimate. It was decided to seal it in a container and dispose of it. Apparently as a delayed effect of some of the analytic procedures, the mud spontaneously separated back into the two criminals, who then burst free of their container. Hydro-Man quickly departed to unknown destinations. Sandman was so traumatized and humiliated by the experience that he renounced his criminal ambitions.

The Sandman formed a friendship with his former enemy, the Thing, who encouraged him to pursue an honest life (see *Thing*). Although still wanted by the police

for past crimes, the Sandman has forsaken his criminal career. He now lives quietly in Brooklyn, New York under the alias Sylvester Mann.

Height: 6′ 1″
Weight: 450 lbs.
Eyes: Brown
Hair: Brown
Strength level: In his sand-like form the Sandman possesses superhuman strength. At the largest size he has been observed to achieve, he can apparently lift (press) at least 85 tons.

Known superhuman powers: The Sandman possesses the ability to convert all or part of his body into a sand-like substance by mental command. His brain has attained a subliminal awareness of all granulated particles of his body. Through conscious effort, he can affect the degree of molecular cohesion between the numerous adjoining surfaces of his particles and thus cause locomotion of discrete volumes, down to individual grains. His radically mutagenically altered body composition and increased density enable him to compact or loosen the particles of sand which make up his form. Consequently, the Sandman can become as hard as sandstone, or disperse his body so that he becomes invulnerable to physical attack. He can shape his sand-state body into any continuous shape he can imagine. He can project his sand particles outward at high speeds and, when in the shape of a bulky object, with the impact of a large sandbag.

The Sandman is vulnerable to heat: temperatures of 3,400° Fahrenheit can cause his highly impure silicate composition to fuse into amorphous silicate (glass). The Sandman maintains mental control of the particles of which his body is composed so that he can reform his scattered grains unless a substantial portion of his body's mass has been isolated. Apparently, he can also convert common grains of sand around him into constituents of his body, to replenish portions he might lose track of during battle. In this manner, he can increase his overall size and volume (to some as yet unknown limit), or that of his limbs.

There appears to be no limit to how long the Sandman can remain in his sand-state. If he were to be rendered unconscious while in his sand-state, he would remain in that state, although the relaxing of his control over his particles would cause him to become an amorphous pile of sand.

The Sandman's mind continues to function in astral form even when he has turned his head into sand, and even when the particles of sand that composed his brain are widely scattered. The limit to how far the particles of his brain can be dispersed before he is unable to reassemble himself is not yet known.

Paraphernalia: The Sandman used to wear a costume designed by his former partner, the Wizard, that had a belt containing a number of chemicals which he could mix with his sand for various effects. For example, he could mix oil with his sand so as to provide a slippery covering for a surface. He could instanteously freeze his sand molecules by releasing tainted liquid nitrogen from the belt. When flame contacted the thus frozen sand, it released a poisonous vapor. Since the disbanding of the original Frightful Four, the Sandman has discontinued use of this uniform.

∎

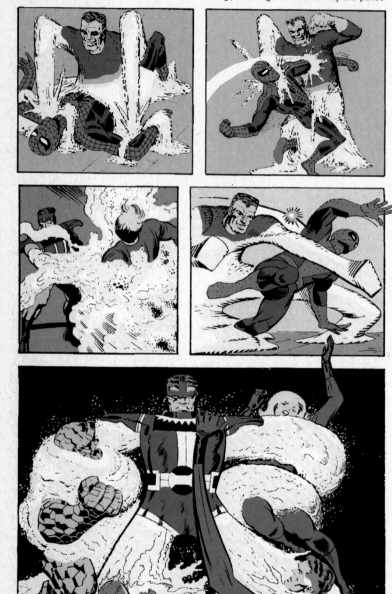

COVER PROCESS

Sketch & Pencils by Mark Brooks

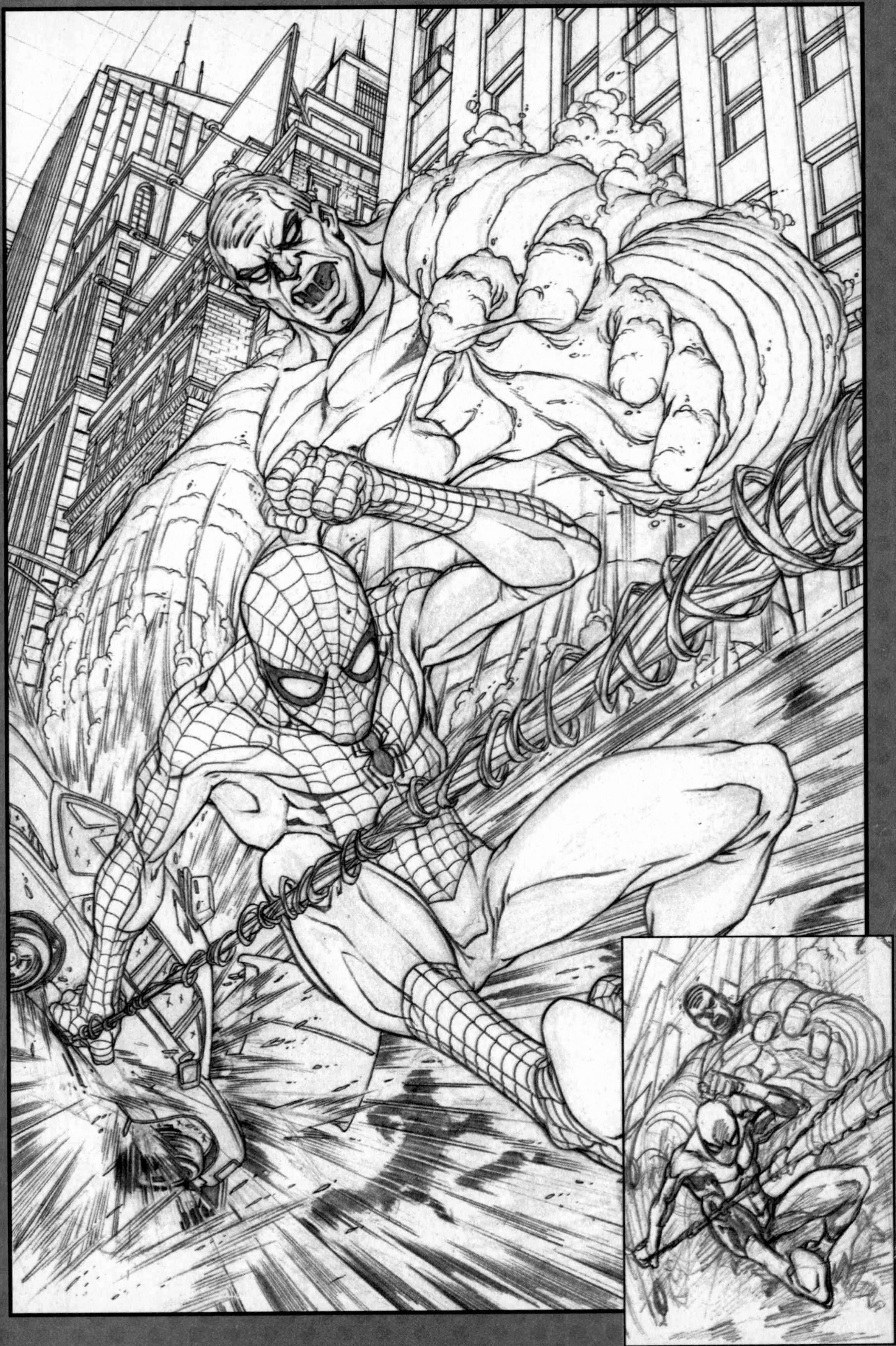

COVER PROCESS

Inks by Jaime Mendoza & Colors by Danimation

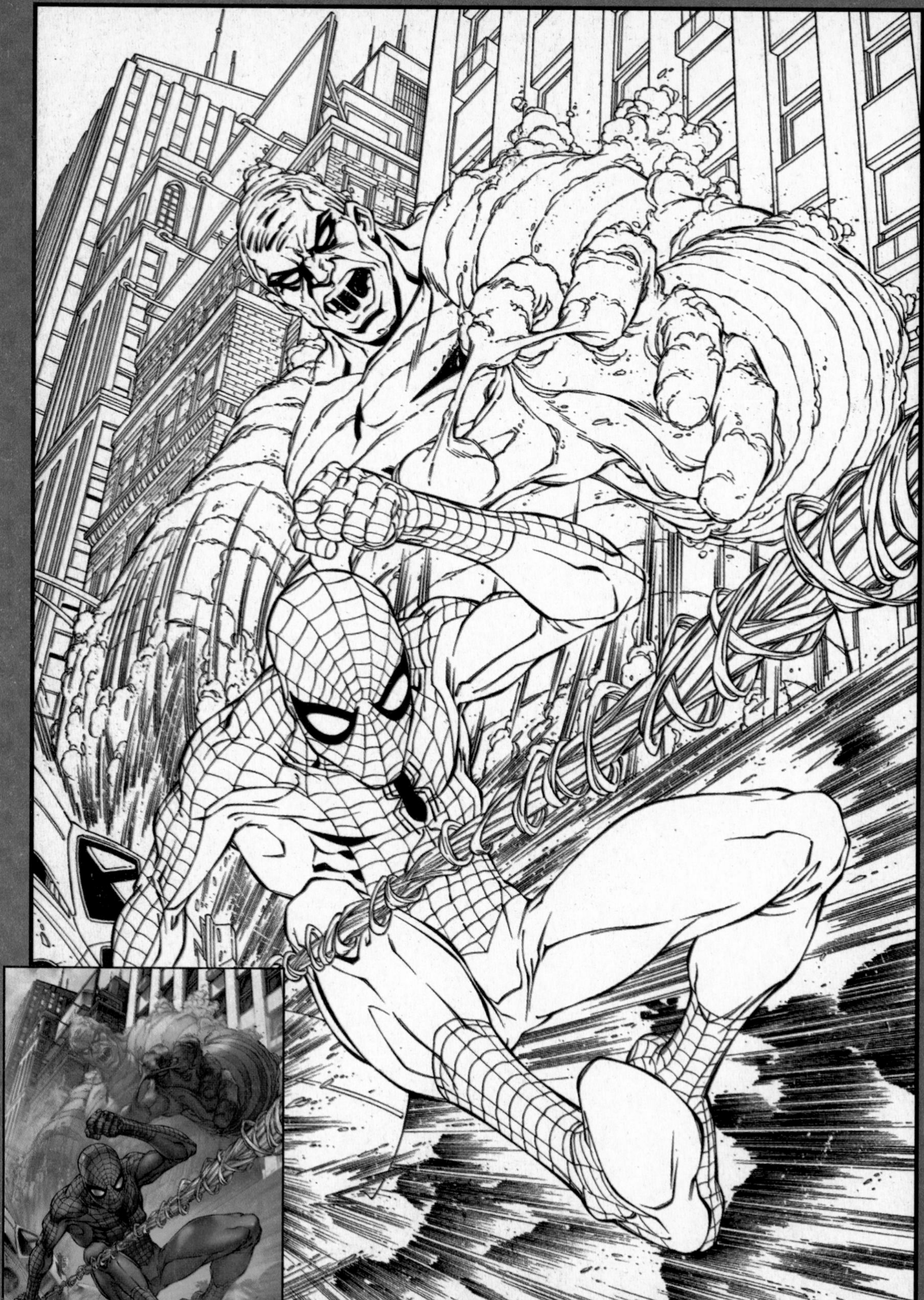